6500 6000 5500 5000 4500 4000 3500 3000 2500 2000 1500 1000 500 0 500 1000 1500 2000

B.C.E. | C.E.

RE-EMERGENCE OF THE GODDESS ■

DOCTRINE OF ASSUMPTION OF VIRGIN ■

■ VIRGIN OF
GUADALUPE

■ WITCH
BURNINGS

■ CULT OF
THE VIRGIN

■ THEOTOKAS; CLOSING
OF LAST GODDESS
TEMPLE IN THE WEST

■ COUNCIL OF EPHESUS,
VIRGIN PROCLAIMED

■ ARTEMIS OF EPHESUS

■ BIRTH OF CHRIST

DEMETER

HEBREW GODDESS

MOSES AND MONTHEISM ■

ANCIENT NEAR EAST:

MINOAN CRETE

AVEBURY

MALTA

■ PRE-DYNASTIC EGYPT

OLD EUROPE

11

12

10

9

7

6

8

4

5

3

6500 6000 5500 5000 4500 4000 3500 3000 2500 2000 1500 1000 500 0 500 1000 1500 2000

B.C.E. | C.E.

The Once and Future Goddess

The Once and Future Goddess

 A SYMBOL FOR OUR TIME

ELINOR W. GADON

HARPER & ROW, PUBLISHERS, SAN FRANCISCO
New York   Grand Rapids   Philadelphia   St. Louis
1817   London   Singapore   Sydney   Tokyo   Toronto

Library of Congress Cataloging-in-Publication Data

Gadon, Elinor W.
  The once and future goddess.

  1. Goddesses.   I. Title.
BL473.5.G33   1989   291.2′114   89–45399
ISBN 0–06–250346–4
ISBN 0–06–250354–5 (pbk.)

89 90 91 92 93 RRD(H) 10 9 8 7 6 5 4 3 2 1

Credits for photos and drawings appear on page 402–6.

For Marie Cantlon

Midwife to the new literary genre documenting women's spirituality and the re-emergence of the Goddess.

Compassionate, worldly and wise, intellectually informed, critically discerning, responsible in relationships, Marie is an exemplar to those of us who seek through our writing to transform our culture into a more just and humane society.

In her gentle and unassuming way, with grace and unfailing good humor, she has worked unstintingly as editor to bring to publication women's vision of the human condition based on their own experience. In breaking the silence imposed by a patriarchy which seeks to suppress a woman's voice, she has caused all of our lives to be enriched.

Contents

Acknowledgments

A book is rarely just the work of the author. It is usually the end product of a personal journey, and the distillation of many influences along the way. I have come to deeply appreciate the value of the collective vision, the place of nurture and support in the creative act. The reemergence of the Goddess is a grass-roots movement, and I have been enriched in my search by the meaning others have found.

My mentors in the way of the Goddess have been Marija Gimbutas, Starhawk, and Carol Christ. I have come to understand the relationship of the life force, the Goddess within, to the creative process through the experience of the artists of whom I write and the many others I was unable to include because of space limitations. The artists' commitment to their vision has been an ongoing source of inspiration. I treasure their openness and friendship.

The mysteries of the Goddess as a living tradition were revealed to me through rituals of two pagan communities of California: Reclaiming, and the Church of All Worlds. Their welcoming acceptance of me affirmed the values of the Goddess spirituality.

A book like mine, which is both a historical interpretation and a critique of contemporary culture, draws on recent scholarship and critical writing in a number of fields. While I have based my arguments on the interpretation of archaeological evidence, I have done so not as a specialist, but as a generalist, interested in the broad perspective, in synthesis, in presenting connections not generally known or acknowledged in our culture. I am indebted to the many whose vision and insight have laid the groundwork for my own reflections. I want to thank in particular four prehistorians for their generosity in so willingly giving of their time and photographic documents—Alexander Marschack, James Mellaart, Marija Gimbutas, and Michael Dames. Other colleagues whose critiques have been so helpful are Donna Wilshire and Mara Keller.

The genesis of this book was in a course I taught in The Women's Studies Program at the Harvard Divinity School in 1979. I am immeasurably grateful for the support of Assistant Dean Constance Buchanan, director of the program, and former Dean George Rupp. Others who encouraged my continuing research that led to this publication are Harvey Cox, Riane Eisler, Claire Fischer, Elizabeth and David Dodson Gray, James Herrod, Frédérique Marglin, Lorna Marshall, and Patricia Reis.

I want to thank Clayton Carlson, publisher of Harper & Row, San Francisco, for his initial and continuing enthusiasm about my project and Janice Johnson, Janet Reed, and all at Harper & Row who made the book into a final reality. My editor, Marie Cantlon, did much to contribute to the clarity of my arguments and the felicity of my prose. I am grateful to Janet Bollow whose design so fully realized my original vision of the integration of text and pictures.

And in conclusion I also want to thank Sophie Dickerson and Caroline Pincus for their invaluable contribution in the tedious but critical details of permissions, photographs, footnotes, and bibliography. Caroline's intelligence, resourcefulness, and competence during the final weeks of preparation of the manuscript were indeed gifts from the Goddess.

Author's Note on Chronology

Archaeologists have developed a complex terminology for dating prehistoric finds for which there are no written records. There are two dating methods, radiocarbon and dendric chronology. Radiocarbon dating, the older, is based on radioactive decay of organic materials found at excavation sites. More recent discoveries revealed that these dates were too late. Corrections are now being made in comparison with tree-growth rates or dendrochronology. The use of recalibrated dating prior to the seventh millennium is controversial. I have used the older radiocarbon dating as given in my sources. In light of recalibration, all pre-historic dates will be older.

Introduction

Mine is a tale about the Goddess as she was in ages past, as she continues to be in many parts of the world today, and as she is reemerging in late twentieth-century Western culture.

My earliest awareness of the Goddess as a living force was in 1967 when I spent a year with my family in Calcutta where my husband was a visiting professor at the Indian Institute of Management. I knew little of Indian culture then but soon realized that I experienced myself as a woman there differently than I ever had in the West. I could not say just how, and surely not why, but being in a culture so utterly different from my own, in which the feminine was celebrated everywhere in sensuous images of great power, both human and divine, was profoundly unsettling.

What happened in India, I came to understand, was that I had experienced myself as sexual, sacred, and powerful in a way no modern women in the West can. Our psychological being has been severed from our biological selves for so long that we are completely cut off from our true natures. Because I was in touch with this strength, with the celebration and fullness of my being for even so limited a time, I could never return to my old ways of seeing the world. When I left India and returned to the United States, there was a radical rupture in the fabric of my being. My erotic self, the deep life force within, had been activated and there was no way to put the genie back in the bottle.

In the ensuing twenty years I have been reflecting on what that pivotal year meant. The focus of my work as researcher, teacher, and writer became the female image—what it means in traditional cultures and in the work of contemporary women artists.

When I tell people that I am writing about the Goddess, they inevitably ask, Which one? While the Goddess has indeed had many names, many manifestations throughout human history, she is ultimately one supreme reality. Only after the patriarchal Indo-Europeans overthrew the cultures where the Goddess had flourished from earliest times and imposed the worship of their sky gods was her identity fractured into myriad goddesses, each with an all-too-human personality. We know these goddesses best from Greek and Roman mythology.

Merlin Stone began her ground-breaking book with the revelation that in the beginning God was a woman.[1] And so she was. Accumulating archaeological evidence affirms overwhelmingly that prehistoric peoples worshiped a female deity. This evidence and the earliest writings document the persistence of Goddess religion for nearly 30,000 years, beginning in the Late Paleolithic, the Ice Age. With the coming of agriculture, in the Neolithic Age that followed, the religion of the Goddess flowered.

As we shall see, Goddess religion was earth-centered, not heaven-centered, of this world not otherworldy, body-affirming not body-denying, holistic not dualistic. The Goddess was immanent, within every human being, not transcendent, and humanity was viewed as part of nature, death as a part of life. Her worship was sensual, celebrating the erotic, embracing all that was alive. The religious quest was above all for renewal, for the regeneration of life, and the Goddess was the life force.

In this context religion is a problematic word; way of life would be more apt. The word *religion* conjures up the great monotheistic world faiths—Judaism, Christianity, and Islam, all revealed traditions. Hinduism and Buddhism, also considered great world religions, do not fit this model because they are not based on revelation. Their followers consider these paths as ways of life embracing the whole, not a dimension of experience separate and apart from the ordinary. All life is sacred. *Religion* is a concept imposed on Eastern practice by Westerners.

The word comes from the Latin *religio,* "to rebind." We might ask then, What was it that became unbound? Before the onslaught of patriarchy and the suppression of the Goddess, all that lived was bound into a sacred fabric, "the larger web of the life force,"[2] part of a whole. All were responsible to each other and responsible for the ongoing rhythms of life, death, and rebirth—humankind, women equally with men, animals and plants, rocks and rivers, the planet earth and its atmosphere. This integration of the whole has never been achieved in monotheistic religions; rather they have led to an ever accelerating severance of nature from culture bringing us, in the late twentieth century, to the brink of species and planet annihilation.

The ancient Goddess cultures that we will explore in *The Once and Future Goddess* were woman-centered, peaceful, and egalitarian. Later the Goddess had to share her power with a pantheon of sky gods, although her worship continued to be widely popular well into the early Christian period.

Outside mainstream Western culture and the Islamic world, female deities are still worshiped almost everywhere; they are agricultural peoples' earth mothers, creator goddesses, objects of fertility cults, and symbols of ethnic unity. Some, like the Hindu Devi, are believed to be the godhead itself. The focus of widespread sects and cults, Devi's festivals are major celebrations during the calendar year. Women in most of the Third World, like those of village India, invoke the presence of the local goddess as a source of strength in the ongoing round of domestic and family events. The female deity presides at rituals that honor the major events in women's lives—first menstruation, marriage, and childbirth.

The demise of the Goddess can be traced back to the invasions of warlike nomadic peoples from the Asiatic and European north who overran the centers of Goddess culture in southeastern Europe, the Near East, and India causing large-scale destruction and dislocation. They brought with them their sky gods who ruled from the heavens like despots. The Goddess, women, and their values were suppressed. Patriarchy, the domination of culture by men, was the new order of society. Even in India where the worship of the Goddess never died out among the common people and was reabsorbed into evolving Hinduism in the first millennium, the culture continues to be patriarchal and the status of women inferior to that of men.

The death blow to Goddess culture was delivered by monotheism in which one male, all-powerful and absolute, ruled both the heavens and the earth. Monotheistic faiths were implacable foes of the Goddess. As we know, the Bible records the continuous battle waged by the ancient Hebrews against the worship of the Goddess.

It is useful to put the ascendancy of the male god, of patriarchy, over the Goddess into perspective (see the timeline in the endpapers). The concept of monotheism is a relatively recent one, first expressed by the ancient Hebrews less than 4,000 years ago. The exclusive authority of one universal male god in Western culture goes back less than 1,700 years to the conversion of the Roman Emperor Constantine in 320 C.E. and his imposition of Christianity as the state religion. Since that time Christianity has actively attempted to convert the rest of the world to one "true" faith.

Still, the last of the Goddess temples was not closed until the fifth century in Gaul. With the suppression of the Goddess much has been lost to human culture. As history was written by the victors, Goddess religion has been portrayed as heretical, bad, "of the devil," the alien other. Women, identified with the Goddess and her ways, were also so branded and denied full participation in society. This transition was not just a gender change from Goddess to God but a paradigm shift with the imposition of a different reality, of different categories of being, that deeply affected every human relationship. Woman, the female, the feminine, was excluded in this shift of consciousness. All that was most valued in the Goddess culture was devalued, given lesser priority, rejected.

When the balance changed, the dark side of the feminine was also suppressed. The Goddess had been a model of women's nature in all its fullness. The irrational, the chaotic and destructive, which had been acknowledged when the Goddess reigned supreme, were split off from divinity and became feared. The power of the feminine came to be seen as threatening to the established social order. Women could no longer express their complete psychic reality. The problems created by these negative attitudes continue to plague us.

Ours is a search for meaning, for what has been lost and for what can be recovered. Our challenge as women and men of the late twentieth century is to open ourselves to other realities, to find other lenses through which to view human life, our relation to each other and to the world around us. To do so we must go beyond the old ways so deeply ingrained in our culture, the "truths" sanctioned by religious and secular authorities, that have come to be accepted as inalienable:

- A male god created the world
- Humans have the right to dominate nature
- Man has a right to dominate woman

As we examine what is known about Goddess religion, myth, and ritual, we must be willing to take an imaginative leap, to discover in living cultures, such as those of Hindu India and Native Americans, clues to the meaning of earlier images and practice. Working with the fragmentary archaeological evidence now being unearthed is like trying to piece together a gargantuan jig-saw puzzle in which some of the pieces are lost and others broken, and there is no picture to show what the completed puzzle looks like. But the surviving evidence for the worship of a female deity is overwhelming. We will use the art and artifacts as keys to our reconstruction. They are tangible records of human experience, meditations on the mystery of the source of our being.

The noted historian of religion Mircea Eliade tells us that symbolic thinking is an essential part of human nature, coming before language and discursive reasoning. "Images, symbols and myths respond to a need and fill a function," bringing "to light the deepest aspects of reality which defy any other means of knowledge. . . . Every historical man and woman carries on, within themselves, a great deal of prehistorical humanity. . . . The mind uses images to grasp the ultimate reality of things." It is the "image of the Mother which reveals—and which alone can reveal—her functions, at once cosmological, anthropological and psychological."[3]

In reclaiming the Goddess, in recovering our full human history as men and women, we can learn other patterns of behavior. We can redress the imbalance between the human species and our natural environment, between men and women, exploring the possibility of living in harmony and justice with all things. This book is not about the idealization of women but about life, connection, and responsibility.

In our own time, in our own culture, the Goddess once again is becoming a symbol of empowerment for women; a catalyst for an emerging spirituality that is earth-centered; a metaphor for the earth as a living organism; an archetype for feminine consciousness; a mentor for healers; the emblem of a new political movement; an inspiration for artists; and a model for resacralizing woman's body and the mystery of human sexuality.

The Once and Future Goddess

In the Beginning:

 PART ONE

Mary Frank, ORIGINS, 1984. Watercolor
on paper. 28 in. x 35 in.

The Sacred Way of the Goddess

The Goddess religion flowered in Europe and the Near East from the Paleolithic into the Late Classical Age. The story is very complex, concerned as it is with an enormous time span encompassing more than 30,000 years of human history and taking in the vast Eurasian land mass. This work draws on the pioneering efforts of intrepid archaeologists and prehistorians, men and women of singular vision and commitment whose creative synthesis of evidence brings these early cultures to life. Through their efforts we only now are beginning to realize that Western civilization has its roots in the Ice Age and that our family tree is a matrilineal one, traceable through the images of the Goddess.

Our first task is an attempt to enter into the mindset of those who lived before history as written record begins. Theirs was a holistic view of life in which the sacred and the profane were not antithetical, and what we now call religion, the search for inner meaning and spiritual connection, was a part of everyday life. Seasonal changes and life-cycles were marked by rituals that continually recharged human connections to community and cosmos.

The word ritual comes from *rtü,* Sanskrit for *menses.* Menses, literally month, is from the Latin, directly translated into English to denote the periods of the yearly calendar. The earliest rituals were connected to the women's monthly bleeding. The blood from the womb that nourished the unborn child was believed to have mana, magical power. Women's periodic bleeding was a cosmic event, like the cycles of the moon and the waxing and waning of the tides. We have forgotten that women were the conduit to the sacred mystery of life and death.

Traditionally we traced the origins of Western culture to Ancient Greece, more recently to the Ancient Near East. History, we were told, began at Sumer in the third millennium B.C.E. with the invention of writing. But human history is much older. We've only begun to dig into our roots. Time-honored notions of history and civilization are being revised as discoveries of lost cultures such as Troy, Crete, and Thera, all prove that truth lies behind myth—that myth is an account of what really happened.

Archaeologists are busy revamping the chronology of human cultural development. Since World War II they have begun to recover a far more remote past than that of Sumer and Greece in the Neolithic centers of Anatolia, Southeastern Europe, and Crete where the glorious Minoan civilizations epitomized Goddess culture. These prosperous trading centers with well-trained artisans—the first people to raise pottery making and weaving to the level of art—are the key to understanding the Goddess. We will examine the civilizations where the Goddess was honored and the implications of her suppression. In these places the major passages of human life, the changing seasons of the year, the agricultural cycle, and the movement of the heavens were woven into a world view that celebrated the ongoing rhythm of life, death and regeneration. As we shall discover, this was what the religion of the Goddess was all about.

The Ice Age: The Earth as Mother

CHAPTER 1

The upper Paleolithic (ca. 35,000–9000 B.C.E.) was a "revolutionary" period in human evolution. There was a virtual explosion of symbolic behavior.[1] Ice Age people were fully evolved humans much like ourselves, capable of speaking and comprehending symbolically based language and of establishing communities with shared norms and values. Like us, they must have speculated about the origin of life and the meaning of death. The earliest human intuition of the sacred was that the earth was the source of all life and ground of being.

Art and religion were born together from a fundamental human passion to express inner life. Although there is no record of these peoples' language, no written myth or stories and therefore no history as usually defined, their art displays a keen observation of nature, the presence of music, of tools, and of self-decoration. Theirs was a rich ceremonial life.

The power of Paleolithic cave art is extraordinary; nothing quite like it has been created since. This achievement seems all the more wondrous when we consider how hard life must have been, lived as it was in the raw, at the mercy of climate and environment that varied dramatically with the expansion and contraction of a mile-high wall of glacial ice. Even the Mediterranean regions were cold and dry. Broad expanses of rich grasslands like the plains of modern Africa covered much of Europe, and vast herds of large animals roamed these flat steppes.

No one knows for certain what life was like for these Ice Age peoples and gatherers and hunters. The men, physically stronger and free from domestic burdens, hunted the large animals while the women gathered plants, which made up the bulk of the food, as they nursed and cared for their offspring.[2] Game might be plentiful but the hunt was not always suc-

🏵 3

cessful. The hardest time was winter when there were no grasses or berries, nuts or tubers to supplement the diet of meat from the hunt. As the seasons changed, people moved about in search of food, often following the migrating herds. The family groups did not wander aimlessly but came back to the same places year after year to hunt the same animals and gather the same plants.

Dwelling places were chosen with great care, always near a reliable water supply, sometimes underneath protecting cliffs that faced south to catch the light and heat of the winter sun, and sometimes overlooking shallows and fords in the rivers where migrating animals such as reindeer might cross. Sites seem to have been chosen because they provided a good view of the surrounding area. "Such vantage points would have been important for observing game animals. . . ."[3]

Much that survives from this time has been found on the floors of these habitation sites under the debris of millennia. Tools, cooking implements, needles for sewing have been uncovered, as well as small, portable art objects whose use has been something of a mystery. There are beads and pendants made from bone, ivory, and even shells, which must have been highly valued since they were brought great distances from the sea. These marked and carved ornaments were probably used in ritual, as our studies of primal peoples inform us that decoration had a sacred function. The most provocative finds on the shelter floors are the small female figures, the so-called "Venuses."

These dwelling sites are one source of Paleolithic art; another is the walls of caves in the heavily forested mountainous regions of northeastern Spain and southwestern France, in southern Germany and Czechoslovakia. The shelters were their places of domestic worship, the caves their temples.

The Sacred Images

The sanctuaries were large caverns, deep within the earth, whose long access through dark and narrow passages was often perilous. Clinging to curtains of stalactites, descending into chasms, negotiating underground waters, our Ice Age ancestors groped their way through the unknown. Some

1

1. THE POWER OF THE ANIMALS, ca. 14,000 B.C.E. Painting on wall. The Rotunda, Lascaux, France.

2. THE SHAMAN-PRIEST, ca. 14,000 B.C.E. Painting and engraving on cave wall, h. 2½ ft. Les Trois Frères, French Pyrenees. Drawing by H. Breuil from original.

2

chambers were too large ever to have been fully illuminated by their lamps, which were small slabs of limestone, hollowed out in the middle to hold burning animal fat. Ever alert to the sounds of danger, the approach of threatening animals, they could hear dripping waters echoing in the vast stillness, terrifying noises. This difficult journey was a rite of passage into sacred time and space back to the beginning. And here, on the walls of the cave sanctuaries, Paleolithic people painted startling panoramas of their environment in brilliant earth colors—wooly mammoth and bison, mountain goat and musk ox, wild horse and deer, all potent with charged energy. Working with stone tools, natural pigments, and charcoal, they brought to life vast herds of these beasts moving across empty space (see fig. 1).

Here we can imagine the shaman-priest invoking the animals' spirits in order to harness their energy and assure their rebirth from the womb of the Mother (see fig. 2). In the dim, flickering light the painted images were transformed into vital, living, breathing presences. Ice Age peoples perceived themselves as one with the animals, not separate species; both were nurtured, like the rocks and the trees, by the life force emanating from the earth itself. Architectural historian Vincent Scully describes the impact the cave paintings had on him: "The forms of the paintings themselves, which create an image of the living beast more persuasive and directly sympathetic than any later art has been able to do, seem to show that the necessary death of the animal, partly induced by magic, was dignified by human respect and admiration for the creature itself and even by human gratitude to it."[4]

Ice Age people also fashioned other images, small icons of the sacred female, from the ivory tusks of the great woolly mammoth, from rocks of glowing, translucent color, and from clay, the very stuff of the earth. Nearly two hundred female figures have been found at dwelling sites all across Eurasia from the Pyrenees in western Europe to Lake Baikal in central Siberia. Perhaps the most widely known, the *Willendorf*, from Austria defines the type (see fig. 3 and color plate 31).

While no two of the unearthed figures are alike, they are almost always faceless with scant attention paid to limbs. All share an emphasis on those parts of the female body associated with reproduction. We are looking at a generalized image whose power lies in its symbolic meaning, icons that embodied the source of life. As Paleolithic people observed the natural processes in a woman's body—menstruation, pregnancy, birth, and lactation—the earth was understood by analogy to be the great womb out of which all life emerged. They believed that the earth was the mother, especially the mother of animals "upon whose continued presence human life depended."[5] Just as the plants withered, died, and fell into the earth, so did animals. Humans also returned to the earth's womb at death, to be reborn again like the plants in the great seasonal round. The dead were buried in the fetal position with their arms across their chests, their bodies marked with red ochre, the pigmented earth, symbolic of life-giving blood.

Early artists represented the sacred female in images that emphasized one part of her body; all else was abstracted or eliminated. Vulva, breast, or buttocks were carved in the round and incised on bone and stone to be worn as beads or amulets. In the Ice Age the part may have stood for the whole, a characteristic of primal thinking, or each body part may have had a different ritual function as Alexander Marschack suggests[6] (see figs. 4–7). All are from the same cultural area in Moravia, whose artists must have been particularly talented in creating powerful visual symbols.

3. THE EARTH MOTHER OF WILLENDORF, ca. 30,000–25,000 B.C.E. Limestone. 4⅛ in. Austria.

Carved from soft limestone, she is naked with pronounced fleshiness, having pendulous breasts, protruding abdomen, massive hips, and a clearly defined pubic triangle. Faceless, her head is capped by carefully arranged curls; she rests spindly arms adorned with a scalloped bracelet on her enormous bosom. Although her legs are broken off beneath the knee, they would have characteristically tapered, ending without feet. The head bent slightly forward, the knees relaxed give the figure a certain awkward sense of movement, a clumsy naturalness, not surprising as she appears to be in the late stages of pregnancy. Still marked with traces of red ochre, an earth pigment the color of the life-giving blood, her figure fits perfectly in the clasped hand.

4

5

7

6

4. Stylized Female with Large Buttocks, Upper Magdalenian, ca. 13,000 B.C.E. Coal. Petersfels, Germany.

A sculpted, highly polished coal pendant depicts a radically simplified female form whose primary features are large buttocks and slightly bent knees.

5. Abstract Female with Breasts, East Gravettian, ca. 20,000 B.C.E. Mammoth ivory. 8.5 cm. Dolní Věstonice, Moravia, Czechoslovakia.

A beautiful, small ivory rod has two full rounded breasts on either side. The body is an extension of the rod, slightly arched and curved backward like the Petersfels pendant. This carefully made, starkly abstract image is notched on all four sides.

6. Abstract Female with Vulva Slit, East Gravettian, ca. 20,000 B.C.E. Mammoth ivory. Dolní Věstonice, Moravia, Czechoslovakia.

Another piece of carved ivory looks more like a two-pronged fork, but on closer examination can be identified as a female form by the narrow slit indicating the vulva at the point where the legs join the torso. The hole at the top shows that it was probably worn as a pendant.

7. Disk with Vulva Slit, East Gravettian, ca. 20,000 B.C.E. Ivory. Brno, Moravia, Czechoslovakia.

Found in a grave, this small coinlike disk carved from a mammoth tooth has a single radial line from the center to the edge. The vulva over time became abstracted to the point where it could be symbolized by a simple circle with a single mark.

The Interpretation of the Female Figures

Paleolithic art has become known only in the past hundred years. The purpose of the cave paintings and the meaning of the female figures have been debated continuously among prehistorians. The discovery of an evolved and sophisticated art dating from thousands of years before recorded history dealt a shattering blow to the theory that viewed "great" art as the reflection of "great" civilizations, such as Classical Greece and the Renaissance. This raised profound and largely unanswered questions about the origins of art as well as about the human condition.

Traditional interpretations looked to tribal societies who employed sympathetic magic and concluded that the paintings on the cave walls were to ensure the increase of game and the success of the hunt. The meaning of the female figures as "mother goddess" and "mother right" have been in and out of fashion. Most often they were lumped together as fertility fetishes or symbols. More recently the image of the Goddess is seen to represent female sexuality, hence the misnomer "Venus," the goddess associated with sexual love in Western culture; but this is far too limited a view.

These figures were not what is commonly understood as cult objects whose sole purpose was to promote the fertility of the land, its animals, and people. Rather, they represent the fecundity of the earth itself in all its abundance, bounty, and creativity. A far more appropriate name would be the Earth Mother, and so we have named her.

Breasts, vulvae, and buttocks are powerful and universal symbols capable of conveying more than one meaning, potent packages that evoke both physical presence and human significance. Breasts, for example, are symbols of nurture *par excellence,* as witness the widely worshiped iconic form of the Virgin nursing the Christ Child (see fig. 106).

In order to interpret these Paleolithic symbols, the work of two scholars is key. The late André Leroi-Gourhan, a leading French prehistorian, laid out the territory by exhaustively examining the wealth of images made over a twenty-thousand-year period in sixty-six of the one hundred known sites in southwestern France and the nearby Spanish Pyrenees. He classified the images, signs, and symbols found on the cave walls by chronology and content. Alexander Marschack, a scientific writer interested in theories of cognition, analyzed the function of this art as he searched for evidence of how our ancestors must have understood the world around them. Both men used the exacting tools of scientific analysis in an attempt to discern underlying patterns. Their task was formidable, since the caves are covered with an endless jumble of human and animal figures, symbols, signs, scratches, and scrawls, often with no obvious relationship. There is overpainting, unfinished work, and the inevitable damage.

The cave panoramas themselves are overwhelming, impressionistic, looking much like grassland seen from far off. Large animals dominate the scenes as they run, gallop, move in steady streams across the walls. Some loom large and crowd the foreground; others recede behind them. Scattered in the midst of all this lively activity are small signs, rows of engraved parallel strokes, splashes or dots, handprints.

The imagery in the shelters is equally confusing. On bits of bone and ivory are carved seemingly unrelated parts of animals, plants, and human bodies that like the cave paintings are overlain with scratches, notches, and cross-hatchings. Marschack demonstrates that the overpaintings, notches, signs, and the like were added over time. But what does it all mean?

Leroi-Gourhan found that the cave artists did not work randomly. There was an underlying structure in the iconography and placement of images. Male symbols were usually associated with female symbols. Musing on his findings Leroi Gourhan comments,

> If we weigh the matter carefully, this answer is at the same time satisfying and laughable, for there are few religions, primitive or evolved, that do not somewhere involve a confrontation of the same values, whether divine couples such as Jupiter and Juno are concerned, or principles such as *yang* and *yin*.[7]

Leroi-Gourhan's comment reveals the mind-set of the patriarchal culture, in which we are still enmeshed, where men and women's relations are confrontational. Riane Eisler in her recent ground-breaking interpretation of prehistoric culture, *The Chalice and the Blade*, posits another model, that of partnership. Analysis of the more obvious sexual symbols such as the pregnant female with the bull (see fig. 9) suggests complementarity of male and female, which continues throughout the prehistoric Goddess culture. This fundamental division between male and female does not directly depict the human sexual act since the representation of anatomical details is rarely realistic. Vulvae and phalli are symbolic representations of the universal life force. What Leroi-Gourhan once read as confrontation can now be seen as complementary.

Although it generally has been assumed that Paleolithic peoples did not understand the causal relationship between sexual intercourse and human reproduction, Marschack suggests that they did know about sexual fertilization in animals[8] and that the female sexual symbol, the vulva, is often found in association with animal and plant life. At times the human phallus is represented within the vulva (see fig. 8).

Leroi-Gourhan's work is a useful reference because it catalogs and organizes a vast amount of visual imagery hitherto known only selectively. His general conclusions are provocative but limited because he does not interpret his findings. There is much work to be done by prehistorians.

Marschack's objective, on the other hand, is to comprehend the way in which the imagery functioned so as to gain a deeper understanding of what went on in the hearts and minds of these early humans. Using such new investigative technologies as microscopy and infrared and ultraviolet photography, which reveal far more than the naked eye can, he examined both the overpainting and the scratches on the cave walls, as well as the notches in the small carved and engraved objects found at habitation sites. His theory suggests that both had ritual use and marked changes over time in the world around them.

He noted that the carved notches record lunar cycles and sequences and that Paleolithic people were aware of the diversity of the seasons. Based on his conclusions, we can conjecture that gathering and hunting peoples whose survival depended upon the ability to adjust to seasonal changes would also have noticed the natural changes in women's bodies and the rutting seasons of animals. The carved notches also might have recorded the menstrual cycle and the lunar months of pregnancy. These marks were not only functional but probably also were part of the ritual process through which all were

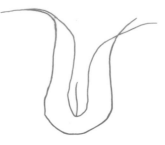

8. PHALLUS INSIDE VULVA, ca. 21,000–20,000 B.C.E. Drawing from engraving on stone. From Isturitz, French Pyrenees. Drawing after Marschack.

connected to the cosmic renewal of life. The world is born, not made; it is a birth process. The earliest rituals may have honored the menstrual cycle, the womb blood that nurtured the new life.

Male animals and human females appear together on ritual objects. Marschack attempts to recover the underlying story, the myth. Examining an enigmatic scene engraved on a bit of reindeer bone that showed the hind legs and phallus of a bison standing over a very pregnant, naked woman, Marschack speculated about several possible interpretations (see fig. 9). Her braceleted hand seems to be raised in worship. Does this scene depict a real woman praying for safe delivery in childbirth, or is she the Goddess in a fertility myth? The scene, Marschack thinks, may be both realistic and mythical, carved as part of a ritual in which a woman and an animal participate in telling a story about the Goddess and a mythical animal. The myth may be part of a ritual to ensure human fertility, the fertility of the earth, or the increase of animals for the hunt.[9]

Beginning with the Paleolithic, a horned and hoofed animal—bison, bull, buffalo—represents the male principle and virility. Ten thousand years ago, the wild bull was one of the most formidable animals in the forests of Europe and the Near East. A shaggy-maned bovine with a large head, short

9. PREGNANT WOMAN WITH BULL, Middle Magdalenian, ca. 12,000 B.C.E. Engraving on reindeer bone. From Laugerie Basse (Dordogne), France.

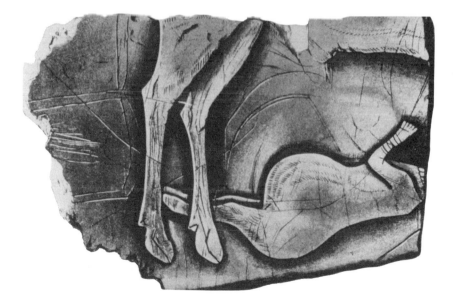

horns, and heavy, powerful forequarters surmounted by a large fleshy hump, the wild bull, standing almost six feet at the shoulders, weighed about a ton.

Why was the male expressed in an animal, the female by a human form? Perhaps it was because the life-giving potential in the woman was readily apparent in her capacity to bear and nurture the young, while man's role in procreation may not have been been fully understood until animals were domesticated and bred. The sexual energy of the great horned animal in the rutting season must have been impressive. The bison and pregnant female on the bone fragment that intrigued Marschack (see fig. 9) symbolize a fundamental life-renewing force; the relation between animal and human seems completely natural.

Another association of the female and the horned animal can be observed in one of the most beautiful Paleolithic females, the bountiful Goddess of Laussel. Unique among the figures of the sacred female, she is carved on a limestone slab at the entrance to a rock shelter in the Dordogne in France. She holds a notched bison horn in her raised right hand while her left hand points to her vulva (see fig. 10 and color plate 33). Traces of the sacred red ochre are still visible on her body, and her abdomen swells gently, perhaps indicating pregnancy.

The mouth of the cave analogous to the entrance to the Mother's womb must have been especially sacred. The Laussel shelter itself was probably a place of ritual. On the inner walls are carvings of several female figures, two animals (a doe and a horse), a fragment of an elegant male who looks as if his arms were raised in ritual gesture, and a curious double image that appears to be a copulating couple.

Marschack suggests that these images may have been part of a complex ritual that associated pregnancy in women with rutting, migration, and calving in animals.[10] The notched horn may represent the crescent moon symbolizing new life. The thirteen lines incised on the horn may mark the months of the lunar calendar.

The woman holding the animal horn is marked with the red color of life and appears to be pregnant, the swelling of her belly emphasized by the natural projection of the rock on which she is carved. Joseph Campbell remarks that "the figure must have represented some mythic personage so well known

10. EARTH MOTHER OF LAUSSEL, ca. 25,000 B.C.E. Limestone. 17 in. Laussel (Dordogne), France.

to the period that the reference of the elevated horn would have been as readily understood as, say, in India, a lotus in the hand of the goddess Shri Lakshmi [see color plate 19a and b], or in the West, a child at the breast of the Virgin."[11] Indeed, the dramatic placement of her image over the shelter's entrance to catch the light of the sun recalls the image of the Virgin on the portals of Gothic cathedrals.

The essential needs of early humans were not very different from our own. Through myth and ritual we humans engage the universal, we go beyond the existential anxieties of our daily life. Marschack conjectures that the small portable objects representing body parts found on shelter floors were used in rituals connected to women's primary biological processes: menstruation, copulation, birth, and lactation. He concludes that the Goddess was conceived to explain the forces Paleolithic peoples observed in human and animal life, and like all symbols, the image of the Goddess was capable of expressing more than one reality at the same time. She was both the sacred female and sacred nature.

The Sacred Triangle Is the Threshold through Which Life Emerges

The visual language established in the Paleolithic for the sacred female is the key to understanding the prehistoric Goddess. The omnipresent sexual symbolism was not erotic in our modern sense of the term, that is, intended to arouse sexual desire, for it indicated not only human reproduction but also the life force, an energy that emanated from the earth. The cave sanctuary was the sacred place of contact with this power where the two great categories of creatures, human and animal, were part of a vision of natural and spiritual forces intermingled.

The ubiquitous vulva takes many forms and shapes (see fig. 11). One, the flower, is universally associated with the Goddess.

11. CARVED AND ENGRAVED VULVA IMAGES from the upper Paleolithic, ca. 30,000–9000 B.C.E. a. Bodrog Kesztur, Hungary, b. Laussel, c. Lalinde, d. La Ferrasie, e. La Ferrasie, f. Les Combarelles, g. Pergouset, h. La Ferraise. Drawing after Marschack.

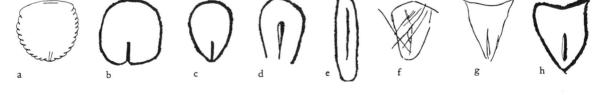

12. BELL-SHAPED VULVAE WITH PLANT, Early Magdalenian. Painting on cave wall. El Castillo, Spanish Pyrenees. The bell-shaped vulvae are painted red and the plant is painted black.

In a cave painting in the Spanish Pyrenees, the connection is clear—the vulva as flower is the sacred threshold through which life emerges (see fig. 12).

The sacred triangle is a natural symbol for women's genitalia. Two women in sculptured relief face each other at the entrance of the cave at La Magdelaine, France. The carving is exceptional in Paleolithic art for the delicate modeling of the human form and the natural rendering that follows the contours of the rock. In the figure at the right, the vulva was deeply cut. It was this sharp-edged triangle that caught the eye of the archaeologist who discovered the relief[12] (see fig. 13). The dual representation of the vulva as both an abstract symbol and as a part of the natural female anatomy shows up again later in the Goddess figures of the ancient Mediterranean and Near East (see figs. 14, 15).

Perhaps we can understand the meaning of the vulva symbol more fully if we look to India where the sacred triangle continues to represent divine power. India would appear to be heir to the iconographic tradition we have identified in the

13

13. RECLINING FIGURE WITH ABSTRACT VULVA, ca. 10,000 B.C.E. Engraved on cave wall. About 1 m. La Magdelaine (Tarn) France.

14. THE CYPRIOT GODDESS, ca. 2500 B.C.E. Clay. Cyprus.

The Cypriot goddess with child in arms, an early Madonna, appears to be wearing a bikini-like garment. On closer scrutiny we realize that what we took for clothing is a prominent sacred triangle.

15. ASTARTE, ca. 1600–1500 B.C.E. Gold. 8 cm. × 4 cm. Syro-Palestinian.

Only the face of the Goddess and her sacred triangle are displayed on the gold Astarte amulet from ancient Palestine.

14

15

Paleolithic. Twenty thousand years after the growing plant was painted among the vulva symbols in a Spanish cave, we find a variation on the wall of a village house in Rajasthan (see fig. 16).

In the Hindu *Shakta* tradition the Goddess is worshiped as the ultimate reality and the *yantra,* the downward pointing triangle, is the ritual diagram used in meditation to invoke her presence. The Kali *yantra* represents *shakti,* the life force, cosmic energy experienced as female. The dot in the center space is the *bindo,* the seed of life (see figs. 17 and 18).

16

17

18

16. Yoni with Vegetation, twentieth century. Wall painting. Rajasthan, India.

17. Kali Yantra, eighteenth century. Gouache on paper. 7 × 7 in. Rajasthan, India.

18. Sages Worshiping the Yoni, twelfth century. Bas-relief, stone. Chausatti Temple. Bheraghat, Madya Pradesh, India

The veneration of the vulva in India is familiar and affectionate. When passing a sculpture of the Goddess it is customary to touch her sacred place, the *yoni*. A twelfth-century relief sculpture carved on the walls of a South Indian Goddess temple is quite explicit about where her power resides. Two holy men are seated at the foot of a giant-sized, rather naturalistic looking vulva, their hands raised in prayer.

In another ritual diagram, the *Shri Yantra*, the downward pointing triangle of the Goddess, intersects with the upward pointing one of her consort, the God Shiva (see fig. 19). *Shri* is a very ancient name of the Goddess used with particular reference to her role as the source of all life, for without *shakti*, primal energy, the male god is dormant, lifeless. There is a popular folk saying in India that without *shakti* Shiva is a corpse. The Hindu Goddess is immanent; every woman is *shakti*. Her presence at ritual is auspicious, life enhancing. A man cannot perform most rituals without a wife. At life-cycle rituals such as puberty and marriage, the presence of the Goddess is invoked and the woman herself becomes the Goddess.

This living tradition gives us first-hand knowledge of the meaning of the sacred triangle, a continuing symbol of the Goddess's power from the beginning of human culture to

19. Shri Yantra, eighteenth century. Gouache on paper. Rajasthan, India.

the present day. The key symbols that carry the underlying meaning of the Goddess religion are already articulated in Ice Age art and ritual: the Earth Mother, the cave that is her womb, the sacred triangle out of which new life emerges, and the horned bovine that represents the male principle. From the beginning male and female symbols complement each other, and both sexes were depicted as necessary for the renewal of life.

What is so startling as we reflect on the opening chapter of the Goddess's story is that the framework of her mythology is already in place, the essential visual language established. The sacred female will evolve into the Great Goddess of Neolithic culture.

The Unfolding of Her Mysteries

CHAPTER 2

With the final retreat of the glaciers northward some twelve thousand years ago, the climate changed dramatically. The weather became wetter and warmer and much of Europe was covered with forests. As the large herds that were the primary source of food disappeared because they could not tolerate the warmer weather, our migrating ancestors were forced to abandon their way of life. Gradually, in different regions at different times, the gatherers and hunters became farmers and breeders of animals, settling down in villages and towns. We call this new age the Neolithic—*neo*, new; *lithic* refers to the stone tools used. Paleolithic was the old, the earlier, stone age.

With the shift from gathering and hunting to agriculture everything changed. As is usually the case in history, radical changes in life-style and technology are accompanied by an ideological transformation. In the Neolithic a profound rethinking of humankind's relation to its environment took place. Before, men and women had been "part of nature, at her mercy, it is true, but also securely in her shelter."[1] Now they had to actively intervene with nature to co-create their food supply.

Agriculture and animal husbandry originated in the well-watered upland plateaus of Anatolia, the region in Asia Minor that is now part of southern Turkey, where the grasses and animals that later became domesticated were found in a wild state. With the disappearance of the large animals, people were hard pressed and for a while had to hunt smaller game such as gazelle and water fowl. Still living in a semi-nomadic state, they began to herd and breed animals that produced meat and milk to supplement their diet of game and seed-bearing grasses.

This eventually led to the sickle to cut wild grasses and a rudimentary silo to store the surplus, inventions that go back as far as 10,000 B.C.E.

Women are now generally credited by prehistorians with the discovery of agriculture. As gatherers of the natural food of the land, they must have observed how the grasses reseeded themselves. Experimenting with the natural seeds, women developed and cultivated grains that were to become the chief foods. They learned to husk, to grind, and to bake wheat and barley into bread. A strong link was forged connecting women as the cultivators of grain, to grain as the bounty of the Goddess, and to bread as the staff of life. Ovens, grain storage bins, and grinding stones became essential ritual furnishings of Goddess shrines. Cakes baked by priestesses were offered to the Goddess in gratitude for the harvest.

With a surplus of food and storage facilities, populations increased, trade became possible, and life was enriched through contact among cultures. The material arts flourished. As Neolithic people learned to spin and weave wool and flax, the natural animal and vegetable fibers, into cloth they were no longer dependent on animal skins for clothing. Clay utensils must have been made in the Ice Age to store food and water, but since they were not fired none have been preserved. With the invention of the kiln, pottery became an art. Weaving and pottery were gifts of the Goddess and the shrines of Old Europe included workshops with looms and kilns.

These changes took place over many centuries; the Neolithic revolution was essentially accomplished by the eighth millennium B.C.E. With agriculture as the economic base, the village or town as the primary social unit, and religion with priestly specialists and shrines institutionalized, the foundations of Western civilization were established.

Simultaneously, a profound revision of symbolic vocabulary took place. The surviving art documents an ideological evolution in human consciousness: People saw themselves in a new relationship to the environment and to other living species. Human, mostly female, representation was growing in importance; the male was still generally confined to a zoomorphic form. Images and symbols of the Goddess that had been part of the artistic production of the Paleolithic are now dominant.

In the new iconography the parts of the female body symbolic of fertility continue to be exaggerated, but now the Goddess is characteristically rendered in the squatting posture of birthing. The head is more naturalistic with facial features shown. Emphasis is on the eyes, indicated by incised clay lozenges or bitumen inlays, the prototype of the Eye Goddess who searched human souls. In time iconographic formulas were developed to express different aspects of the Great Goddess. These are the foremothers of the goddesses we know from ancient mythology and perhaps reflect an evolving psychological sense of self.

Animal and human identities continue to overlap, but their relationship is expressed in new ways. Totemic figures, half-human, half-animal, manifest animal powers in human bodies. The Old European bird and snake goddesses are cosmic creators, guardians of the life-giving waters above and below, the rains and the underground streams. The many animal epiphanies of the Goddess symbolize qualities needed for survival—the regenerative powers of the butterfly, the fabled nurture of the bear for her cubs, and the prodigious fecundity of the pig. The ritual terracotta masks of Old Europe provide insight into the role of the priestess who impersonated the animal spirit she was evoking.

With the working of the soil came a new understanding of the landscape as sacred. The hills, the rivers, and the mountains were seen as parts of the Great Mother's body. Her sanctuaries in Crete were sited in direct relation to these natural symbols. The megalithic builders of Western Europe connected the sacred landscape with the paths of the heavenly bodies.

In the following chapters we will look at aspects of the Goddess religion through analysis of the meaning of the sacred art of five different cultures, Çatal Hüyük, Old Europe, Malta, Avebury, and Crete. Although conditions of life radically altered and would continue to do so in ages to come, the human impulse to conceive the divine force as female would remain a constant.

What previously had been an intuition of the earth as the ground of being and source of all life, imaged as the sacred female, now developed into a belief system and ritual practice whose values were the relations of humans to the land and to all living creatures. The role of the Goddess was understood as both life giver and life taker; burial in her great womb meant rebirth. Self-creating, autonomous, she was the all powerful Mother. The vital connection between the magical power that provided food necessary to sustain life, woman as birth-giver and nurturer, and the female deity was expressed in art and ritual.

Evidence for the worship of the Goddess in Europe and the Near East is accumulating. Just cataloging the finds of female figures and other archaeological records—tools, weapons, eating utensils, ritual objects, burial sites, and dwelling places—would fill several volumes.[2] During the Neolithic we find the clues that Marschack was looking for in the Paleolithic, those that reveal how early humans thought about themselves and their world. There is abundant visual material from which to reconstruct the story, myth, and ritual that celebrated the power, sensuality, and sacredness of women's bodies.

Perhaps the most provocative discovery of recent archaeological research is that nowhere in Neolithic Goddess cultures is there any sign of warfare. There is no evidence of fortifications, of violent death, invasion, or conquest. We can only conclude that there was some direct relation between Goddess religion and peaceful coexistence. Neolithic Goddess culture was woman-centered, peaceful, prosperous, and nonhierarchical.

Çatal Hüyük: Birth, Death, and Regeneration

CHAPTER 3

Çatal Hüyük, in Anatolia, is the most important Neolithic site in the Near East. Monumental images of the Goddess emblazoned on the walls of the shrines celebrate her powers as life giver and life taker. She is shown in the act of giving birth, at that moment of "crowning" when life first emerges from the womb. A powerful naked figure modeled in bold relief with arms and legs spread wide—although her face is not human and her body is catlike, she clearly represents the female principle (see fig. 20). Also the life taker, she is symbolized as a great vulture swooping down to devour the flesh of the dead (see fig. 21).

The Goddess is the fountainhead of regeneration. Beaks of the life-taking vultures embedded in plaster breasts, symbols of life-giving nurture, line the walls of yet another shrine. Responsible for the ongoing round of life, the Goddess lived directly among her people. Her shrines were built in the midst of their dwelling places, one for every four or five houses. The discovery of Çatal Hüyük by British archaeologist James Mellaart in 1961–63, with a wealth of intact shrines in an exceptional state of preservation, has opened up a whole new perspective on the worship of the Goddess.

Çatal Hüyük, the First Known Urban Center

Mellaart is aware of the potential of Çatal Hüyük for reconstructing the human narrative. Sensitive to the place of religious belief and practice in this story, his publications document fully all surviving evidence of cult and ritual. His interpretation is radically innovative, revealing a more com-

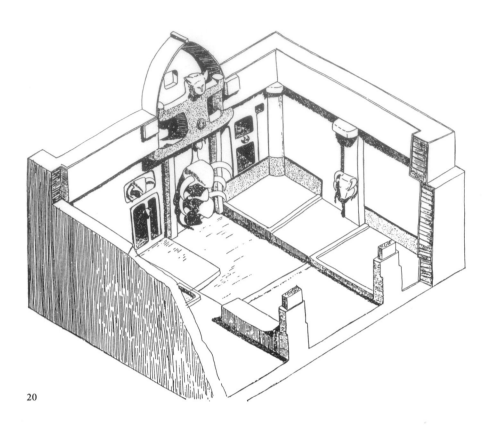

20

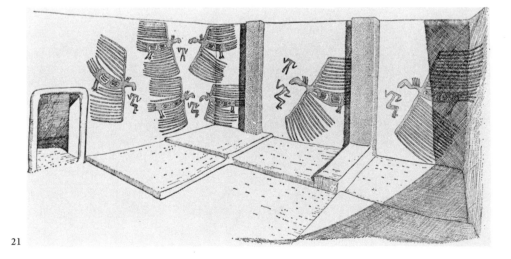

21

20. THE GODDESS AS LIFE GIVER, seventh millennium B.C.E. Bas-relief. 4.5 m. Çatal Hüyük.

The Goddess is giving birth to a bull. Three life-size plaster heads are superimposed in the wall below; actual skull plates with attached horns of the animal are embedded in the plaster.

21. THE GODDESS AS LIFE TAKER, seventh millennium B.C.E. Bas-relief. Çatal Hüyük.

Vultures with wing spans of five feet, swoop down on the headless human corpses. Three fly to the right, four to the left in a continuous mural that wraps around the walls of the shrine. What awe and terror they must have inspired!

prehensive understanding of the meaning of the Goddess by Neolithic peoples than previously had been accepted by scholars.

The first known urban center, Çatal Hüyük is a remarkable city that flourished in the seventh millennium B.C.E. Built in the midst of the fertile wheat fields of the Anatolian plain, the early city included woods and parkland where red deer and wild cattle freely roamed. The primary sources of wealth lay in abundant agricultural products and trade in obsidian, a precious black volcanic glass prized for its hardness because it could be used to make knives.

A cosmopolitan community, the citizens could afford luxuries like obsidian mirrors, elegant stone ceremonial daggers, and trinkets of metal, beyond the reach of any of their known contemporaries.[1] Artisans were well trained and highly specialized. Copper and lead smelted and worked into beads and small tools was the beginning of metallurgy. Their textiles and pottery are the earliest known and much like those still being made in modern Turkey. A peaceful society, there is no sign of fortifications or warfare in eight hundred years of settlement.

The fifty-foot Neolithic mound at Çatal Hüyük explored thus far reveals twelve successive layers, the remains of twelve different cities, one built on top of the other. By 1963 only one acre of the thirty-two-acre site had been excavated when the Turkish government halted the project. What has been recovered makes what remains buried tantalizing. It is an ideal site for archaeologists because no buildings have been erected since the Neolithic period, and the city was undisturbed except for the natural damage to the surface layers caused by wind and soil erosion. The buildings below the top level were well preserved.

Well organized, the city was laid out like a pueblo without streets, large plaza, or palace. Flat-roofed, mud-brick houses and shrines were built around open courtyards. The buildings showed little variation in size or in the wealth or possessions of the occupants. Entrance was by ladder through an opening in the roof. The interiors were found in immaculately clean condition. Every room, large and small, had built-in furniture—sleeping platforms, benches for food preparation, oval ovens, and hearths with adjacent storage space for grain. Clay boxes served as tool kits, rush matting was used for cushions, and textiles provided bedding just as today in much of the Near East.

The dead were buried under the platforms used as beds. The large main platform on the north wall belonged to the mistress of the house. Children were buried with their mother, suggesting a society in which descent was through the mother. Men's platforms were smaller and not in any fixed place.

Çatal Hüyük appears to have been a city of shrines and may indeed have been the sacred center for other settlements on the surrounding Anatolian plain. In plan and construction the shrines were no different from the ordinary dwellings and included all the same built-in furniture. They can be identified easily as sanctuaries by their relief sculpture and wall paintings. At the time of Mellaart's excavations, altars were still in place and cult statues still lay on the floor where they had been left when the city was set ablaze by fires from the eruptions of nearby volcanos around 5700 B.C.E. After serving a ritual function, the paintings and sculpture had been covered with whitewash, sometimes as many as a hundred layers.

Images of the Great Goddess

The oldest shrines in Çatal Hüyük show the transition from a gatherer-hunter to an agricultural society. As in the Paleolithic caves, the earliest walls are covered with pictures of animals, manifestations of divine power. The act of painting was part of ritual to invoke the animal's spirit. When a shrine was abandoned, the numinous power of the relief sculptures had to be ritually desacralized by destroying the heads and feet of the image. Also, as agriculture replaced hunting, the first Goddess images began to appear on the shrine walls.

22. THE MAIDEN, seventh millennium B.C.E. Bas-relief. Çatal Hüyük.

The Maiden, the Youthful Goddess, arms and legs stretched wide, is running, dancing, whirling, her hair floating behind her in the wind.

23. THE MOTHER, seventh millennium B.C.E. Terracotta. Çatal Hüyük.

The Mother, her full maternal body in the squatting birth posture characteristic of the Neolithic, gently presses her hands to her bosom.

24. THE CRONE, seventh millennium B.C.E. Marble. Çatal Hüyük.

The grim-faced Crone, the Goddess of Death, was found kneeling beside a bird of prey.

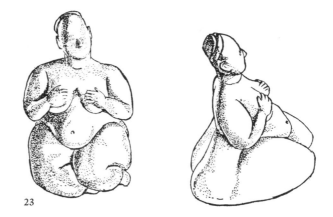

23

24

The Great Goddess in the fullness of her being took on various roles. The names in other Near Eastern and Mediterranean cultures may have been different, but the basic personae were the same as in Çatal Hüyük. We can easily identify the Triple Goddess—as a young maiden, a birth-giving matron, and an old woman or crone—who represents the life cycle of women (see figs. 22–24).

The Triple Goddess was associated with the three phases of the moon—waxing, full, and waning—as well as with the three worlds—heaven, earth, and the underworld. In her third aspect as crone, she represented old age or death, "the inevitable destruction or dissolution that must precede regeneration."

> The Crone also represented the third, post-menopausal, phase of women's lives; her shrines were served by priestesses in this stage of life. Because it was believed that women became very wise when they no longer shed the lunar wise blood but kept it within, the Crone was usually a Goddess of Wisdom.[2]

The rich finds at Çatal Hüyük and the fact that the site was self-enclosed make it possible to follow the development of the Goddess image and observe how her fully three-dimensional naturalistic icon evolved out of unshaped stone. In more ancient times before the city was built, the Goddess was worshiped in the caves of the nearby Taurus Mountain in the form of a stalactite, a limestone accretion that hung from the ceiling. The elemental form of the Goddess is a natural one, a sacred rock or stone, charged with the energy of the molten fires deep in the earth out of which all matter was formed.

She is the earth. Early crudely carved figures were inspired by the mysterious stalactites, ever dripping, ever growing in the mountain caverns that were believed to be the haunt of the Earth Mother and the realm of the dead. When the urban people of Çatal Hüyük built their first shrines, they continued to worship the natural forms from the caves, sometimes carving just the top of a stone into a crude human head. A small blue limestone boulder incised with a few lines for eyes and mouth was sufficient to turn it into a pregnant woman.

This formal progression to a naturalistic three-dimensional form was not always steady; old forms continued to be made and overlapped with new ones. We can observe the evolution of the Mother of the Earth into the Great Goddess through her changing image. The elemental forms continue to be worshiped along with the newer ones. The mysterious powers of the Earth Mother were never forgotten.

Male and Female in Complementary Relationship

As in the Paleolithic caves and shelters, the symbols for male and female appear in complementary relationship. The Life-giving Goddess is the dominant image, sometimes projecting into an arcaded niche above the roof line with bulls' heads embedded in the wall below (see fig. 20). The female principle is represented by the Goddess, the male by the bull or other horned beast. Bulls' horns and female human breasts were molded on the wall side by side. Together they represent new life.

No two shrines are alike. There is a play and variation in the representation of the male and female. Ram and stag sometimes stand in for the bull. The Goddess gives birth to a bull and to a ram. This affinity between human and animal is a continuation of Paleolithic sensibility.

Wild bulls were venerated in the Near East long before the animal was domesticated. Bull skulls were found in the walls of houses in the Middle Euphrates region in the late ninth millennium B.C.E. The image of the bull is everywhere at Çatal Hüyük. Marija Gimbutas comments that the sacredness of the bull was expressed in particular through emphasis on its horns.[3] With mysterious powers of growth and regeneration, horns were already a lunar symbol in the late Paleolithic relief at

Laussel (see fig. 10). The schematized bull's horns, one of the basic symbols of the Goddess religion, is used as the altar of consecration throughout the Neolithic and Bronze ages. This is a particularly compelling multidimensional symbol because of its formal resemblance to women's organs of reproduction, the fallopian tubes and the uterus.[4] In the early shrines, bulls' heads are usually modeled in clay and plastered with enormous upturned horns. Centuries later the actual horns and frontal bones of the wild bull were used, enhancing the awesome power of the animal symbol (see fig. 25).

The bull continues to be identified with the male in the Indo-European symbol system as the animal form of gods like the Greek Zeus and Hindu Shiva. The same two symbolic forms, the one, the bovine—bull or buffalo—and the other, the anthropomorphic image of the Goddess with emphasis on her procreative body parts, continue to represent the male and female life force from the earliest known visual art to the living traditions of India.

25. BULL, BUCRANIA, AND BULLS' HEADS, seventh millennium B.C.E. Bas-relief. Çatal Hüyük.

Life-sized silhouettes of the bull, lively and naturalistic, were cut into the plaster wall and painted bright red. Bucrania, stylized bull heads and horns set on pillars, served as altars and ritual benches.

Birthing Room

One shrine at Çatal Hüyük is strikingly different from all the others. Excavator James Mellaart was at a loss to explain its curious features. The walls and floor were painted red. The floor of burnished limestone had been relaid at least twice. A molded plaster porthole enabled an observer to look in. Gutters ran alongside the raised sleeping platform. Dorothy Cameron, the Australian artist who was part of Mellaart's research team, suggests that this was a birthing room where women went for delivery.[5] Red was the color of life, of birth. To find such a shrine in a society whose central cult image was of the Great Goddess giving birth seems reasonable.

Cameron's provocative identification of the frieze painted on the west wall of this shrine as symbol of the birth process further supports her interpretation. She sees the cream-colored circular forms with red centers and outlined in red as the cervix, that ring of muscle below the uterus through which the baby begins its journey out of the mother's body. The thick line underneath the circles painted in the same cream color and also outlined in red is the umbilical cord; the thin wavy lines covering both "cervix" and "cord" is the amniotic fluid in which the baby is suspended during pregnancy. According to Marija Gimbutas zigzags, wavy lines, and interlocking spirals, common features of both Paleolithic and Neolithic art, represent the waters of life, the cosmic deep from which all life springs.[6]

If we accept Cameron's theory, the architectural features and furnishings that so puzzled Mellaart were for the practical business of childbirth. The long red runnels carried the plentiful water needed during confinement, the floor burnished and hardened for easy cleaning. Perhaps the porthole was like the observation window in a modern hospital, to check up on what was going on inside. When we reflect on the awesomeness and danger of human birth we can well imagine that Neolithic women would seek the protective power of the Great Mother at the time of delivery, and that her priestesses would have served as midwives. Cameron's theory is congruent with the holistic character of the Çatal Hüyük cult in which birth and death were so powerfully portrayed.

26. BURIAL RITE, ca. 6150 B.C.E.
Reconstruction of shrine at Çatal Hüyük.
After Mellaart.

Funerary Ritual

A funerary rite, with priestesses ceremonially dressed as great birds, has been reconstructed based on the discovery of wall paintings of vultures with human legs. Human skulls were found on the platforms below them (see fig. 26). Secondary burial, excarnation, was widespread in the Neolithic. The bodies of the dead were first exposed to the vultures who stripped the bones clean. The wall paintings at Çatal Hüyük illustrate this preliminary process. Later, the bones were wrapped in cloths or placed in baskets and buried underneath the sleeping platforms in the family home.

Popular lore unfairly maligns vultures, which are neither aggressive nor predators, but scavengers. In the ancient world the vulture is sacred to the Goddess and is referred to as her compassionate purifier,[7] which cleaned up the rotting flesh of death. Vultures still play this role for Zoroastrians in Iran and India who expose their dead in high towers. At Çatal Hüyük, skulls of vultures, foxes, and weasels, all scavengers who thrive on carcasses, are embedded in rows of "mothers' " breasts. The people must have seen life and death as complementary rather than opposed.

These dramatic images reveal the forms in which the divine presence was invoked, but we are still thrown back on our imaginations to reconstruct the ceremonies that took place there. We do have a few clues. In one of the shrines of the Life-giving Goddess, burnt grain was placed on the bucrania, the stylized bull horns that served as ceremonial altars. Perhaps like biblical sacrifices, they were a gift of the fruits of the first harvest.

In the grain bin adjacent to this shrine a small votive image was found lying on the floor, the Goddess represented as the "Life Giver" in a fully human form (see fig. 27).

The Goddess's association with wild animals reflects her original role as provider of game, the Patroness of the Hunt. Embracing all life in its myriad forms, her divine nature includes the animal as well as the human. The leopard is her representative and lends its strength and dignity to enhance her powers. As Mistress of the Animals, she ultimately evolved into Artemis of Ephesus (see color plate 35) whose cult was so popular in the ancient world. The memory of the power of the animals on the walls of the great cave sanctuaries was still potent.

The purpose of the ritual at Çatal Hüyük was the same as that in the Paleolithic caves. The Goddess was placed in the grain bin to promote the fertility of the crops. Another clue was the handprint left by the worshiper—a child's print on a mother's breast, an adult's on a bull's head, rows of handprints on wall panels made by pressing a hand against the wall and painting around it. The hand is the most versatile of instruments, the symbol of creation, of effort, and of humans themselves, the mark "I was there." Its ritual use is universal and still practiced by Native Americans, Hindus, and traditional peoples worldwide. "It is the hand which sought blessings in prayer, the hand which caressed and the hand which warded off evil."[8]

A male god was also part of Goddess iconography, even if his role was subordinate. His presence acknowledges that the male and female were complementary and integral to under-

27. Votive Image of the Goddess as Life Giver, seventh millennium B.C.E. Terracotta. Çatal Hüyük.

Her posture is regal. Elegantly costumed and coiffed, she gives birth enthroned between two leopards. The leopard is both her guard and her pet. She reaches out to pat him on the head. He supports her in her confinement, his tail curls around her shoulders. She wears his skin as her dress. Mother of animal and human, she holds two leopard cubs, one in each arm.

standing the religion of the Great Goddess. Mellaart speculates on the basis of later mythology that the young male shown riding the leopard is probably her son, the older bearded man on the bull, her consort. We know from historical accounts that the union of the Goddess with her lover-consort was an annual ritual, usually enacted at the New Year to ensure the fertility of the land (see fig. 28).

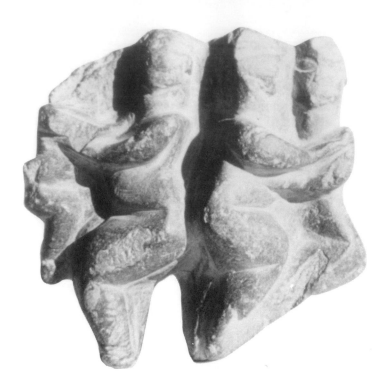

Four figures carved in bold relief on a greenish-grey schist plaque may represent two successive states in the Sacred Marriage Rite, the *hieros gamos*. On the left, a couple embrace; on the right, the mother holds a child, the fruit of their union, symbolic of the whole community's well-being. This iconography suggests that the causal relationship between intercourse and procreation was now fully understood.

A Religion Aimed at Conservation of Life in All Its Forms

At Çatal Hüyük, the earliest known culture documenting the Goddess, religion displays the full range of her iconography. The mood is joyful, the dominant themes celebrating the renewal of life. The art expresses a spontaneity and free spirit, a healthy respect for the life force in both men and women, along with an acknowledgment of the dread power of death and the mystery of the unknown.

Religious practice was intimate, personal, integrated into rhythms of ordinary life. The shrines were next to the dwellings, sharing the same courtyard, with the same structure and the same furniture. The priestesses and their families were part of the community, sharing common space, common tasks like ritual bread making.

Çatal Hüyük has given us a picture of the development of the Neolithic Goddess religion and is most important for our reconstruction of her full story. What were the conditions that made this possible? Mellaart speculates that when agriculture replaced hunting, women came to control both the new food supply and the wealth it generated. They were responsible for the agricultural revolution in the first place and continued to be in charge of its production.

> As the only source of life she became associated with the processes of agriculture, with the taming and nourishing of domesticated animals, with the ideas of increase, abundance and fertility. Hence a religion which aimed at exactly that same conservation of life in all its forms, its propagation and the mysteries of its rites connected with life and death, birth and resurrection, were evidently part of her sphere rather than that of man. It seems extremely likely that the cult of the goddess was administered mainly by women, even if the presence of male priests was by no means excluded. . . .[9]

Mellaart's conclusion that with economic and social power women were able to transform society in terms of their own values sounds strikingly modern, not unlike contemporary feminist objectives. Although we must always be cautious about interpreting the past in terms of the present, we can speculate on the basis of the visual evidence. As historian of religion Ann Barstow comments, "If ever an early society tried to communicate through its art, this society tried, through these lively, natural, life-like figures."[10]

While Çatal Hüyük was flourishing in the Near East, another women-centered Goddess culture was evolving in southeastern Europe. Archaeologist Marija Gimbutas has identified the earliest European civilization as Old Europe (ca. 6500–3500 B.C.E).

Old Europe:
Cosmic Creation and the Maintenance of Life

CHAPTER 4

In Old Europe the spirit of the Goddess was manifest in the creatures of the woodland and farmyard whose powers were different from those of the wild animals painted on the walls of the Paleolithic caves. While worship of the Goddess was integrated into the daily lives of her devotees at Çatal Hüyük with her shrines adjacent to their homes, her cult images as life giver and life taker project an awesome presence. In Old Europe the divine is on a more intimate scale, brought into the cottage as it were, and expresses the everyday concerns of a people who believed they had much to learn from the animals. We discover there the beginnings of a mythology whose folklore and fairy tales still delight us. The epiphanies of the Goddess were the bird and the bee, the toad and the duck, the bear and the snake. Their terracotta images were ritual objects full of humor and fancy. When we find a model of a Bird Goddess shrine in the form of a birdhouse complete with a round hole for her symbolic visit, we are filled with wonder at the playful imagination displayed (see fig. 41).

There was no sharp break between the Paleolithic and the Neolithic in Old Europe. Our understanding of life in the earlier culture is still speculative because the evidence is so fragmentary. We are on firmer ground in Old Europe because so much more has survived, and we have the ground-breaking interpretation of Marija Gimbutas as our foundation.

More Than Three Thousand Settlements

Çatal Hüyük was one isolated site; nothing like it has been discovered outside the Near East. Old Europe with its more than three thousand settlements was the link between the

Paleolithic and Greek cultures on which Western civilization is based. Old European civilization was savagely destroyed by patriarchal Indo-European invaders, but the mythology, imagery, and practices of their Goddess religion survived as a fertile substratum underlying later European cultural developments that continued to enrich the European psyche well into the Renaissance. Long after Christianity had dealt a death blow to the Goddess religion, remnants were still alive among agricultural peoples.[1]

Geographically, Old Europe extended from the Adriatic to the Aegean, including the islands, and as far to the north as Czechoslovakia, southern Poland, and the western Ukraine. This area, opened up archaeologically since World War II, has pushed back our knowledge of European culture three to four thousand years.

The germinal work of Gimbutas is fundamentally important in recovering the religion and culture of Old Europe. With penetrating intelligence seasoned by first-hand knowledge of Neolithic and Copper Age cultures, she has looked at the archaeological evidence with fresh eyes, identifying a coherent mythology that is the key to the continuity of Goddess symbolism. Neolithic deities evolved out of Paleolithic symbols. "The beginning is deep, deep in the past."[2] Although she was not the first to take the larger view, Gimbutas is the first to have analyzed European iconography of the Neolithic and Copper Age systematically in order to reconstruct the underlying belief system.

Her approach looks to the decorative motifs on the artifacts as well as the form of surviving structures to recover the mythology. Her prodigious task has engaged her for forty years. "By 1974 when Gimbutas first published a compendium of findings from her own excavations and from over three thousand other sites, no less than thirty thousand miniature sculptures of clay, marble, bone, copper, and gold had been uncovered, in addition to enormous quantities of ritual vessels, altars, temples, and paintings on both vases and the walls of shrines."[3] Her interpretations are often sparked by her extensive knowledge of folklore. Over and over again, she offers anecdotes and makes associations that sensitize us to the staying power of the mythic image as its meaning is absorbed by one culture after another. Lithuanian born, she spent her summer holidays among farming people whose Christianity was only a thin veneer over old pagan ways, and she was deeply influenced by their respect for all life. Just as in Old Europe, the animals were the teachers.

The Cult of the Fish Mother, a Transitional Iconography

The sanctuary built by the hunting and fishing peoples of Lepinski Vir, a transitional culture of the late seventh and early sixth millennium B.C.E, in the scenic Danube River Basin in northern Yugoslavia, introduces us to the Old European cosmology and symbol system. The river basin is "one of the most remarkable natural regions in Europe."[4] The isolated gorge, not quite a hundred kilometers long, is a world of incredible natural beauty, restricted but "infinitely varied and dynamic. . . . Nowhere else in a single area are there so many different landscapes, so many forms of forest, scent and colour."[5] There are huge oak, beech, and walnut trees, and the steepest slopes are covered with great masses of lilac. "Two practically inexhaustible food sources were to be found at the site: the forest, full of game and with an abundance of fruit-bearing trees, and the river, rich in fish."[6] Furthermore a variety of rocks and minerals were accessible for building materials.

In the rocky hinterlands above the shrines are grey-green sandstone, reddish limestone, and bluish grey marl. A little farther on, the waters laid bare formations of porphyrite and reddish limestone. When the water is low the Danube leaves on its bank a brilliant mosaic of ores and minerals brought down by swift-flowing tributaries from the mountains.

The Danube at this spot flows at great speed, creating big whirlpools and carving gigantic monoliths from rocks that rise from the river's edge.

> Two kilometers to the north and six kilometers to the south, high cliffs constrict the river, shut out the view and form a huge isolated amphitheatre. . . . Out of the river bed upstream rise two enormous porphyry rocks. . . . Here the river becomes a terrifying force in constant movement.[7]

The peoples of Lepenski Vir saw the mystery and power of the Goddess manifest in the great whirling pools of water and built their shrines on the sunny bank of the river aligned with them. Across the river, monolithic rock walls stood like sentinels guarding the sanctuary. The earliest were built into the stony shore and arranged in a semicircle conforming to the natural contours of the land as it rose sharply from the river bank. The later shrines farther up the slope were accessible by ramp or stairs (see fig. 29).

29. SANCTUARY FOUNDATION, sixth millennium B.C.E. Lepenski Vir.

30. FISH MOTHER, sixth millennium B.C.E. Sandstone. 50 cm. Lepenski Vir.

More than fifty shrines have been discovered. They differ in size but all have trapezoid floor plans with rectangular hearths sunk below the floor level.

Large stone sculptures covered with red ochre were set into lime plaster floors in front of the hearths. Some are natural egg-shaped river boulders carved to resemble a fish or with half-fish, half-human features and are decorated with meandering, labyrinthine lines, diamonds, and chevrons representing water. One has female breasts. The sculptures seem to represent a female divinity who "incorporates aspects of an egg, a fish and a woman and which could have been a primeval creator or a mythical ancestress. Standing at the hearth she was probably a guardian of the house"[8] (see fig. 30).

The sculptures also served as altars; more than twenty have depressions carved into the top. In the hearth are the charred remains of dog, deer, and fish sacrifices. Nothing else like the fish sculptures has been found anywhere in Neolithic Europe. They would seem to be "specifically connected with the cult practices of a people whose main concern and subsistence was fishing."[9]

The shape of the shrines and their interior arrangements represent a microcosm of the universe that was imaged as the body of the Goddess. Here again we find the sacred triangle is her symbol. The trapezoid floor plan is merely a triangle with its top cut off, the red color of the floor is the life-sustaining blood. The stones of the forecourt leading into the elongated central hearth may represent the entrance into the Goddess's womb, and the waters and their creatures, new life. According to Gimbutas the fish sculpture at the end of the hearth is one of her manifestations.

The interrelated symbols at Lepenski Vir—the floor plan, the red limestone, the red painted fish-shaped sculptures—all stand for regeneration and reinforce each other. The symbolic identification of fish with rebirth goes back to the Paleolithic. Marschack has shown that images of the fish, like the salmon whose spawning is so dramatic, typically appear in the seasonal representations of early spring, and are frequently associated with new shoots and young animals.[10]

Symbols, particularly those related to gender and sexuality, have a long life and a power deeply rooted in the human psyche. The fish is a worldwide symbol of the Goddess. The

uterus is said to be fish-shaped. Fish and womb (*delphos*) are synonymous in the Greek language, and the sanctuary at Delphi, the place of prophecy, was believed to be the navel of the earth, the connector to the womb (see fig. 31 and color plate 25). Christianity incorporated the Goddess's fish into its own symbol system as the *vesica pisces,* the pointed oval sign for the womb. The Christ Child frequently appeared inside a fish. The early Christians chose the fish as the symbol of Christ; was it coincidental that the Greek word for fish, *ichthys,* was also the acronym for the most common title of their savior?

31. OUR LADY OF THE BEASTS, seventh century B.C.E. Painting on terracotta amphora. Boêotia.

A seventh-century B.C.E. Greek amphora shows the fish inside the body of the Goddess symbolizing the regenerative powers of her womb.

The Many Manifestations of the Great Goddess in Old Europe

The interrelationship of symbol, image, and ritual setting at Lepenski Vir reveals the way in which mythology and cult practice evolved in a specific natural environment. At the same time, in the seventh millennium B.C.E, in the more open areas of southeastern Europe, agricultural peoples began to domesticate plants and animals and to settle down in villages. During the next two thousand years, as they became increasingly efficient in using the resources of the fertile river valleys, their material life improved. Expanding trade and communications on the rivers and the surrounding Mediterranean Sea must have provided a tremendous impetus to cultural exchange.

In time a complex social organization of small townships with government and religious institutions developed. Houses and shrines were built out of "wattle and daub": poles set in the ground, interwoven with slender branches and reeds, and then plastered with earth. These individual structures, one or two stories high, were roofed with thatch. Weaving, pottery, and stone and metal working provided material comforts. Old Europeans learned to work copper and gold to make elegant tools and luxurious ornaments.

As always economic and social change led to a new understanding of the spiritual forces on which well-being depended. The rich mythology and imagery reflect a host of associations that an agricultural people brought to their sacred life. The dominant motif of Old European symbolism was regeneration, the maintenance of life. With agriculture, grain became the sacrament, the symbol of divine reality. We noted the presence of the Life-giving Goddess in the grain bin at Çatal Hüyük. The sacred female of the Ice Age now becomes the Pregnant Vegetation Goddess in Old Europe. In time she will evolve into Demeter, the Grain Goddess who presided over the Mysteries, the personal salvation religions that flourished in late antiquity.

In Old Europe the power of the Great Goddess continued to be expressed in the massive volumes of her body. Characteristically, her forearms are placed on her breasts in a gesture of nurture. The most common image shows her squatting, in the posture of birthing. A complex persona, the European Great Goddess had many manifestations. She was the Bird Goddess, the Snake Goddess, the Mistress of the Waters who creates the world, the Pregnant Vegetation Goddess who was fertility itself. Her epiphanies were the animals and the insects, the bees and the butterflies through whom she projected her powers of regeneration.

Cosmic Creator and Regenerator

Almost all Old European Goddess images are composites. The notion of a hybrid human and animal known in the Paleolithic continued to serve as divine incarnations throughout prehistory in Eurasia.

Gimbutas identifies the parallel lines, chevrons, and the rhythmic meandering patterns found in Paleolithic cave paintings and on their ritual objects, as the primal waters, the rains from above (see fig. 32). These decorations are the marks of the bird and snake goddesses, the cosmic creators in Old European mythology. Moisture, rain, the divine food was metaphorically understood as mother's milk and these goddesses are the nurses. "The presence of the Bird and Snake Goddess is felt everywhere—on earth, in the skies and beyond the clouds where primordial waters lie."[11]

"The Snake Goddess and the Bird Goddess appear both separately and as a single divinity. Their functions are so intimately related that separate treatment is impossible. She is one and she is two, sometimes snake, sometimes bird. She is the goddess of waters and air, assuming the shape of a snake, a crane, a goose, a duck, a diving bird."[12] The water bird who lays the cosmic egg is a universal creation myth (see fig. 33). The veneration of waterfowl goes back to the time of the gatherer-hunters who depended in part upon the seasonal return of the great bird for their food supply. They associated the seasonal migration with the origin of life and created hybrid waterbird and female figures connecting the water sphere where all life begins with the magic vulva of the Goddess. Late Paleolithic images with silhouetted egg-shaped buttocks like the schematic figures made of coal from Petersfels (see fig. 4) probably represent the Goddess pregnant with the cosmic egg (see figs. 33, 34).

The emphasis on the phallic neck marks the waterbird divinity as bisexual, symbolically linking it to the snake.[13] The snake and its abstract derivative, the spiral, are the most popular motifs in the art of Old Europe. "The mysterious dynamism of the snake, its extraordinary vitality and periodic rejuvenation, must have provoked a powerful emotional response in the Neolithic agriculturalists, and the snake was consequently mythologized, attributed with a power that can move the entire cosmos"[14] (see fig. 35).

32. IDEOGRAMS OF THE BIRD GODDESS, ca. 4000 B.C.E. Drawing from a terracotta vessel. East Balkan. Drawing after Gimbutas.

The double divinity of bird and snake was linked with its aquatic environment. Inspired by the rippling of the waters, the sinuous movement of the snake and the dance of the water-bird ideograms are used to decorate ritual vessels and sacred images.

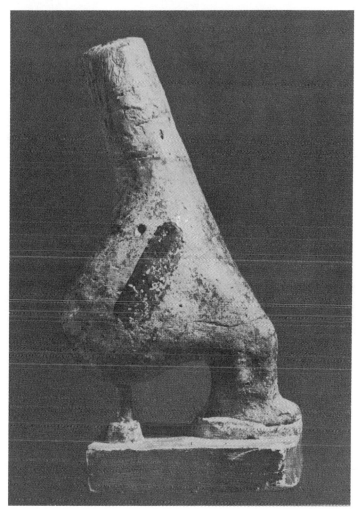

33

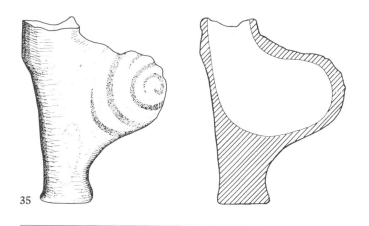

35

33. The Bird Goddess Pregnant with the Cosmic Egg, early sixth millennium B.C.E. Terracotta. Vinca. East Balkan.

The Old European image with the cylindrical neck and large buttocks suggest a half-bird, half-woman. Her body contains an egg just like the bodies of birds painted on the Minoan vases.

34

34. Design of Birds with Large Eggs Inside Them, ca. 1500 B.C.E. Minoa. Drawing after Gimbutas.

35. Figurine with Egg Hollow Inside the Buttocks and Snake Winding Around Them, early sixth millennium B.C.E. Drawing. Central Balkans. Drawing after Gimbutas.

The snake was the vehicle of immortality. A gigantic snake was thought to wind or stretch over the whole universe—over the sun, the moon, the stars, and the rain torrents. "The universal snake winds around the universal egg like a continuous flow of water."[1] The snake was the stimulation and guardian of spontaneous life-energy winding above or below a growing plant, coiling around the pregnant mother's belly.

36. CROWNED SNAKE GODDESS,
6000–5000 B.C.E.. Terracotta. Kato
Ierapetra, Crete.

"The phallus, horns, snake, water bird and
water life are closely interrelated in myth and
cult. The mystery of life lies in the waters, in
oceans, deep seas, lakes or rivers. . . . To the
poets and philosophers of ancient Greece
water was the primordial element, able to
produce life, stimulate its growth and nurture
its damp warmth. This concept of the genesis
of the universal from an elemental aqua
substance surely extends back to the
Neolithic."[2]

From the early Neolithic to ancient Greece, the snake appears
in human form as the Snake Goddess. Her body is usually
decorated with stripes and spirals, while her arms and legs are
portrayed as snakes or as entwined by them (see fig. 36).

The Pregnant Vegetation Goddess

While the bird and snake goddesses were the creative energies
of the waters, the Vegetation Goddess represented the fertility
of the earth. A goddess symbolizing earth fertility was the

37. PREGNANT VEGETATION GODDESS, ca. 4500 B.C.E. Terracotta. Central Bulgaria.

The vegetation goddess is portrayed naturalistically as "a pregnant female with hands above the belly."[3] On each buttock are two large lozenges placed there not as decoration but to stress her function as the fertilizer of the earth, responsible for germination, sprouting, growing, and ripening of plants. Her center of gravity in the abdomen draws her downward toward the earth of which she is a part.

natural response to an agrarian way of life. When the role played by the seed in germination and growth was understood, the pregnant belly of a woman came to stand for the fertile field. The belief that a woman's fertility influenced the growth of the crops is commonplace in European folklore. "Barren women are regarded as dangerous; a pregnant woman has magical influence on grain because like her, the grain 'becomes pregnant'; it germinates and grows."[15]

Like the Bird Goddess, the Vegetation Goddess can be identified by her sign, "a dot in a lozenge, the diamond shaped pattern, incised or painted on her belly, thighs, neck or arm" (see fig. 37).

The Mother of the Dead

When the goddess appears as the Mother of the Dead, her body language is reversed. Carved from thin slabs of bone or ivory, without the ruddy coloration of life, her body is stiff and rigid, her arms folded tightly beneath her breasts, pressed against her body in the fetal position (see fig. 38). "Placed in graves singly, in pairs, or even dozens, . . ."[16] they are marked by an enormous sacred triangle. Gimbutas suggests that perhaps the artist through the act of engraving "visualized the universal womb, the inexhaustible source of life, to which the dead . . . return in order to be born again."[17]

The dead were buried with their arms tightly pressed to the body, in the fetal position, their bodies sometimes squeezed into egg-shaped earthen grave pots (*pithoi*).

The Phallic Goddess:
The Self-Fertilizing Virgin Mother

In other images, her phallus-shaped head and neck and nurturing breasts suggest that her nature is androgynous; "divine bisexuality stresses absolute power."[18] These symbols of gender identification have nothing to do with twentieth-century notions of sexuality but refer to fertility and the life force. The phallus like the vulva can symbolize creative energy (see fig. 39).

Two seemingly contradictory notions coexisted in Old European religion. The Great Goddess encompassed all that was alive, both male and female, within her being. She was the self-fertilizing virgin mother. In addition, with the domestication and breeding of animals, the causal relation between the sexual act and reproduction came to be understood, and the critical role of the male in engendering new life was ritually honored.

A "whole group of interconnected symbols—phallus, ithyphallic, [that is, with erect penis,] animal-masked man, goatman and the bull-man—represents a male stimulating principle in nature without whose influence nothing would grow and thrive." This family of symbols goes back to the origins of the early agricultural era when domesticated goat and cow herds first existed.[19] The male sexual act was seen as the

38. MOTHER OF THE DEAD, ca. 4500–4000 B.C.E. Bone. Bulgaria.

39. PHALLIC GODDESS: THE SELF-FERTILIZING VIRGIN MOTHER, ca. 6000 B.C.E. Terracotta. Sesklo, Thessaly.

40. HUMAN-HEADED MASKED BULL, 5000–4500 B.C.E. Terracotta. Vinca. East Balkan.

Male figures wearing enormous bull masks have powerful shoulders shaped like a bull's rump, the place where the animal's strength is concentrated. Standing firmly on short legs, the bull-man seems a monumental, formidable presence. "Such hybrid creatures must have been regarded as possessing a greater potential than either a man or a bull alone."[4]

39

40

plowing necessary for the seed to germinate within the fertile field that was the Goddess's body. In order to assure the cyclical renewal of nature, the Vegetation Goddess would mate with her young lover, the Year God, who was then sacrificed either literally or symbolically.

The Year God

The male principal is represented by the naked ithyphallic Year God seated on the throne. He is the ecstatic dancer, goat- or bull-masked, the prototype of Dionysus, the God of Vegetation and the male consort of the Goddess. The male god continues in the image of a bull (see fig. 40). We already know the bison as the symbol of male potency in the Ice Age. The return of the herd in the early spring was a harbinger of seasonal changes that meant an increased food supply. The death of the animal in the hunt was viewed as a gift, an exchange of energy that had to be ritually sanctified. The sacrifice of the Year God to ensure the growth of a new crop in the spring adapts this fundamental belief of the gatherer-hunters to the context of an agricultural society.

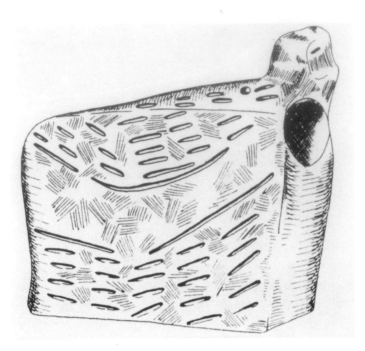

The Temple Is the Body of the Goddess: Birdhouses and Snake Dens

The numinous presence of the Bird and Snake Goddess inspired a most fanciful sacred architecture in Old Europe. Miniature clay models of the temples, small enough to be held in the hand, were found near the sites of altars. Probably dedicatory gifts to the Goddess, they are "doubly revealing: they not only reproduce the temple's configuration, but they are also often elaborately decorated with symbolic designs. Frequently a divine image in relief adorns the gables, rooftops, or roof corners."[20] Temple buildings seem to have been constructed as the literal "body" or "heart" of the deity. Some are distinctly bird shaped with numerous incisions on their sides to indicate plumage. And one is a birdhouse with a round opening to accommodate the manifestation of the Goddess in the form of a bird (see fig. 41).

Other models are the domain of the Snake Goddess, their walls decorated with meanders and figurative representations of the snake.[21] Vertical panels on either side of the entrance of a Vinca temple model from northwestern Bulgaria are

42. LADY BIRD, fourth millennium B.C.E. Terracotta. Vinca. East Balkan.

inscribed with the Goddess's signature, intertwined double spirals, clearly resembling the pairs of double snakes with opposed heads so often found on cult vessels. Above the temple model's entrance are bands of dots and zigzags, snake-skin designs. A schematic head in the center probably represents the Goddess of the temple, the masked heads on the corners, her priestesses.

Ritual Theater

The playfulness of the birdhouse shrine is characteristic of Old European culture. The wealth of figures with animal masks from the Central Balkan Vinca culture (5500–3500 B.C.E) have a charm and vitality that bring to life the ceremonial world in which they were the actors, helping us to imagine what ritual must have been like. Priestesses and priests wearing the masks must have invoked the spirit of the divine animals to harness their creative energies and enhance their own lives. The use of the mask is as old and universal as art and religion. Neolithic people followed a tradition established by Paleo-lithic shamans, adapting the animal mask to their own modes of ritual and artistic expression. The stylized features of the masks with their angular projections are startling, capturing the essence of the creatures being mimed: bird, duck, bear, or ram. At the peak of Old European civilization, a sophisticated image of the Bird/Snake Goddess appeared wearing an elaborate dress and a mask (see fig. 42).

The Offering of Grain, the Sustenance of Life

The remains of an actual shrine in Soviet Moldavia give us an even fuller picture of cult practice (see fig. 43). There were thirty-two female figures in the shrine, human women taking part in the ritual bread making, and votive images of the Goddess on the altar (see fig. 44). There must have been someone in charge of the ritual preparations, probably a priestess who sat in the life-sized chair.

The exaggerated body proportions of the female figures characteristic of the Neolithic goddess symbolize fertility, and

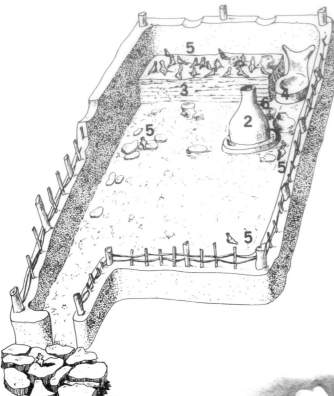

43. SHRINE OF SABATNOVKA, ca. 5000–3500 B.C.E. Soviet Moldavia. Plan. Drawing after Gimbutas.

The wattle and daub building is large, 70 meters square; its entrance on the long side was through a narrow passage paved with flat stones. The rest of the floor was plastered with clay. A Goddess figure carved from bone was found lying on the threshold. Again there was a large oven and some querns, the primitive hand mills used for grinding grain. The large vessels include a dish filled with the charred bones of a bull. Against the far wall opposite the entrance was an altar, a raised platform. On the altar were sixteen Goddess figures all sitting on horn-back stools. In the corner next to the altar was a throne-like chair; its ample, one-meter-wide seat had originally been covered with split planks.

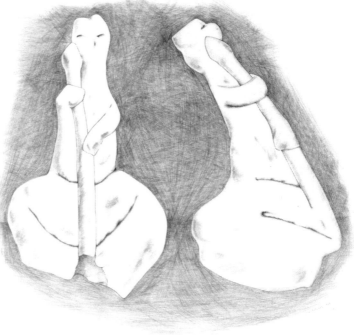

44. GODDESSES ON THE ALTAR. Detail of Shrine of Sabatnovka.

All were schematically rendered with the same massive buttocks, fat thighs, tiny breasts, and snake-shaped heads. Except for one holding a baby snake, they had no arms. None had feet, and their legs tapered like those of the Venus of Willendorf.

the hand held to the breast, nurture. The sacrifice of the bull was the male potency necessary to fertilize the seed. In the Old European agricultural society grain made into bread was the staff of life. The Great Goddess's forces were the life-giving waters and the life-fertilizing earth that make possible a good harvest. Bread was the sacrament in ritual that was a perpetual thanksgiving to the Goddess for her bounty.

The Life Force of the Goddess Fully Manifest in the Lives of Women and Men

Analysis of the symbols and images of Goddess religion in Old Europe carries us back to her Paleolithic origins and affirms what we already sense by now, the continuity of the tradition. The Old European Goddess is a composite image with an accumulation of traits from both pre-agricultural and agricultural eras.[22]

The exuberance of this imagery suggests a culture in which the life force of the Goddess was fully manifest in the lives of women and men and in which the creative spirit was celebrated. Indeed the Goddess was the patron of the arts. Artisans were in her service: Their workshops were attached to her shrines.

Gimbutas suggests that Old European culture was matrifocal, that is, woman-centered, and matrilineal, where descent was through the mother. Woman-centered does not imply a matriarchy that is the opposite of patriarchy, a society in which one gender exercised power at the expense of the other. Although female images greatly predominate, male and female principals were manifest side by side. The male divinity in the shape of a young man or a male animal appears to affirm and strengthen the forces of the creative and active female. Neither is subordinate to the other; by complementing one another their power is doubled.[23] "The male element, man and animal represented spontaneous and life-stimulating—but not life-generating—powers."[24] The role of a woman was not subject to that of a man. Gimbutas concludes that much that was created in the Neolithic was the result of a "structure in which all resources of human nature, feminine and masculine, were utilized to the full as a creative force."[25]

Other European Neolithic peoples built great stone monuments to the Mother, temples and tombs in the shape of her body. Where these megalithic builders came from is still a mystery, but the ruins of their prodigious structures still dominate the landscape in parts of the western Mediterranean islands and Atlantic Europe.

Malta: The Temple as the Body of the Goddess

CHAPTER 5

An island sanctuary, Malta was a place of pilgrimage and a healing center with more than thirty temples built with a floor plan in the shape of the body of the Goddess (ca. 3500–2500 B.C.E). To enter the temple was to be within the body of the Goddess and to be in touch with the elemental force that creates and maintains life (see figs. 45, 46).

The Maltese archipelago lies off Sicily less than two hundred miles from Africa. German archaeologist Sybille von Cles-Reden describes the islands:

> The main island rises out of the glistening Mediterranean like a bare, steep-sided raft of solid rock. Its area is ninety-three square miles, the neighboring island of Gozo is one-third as big, and the other islands . . . are small reefs of rock. . . .
>
> The fierce sun, the desert wind from the south and the salty sea-breezes, scorch and blow away the almost treeless islands' scanty soil.
>
> Gozo is greener than Malta, but like Malta has no real springs; only surface water and a brief rainy season when its strong nakedness is veiled by a shimmer of rapidly blooming and fading flowers. . . . The sea that surrounds the dead, sun-bleached rocky mass sparkles like diamonds and fills the inlets in the fissured shore with deep blue, green, and violet shadows.[1]

"The Maltese islands cover only 314 square kilometers but there is probably no other area of this size in the world with such a number and variety of archeological sites."[2] The temple ruins are important because they richly document developments in the religious life of prehistoric peoples that are only now beginning to be understood.[3] Research into Malta's past has been going on for three centuries or so, but professional archaeological excavation began only in the 1880s. The origins

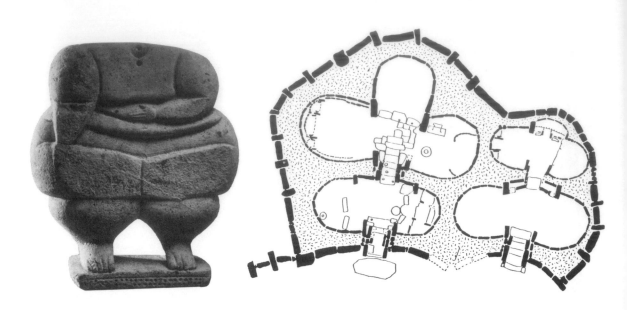

of the temples and the meaning of their unique form continue to be controversial among prehistorians and archaeologists. Of extraordinary dimensions, the temples were made of huge rough-cut stone called megaliths. Many of the honey-colored temples were spectacularly sited on bluffs overlooking the blue-green sea; all were in places of great natural beauty (see fig. 47).

We know nothing about the people who built the temples, neither their everyday life nor their social, political, or economic organization. "All their creative energies seem to have been concentrated on a religious experience of overpowering intensity and to have been dedicated exclusively to it."[4]

Archaeologists believe that the first settlers arrived from Sicily in the sixth millennium B.C.E. Occupied continuously since then, the earliest shrines at Malta were cave sanctuaries, hallowed places where the dead were buried. Burial in the womb of the earth promised rebirth. The dead were placed in fetal position with their knees drawn up to their chests, their bodies sprinkled with red ochre. Like the Anatolians at Çatal Hüyük and most Neolithic peoples, the Maltese practiced excarnation. A preliminary individual burial was followed by a secondary collective one in which the bones of the dead were placed in mass graves.

Later burial chambers were artificial caves or dolmens, vaulted over with huge stones and built in the form of the

45. THE MALTESE GODDESS, ca. 3600–3000 B.C.E. Limestone. Malta.

The Maltese Goddess is characterized by grossly exaggerated fleshiness in her upper arms, thighs, and buttocks and, notably, no overt indication of breasts or vulva.

46. PLAN OF GGANTIJA TEMPLES, ca. 3600–3000 B.C.E. Malta.

Their silhouette mirrors the massive rounded forms of the Goddess image. The raised threshold can be read as the vulva, the entrance to her body.

47. Mnajdra Temple, ca. 3300–2500
B.C.E. Photograph.

earlier natural sanctuaries to keep in touch with the numinous power. The dolmens evolved from oval, womb-shaped tombs, dug slightly below ground that "looked as if they had been scooped out by a giant hand"[5] into elaborate, lobed chambers extending both horizontally and vertically, covering extensive territory. They were used for public worship and burial rituals.

The first megalithic temples were one-celled, round structures, a variant of the womb-tomb shape of the earlier natural cave sanctuaries. Later temples were enlarged with interconnecting chapels arranged in the form of a woman's body (see fig. 46). All three structures—cave, tomb, and temple—were ritual spaces experienced as being within the body of the Great Mother. The cave extending into the earth was the womb of the Goddess, the original place of emergence of life. Pottery found in the cave-shrines was decorated with vulva symbols.

The Maltese temples are the earliest known free-standing roofed stone buildings and the earliest known megalithic structures. Their construction was an incredible achievement by the inhabitants of the islands who had no metal, only stone and horn for tools. The scale of the buildings was enormous, their construction called "cyclopean." Some of the megaliths weighing forty or fifty tons are as big as houses. The task of moving these stones was prodigious and must have engaged the energies of the entire community for centuries, much like the construction of the Gothic cathedrals in Medieval Europe when the faithful yoked themselves together to haul granite blocks from the quarries to the cathedral site. As the Gothic cathedrals represented the heavenly Jerusalem, so the Maltese Goddess temples symbolized cosmic order and were the center and focus of community life.

The Oldest Temple, Ggantija, the Giant

The oldest great temple, appropriately named Ggantija, the Giant, stands on a hill on Gozo.

> None of the later shrines reached the colossal proportions of this building. Its grey stone masses dominate the landscape, which falls away in long folds and furrows down to the rugged coast. The great curving façade faces the rising sun and looks towards Malta, which is separated from Gozo only by an arm of the sea.[6]

Entrance to Ggantija is through a concave stone wall opening into a courtyard. Within the walled area, two temples are set side by side, with their façades roughly in line, one larger than the other, sometimes identified as mother and daughter Goddesses (see fig. 46). All the other sacred buildings on Malta were modeled on Ggantija.

A legend still lingering among the people of Gozo tells of a female ruler, a woman with a baby at her breast, who built the temples. Fortified by a meal of magic beans, she is said to have moved all the huge stone blocks to the site in a single day and to have built the walls that night. Was the woman with the baby at her breast the Goddess?

Perhaps so, because on Malta the Goddess was envisioned as giant in size. One of the sensational discoveries within the South Temple at Tarxien was a fragment of a colossal statue, colloquially known as the "Fat Lady," still standing in her original place (see fig. 48). Unbroken, this colossus would have been eight feet high. Sadly, time, the weather, and the local farmers have reduced the statue so that only her impressive lower parts survive. Based on other female figures found at Tarxien, we can imaginatively reconstruct the image. She would have had a small head and feet, bulbous arms with tiny hands, and a flat chest. Nude to the waist, she would have worn a bell-shaped, fringed skirt and a necklace as ornament.

48. COLOSSUS AT TARXIEN, ca. 3300–2500 B.C.E. Globerina limestone. Fragment, 1 m. high. Tarxien.

49. THRESHOLD STONE OF INNER SHRINE, ca. 2400–2300 B.C.E. Central Temple at Tarxien. Malta.

Passing a spiral barrier into an inner sanctuary seems, like the passage through the labyrinth, to have been a necessary passport into the sacred realm. This realm of immortality is reached by a real or symbolic death from the relative and transient natural world, and rebirth into the land of the dead—or the next world. The theme is found throughout the megalithic and Neolithic worlds: in much of Europe, in Mexico, in China, and in Egypt. Such spirals demonstrate the evolutionary nature of the journey being made. At Tarxien they suggest the balancing of opposing vortical energies, by which the state of wholeness or enlightenment is reached.[5]

The Tarxien complex is the most elaborate group of megalithic remains on Malta and, because of its strong and harmonious proportions and fine sculptural reliefs, the most elegant (see fig. 49). In the central temple, a low altar lies across the threshold of an inner shrine, perhaps a sacred precinct. Carved on the face of the stone altar are magnificent double spirals unfolding into plantlike forms.

On a nearby block, a bull and a sow with her thirteen piglets march toward the altar in solemn procession, thirteen being a recurring number of the Goddess. The fertility symbolism is obvious "given the association of the very male bull and the patently female sow."[7]

The majestic temple ruins at Malta are the most complete survival of the Neolithic vision of rebirth in the body of the Goddess. The temples were built with enormous double walls, rubble and earth piled in the space between the inner and outer walls, so the effect was to have the temple *inside the earth,* surrounded by the earth.[8] To sleep within such a shape, as the faithful apparently did, would have been a return to the womb of the Mother, an analogy to actual death, implying the attainment of a kind of eternal rebirth.

The Hypogeum: Center of Healing

Surely the most spectacular monument on Malta is the enormous, labyrinthine, underground sanctuary known as the Hypogeum, which may have been the ceremonial center of the islands. Like the rest of the underground sanctuary, the Main Hall of the Hypogeum was carved out of living limestone. A remarkable example of sculptural architecture, this catacomb-like structure seems to have been at once temple, tomb, and healing center. Encompassing more than 6,000 square meters in three levels, the Hypogeum goes down thirty feet to bedrock and water. Spaces flow freely into each other in a series of interconnecting, egg-shaped chambers: Some are natural caves, others are enlarged or entirely human-made and must have served as chapels for funerary rites. The remains of 7,000 Maltese, along with their personal ornaments, amulets, and pottery offerings were found there.

The feeling in the Main Hall is not that of a cave but rather of structural architecture reproducing the balanced concave proportions of the temple façade at the entrance. Inside, the upright posts framing the doorway and vaulted ceiling are typical of Maltese temple construction above ground. Unlike the rough surfaces of the other rock-cut rooms of the Hypogeum, the Main Hall's red-ochred walls are highly polished, giving this sanctuary an air of serenity and solemnity.

This "Holy of Holies" leads into the Oracle Room named for a curious hole in the wall close to the ground. The sound of a human voice spoken into this hole echoes throughout the entire Hypogeum. In the ancient world oracular pronouncements were frequently delivered through such an acoustical device; the awesome words of prophecy would reverberate throughout the shrine. Oracles were generally considered predictions of subterranean powers whose wisdom was that of the Earth herself.

An oracle hole was a common feature of healing chambers in ancient sanctuaries. Although we have no record of what went on in the Oracle Room in the Hypogeum at Malta, we can speculate from what is known about such practices in other places in the ancient Mediterranean world. Divination, the art of foretelling events or discovering hidden knowledge, usually by interpreting omens or dreams, was also practiced in healing temples. Altered states of consciousness, often brought on by drugs and sometimes snake bites, induced dreams and visions. A subterranean pit in the Oracle Room, two meters deep with concave walls, would have been well suited for keeping snakes.[9]

> Much like mescaline (a product of the peyote cactus) or psilocybin (found in certain types of mushrooms), both used as sacraments in some North American Indian religions, the chemical makeup of certain types of snake venom may have caused a person, especially someone in the expectant frame of mind, to feel in touch with the very forces of existence and a sensation of perceiving the events and meaning of the past, present and future with great clarity and comprehension. . . . The sacred serpents, apparently kept and fed at the oracular shrines of the Goddess, were perhaps not merely the symbols but actually the instruments through which the experiences of divine revelation were reached.[10]

Pilgrims who journeyed to Malta may have done so for dream communion, for divination, and for healing as they did to Epidauros in Greece.

On the ceiling of the Oracle Room four stylized trees with red fruit were painted. An important clue to what took place here is two identical small sculptures of a woman found lying on the floor where they were probably left when the shrine was abandoned. She is lying on her side on a low couch, one enormous right forearm underneath her head, the other draped across her heavy breast (see fig. 50). Like the colossus from Ggantija, she is ample-hipped and topless, dressed in a full length, bell-shaped skirt. She clearly appears to be asleep, almost visibly dreaming, but who was she and what was she doing asleep?

The "Sleeping Lady" is probably a healer, a priestess acting on behalf of the Goddess. In Classical Greece and Rome dream incubation was closely associated with cults of healing. The most famous, that of the healing God Asklepios at Epidauros, had gained a wide reputation for effecting cures by

50. "Sleeping Lady," ca. 3800 – 3600 B.C.E. Brown clay with traces of red ochre. 7 cm high, 6.8 cm wide, 12.2 cm long. Malta.

the fifth century B.C.E. This center included an amphitheater for ritual drama and a dream incubation temple. The treatment began with fasting and bathing, followed by a stay overnight in the temple.

> The sick . . . would "await a vision that would come during sleep, perhaps in the form of a visit by a god or goddess, perhaps in the form of a vision of some deed or mission which [they were] meant to accomplish in order for the healing to take place. While some material means of physical cure were practiced by the healers, . . . for the most part healing was accomplished via a deep psychic or psychological or spiritual insight and transformation of life purpose. After the divine visitation or healing vision had been received, it was customary to enact what had been seen for the benefit of the whole community—perhaps immediately in the theater.[11]

The red fruit painted on the ceiling of the Oracle Room may be pomegranates, whose redness symbolizes a woman's womb, the abundance of seeds its fertility and source of eternal rebirth. Barren women may have come to the center seeking a cure for infertility. The pomegranate is associated with Persephone, the daughter of Demeter, whose descent into the underworld and return depicted death and the rebirth of life. The connection between these practices will be strengthened if the suggestion of Malta as a possible source of the Mysteries of Demeter, the most important of the ancient Greek religious festivals, is confirmed.[12]

The Hypogeum at Malta was itself the womb and the place of burial where the dead returned to the Mother. While we know nothing directly of the rites that took place there, this was a sacred precinct, under the ground, that privileged place associated with the chthonian Goddess where communication with her and the spirits of the dead in the underworld was possible.

Archaeologists have puzzled for decades over the temples on Malta and the meaning of their singular architecture, unable to read them as Goddess forms. Perhaps these ancient megaliths have remained a mystery because we have "lost confidence in the ability of artifacts and structures to contain and transmit meaning directly without first being converted into written words."[13]

In traditional cultures, architecture conveyed meaning through recognizable symbols and images. The *kiva,* the ceremonial chamber of the Hopi Indians, is the womb of the Earth Mother. The cruciform church, a three-dimensional symbol that the worshiper could enter and achieve total union with God, was consciously designed to reproduce the crucified Christ (see fig. 51).

Architectural Forms Expressed Significant Human Experience

In the Neolithic, when the godhead was a woman, a temple shaped in her form is not surprising. Only in the modern world have architectural forms become abstract. For ancient peoples and for primal peoples everywhere still, all material objects that support daily life, from the smallest to the largest, are charged with extra meaning.[14] Architectural forms expressed significant human experience. Maltese sanctuaries were the symbol of death and rebirth. With their insistent curved lines, they represent the cosmic womb, the continuous state of pregnancy and fertility of the Goddess,[15] pregnant not with child but with all possibility.

The spiral motif, so frequent on the entrance walls and altars of the inner sanctuaries, symbolizes cosmic renewal, a passage into the center and out again, rebirth and transformation (see fig. 49 and color plate 51).[16]

Giulia Sorlini, an Italian anthropologist, suggests that besides being places of worship the temples also could have been storage places. Here the Goddess presided over the distribution of wealth, in this case staple foods, as she did at Çatal Hüyük whose grain storage bins were adjacent to her shrines. One possible link between the Maltese goddess and the Grain Goddess is a row of primitive querns, or grinding mills, engraved on the base of the colossus of Ggantija.[17] Actual querns also were found in the temples, and archaeologist D. H. Trump speculates that grain was stored on the lowest level of the Hypogeum.[18] Querns have been excavated at Malta, and, as in Old Europe, may have had both ritual and domestic use.

> This double function of the temple could have been later diversified and transformed into the earliest form of the Demeter cult and the Maltese archipelago may have been its place of origin. . . . The Maltese mysteries might have had rites that re-enacted the decay and birth of the vegetation and, at a deeper level, the spiralling cycle of Life and Death over which the Goddess presided and of which the Goddess knew the secrets.[19]

Sorlini goes on to comment that the inexpressible happiness of the Eleusinian initiates described in classical literature may have resembled the almost tangible state of communion that people felt when they were in the Goddess's temple womb.[20]

Modern visitors to Malta's Neolithic ruins speak with awe of the congruence of internal and external space. The rounded outer walls are mirrored in the inner curvilinear structures. There are no sharp angles; all shapes are rounded, curved. In architecture, the interior space is as important as exterior space, if not more so. Instead of leaving the occupant in a boundless world, an interior space encloses like a self-contained world of its own. Undoubtedly, prehistoric pilgrims came to Malta for spiritual renewal. To worship within the Goddess's temple was to return to the Mother and experience rebirth.

Tarxien was apparently the last of the temples built by the original Maltese settlers before they were invaded from the European mainland in the mid-second millennium B.C.E. These warlike people had formidable weapons—copper daggers and axes and sharp obsidian arrowheads. The builders of the great temples vanished, leaving behind the mystery of the Goddess religion as practiced in their megalithic temples. We can only conjecture with other scholars about their rituals and imagine that perhaps "the ancient ideas about the Earth Mother and the dead were resurrected from deep levels of the mind in the mystery cults of classical times."[21]

Avebury: The Great Seasonal Drama of Her Life Cycle

CHAPTER 6

Megalithic structures, rock-cut tombs, and burial mounds were also built from the late Neolithic into the Bronze Age in the western Mediterranean, along the Atlantic coast of Europe, and in the British Isles. Their connection with the Maltese temples is another perennial controversy among prehistorians. Where did the Maltese people go when they were driven from their island home by threat of famine or invasion? Sculptor Cristina Biaggi's comparative study of the Maltese and Scottish megalithic structures conclusively demonstrates a direct relation between their form and function. Biaggi is interested in the meaning of these architectural forms and how they suggest the worship of the Great Goddess. The monuments at Avebury speak powerfully to her presence in Stone Age Britain.

In the third millennium B.C.E. the life story of the Goddess was celebrated at Avebury in a seasonal round of festivals. The major events in her life—puberty, marriage, childbirth, and death—were the themes of dramatic rituals in which the entire community participated. The great monuments were built to symbolize these transformative rites.

Avebury was a religious center and may have drawn worshipers from the whole of Britain. The monuments here are the most important Neolithic group in the British Isles and include England's tallest artificial hill and largest prehistoric tomb, the foundations of a monumental stone circle much like that at Stonehenge and the remnant of two stone avenues, each a mile and a half long. These mighty forms lie on the rolling chalk downs of the beautiful, ever green countryside of southwestern England. The waters of the landscape—two rivers, the underground streams, and springs—were also part of the ritual structure (see fig. 52).

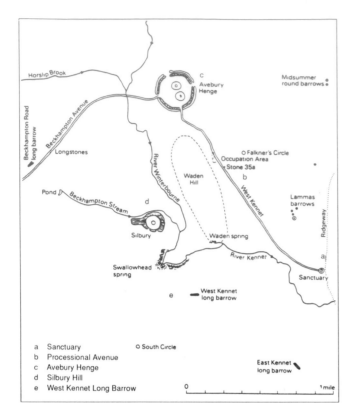

52. MAP OF AVEBURY MONUMENTS. a. sanctuary; b. processional avenue; c. henge; d. Silbury Hill; e. long barrow. After Dames.

Map labels:
- Horslip Brook
- Beckhampton Road long barrow
- Beckhampton Avenue
- Longstones
- River Winterbourne
- Pond
- Beckhampton Stream
- Silbury
- Swallowhead spring
- Waden Hill
- Waden spring
- c Avebury Henge
- Midsummer round barrows
- Falkner's Circle Occupation Area
- Stone 35a
- b
- West Kennet
- d
- Lammas barrows
- Ridgeway
- River Kennet
- a
- Sanctuary
- e West Kennet long barrow

Legend:
- a Sanctuary
- b Processional Avenue
- c Avebury Henge
- d Silbury Hill
- e West Kennet Long Barrow
- South Circle
- East Kennet long barrow

0 _____ 1 mile

Michael Dames, a British artist used to honoring his visual experience, gives his book on Avebury's artificial hill, *The Silbury Treasure,* the subtitle, *The Great Goddess Rediscovered.* He urges us to break out of our habit of seeking meaning only in history that is acted out in linear time and to look to the recurring cycles of myth, symbol, and folklore, the circular time that is the "product of a cultural period in which life had not yet broken away from the harmony of Nature."[1] Mythic time is always concerned with both the natural process of the seasonal round and the narrative events in the human life cycle.

Dames argues that the Avebury monuments were created to stage a religious drama that took place over the course of a year. Each structure, human-made or natural, offered in turn a setting for the celebration of a particular event in the agricultural year that matched the corresponding event in the life cycle of the Goddess, for example, the harvest and childbirth.

The "architecture" of the entire cycle was designed to be read as a sequence of visual images as the Great Goddess changed from child to maiden, to mother, to crone. These gigantic forms were regarded as living characters whose transformation from one role to the next was confirmed by the disappearance and reappearance of the local rivers at different seasons.

In the unified premodern view, the body of the deity is the pattern of the world encompassing its physical totality, geographical and topographical. All sacred places are contained within her body. At set times during the calendar year, the community reenacts the creation of the earth. Symbols are the key and, when activated by ritual, tell the community's master story—the narrative that explores, regulates, and perpetuates the existence of the people in harmony with the divine. The story is repeated every year because mythology has to be experienced continuously in order to transform lives.[2]

In this way the power of the Goddess inherent in the landscape that is her body is revitalized and the interconnection of nature, the human, and the divine realized. Just as the Maltese modeled their temples in the shape of the body of the Goddess so that, when they were brought into intimate relation with the whole, they could then find the divine within the depths of their own being, so the people of Avebury reshaped their landscape to have her physically present among them throughout the seasonal cycle.

The prehistoric religious impulse was to find, to express, and to benefit from the identity between the microcosm and the macrocosm. In the Avebury ritual cycle we find sacred order as understood by an agricultural community that observed the movements of the sun and were aware that the relation between the earth and the sky reflected the cyclical progression of the seasons. Each season was different in character, yet each was linked to the others. The seasons affected the crops and their animals, the surrounding untamed flora and fauna, and almost every aspect of human behavior.

The equating of seasons with the stages of the human life cycle is a universal one. Spring and childhood correspond, summer and youth, autumn and adulthood, and, at the close of life, winter and old age. These transformations are reflected in the four quarters of the agricultural year. The farmer sows the crop in the spring, tends to its growth in the summer, reaps the harvest in the autumn, and allows the dying fields to lie fallow during the winter months.

At Avebury, the seasonal rites reenacted nature's cycle of life and death over which the Goddess presided, just as the Christian sacraments honor the rites of passage in human life. The agricultural seasonal changes were marked by rituals acknowledging their sacred character. The dates of the holy days were determined by the movements of the heavens, the relation of the sun and the moon to the earth. "The village year was divided into four quarters, with each quarter straddling either equinox or solstice. Each quarter was ushered in by a major folk festival."[3] Vestiges of the tradition of Quarter Day Festivals are still alive in rural communities in the British Isles. Even in contemporary America we make much of Hallowe'en, of All Soul's Day, that liminal time when the boundaries between the worlds of the living and dead grow dim.

The Quarter Days marked the activity of the Goddess in the natural world. The old names still in common use in England and Ireland provide clues to their original meanings and rituals. On Candlemas, in early February, a procession of lighted candles or torches welcomed the first signs of spring and the return of the Goddess from the underworld. Beltane, the Celtic May Day, marked the first flowering of the land when the fruit trees blossom and the countryside was a blaze of color and the herds were sent to the hills to graze. Lammas, the First Fruits Festival in August, was named for the loaves of bread made from the first ripe grains harvested and consecrated that day. The early November festival called Samhain, Summer's End, or Martinmas (from "mart," the Old English word for the ox that was fattened for slaughter) marked the season when the grass died and there was a shortage of winter fodder, the time when the Goddess went underground and all of nature lay dormant.

Puberty Rites/The Goddess's Time of Becoming

Let us follow the events at Avebury as the Goddess's life story unfolds. We will begin our annual round in early February, at

Candlemas when the farmers begin to prepare for the sowing of the crop. Spring comes early to Britain. Candlemas, like puberty rituals formally acknowledging a young girl's biological capacity to bear children, is the Goddess's time of becoming.

According to Dames's hypothetical reconstruction, puberty rites of the Goddess were reenacted in a small wooden temple that once overlooked the headwaters of the River Kennet in Wiltshire. All that remains today are concrete markers indicating the position of stones and wooden posts, yet the site is still known locally as the Sanctuary. The eighteenth-century antiquarian, William Stuckley, whose field survey was the first comprehensive study of Avebury, made at a time when much more of the site survived, identified the temple as that of Ertha, the Northern European Goddess of Spring and Fertility after whom the Christian Easter is named.

There is little surviving evidence to document the nature of the rituals held there but what there is relates to fertility. An extraordinary number of snail shells found in the stone and post sockets at the Sanctuary site must have been brought from lower and wetter ground because their spiral shape symbolized eternal fecundity. In primal and archaic religions, snails participate in the sacred powers that are concentrated in the waters, in the moon, and in women.[4] The Sanctuary ground plan itself was an enlargement of the snail shape. As puberty marks the passage from childhood to adulthood, spirals, like labyrinthine mazes, are the paths of entry into the sacred realm.

We can look to anthropologists' accounts of primal peoples for corroboration of Dames's interpretation. Bruce Lincoln in his study of women's initiation rituals (1981) cites the Navajo Indians as exemplars because their religious system is extremely rich in symbol and ceremonial.

> Among the Navajo a young girl's first menstruation is cause for general rejoicing, because it indicates that she is ready to bring forth new life. . . . Menarche is "regarded as the fulfillment of a promise, the attainment of reproductive power." Physiological maturity alone, however, is not sufficient for the fulfillment of this promise. The girl must also be ritually transformed, made over, before she takes her place as a woman.[5]

Ritual Sexual Initiation/
The Wedding of the Goddess

Although material evidence connecting the Sanctuary with puberty rituals is scanty and controversial, this identification is important to Dames's overall schema. His conjecture is that while a girl's first menstruation might be any time during the calendar year, the puberty ritual would be collective and communal. Once a young girl had been initiated into womanhood, her sexual initiation was celebrated on the next Quarter Day, the first of May, the time of the flowering of all nature, at the Avebury Henge. A henge, as in the well-known Stonehenge, was a great circle of huge rough-cut stones pitched end to end and surrounded by a ditch and an earthen bank. The Avebury Henge was so large that the entire modern village fits within its circle (see fig. 53).

The henge was linked to the Sanctuary by a processional avenue lined with a double row of monoliths appropriately

53. Avebury Village and the Remains of the Henge. Aerial photograph.

called "bridestones." The monumental avenue was fifty feet wide and a mile and a half long and was complemented by another, now demolished, of identical length, coming to the henge from the opposite side, presumed to be for the young men (see fig. 54).

Dames interprets the wavy path as the symbol of the serpent energy generated by the puberty rites. In village India, the awakening sexuality of the young girls is linked to the uncoiling of the snake.[6] As we have already seen, the snake is one of the Neolithic goddess's most important incarnations. In Old European mythology she was the Creator of the Universe. And in Minoan Crete the snakes coiled round the arms of the priestess were the emblems of her power.

The henge itself was designed for the communal May Festival in which the union of the Goddess with her male consort could be ritually reenacted. The stone circle had to be large enough to accommodate the worshiping congregation so that

54. BRIDESTONES ON PROCESSIONAL AVENUE. Photograph.

its vast circular interior space could be experienced communally as the sacred vulva of the Goddess. "The deep trenches around the henge were probably dug to tap the water which collects above the chalk rock embracing the sacred arena with a colossal water serpent."[7]

May Day is still celebrated with circular dances in rural Europe. In old Avebury the observances may have included ritual sexual initiation in which the lovers absorbed the power of the sacred ground, the fertility of Mother Earth. At dawn the young women, no longer maidens, could look across the downs of Avebury to the top of Silbury Hill, the Pregnant Goddess, and know that they would carry her child as they and the landscape were now one. "Cultic sexual activity was an essential aspect of religions" that venerated the mysterious life cycle of nature conceived as female.[8] As Dames informs us, Silbury "was built to participate in dynamic processes—the fattening of the moon, the transformation of corn from green to gold and the stirrings of an unborn child"[9] (see figs. 55, 56, 57).

The Pregnant Goddess Gives Birth at the August Harvest

The Goddess gave birth every year at Lammas on the August Quarter Day. The ancients came to Silbury to be with their pregnant Goddess when she was near her time. Seeds put in her womb in the spring had grown big. The moment of joy was at hand, the harvest was about to begin. For Silbury to have a good birth she had to begin labor at night when the moon was full. Then she squatted down and brought forth the corn harvest. Her delivery of the new crop was celebrated as the First Fruits Festival. Farmers came bringing their sickles and offered her the tall green corn, the first fruits of the season, in deep gratitude for her bounty.

It was believed that after Lammas the corn ripened as much by night as by day.[10] The moon has been linked with the fertile female at least as far back as the Paleolithic when the Goddess of Laussel, proudly displaying the crescent horn, was carved over the shelter entrance (see color plate 33). The

55. SILBURY HILL WITH SURROUNDING WATER-FILLED MOAT. Photograph.

Silbury Hill is the Great Goddess pregnant. Her womb is the mound, 130 feet high and more than 550 feet in diameter.[6] The rest of her body is defined by a water-filled moat that was carefully dug out of the surrounding quarry. The mighty female's body is seen in profile. Her head and neck, her breast, back, and thigh are water. Her head extends toward the west, her back faces north, and her breast and knees point south; all are plainly delineated by the outer edge of the quarry. The hill or womb is composed of material derived almost entirely from the quarry. She appears to be squatting, ready to give birth to the unborn child within like the Pregnant Vegetation Goddess of Old Europe (see fig. 31).

56. PREGNANT VEGETATION GODDESS, ca. 4300 B.C.E. Drawing after Dames.

57. SILBURY HILL IN PROFILE. Drawing after Dames.

From her head to her thigh, the Mother measures almost 1,400 feet. Silbury was not intended to be viewed from a distance but to be experienced directly. The vastness of her womb can only be appreciated by climbing up the steep slope and slowly walking around the top. In this way the whole complex of meanings is revealed as it would have been experienced in ancient ritual.

1. GORGON, sixth century B.C.E. Colored marble. From the pediment of the Temple at Syracuse.

In ancient Greece, the terrifying image of the Gorgon represented an archaic level of religious history, the dark side of the Goddess representing death and destruction.

2. THE COSMIC VICTORY OF DURGA, THE
UNASSAILABLE ONE, eighth century.
Sandstone, India.

Durga, the most popular manifestation of the
Great Goddess in modern India, stands confi-
dently poised for her triumph over the buffalo
demon, oppressor of the earth and its peoples.
Planting one foot firmly on the demon's shoul-
der, she raises her arm to strike the blow that
will sever his head.

3. Mary Frank, PERSEPHONE, 1985. Terracotta,
25 in. × 74 in. × 38 in.

The fragmentary reclining figure of Persephone
with her great mane of hair is an image of devastation, a powerful expression of the mythic
theme of abduction and rape.

2

3

4. EARLY FEMALE FIGURE, mid-fourth millennium B.C.E. Terracotta, paint, 11½ in. Egypt.

Her arms raised high, the bird-faced Goddess of pre-dynastic Egypt brings the life-giving energy of the sun to the earth.

5. GODDESS AND HER DEVOTEES DANCING IN ECSTACY IN A FIELD OF LILIES. ca. 1500 B.C.E. Gold signet ring. From Isopata near Knossos, Crete.

From earliest times, dance, celebrating body and spirit, has been a form of worship.

6. PAINTED POT IN THE FORM OF THE GOD-
DESS, fifth millennium B.C.E. Terracotta with
obsidian. Hacilar, Turkey.

The vessel universally represents the Great
Mother, its interior space, her womb.

7. TLAZOLTEOTL GIVING BIRTH, fifteenth
century. Aplite with garnets, 8 in. Aztec,
Mexico.

The Great Mother was the genetrix in the
matriarchal culture of the pre-Columbian
New World, primordial goddess of matter,
and mother of the gods. Her home was in
the West, the place of women and the primeval hole of the earth out of which humankind once crawled, as well as the place where
the sun descends, the archetypal womb
of death.

8. Judy Chicago, EARTHBIRTH, 1963. From the *Birth Project*. Quilting over air-brushed fabric, 63 in.
× 135 in. Painting by Judy Chicago, quilting by Jacqueline Moore.

The Earth Mother gives birth to herself, extruding the primal matter in a great wave spouting from
her mouth.

9. Beth Ames Swartz, MOVING POINT OF BALANCE #1, 1983. Acrylic and gold leaf canvas, 84 in. × 84 in.

Swartz believes that art is a quest, a healing and devotional act. *Moving Point of Balance,* a healing environment in which the viewer participates, is based on the chakra system, body connected energy centers that provide a way to check into the body to review the state of one's physical and mental well-being. The first of the seven paintings in the installation is the point of visualization at the base of the spine, the symbolic seat of all of our most primal bodily responses.

11. Deborah Kruger, BIRTH MOTHER, 1985. Acrylic, oilstick, pastel, 30 in. × 22 in.

At the end of her first pregnancy, the artist, apprehensive at the coming birth, dredges up from deep within the supportive image of the somber Earth Mother, herself in labor.

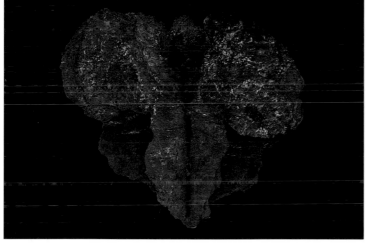

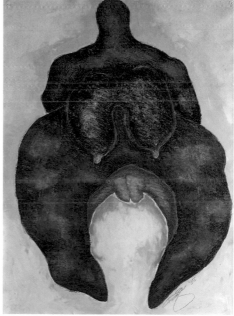

10. Beth Ames Swartz, THE RED SEA #1, Honoring Miriam, 1983. Fire, earth, sunlight, mixed media on layered paper, 41 in. × 47 in.

Part of a ritual series of earthworks, made when the artist went on pilgrimage to the ancient sites in Israel, in search of her roots as a Jewish woman, *The Red Sea* honors Miriam, sister of Moses. Swartz expresses the deep connection she felt to the sacred female presence symbolically in the form of the female reproductive organs.

12. Jim Ann Howard, REUNION, 1988. Oil on wood panel, 92 in. × 23½ in.

Timeless symbols of renewal abound as the archetypal image reemerges in the modern artist's consciousness: the murky waters of birth, the spiral, and the moon. For all its compelling power, Howard's Goddess is not fully manifest. The surface waters press down on her head. We have to face the death of old values before the healing can begin.

13. Faith Ringgold, WEEPING WOMEN #2, 1973. Beads, raffia, and sewn cloth.

Ringgold's women weep because of the double oppression of being black and female in our culture; their mouths open in the need to speak out.

12

13

14. Sudie Rakusin, HECATE, 1984. Oil on canvas, 30 in. × 24 in.

Rakusin projected onto her life-sized icon her own need for wholeness and the acceptance of all that she is. She becomes the wild Hecate.

15. VIJALI AS THE EARTH MOTHER, 1987. Performance, "World Wheel: Western Gateway," Malibu, California.

In ritual performances to resacralize the planet, the artist appears as the primordial goddess, her body covered with earth, her hair wildly tangled.

16. Asungi, DUNHAM'S LIFE SONG, 1982. Pastel, 23 in. × 32 in.

Out of her need to see images of strong, self-contained and focused black women, Asungi created a series of Amazons inspired by black cultures' tales, myths, goddesses, and other spiritual realities.

16

17

18

17. Nancy Spero, REBIRTH OF VENUS, 1984 (detail). Handprinting on paper.

Spero's new woman is fully empowered, celebrating her body, freely sexual, aware of her spiritual heritage as the embodiment of the Great Goddess.

18. Faith Wilding, CATWOMAN, detail from *Leaf-Scroll,* 1986. Gouache, goldleaf, watercolo paper, 16 in. × 30 in.

A shamanic figure with a human body and animal mask. *Catwoman* represents the animal-human nature we all share. Inscribed within a circle representing the microcosm, the totemic figure is surrounded by the universal symbols of earth, air, and fire.

55

56

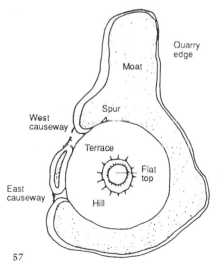

57

association of the moon with pregnancy and birth has been so compelling because the dramatic rhythms of its periodic waxing and waning, of growth and decay, have been there for all to see. For premodern peoples metaphor defined reality. "It is not surprising, . . . that [in ancient belief the moon] governs all those spheres of nature that fall under the law of recurring cycles: waters, rain, plant life, fertility. . . . 'Becoming' is the lunar order of things."[11] Like the ebb and flow of the tides, women's menstrual cycles are tied to the phases of the moon. More women give birth at the time of the full moon than at any other.

The Goddess squatted in labor because this is the normal position for women to give birth in most parts of the world and was also the birthing posture in the West until the eighteenth century when the male medical establishment took over prenatal care and delivery from midwives. Female figures in the birth-giving posture have been found in abundance at all Neolithic sites and in Native American, Mexican, Central and South American, and Pacific Island cultures (see color plate 7).

The belief in a squatting goddess giving birth at the August harvest persisted in the British Isles long after the Neolithic Age came to an end. Harvest festivals like the First Fruits at Avebury were celebrated well into the twentieth century and were known in Ireland as Big Sunday. It was a time when friends and relatives gathered together. Big Sunday marked the end of the period of waiting for the new crops to mature and the first opportunity to enjoy the food of the new harvest. This was the day when the first potatoes were dug. To dig before the right day would stunt the growth of the rest of the crop; on the other hand, if the first root was not lifted at the proper time, the crop would become blighted. Women, men, and children came to participate in the birth and to celebrate the happy event. The first fruits of the harvest were eaten at a ceremonial meal. On Big Sunday itself the whole local population assembled at one of hundreds of traditional hilltop sites scattered throughout the countryside. In Ireland, in 1942, one hundred and ninety-five sites were known, and formerly there must have been many more. Big Sunday was the most joyful time of the year. In the old days, booths were set up at the summit to sell country wares. There were round dances, contests and games, berry picking, and after the descent from the hill, dancing in the kitchen and at the crossroads. Musicians with fiddles, melodeons, and flutes played for the dancers.[12]

And so the yearly round of life was intimately connected with the seasonal changes in the land. The land was the Great Mother. "The need for community affirmation of this truth led to the search for a local isolated hillock where she could be easily seen [and worshipped] on a sympathetic scale."[13] Almost all traditional sites are conical in shape and sometimes flattened at the top. They rise out of the flat farmland and were revered as the universal mountain where the sacred energy was consecrated. Many, like the Paps of Anu in Ireland (see color plate 23), are named for regional goddesses whose narratives are recounted in local legend. The analogy of the contours of the landscape to the body of the Mother was a generalized concept. The hills could represent her breasts as they do in County Kerry, Ireland, her womb at Silbury, or her sleeping form as in northern California where Mt. Tamalpais was revered by the Native Americans as the Sacred Woman.

Artificially constructed harvest hills, re-creating their natural counterparts, were built to facilitate union with the Goddess.[14] Like the natural hills, Silbury was womb shaped and like them probably covered with soil, alive with the continuously reborn plants and their stabilizing roots. "Indeed, the experience of the soil could be said to sum up the Neolithic fusion of nature with culture, since the natural ground paradoxically required endless expenditure of human skill and attention, in order to promote the natural miracle of harvest."[15]

The Horned God

Their vision of Silbury was inclusive, embracing all that was human, male as well as female. Stag horns found in the silt at the bottom of the ditch and marks in the chalk cliffs show that the original builders had chosen red deer antlers as picks because of their sacred character. Antlers seem especially appropriate symbols for her male counterpart, as their new growth is closely connected to reproductive activity, morphologically connected to the waxing and waning of the moon. Antlers are not permanent body parts. The stags usually shed them between late February and late March, the time of the spring planting.

> By April the new set are beginning to show; by May a sensitive covering of hair and skin envelopes the growing bone, called velvet . . . By June, the form of the antler is well established, and in July the tines are almost fully grown; the development is completed in August, when the velvet is shed to reveal hard, white tines.[16]

The Horned God is the Goddess's consort in the Celtic tradition and modern paganism, and to this day harvest festivals in Great Britain include a Stag Dance in which men wear antlers on their heads (see fig. 58).

Winter: The Crone Goes Underground

The August rites at Silbury ushered in the harvest and the life-giving powers of the Goddess. As the seasons turned so did the life and cosmic cycles. Three months later, the next quarter, the Goddess officiated in the underground burial chambers.

Called Samhain, Summer's End, or alternatively, Winter's Eve, this time was regarded as the most perilous of the year, very different from the merrymaking at Lammas, and was marked by solemn festivals at the ancient burial grounds. For Winter's Eve there was no full "birth moon" but the pitch blackness of the new moon, deepening the mood of desolation that sets in when the leaves fall, the frost comes, and the land dies. Memories of this frightening time linger beneath the masquerades of Hallowe'en. Witches, goblins, and ghosts with their threats and tricks are projections of the fear of winter's harshness in northern climates.

At winter's approach, the Tomb Lady took over from the Harvest Goddess and invited her people to follow her retreat into the underground, into the megalithic tombs (see figs. 59, 60a and b).

The Harvest Mother did not vanish from the earth but entered it to receive the dead into her hollow body. Water was

58. HORNED GOD. Detail of Gundestrup Cauldron. Silver. Jutland, second century B.C.E.

the lifeblood of the Goddess. Where a few months previously running streams had supported fish, insects, and water plants, all died as the vital water dried up in late autumn. And the November landscape was bare of sap. The setting of the barrow tomb high above the valley ensured dryness through the

The Long Barrow S. of Silbury Hill.

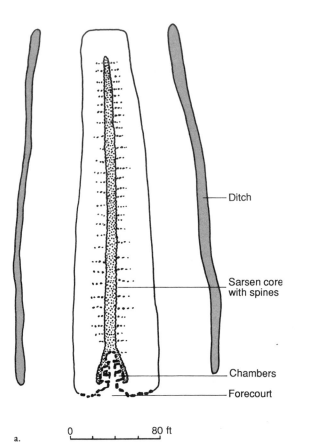

Ditch

Sarsen core
with spines

Chambers

Forecourt

0   80 ft

a.

59. West Kennet Long Barrow in 1723. Drawn by William Stuckley.

60a. Interior Plan, West Kennet Long Barrow. Detail of the tomb. Drawing after Dames.

The West Kennet Long Barrow is an enormous 340-foot earthen mound whose eastern end opens into underground burial chambers constructed, like the Maltese tombs, in the form of the Goddess.

60b. Entrance to the Underground Burial Chambers, West Kennet Long Barrow. Drawing after Dames.

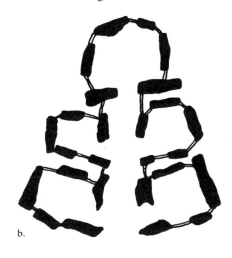

b.

The Mother-turning-into-Hag is still woven in rural England. As a symbol can, the Corn Dolly functions through her ambiguity, taking two contradictory forms. The most common one was big-hipped, squatting; the other, long and thin, corresponded to the shape of the barrow. Like the Pregnant Harvest Goddess who, transformed into the Long Barrow, went into hibernation, the Corn Dolly was shut up in the barn every winter to be returned to the fields the following spring so that the eternal round could once more be renewed.

long, barren months until late winter when the underground waters began to replenish themselves.

The great hummocky barrow mound was defaced by centuries of digging for bones to be ground into medicine. Its central core or spine made from local sandstone boulders six feet high is the desiccated skeleton of the Goddess. A mass of chalk rubble quarried from the two flanking ditches lay over these "bones." The burial chambers were topped by a thin cover of dark, turfy material, blackish, decomposing vegetable matter. The slow fermentation was the Great Mother at work garnering the seeds for the next creation.[17]

The tomb contained the primary chaos of natural and human-made things, undifferentiated rubbish from which new life arose every year. Within the tomb there was a blurring of distinctions between the living and the dead. Clay pot and skull, both rounded containers, seem to have been used interchangeably in underground ritual.

In our denial of death, we avoid confrontation with a basic reality. We conceal the ravaged face of death with cosmetics and bury our dead in costly metal boxes outfitted with luxurious bedding to provide comfort and security and to ignore the inevitable decay of the flesh into a pile of bones. In our avoidance of the reality of death, we do not face our fears of the great unknown. In separating death from life, we have severed our connection to the universal chain of being in which plants and animals, the earth and its atmosphere, the planets and galaxies are united in a never-ending cycle of life, death, and rebirth.

We can look to living tradition in India for the survival of Neolithic belief and ritual. In Tantric worship of the Goddess Kali, the seeker (*sadhaka*) must confront and assimilate the meaning of death in its most concrete form. Kali is both the loving mother who gives birth and the devourer of flesh who dances on the corpse in the graveyard. In loving her, with all her contradictory ways, the devotee overcomes the fear of death.

As Silbury is an image of the Squatting Birth Mother, so the Long Barrow is the same being in her Old Hag guise. "Like all female elders, hags have generally been cursed with pejorative meanings in patriarchal society. . . . The popular cartoon image of the hag as an ugly old witch loses sight of her original meaning. A hag used to be a 'holy woman' or wise woman: the female shaman of pre-Christian Europe, or the tribal matriarch who knew the wise ways of nature, healing, divination, civilized arts, and the traditions of the Goddess. Like the word *crone,* the hag once connoted an elder woman with the spirit of the Goddess within her, just as after menopause her 'wise blood' remained within her body and brought her great wisdom."[18] Long barrows represent the Winter Goddess as gigantic. In Celtic tales the Hag is giant-sized because she eats so much. Prehistoric tombs in Germany, Denmark, and Holland were named "giant."[19] The Great Provider has become the Great Devourer. The Corn Dolly woven from the last of the wheat straws, the vital stuff of the community's life, symbolized the Winter Goddess (see fig. 61).

As we have seen, the Avebury cycle was designed as a sequence of visual images of the Neolithic deity. The Great Mother's gigantic forms were regarded as living characters, brought, each in its turn, to a state of life-enhancing power by the sequence of human rites conducted within them annually. Such an attitude was characteristic in prehistoric times, when "the whole of creation was thought of as a giant human being."[20]

The movement of the heavens dictated the choice of Avebury as the site of this great religious drama. The Goddess was seen to be active there because of the accidental alignment of the underground river sources with the sunrise and moonrise positions at the summer Quarter Day. The vital waters that nurtured the Goddess were fed from two springs. This extraordinary coincidence was interpreted as a divine exhibition of harmony between the underworld, the terrestrial plane, and the sky.[21] The ritual cycle at Avebury is a vision of cosmic unity and its monumental forms symbolically convey that harmony.

The fertile countryside surrounding Avebury has been continuously occupied since the Stone Age. As one age succeeded another, the unified worldview at the core of the ritual cycle was eventually lost. All that remains of prehistoric Avebury today are the broken monuments. In the eighteenth century when interest in prehistoric Avebury revived, excavators were searching for a royal tomb. According to one local tradition Silbury Hill was a great mausoleum, the burial place of the legendary King Sil whose myth was created by generations of antiquarians on a treasure hunt. It was believed that the magnificence of Sil's treasure was likely to match the unique size and importance of the mound.[22]

A Viking bridle discovered at Silbury in 1723, buried just below the summit more than three thousand years after the hills were constructed, was exhibited as proof of the existence of the mythical royal horseman. Since the hill occupied five and one-half acres, locating the burial spot was no easy task. For more than two hundred years prehistorians have tried to reconstruct Avebury's history to conform to the patterns and priorities of a patriarchal warrior society.[23]

Ironically, the archaeologists who through excavation and restoration have done so much to provide additional data about the Avebury monuments are reluctant to explain how they relate to each other, beyond confirming that they should be regarded as a group built for an unknown religious purpose.[24]

> "Yet as we have seen, linear chronology has so far produced no overall picture and no narrative whatsoever for our greatest group of prehistoric monuments. In fact one can only get deep into prehistory either by going round and round, or by following anthropologists into the jungle. There, among living Neolithic communities, one discovers that "myth of its very nature repels historicity," and, in mythic awareness, "time itself is regarded as a recurring cycle. For such thinking there is no chronology."[25]

Both prehistorian and archaeologist are locked into old paradigms and cannot see the forest for the trees. Without written evidence, they feel that they can only be silent. The Avebury treasure, an integrated worldview, is far more valuable than gold or precious jewels. These monumental symbols have much to tell us as we learn to read their nonverbal language.

Crete: Fulfillment and Flowering

62. SNAKE GODDESS, ca. 1600 B.C.E. Faience and gold. From the temple repositories, Palace of Knossos, Crete.

Her eyes fixed in a trance-like gaze, the Minoan Goddess invokes the powers of the snakes, forces of regeneration, wrapped around her arms.

✿ CHAPTER 7

The apogee of Goddess culture was Minoan Crete (3000–1500 B.C.E.), a free, joyous society, where people lived in peace and in harmony with nature. The whole of life was pervaded by an ardent faith in the Goddess, which reflected and reinforced a woman-centered society. Sexuality and the human body were celebrated in images of compelling beauty and power in the brilliantly colored paintings on the walls of their great palace-shrines (see fig. 63). "The Cretans saw the supreme divine power in terms of the feminine principle, and incarnate in a woman whom they portrayed exactly like one of themselves . . . comfortable with her beauty, her body and her power" (see color plate 42). "This dedication to a goddess involved also a glorification of the meaning of sex. Fertility and abundance were the purpose and the desire, sex was the instrument, and for this reason its symbols were everywhere."[1]

The artistic tradition of Crete was unique in the Mediterranean world, expressing a sensitivity to and delight in all that was alive. Nothing quite like it had ever been seen before. The artist's impulse was to capture life fully present in the fleeting moment, like the leap of the flying fish on another fresco. "Quick, full of life, mouths agape, they flutter there for an instant, in their own element," quite free from humans and their purposes.[2] The artist's uncanny genius was to capture the essential spirit of the creature in its natural habitat like dolphins frolicking in an azure sea or a blue bird "poised for flight from a fantastic rocky outcrop with various slender plants waving round it and enhancing the suggestion of rising flight."[3]

The same rhapsodic mood celebrating nature is conveyed in the miniature scenes engraved on the gold signet rings that most fully capture the Cretan vision of the Goddess. On one

we find her sitting casually, knees up, under a tree to receive offerings of fruits and poppies (see fig. 73). This is perhaps a summer festival. On another ring the Goddess is descending to join ecstatic devotees who dance in a meadow full of lilies (see color plate 5).

Art is everywhere and at all levels of the culture. Much has been recovered from the palace treasures, refined and elegant sculpture in faience like the famous Snake Goddess (see color plate 42). But we also find a simpler ceramic art at the village level, playful and full of humor like the miniature shrine with the Goddess at the door. She is bright-eyed and grinning, and a cat is playing on her rooftop.

Play in its most profound meaning, that of the deep connection to the wellspring of creation eros, is the leitmotif of Minoan Crete. Minoan civilization most fully expresses the life of grace, which is the revelation of the Goddess.

63. Tribute Bearers to the Goddess, fifteenth century B.C.E. Fresco. Corridor of the Procession, Knossos.

In a ritual scene painted on a corridor wall of the palace-shrine at Knossos, two converging lines of men attend the Goddess. Some raise their arms in homage, others carry wine offerings in large rhytons. The Goddess or her priestess stand-in is a handsome woman, fashionably dressed, and coiffed. She wears a tight bodice, open to reveal her full breasts, a waist-cinching girdle, and flounced skirt. Her dark hair is carefully arranged in long ringlets that frame her face, crown her head, and fall down her back to her hips. Both male attendants and divine female frankly exult in their physicality, with erect carriage, proud movement, and graceful gestures.

Crete, an Unspoiled Paradise

Hesiod, the eighth-century Greek poet, sang of Crete, the golden land where "the earth poured forth its fruits unbidden in boundless plenty. In peaceful ease they kept their lands with good abundance, rich in flocks and . . . did not worship the gods of war." The island was first settled in the seventh millennium B.C.E. by hunters and fishermen from Anatolia who brought with them the culture and religion we know from Çatal Hüyük. Crete was an unspoiled paradise, having fertile soil, plentiful sources of water, luxuriant forests, and a gentle climate of extraordinary range for the size of the island. Cultivation of slopes and upland plains thousands of feet above the sea meant a succession of harvests, spread over many months. The islanders prospered, cultivating wheat and barley, grapes and olives, figs and apples, raising sheep, cattle, goats, and pigs. They exported their agricultural surplus and built sailing vessels for overseas trade.

The religion of these early Cretans was conditioned by their close links with and the value attached to everything that came out of the soil. They worshiped the Great Goddess who was also the Mistress of the animals and the sea, and who ruled over the powers within the earth. "The rich fertility of the island was a measure of her devotion to its inhabitants."[4] She showed her displeasure in devastating earthquakes.

At the beginning of the Bronze Age (ca. 3500 B.C.E.) new waves of population came to Crete from Anatolia and from Libya in North Africa. Together they created Minoan culture, the first great civilization of Europe. Easily accessible to all parts of the ancient world, with good natural harbors and plentiful timber for shipbuilding, Crete became the maritime center of the Mediterranean and grew rich on commerce and trade.

Cretan towns developed primarily from settlements that grew up around the harbors where the marketplace was the center of exchange as well as the hub of religious and social activity. The city-states that developed on Crete seem to have been loosely united under the strongest of their number and to have shared the advantages of a common culture while retaining separate traditions.

Protected by the sea from invasion, the islanders were able to seek trade rather than make war and to hold onto their wealth. Vast multistoried palaces, villas, farmsteads, well-designed cities, harbor installations, networks of roads crossing the island from end to end all testify to the quality of life.

At some time around 2000 B.C.E. and for reasons not yet clear (some think new people arrived; others only new ideas), the Minoans began to build their famous palace-shrines. These sprawling, multistoried complexes of as many as one thousand, five hundred rooms, were the ritual centers of late Minoan civilization. Their splendors were known only through myth until the early twentieth century when Sir Arthur Evans discovered the ruins of the palace at Knossos, revealing an entire previously fabled civilization. He spent the rest of his life reconstructing this wondrous palace culture so that the world at large could know the glory of Minoan Crete.

Manifestations of the Goddess

However, the primary holy places remained the caves and the mountains. Throughout the most splendid periods of their material achievement, Cretans continued to perform their rites on steep, almost inaccessible slopes, on the tops of mountains, in caves, in household chapels, and rustic shrines by groves and springs. Ritual remained close to its origins in nature and the earth, preserving the connection to the cave, the pillar, the tree—all manifestations of the Goddess.[5] The tree, like the cave, is a primordial form of the Goddess, symbolizing birth, death, and regeneration. Rooted in the earth, it sprouts, flowers, ultimately withers, and dies only to rise again from its own seed.

As in Malta and at Avebury the sanctuaries were built in relation to the sacred body of the Goddess. Architectural historian Vincent Scully shows us how the setting, orientation, and design of the palace-shrines made conscious use of the omnipresent symbols of the Goddess—her anthropomorphic form, the labyrinthine cave, and the bull's horns (see fig. 64).

> From roughly 2000 B.C.[E.] onward, a clearly defined pattern of landscape use can be recognized at every palace site. . . . [E]ach palace makes use, . . . of the same landscape elements . . . first, an enclosed valley of varying size in which the palace is set; . . . second, a gently mounded or conical hill on axis with the palace . . . and lastly a higher, double-peaked or cleft mountain some distance beyond the hill but on the same axis.[6]

The conical hill would be seen as the earth's fertile body, the twin peaks as the horns of the bull, the symbol of her activating power.[7] The palace-shrines located in the enclosed valley would

64. Sacred Horns and Sacred Peak. Southward view to Mt. Jouctas from the Palace temple of Knossos. Photograph.

be constructed to re-create the labyrinthine passages of the cave, the hollows sacred to the Goddess, her womb, and would be the ritual center. "All these forms, natural and man-made, create a ritual whole, in which man's part is defined and directed by the sculptural masses of the land and is subordinate to their rhythms."[8] The notched peak of Mt. Jouctas can be seen rising directly to the south of Knossos. In Minoan times, there was a cave sanctuary of the Goddess within the mountain.

The Goddess belonged to both the cave and the mountain-peak sanctuaries that were places of healing (see fig. 65). Dream incubation was practiced there as in the Hypogeum at Malta and at Epidauros. Caves also were associated with childbirth and the maternal nature of the Goddess. The cave has always been a womb image and those in the great mountains were probably visited by women who wanted children, or protection in childbirth.[9]

One of the oldest cave sanctuaries was dedicated to Eilei-thyia, the Greek Goddess of Childbirth, and was the center of her cult from Minoan to Roman times, where the Goddess was worshiped in the form of a nearly cylindrical stalagmite enclosed by a low stone wall deep within the cavern. Other

stalagmites have ritual markings from the Neolithic recalling the worship of limestone concretions in the Taurus Mountains near Çatal Hüyük. The supplicants who went there seem to have been humble people, for they left no rich offerings, only crude pottery images, a couple in embrace, a mother and child.[10] Outside the Cretan cave sanctuary was a fig tree, sacred to the Goddess because of the pulpy fruit's resemblance to a woman's fertile womb (see color plate 45).

Even the gods were sometimes born in caves. An early cave sanctuary dedicated to the Goddess was the legendary birthplace of Zeus on Mt. Dikte. According to classical mythology, Zeus's mother Rhea fled from the deadly clutches of her husband Kronos whose habit was to devour his own offspring so they would not grow up and usurp his power. On Crete she gave birth in a cave to her immortal son.

There is an enigma about Zeus in Crete. According to early pre-Olympian myths known to both the Cretans and the

65. IBEX AT PEAK SANCTUARY. Detail of a steatite rhyton. Formerly covered with gold leaf. From the Palace at Kato Zakro.

Greeks, he was born, grew to manhood, and was buried in Crete. Zeus's place of burial is said to be on Mt. Jouctas where there was a cave sanctuary dedicated to the Goddess in Minoan times, later converted into a sanctuary to Zeus. Jouctas is the mountain peak most sacred to the Goddess on Crete. A seal impression from Knossos shows her standing on the top of the mountain surrounded by her lions (see fig. 68).

This heterodoxy of the Cretans persisted into classical times.[11] Why did the first Greek settlers identify their sky-father with a god who lived and died like a man in Crete? The reasons are complex and there is much that has still to be recovered and understood. Zeus was, of course, an Indo-European god introduced to Greece by the invading Achaeans. The poet Hesiod, living about a century after Homer, accepts the legend that Zeus was born in Crete and was the Year God of the Cretan Goddess of the Caves.[12] The lasting power of the Goddess was so strong "that the Greeks allowed her to capture the origins of their sky Father, to pull him down from self-created majesty on Olympus to wailing infancy in a Cretan cave."[13]

Today there are still remains of ancient rituals in this cave. In an upper grotto, a sacrificial deposit of horned animals' ashes and bones many feet deep lies beside an altar. Double axes, the *labrys* (see color plate 44), another symbol of the Goddess, still stand where they had been thrust into the stalagmite columns in a cavern below. The stalagmites, like the tree and the sacred pillar, embodied the numinous presence of the Goddess. At Crete we witness the transformation of the natural symbols of the tree and the cave into art.

Symbolically the sacred pillar is a variant form of the tree and, as in many cultures, represented the Goddess in Minoan shrines. Contact with the Goddess was believed to be established by pouring blood or other sacred liquids on pillar altars. Every household from the royal palace on down had a shrine room, a windowless crypt resting on heavy pillars that had trenches cut around them, or vats standing in front of them, for ritual libations. Occasionally the horns or bones of sacrifice or a ritual vessel were also found lying nearby.[14] Some scholars now believe the palace-temple was a burial sanctuary and the ceremonies there were funerary.

Miniature shrines representing the Goddess show doves resting on her sacred pillars, and in small votive figures of the

Goddess found at household shrines she wears doves in her headdress (see fig. 66).

Later, Greek and Roman mythology reveals the dove as another of those complex symbols representing the fullness of the Goddess as bearer of both life and death. The emblem of the Goddess of Love and Beauty, Aphrodite/Venus, the bird stands for sexual passion and the soul returning to her after death. Aphrodite was both the bringer of death and peace. Romans called her Venus Columba, Venus-in-the-Dove. Her catacombs, mausoleums, and necropoli were known as *columbaria,* dovecotes.[15] Christians later adopted the dove as the sign of the Holy Ghost, but originally the bird stood for Sophia, God's female soul. Jacquetta Hawkes in her colorful narrative history of Minoan and Mycenaean times, *Dawn of the Gods* (1968), comments on how the attributes of the Goddess reveal her as both the One and the Many (see fig. 67).

The famous faience Goddess from the palace-shrine at Knossos, her arms entwined with serpents, invoked their chthonic powers (see fig. 62 and color plate 42). The snake, the guardian genius of the household and its possessions, was believed to be in touch with the powers of the earth out of which it comes. Friendly reptiles were kept like pets in palaces and humbler houses as they still are in peasant homes in many parts of the world.[16]

Scenes of worship in the wild places were engraved on exquisite gold seals and signet rings (see color plate 5). The Vegetation Goddess is shown again and again dancing in meadows and groves with her priestesses or with her young god, "pulling down the bough from the sacred tree, receiving blossoms, fruits and poppy seeds." Like Dionysus's in classical Greek religion, her ritual dance is orgiastic.

"Equally of the wilds, but chaste and free, was the mistress of the wild animals, huntress and later tamer of the beasts."[17] We first encountered her with her animals in the grain bin at Çatal Hüyük where as the life giver she sat between two leopards to give birth (see fig. 27). In the later days of Minoan culture she is often seen standing between wild creatures on a mountain top (see fig. 68). However, Rachel Levy, the English scholar whose study of Stone Age religion, *The Gate of Horn* (1948), is a classic, finds little resemblance between

66. Epiphany of the Goddess: Doves on Sacred Columns. Detail of miniature shrine. Clay. From the Old Palace of Knossos.

67. GODDESS WITH POPPY SEEDS IN HER CROWN, ca. 1350 B.C.E. Clay. Gazi.

The most common image of the Goddess found in household shrines has a tubular shaped lower body as if she is half emerging from a pillar or tree, a comment on her origins. Her upper torso is that of a woman with arms raised in prayer. In her crown she wears one of the emblems of her cult: the poppy seeds that will induce trance, the horned altar of consecration, or the messenger dove from the upper air.

68. THE MOUNTAIN MOTHER BETWEEN LIONS, ca. 1600 B.C.E. Impression of seal. Knossos. Drawing after Levy.

the personality of the Cretan Mistress of the Wilds and the Asiatic goddess of human fecundity found at Çatal Hüyük. Rather "she is a creation of Minoan independence . . . the forerunner of Artemis and Diana."[18]

The Golden Butterfly

The supreme emblem of the Minoan Goddess, carried by both her and her priestesses, is the puzzling double axe, the *labrys* that might be made of bronze of gigantic size, or very often smaller in gold[19] (see color plate 44).

Hawkes traces the origin of its name and connection to the labyrinth.

> It was known as the *labrys* from its Lydian name, and the palace of Knossos was known as the Labyrinth in the sense of the House of the Double Axe. It was only later, when visiting Greeks saw the bewildering ruins of the ancient palace, that the name came to be applied to the maze, and the sign of the maze was set upon the Cretan coinage. In the palace as everywhere else the symbol was displayed as frequently and conspicuously as the cross in Christian buildings.[20]

The way the *labrys* must have been set up in shrines appears clearly in a scene on the Hagia Triada sarcophagus (see fig. 69). "A priestess is pouring a libation into a vessel standing between two towering obelisk-like shafts, set on stepped bases and crowned with ornate double axes in gold."[21]

According to Gimbutas the double axe is the symbol of rebirth in the form of a butterfly.

> The shape of a butterfly emerges on Çatal Hüyük frescoes and is incised on European Neolithic pots. . . . These schematic butterflies are the prototypes of the Minoan 'double-axes' which we find portrayed between the horns of a bull. The emblem of the Great Goddess in its origin has nothing to do with the axe; it antedates the appearance of metal axes by several thousand years.
>
> The process of transformation from a butterfly to a double axe must have been influenced by the similarity of shape between the two or by the influence of the nearby Indo-Europeans (Mycenaeans), to whom the axe of the thundergod was sacred since it was imbued with his potency. Whereas the Indo-European axe was the weapon of a male god, the Minoan

69. Funeral Scene from Hagia Triada Sarcophagus, ca. 1400 B.C.E. Fresco on limestone.

double-axe was never shown in such a context. It appears as an emblem held by the Goddess in each hand in frescoes and on |stone| plaques.[22]

The double axe of the Goddess stood for regeneration while that of the Indo-European god meant death.

The Bull and the Goddess

The most singular aspect of Cretan religion was the ritual bull dance performed in the Great Hall of the palace-shrine of Knossos (see fig. 70). The objective of the young bull dancers was not to conquer but to adjust their human rhythms to those of the animal, both being living creatures, part of the Goddess and nature. "The love for the free movement of the

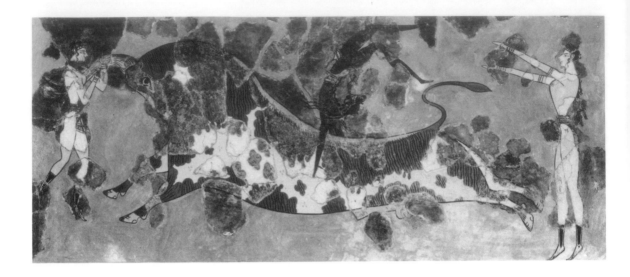

beast which is demonstrated by the paintings of the Paleolithic caves now broadens its conceptual base and grasps the beauty of the movements of man and beast together . . . ."[23] This was quite unlike the cruelty and contradictions of the Spanish bullfight, in which the animal is seduced, enticed, maddened by the red cape waved before his eyes, his power broken through bloody conquest and his death a victory. In Crete, "the final sacrifice of the bull to the Goddess should itself also be seen . . . as an act of reverence to the animal, since it dignified with ceremony and hallowed with gratitude the everyday deaths of his kind"[24] slaughtered for food.

> In trying to imagine the general atmosphere and expectation of the bull leaping [ceremony], it may be helpful to recall a great circus tent or hall where trapeze artists are performing without nets. The tension and excitement are stimulated by awareness of mortal danger, yet it is assumed that all will be well, and death is in fact [rare] . . . The . . . enjoyment of the audience is in the supreme skill and grace of movement. "The fact that men and women perform together and entrust their lives to one another adds a distinctive flavor."[25]

In the palace frescoes it is conventional to depict men as brown skinned and women as white. So we can easily identify their slim, well-built, and athletic bodies, performing in concert, first grasping the horns of the huge charging beast, then

70. YOUNG MEN AND WOMEN BULL-LEAPING, after 1600 B.C.E. Fresco, Knossos.

Young men and women, votaries of the Goddess, confronted the charging bull in daring acrobatic leaps, seizing the animal's horns, the symbol of his power, their bodies in perfect tune with his animal nature.

somersaulting onto its back and over once again into the arms of a waiting companion.

In the Cretan arena the strong emotions of religious significance would be evoked. The bull was sacred and a universal symbol of potency (see fig. 71). The performance would begin and end with libations and other ritual observances; the bull dance would be seen to serve the divine power of the Goddess who would, in turn, bring fertility and well-being.[26]

The bull came to be the symbol of Minoan civilization but was not worshiped by the Cretans. His was the masculine counterpart to the Goddess's female power. In the celebrated bull leaping, he embodies the raw animal power of nature. We have seen his schematized horns become the altar consecrated to the Great Goddess, a core symbol of the Goddess religion. In later Greek mythology the life-enhancing power of the bull is perverted. Zeus disguised as a bull rapes Europa (see fig. 74) and Pasipaie, King Minos's queen, mates with the beautiful white bull from the sea.

In Minoan religion the horns of consecration are used to mark the sanctity of an enclosure or the neighborhood of a shrine or to denote the presence of deity or ritual object. Anointed with bull's blood, the horned altar was nearly always small and was used as the base in which the double axe's shaft rests. The complementarity of the male and female principals continues to evolve as a fundamental aspect of Goddess religion.

The Role of Women in a Goddess Culture

In the fullness and flowering of Goddess religion what was the role of women? Minoan art and artifacts provide unambiguous evidence of the prominent role that Cretan women played in that relatively free and rich society. Opulent, sophisticated, Minoan arts and crafts were unparalleled in the ancient world for their beauty and refinement. Their imagery was realistic, yet imaginative and exuberant, and drew on the natural environment, on everyday life and on sacred ritual, leaving us a fuller record of their world than that of other prehistoric peoples.[27]

The way in which Cretan men and women dressed is especially revealing of cultural attitudes and suggests a frank enjoy-

71. CRETAN BULL RHYTON, 1550–1500 B.C.E. Black steatite with rock crystal eye and wood gilt horns. Little Palace, Knossos.

ment of sexuality that would go along with the high status of women. In public, women appeared graceful and elegant in dress and seemed to be uninhibited, lively, and free in mingling with men.

For rituals men and women often dressed alike, implying that their roles were interchangeable.

> The women bull leapers wore the loincloth and codpiece of the men, and in funerary rites [they all] wore identical sheepskin skirts. In other rituals in which both sexes took part, men donned long flounced robes, initially the garb of the priestess and usually worn by women. They wore metal belts around their very slim waists, both used a great deal of jewelry— bracelets, armbands, collars, and headbands. Both wore their hair in the same way—long and curly, falling down their backs, with locks hanging in front of the ears. Clothes accentuating the penis and female breasts are equally revealing, indicating a frank acceptance of the human body.[28]

The Goddess was an impressive and pervasive presence. She is pictured with her priestesses and votaries in every aspect of the natural and social ambience of Crete. Women were the central subjects, and those portrayed most frequently were shown in the public sphere. In one large fresco documenting a festival, mature women are shown in the midst of the foreground action, gossiping and relating to each other warmly and intimately. Women were artisans, weavers, and potters. The famous Cretan "pottery was as thin as porcelain and decorated with vibrant geometric patterns of flowers and leaves, shellfish and flying fish, birds and animals and dancing women"[29] (see fig. 72).

Women and men, animals and plants are shown in free and close communion with each other. Young men and women hunted the wild bull with staves and nooses, entrusting their lives to one another. In one scene of a bull hunt, engraved in high relief on a gold cup, a masterpiece of uninhibited straightforward story-telling art, a male hunter is thrown by a bull while his woman companion wraps her whole body around the animal's horns in an effort to subdue it.

Women were the midwives and probably the healers as well (see fig. 73). No one knows whether the woman holding three poppyseed heads is the Goddess or flesh and blood woman, perhaps a priestess performing a healing ritual.

72. POTTERY GROUP OF DANCING WOMEN
FROM PALAIKASTRO, ca. 1500 B.C.E.

The Minoans, particularly women, had a
passion for dancing in a ritual circle. Again
and again they are shown in the meadows
and groves before the Goddess and her altars.

73. GODDESS OR HER PRIESTESS
PERFORMING A HEALING RITUAL, ca. 1500
B.C.E. Drawing from impression of seal.

The lily, poppy, crocus, and iris, favorite
subjects of Minoan painters, potters, and seal
cutters, were especially sacred, associated with
the Goddess in her aspect as deity of
vegetation. The lily was used to check
menstruation and the poppy seed was used
for medicinal as well as religious purposes.[7]

Was Crete a Matriarchy?

A number of scholars are convinced that Crete was a matriarchy, a theocracy ruled by a queen-priestess.[30] No single representation of a king or dominant male god has yet been found, and this may simply mean that there was no central ruling figure on the island. But since there are two thrones in the palace at Knossos, one in a room consecrated to religious ritual, the other in a public audience chamber in the residential quarters, someone must have been occupying them (see color plate 38).

In the palace frescoes male figures are always young men, and often are represented as smaller than the prominent female who can be read as the Goddess or the high priestess who represented her. When the Goddess presides over religious rites she is always accompanied by priestesses or female votaries. Participation by men in the cult was a late development that suggests a shift in the male-female dynamic or perhaps shows outside influence, an increasing Mycenaean patriarchal presence. In the ritual scenes engraved on the stone seals, is it the high priestess who takes her place on the seat of the Goddess in the outdoor festivals and who sits on the mountain peak to receive offerings from her acolytes and the faithful? Living women enacted the role of the Goddess, and the famous faience image of the woman with the snakes may represent a priestess impersonating the Goddess.

In miniature scenes not only is the Goddess always the central figure, she is sometimes sitting on a throne. If a king did rule as the consort of the Goddess, one would expect that at the royal court there would have been a throne for both as the human reflection of the divine order, the usual situation in the Near East.

On seals and elsewhere, griffins, those fabulous beasts that are part eagle and part lion, symbols of nature's creativity, attend the Goddess. In the palace restoration the gypsum throne is guarded by a pair of monumental griffins reclining amidst tall papyrus whose graceful white stems shimmer against the deep red background. "The occupant of the throne would therefore have appeared as a figure between two confronted beasts, a ritualistic motif originating in the Orient and often reproduced in Minoan . . . art."[31]

The graves of two women who could have sat on the throne have been found a few miles from the palace, the first noble tombs found on the island that had not been plundered. One was buried in a gown of gold, richly adorned with one hundred and forty pieces of gold jewelry and tiny gold amulet boxes.[32] The other "wore a necklace of astonishing beauty, each of its gold parts shaped like a paper nautilus shell. She lay on her left side, facing Mount Jouctas, and held in her hands a copper mirror, a stunning image of death."[33]

The Mystery of Minos

Minos was probably a member of the dynasty established at Knossos by the Mycenaeans who overran Crete in the late fifteenth century B.C.E. when their civilization had been weakened by the devastation of earthquakes, floods, and fires. The fertile land was colonized and most of the people enslaved. Minoan, thus, "is a misnomer for the earlier period."[34]

Myths are stories that ostensibly tell how it was in the beginning, usually to explain the origin of certain practices, beliefs, or institutions. The complex scenario of King Minos's "history" was rewritten by the Greeks to explain the takeover of Crete by their Mycenaean ancestors. What can we learn from these tales about the original Cretan story concealed within the myth?

In Phoenicia, Zeus met Europa, daughter of the King, walking by the seashore picking flowers. He fell in love with her at first sight; in order to seduce her, he transformed himself into a handsome bull. Attracted to the playful beast, Europa mounted his back. Against her will, he raced off with her across the winds of the sea and brought her to Crete (see fig. 74). She bore him three sons of whom Minos was the oldest.

Once when Minos wanted to offer a sacrifice, the King of the Sea, Poseidon, sent him a dazzling white bull, which stepped out of the waves as the intended victim. Minos, much taken with this prize, decided to keep the white bull for himself and sacrificed another in its place, outraging Poseidon. To punish Minos, the god had Pasiphae develop a consuming passion for the animal. A clever palace engineer, Daedalus, fashioned a model of a cow in which he concealed the Queen,

who thus satisfied her lust for the bull. Out of their union was born a monster, the Minotaur, with the head of a bull and a human body, who was imprisoned in the heart of the Labyrinth. Daedalus, it is said, built the complex structure to hide the monster and his mother from the world.

According to Greek legend, Athens, a tributary of Crete, had to send seven youths and seven maidens every year to Knossos to satisfy the rapacious appetite of the Minotaur. Theseus, the son of the King of Athens, volunteered to go to

74. EUROPA AND THE BULL, ca. fifth century B.C.E. Painting on vase. Greek.

Crete to kill the Minotaur. With the aid of a ball of string given to him by Ariadne, the daughter of Minos who had fallen in love with Theseus, he found his way out of the Labyrinth (see fig. 75).

Theseus's victory is the metaphoric deathblow to the way of the Goddess. His story is the myth of the patriarchal hero who defied death in killing the bull-headed monster who had become the king of the underworld. Theseus kills him with the double axe, the emblem of the Goddess, at the center of the Labyrinth, which is her body. Theseus has usurped the power of the Goddess. The Labyrinth, her sacred space deep within, her "holy of holies," was transformed into the dreaded kingdom of the dead, a complete reversal of Goddess values. Death was no longer viewed as rebirth in the body of the Mother.

75. THESEUS AND THE MINOTAUR, fifth century B.C.E. Painting on vase. Greek.

Europa is the manifestation of the Great Goddess as the mother of an entire continent. Her name means "full moon," and like the Egyptian Hathor and the Greek Hera she was embodied in the moon-cow. The rape of Europa can be read as the triumph of the sun-bull of the Olympian sky gods. Zeus, their king, triumphed over the Great Goddess by rape. Rape metaphorically describes the actual plunder and suppression of the Goddess and her culture, as well as the changing attitude toward women with the onset of patriarchy.

Evans's discovery of the actual palace at Knossos revealed the labyrinthine complexity of its structure. The ritual center was deep within the palace; the discovery of the *labrys* emblazoned on the walls gave credibility to the historical origins of the myth. This was the secret place out of which the Greeks created the mythical Labyrinth.

Scully re-creates the awesome mood of a ritual procession moving down into the shrine of the Goddess from dark to light to dark through lighted stairwells to cavernous dark apartments to open courts culminating in the innermost dark shrine that was the hallowed earth of the Goddess. The processional space was fluid and moving like the bull dance. The water that ran through it was the Goddess's gift and was collected in lustral basins wherever it found its level in her hollows. All was in constant motion up and around the innermost shrine, the sanctuary where the priestess of the Goddess sat on her throne between the two griffins[35] (see color plate 38).

The universal mystical meaning of the labyrinthine form is as a symbol for the journey into the other world and the return, a death to one state and rebirth into another. The classical Labyrinth is not a maze in which to get lost. Rather there is only one pathway, in and out. The Hopi Indians call the labyrinth the symbol of Mother Earth and liken it to the kiva, their underground sanctuary out of which the Hopi people emerged into the world. "All the lines and passages within the maze form the universal plan of the creator which [humans] must follow on [their] Road of Life."[36] Mazes are sometimes found in Christian cathedrals as at Chartres. "He who knows how to follow or make the diagram has his passport to the other world and resides in the God—or rather, because the maze honors women and the belly, the God-

76. Cretan Coin with Labyrinth, ca. 1200 B.C.E. Drawing. Knossos.

dess."[37] The Cretans engraved the symbol of the labyrinth on their coins (see fig. 76).

People do not lightly give up a belief system in which their reality is grounded and their humanity affirmed. Much of the Goddess religion of Minoan Crete was absorbed and transformed by the Greek religion that replaced it. But the seamless unity of Goddess culture was lost and with it the grace of life that flowered in Minoan Crete.

Part of the contemporary fascination with Minoan culture is its heady combination of elemental forms of worship with a sophisticated and refined aesthetic. The Cretans tapped directly into the forces of nature that transfused their life with a passion and beauty never known before or since in Western culture.

Minoan culture realized the fulfillment of the sacred way of the Goddess and was one major source for Greek civilization; another was the Indo-European. We will look next at the transformation of the Goddess under the sky gods' hegemony.

The Patriarchal Takeover:

 PART TWO

City Shrine Surrounded by Signs of
Inanna: The Rosettes, Her Face, and
Her Gateposts, 3000 b.c.e. Cylinder seal.
Tell Agrab. Mesopotamia.

The Taming of the Goddess

Minoan civilization fell to the combined onslaughts of natural disasters, floods and earthquakes, and the invasions of the Achaeans, Greek-speaking peoples from the mainland usually referred to as Indo-Europeans. These were the same warlike people who overran Old European civilization and imposed their male-dominated hierarchy and the worship of their sky gods on Goddess cultures wherever they settled.

These invasions occurred in different places and at different times over millennia as wave after wave of Indo-Europeans arrived on the scene. By 1500 B.C.E. they were firmly established in Old Europe, the Near East, and the Mediterranean. Wherever the Indo-Europeans ruled, the Goddess would have to share her domain with male gods.

In some places the transition was precipitous and brutal, in others gradual, as her powers were co-opted one by one. The new divine order led to far-reaching changes in the social fabric, in the relations of men and women with the gods, with each other, and with nature. It seems that everywhere that the sky gods took over, life became less free, less creative, and less joyful.

The origins of patriarchy and the identity of the invading peoples is a most vexing problem.

Modern scholarship no longer uses the term Indo-European as racial identity. Indo-European refers to a group of languages with common roots that are found from the British Isles to the Bay of Bengal. The more recent field research of physical anthropologists demonstrates that the so-called Indo-Europeans were of different racial stocks. The original use of the term by western European scholars in the late eighteenth and nineteenth centuries to refer to both race and language was part of a commonly held ideology that sought to classify the world by race, placing great value on racial purity, which they saw as affirmed by the Hindu caste system.[1]

The concept of racial purity has been thoroughly discredited by Nazi use to justify their own policies of genocide and wars of conquest, but the term Indo-European has stuck.

The most concrete evidence that we have to account for the demise of the woman-centered Goddess cultures is archaeological. Remains have been uncovered that show a pattern of disruption, invasion, and natural catastrophe in Anatolia, Old Europe, Malta, and Crete leading to a period of regression and stagnation. As we have already noted, interpretation of such evidence is an enormously complex business. The archaeologist must extrapolate the culture from the reassembled fragments found in burial grounds, sacred sites, and dwelling places. Artifacts from graves are particularly helpful because of what they tell about the status of the dead and beliefs in the afterlife.

From such findings Gimbutas identifies the invaders of Old Europe as the horse-riding Kurgan peoples from north of the Black Sea who with their newly acquired skill of metallurgy forged lethal weapons from copper and bronze to kill, plunder, and enslave. Neolithic peoples had long known how to work metals like copper and gold but used them for ornamental and religious purposes.[2] Kurgan warriors were buried with their weapons on which were engraved the earliest known representation of the Indo-European gods, abstract images in which the deity is represented by his weapon alone or in combination with a belt, necklace, double spiral pendant, and divine animal, either a horse or stag.[3] The weapons, axes with long shafts and daggers, symbolized the god's powers and were worshiped as the god himself.

Historian Gerda Lerner, working from the earliest written documents, argues that patriarchy is a historic creation formed by men and women in the ancient Near East in a process that took nearly 2,500 years, beginning in the third millennium B.C.E. and was well established by the time of the writing of the Hebrew Bible.

> In its earliest form patriarchy appeared as the archaic state. The basic unit of its organization was the patriarchal family, which both expressed and constantly generated its rules and values. . . .
> The roles and behavior deemed appropriate to the sexes were expressed in values, customs, laws and social roles. They also, very importantly, were expressed in leading metaphors, which became part of the cultural construct and explanatory system.[4]

The social system that ultimately evolved in the lands conquered by the Indo-Europeans was based on a system of dominance that mirrored the interpersonal relationships in their pantheon. We are only now becoming aware that patriarchy has become so embedded in our belief system that we accept its premises as natural and inevitable.

Lerner looks to the analysis of class structure, men being the dominant, women the underclass, for her understanding of the root causes of patriarchy.

> Women . . . became a resource, acquired by men much as the land was acquired by men. Women were exchanged or bought in marriage for the benefit of their families; later, they were conquered or bought in slavery where their sexual services were part of their labor and where their children were the property of their masters. . . . Since their sexuality, an aspect of their body, was controlled by others, women were not only actually disadvantaged but psychologically restrained in a very special way.[5]

In Mesopotamian societies the institutionalization of patriarchy circumscribed and finally eroded the sexual rights of upper-class women.[6] Lerner argues that "the lifelong dependency of women on fathers and husbands became so firmly established in law and custom as to be considered natural and God-given. In the case of lower-class women, their labor power served either their families or those who owned their families' services. Their sexual and reproductive capacities were commodified—traded, leased, or sold in the interest of male family members." However, she goes on to comment that "even then powerful women in powerful roles lived on in cultic service, in religious representation, and in symbols."

The Great Goddess of prehistory was manifest in historical time in many personae—in cult images and in the role of priestesses who embodied her presence, an active force in daily life and popular religion, even as her supreme powers were being eroded.[7] "Mesopotamian men and women in distress or sickness humbled themselves before [the] goddess and her priestly servant . . . they praised and worshiped the goddess's power. . . ."[8] The petitioner would buy appropriate offerings: food, a young animal for sacrifice, oil, and wine. For the goddess Ishtar such offerings quite frequently included images of the vulva, fashioned out of precious lapis lazuli and offered up to her in praise, celebrating "the sacredness of female sexuality and its mysterious life-giving force which included the power to heal."[9]

One cannot help but wonder at the contradiction between the power of the goddesses and the increasing societal constraints upon the lives of most women in ancient Mesopotamia,[10] a situation not unlike that of contemporary India where the Goddess is widely worshiped as the all-powerful Absolute Being and the oppression of women is widespread. In a patriarchal culture—and modern India is a very patriarchal society—there would seem to be little direct relation between the status of women and the worship of the Goddess. The status of women is a function of socioeconomic structure. There is much to reflect upon. In changing our consciousness we need not only to create new symbols but also to live our lives in accordance with the underlying values they embody. We will return to this social dynamic later when we look at the impact of the re-emergence of the Goddess now under way in our culture.

We first will look at two Goddess cults under patriarchy, the Sacred Marriage Ritual in Sumer and the Mysteries of Demeter in Greece, for insight into the impact of male-dominated cultures on the sacred values of the Goddess. Next, we will consider the fateful confrontation between the Goddess and monotheism. Then, we will turn to the Virgin who has carried the powers of the divine female into our own time, albeit severely handicapped by Christian attitudes toward sexuality and the body. In conclusion, we will consider what has been lost and the price Western culture has paid for the suppression of the unified worldview of the Goddess culture.

The witch persecutions of the fifteenth to the eighteenth centuries are the ultimate example of misogyny. As many as nine million people, mostly women, were tortured and put to death in a fanatical outburst against that constellation of beliefs and practices we have come to recognize as the way of the Goddess. The social and political forces that led to this holocaust—an apt name, for in some villages in Europe there were no women left alive—are complex, but the root cause was fear of the power of women.

The visual documentation of the major paradigm shift we are following in these chapters is not easy to interpret. There is no dearth of images of the Goddess in all her glory. Small devotional figures continued to be mass produced everywhere in Europe and the Near East until Christianity and Islam were well established. But we are now in historical times and also have to deal with scripture and other texts that were usually written from the viewpoint of the victor whose interest was to vilify the vanquished deities.

The iconography of the Virgin absorbed many of the Goddess's powers and attributes. Mary was the most venerated figure in Christianity, often more widely worshiped than her son, Jesus, the object of widespread devotion and a major source of inspiration for late Medieval and Renaissance art. The womb/vulva, primary symbol of the Goddess and her life force, takes on new meaning in Christianity as the pure vessel in which the new god was first nurtured and out of which he was born.

Mary takes over many of the maternal and fertility functions of the Goddess and in time cosmic ones as well. With her Coronation she becomes the Queen of Heaven and rules alongside God the Father and God the Son. Although Christian doctrine says her powers are mediated through the Father and Son, in devotional practice she became the ultimate source of divine intervention in human affairs.

The power of the image to contain, express, communicate, and sustain faith is almost unlimited. In the example of the Virgin, the visual evidence belies theology and doctrine. In the case of the Goddess, this power is reinforced when the image is made from clay, from the earth, the stuff of the Goddess's own body. The relationship of the worshiper and icon is very intimate when the object of devotion is held in the hand. The Protestant Reformation, with its unequivocal rejection of the veneration of the Virgin and use of devotional imagery, was so successful in making a radical break with old ways because the primary psychological and emotional connection to the

sacred female image was completely severed. The full impact of iconoclastic Protestantism is felt in the United States where
no existing tradition of glorious Christian
art counteracts the absence of divine
images in Protestant churches.

While the onset of Protestantism in the
late fifteenth century was not the cause of
the witch burnings, their historical coincidence dealt the final blow to Goddess
values, to the freedom of women to practice a faith honoring the spirituality of
nature and their own bodies.

We now return to the early historical
time of the third millennium B.C.E. to pick
up the story of the Goddess as she confronts the patriarchy in the Near East,
because that is where the historical record
of the takeover is most fully documented.

Sumer: The Descent of Inanna

✿ CHAPTER 8

The Goddess was continuously worshiped for thousands of years (ca. 3500–500 B.C.E.) in the ancient Near East "during the ascendance and decline of civilizations that flourished and were conquered."[1] Her names were many: Ishtar, Astarte, Anahita, Ma, Asherah, but she was first known as Inanna, the beloved and revered deity of Sumer.

Despite hostile intrusions into her domain by the patriarchal sky gods, Inanna continued to be revered as the awesome Queen of Heaven and Earth. "Her womb was the vessel of Creation from which flowed grains, fruit, and legumes. Hers was the nourishing breast of nature. Hers was the bountiful lap of nurturing mother earth. As the radiant Morning Star, she is birth, potential, all possibility; as Evening Star, she is completion and fulfillment."[2] Inanna is the Goddess of Love, giving forth "desire that generates the energy of the universe."[3]

Inanna played a greater role in Sumerian myth than any other deity. Her life inspired the poets of Sumer who transformed the much older myths into a cycle of impassioned, rhapsodic verse, *The Hymn to Inanna*. Ecstatic hymns and songs were sung in her temples throughout the Near East. Inanna's sacred narrative includes "the world's first love story, two thousand years older than the Bible—tender, erotic, shocking and compassionate. . . ."[4] And her journey to the underworld illuminates for us the relation between sex and death and the meaning of sacrifice.

Archaeological finds have been our primary resource in the search for the meaning of the Goddess. Now we will include the poet's image and metaphor. Inanna's story has been restored through the collaboration of Diane Wolkstein, a gifted storyteller and folklorist, and Samuel Noah Kramer, the preeminent expert on Sumer. Kramer translated, ordered, and combined the fragmented cuneiform tablets comprising the "Cycle of Inanna." Wolkstein took his literal translation and wove it into contemporary poetic form to create an authentic portrait of an archetypal Goddess.

The *Hymn to Inanna* was sung at the sacred marriage rites between the Goddess and the Sumerian king to ensure the fertility of the land and to legitimize the king's rule. The sacred marriage (*hieros gamos*) was celebrated annually throughout the Near East. The role of the Goddess in the ritual sexual union was taken by her priestess, the hierodule, believed to be an embodiment of the Goddess herself. "Union with the goddess was of paramount importance for rule on earth."[5] The cosmic powers of the Goddess had to be transferred to the king to ensure his powers of leadership and fertility. Their sexual union was necessary to activate the annual cycle of life.

The model for the sacred rite was the marriage of the Goddess Inanna to the Shepherd King Dumuzi. Every year Inanna, the Queen of Heaven and Earth, descended from heaven at the time of the autumn equinox to consummate her marriage to Dumuzi in her temple at Uruk. The sacred law of Sumer, which dictated the order and form of things, ordained that day as the beginning of the New Year when the earth awakened and the winter crop of barley from which they made their bread and beer was planted.

While the surviving record is written from the vantage of those who would suppress the Goddess, a critical rereading in the light of what we already know about her culture helps us to understand the dynamic of change as well as the key issues involved.

The land inhabited by the ancient Sumerians in the alluvial valleys of the Tigris and Euphrates rivers is an area of approximately 10,000 square miles. It lies in the southern part of what is modern Iraq, roughly between Baghdad and the Persian Gulf. The unpromising land seemed doomed to poverty and desolation, with its hot, dry climate and windswept soil. There are no minerals and very little stone or timber. "But the Sumerians were a gifted, energetic, innovative people, technically inventive and ideologically resourceful, and with the help of irrigation and a relatively pragmatic view of life and its mysteries, they turned this deprived land into a veritable Garden of Eden."[6]

In the third millennium B.C.E., Sumer consisted of a dozen or so city-states, large, walled cities surrounded by villages and farms, "dominated architecturally and spiritually by a many-storied temple, or ziggurat, constructed to house the [ruling] deity under whose auspices the city was thought to live out its destiny and to prosper."[7] "[The] lofty ziggurats, or temple towers, rose skyward, filling the citizen's heart with awe, wonder and pride."[8]

Inanna's city, Uruk, identified with the biblical Erech, was on the Euphrates River. German archaeologists, systematically excavating there since the late nineteenth century, have uncovered levels of the city dating from the fourth to the first millennium B.C.E. Important to our knowledge of Inanna and ancient Sumer are those levels dating from 3500 to 2900 B.C.E. providing evidence of an urban civilization. The sudden transition from village to urban life suggested by the archaeological remains makes credible the story of Inanna's gift of civilization to her city. Sacred narrative often preserves memories of how people experience cultural changes.

Inanna's Temple, The Sacred House of Heaven

"The sacred house of Inanna," called Eanna, the "House of Heaven," is the oldest preserved temple at Uruk. An enormous mud-brick construction, more than 30 × 30 meters in size, the main temple is set on a limestone base, an unusual feature in a region where stone is so rare. The temple has a three-part plan composed of two aisles flanking a nave, and at the end of the nave, a rectangular central shrine, the "holy of holies." The main temple is connected to a smaller shrine by an astonishing portico that is supported on colossal circular columns of mud brick. The portico faces a broad open court whose walls are covered with bold and colorful geometric mosaics in red, black, and yellow. A statue of the Goddess stood in a niche in the shrine.

Temple statues from Sumer show a startling emotional and spiritual intensity: the whites of their boldly staring eyes, heavily outlined in black, their pupils set with deep blue lapis lazuli. Usually standing or seated in rigid frontal posture, their bodies are tense and arms closed (see fig. 77).

Male and female figures both wear a long flounced garment. Often we cannot distinguish between the representation of the deity and the priestly functionary (see fig. 78).

While the priestess was a surrogate for the Goddess, it is important to realize that people of Sumer believed that the Goddess actually lived in her temple (see fig. 79).

The center of Inanna's cult was the temple with priests and priestesses, musicians and singers, castrates and hierodules, who performed sexual rituals. Women and men served equally in the temple.[9]

Surrounding the shrine were rooms used by the priests and priestesses who administered the Goddess's vast agricultural holdings. The temple was a court of law and a healing sanctuary as well. Throngs of scribes, judges, and witnesses of legal documents, healers, diviners, and prophets milled about.

77. GODDESS, mid-third millennium B.C.E. Copper, lead, and lapis. Treasure of Ur, Mari.

78. GODDESS OR PRIESTESS, mid-third millennium B.C.E. Alabaster. 0.36 m. Temple of Ishtar, Mari.

79. City Shrine Surrounded by Signs of Inanna: The Rosettes, Her Face, and Her Gateposts, 3000 B.C.E. Cylinder seal. Tell Agrab, Mesopotamia.

Inanna's awesome facial features loom large over her temple. Its identifying gateposts are the rolled-up bundles of reeds, still used by modern Iraqis to frame their doorways. The rosette-star is her symbol as the Goddess of the Morning and Evening Star.

The scene was probably something like that in the temple of Jerusalem at the time of Jesus.

By the third millennium B.C.E. the unified worldview of the Great Goddess had already been shattered in the Near East, her powers divided. The Sumerians believed that the universe was controlled by a large pantheon of gods and goddesses "human in form but superhuman in nature and powers" who were always present. These beings ". . . guided and controlled the cosmos in accordance with well laid plans and duly prescribed laws"[10] but like humans they ate, drank, slept, loved, and reproduced. They fought and were in turn jealous, angry, wise, and compassionate. Divine power was not grounded in gender. Male and female divinities both shared "the awesome powers to judge people, decree their fate, initiate violence, and control fertility."[11] The lives of the gods mirrored a complex, class-stratified society. Their human representatives, the high priests and priestesses, known as *en,* ruled the main temples in each Sumerian city-state.

One of the most famous priestess-rulers was Enheduanna, the daughter of Sargon the Great, the Akkadian ruler who took over the political control of Sumer ca. 2300 B.C.E. Sargon appointed his daughter high priestess at the temple of the moon god Nanna at Ur and possibly of the heaven god An in Uruk as well. "It was her devotion to . . . Inanna that helped the process of political union by her fusion of the Sumerian Inanna with the Akkadian Ishtar."[12]

Enheduanna was the first in a long line of royal high priestesses who presided over temples in Sumer and Akkad (Old

Babylonia) for the next five hundred years. Enheduanna was also a brilliant poet whose influence on subsequent sacred literature contributed significantly to Mesopotamian theology. She eulogized the Goddess in her hymn, "The Exaltation of Inanna," describing her as the consort and equal in rank to the god An, the head of the Sumerian pantheon.[13]

Inanna's status reflects widesweeping cultural changes. Some time in the third millennium the supremacy of the Great Goddess was taken over by a male god, An, who ruled like an absolute monarch. The numinous power of the sky, he lived in the highest heaven and never came down to earth.

Scenes from the myths, which recounted the stories of the deities' lives and the rituals through which human worshipers encountered them, were carved on cylinder seals, small tubes of stone. The design becomes clear when the cylinder is rolled over a clay tablet. The most popular show a worshiper petitioning a deity (see fig. 80). The seals served a ritual function; they were like a permanent prayer. On one a barefooted worshiper is led before the majestic Inanna seated on an elaborate throne who raises her hand in greeting.

80. WORSHIPER PETITIONING INANNA, ca. 2250 B.C.E. Cylinder seal, Lapis lazuli. Sumerian.

The invention of a practical system of writing with cuneiform or wedge-shaped characters inscribed onto clay tablets with a reed stylus was the Sumerians' major contribution to civilization. Cuneiform script began as a series of pictographs devised by temple priests and priestesses primarily for the purpose of keeping the temple accounts. But some five to six thousand tablets and fragments were inscribed with literary works including myths, epics, hymns, poems, love songs, and laments that reveal the religious beliefs, ethical ideals, and spiritual aspirations of the Sumerians.[14]

Inanna's Story

The hymns to Inanna acknowledge her myriad achievements and aspects, but one verse cycle follows the same pattern as "the archetypal Moon Goddess: the young woman who is courted; the ripe woman who enjoys her feminine powers and generously offers her bounty; and the mature woman who meets death in the underworld."[15] While Inanna is a powerful goddess, the anonymous Sumerian poet tells her life story in human terms, through a range of emotional experiences, fears, and anxieties that modern women can identify with. Pieced together gradually over a period of fifty years by Kramer from tablets and fragments inscribed around 1750 B.C.E., the poem is based on material dating back to the early third millennium when Inanna's temple was being built at Uruk. The tablets lay buried and forgotten in the ruins of Nippur, which later became Sumer's spiritual and cultural center, for close to four thousand years.

The Tree of Knowledge

The cycle opens with the creation of the world. The symbol of new life is the *huluppu* tree, which emerges out of the ground into the light and grows toward the heavens. The tree was the axis of the three worlds, connecting the underworld, the earth, and the heavens. "The wonder of the tree continues to exist today, for although we cannot explain the mystery of the *first* seed, we can take the seed with our hand and say, here is the beginning of life." In the Sumerian creation story, the *huluppu* tree, like the biblical Tree of Knowledge, embodies the forces of a culture now polarized—"consciousness and unconsciousness, light and dark, male and female, the power of life and the power of death."[16]

We first meet Inanna as a woman fearful, anxious about her awakening sexuality and her future responsibilities as queen of the land. As the story unfolds she discovers her feminine powers, her strength as a leader, her spirituality, and ultimately her wisdom. While her powers are potentially prodigious, befitting a great divine being, her emotions are all too human. Her personality is very appealing; her relationship to her people must have been a deeply personal one.

Inanna rescues the tree of life from the world flood and plants it in her garden (see fig. 81). She wants to make a shining throne and a sacred marriage bed from the growing tree, claiming her queenship and her womanhood. First, she must get rid of the unwelcome intruders who live there—the serpent who "made his nest in the tree," the anzu bird who "set his young on the branches," and the "dark-maid Lilith" who "built her home in the trunk." Inanna is powerless before them; they will not leave. She must call on her earthly brother Gilgamesh for help. "Gilgamesh is the brazen young hero, full of his manliness and the signs of his physical strength— his heavy axe, which weighs 450 pounds, and his great armor, which weighs 60 pounds."[17] In defeating lawless nature, he enacts the role of the epic hero-king.

In Sumer, nature is no longer to be worshiped directly. Inanna brought the *huluppu* tree from its free floating state in nature into her enclosed garden. "In order to produce a throne and a bed, a green tree must be changed into a hewn tree."[18] Gilgamesh, using the bronze axe, "the cutting weapon of civilization," defeats "the serpent who could not be charmed"[19] and cuts down the tree. The bird then flies with "his" young to the mountains and Lilith "terror-stricken"[20] "smashed her home and fled to the wild, uninhabited places."[21] Although Anzu's gender is masculine in the Sumerian language, the bird, like the snake and Lilith, was probably originally a form of the Goddess now outlawed by patriarchy. The mother bird is the one who usually cares for the young in the nest.

81. PLANTING THE TREE, ca. 2500 B.C.E.
Relief vessel. Steatite. Mary, Syria. 20 cm.

The Uncontrolled Sexuality of Lilith

Although Lilith does not appear in any other Sumerian texts, she is represented in terracotta plaques roughly contemporaneous with the Inanna poems as a hybrid bird-woman, her sensuously modeled nude body contrasting awkwardly with powerful clawed feet (see fig. 82). Guarded by the bird of wisdom, the owl, and the king of the beasts, the lion, she wears the stepped crown and holds the rod and ring of Sumerian royal authority, suggesting that she indeed was a figure to be reckoned with.

To understand Lilith's reputation as a sexual temptress, we must look to later Hebrew legend in which she first appears as Adam's intended wife. Insisting on equality in their relationship, she refuses to have sex with him in the conventional position because she is unwilling to lie beneath him and runs away. Remaining forever outside of human relationships or regulations, Lilith surfaces in medieval Hebrew esoteric tradition as a demonic creature, possessed by an insatiable sex-

82. LILITH, ca. 2000 B.C.E. Bas-relief. Terracotta.

uality. She holds dominion over all instinctual, natural beings. Discovering the roots of Lilith's bad reputation in this curious solo appearance in the Inanna cycle is cause for sober reflection on the origins of the notion of uncontrolled female sexuality as evil, already so forcibly expressed in the earliest written material of Western culture. Raphael Patai, the expert on the Hebrew goddess, suggests that while a citizen of Sumer in the mid-third millennium may have "had very little in common" with an Eastern European Hasidic Jew in so far as the so-called "higher levels of religion were concerned, they would have readily recognized each other's beliefs about the pernicious machinations of Lilith. . . ."[22]

83. INANNA WITH CROWN AND STAFF, ca. 2000–1600 B.C.E. Clay plaque. Mesopotamia.

Inanna stands in full regalia, wearing the high crown with its multiple horns and the flounced robe of divinity, holding the lion-headed mace of her royal office in her outstretched hand.

The hybrid bird-women, creatures of foreboding, are well known in archaic Greek art and myth as sirens and harpies. Lilith is identified as the dark maiden and called "screech owl" in a biblical passage from Isaiah.[23] When we consider the prominent role of the Bird Goddess as Cosmic Creator in Old Europe, her reappearance as threatening female power is a telling example of the reversal of the symbol's meaning under patriarchy.

Once Lilith, like the Neolithic Bird Goddess, helped women in childbirth and nursed infants. In a seventh century B.C.E. tablet inscribed with a prayer chanted by Assyrian women giving birth, Lilith appears as a winged sphinx.[24] In medieval Jewish texts she becomes the dreaded demon who causes small children to die in their sleep.

With Nature Tamed Inanna Is Ready to Rule

In the Inanna narrative, the life force of the Goddess is still recognized as powerful and creative, but nature is no longer revered as sacred. The symbols of her authority as ruler of Sumer, her throne and her bed, rest on nature tamed. The world tree must be cut down, instincts curbed. The later proscriptions of Judeo-Christian religion that link the sacred with the moral order is a legacy of this emerging patriarchy that always seeks to control. The earlier morality of nature in which the ebb and flow of the life process is the highest good is of a different order.

Out of the wood of the world tree Inanna fashions her throne and her bed. "When [she] begins her rule, she will be sitting on the throne of the *huluppu*-tree, and her understanding of life and death, consciousness and lack of consciousness, will be increased accordingly. Likewise, when she holds a man in her arms, the bed will murmur to them both the secrets of life and death, light and darkness." The multivalent symbol of the tree retains the memory of a prehistoric time before patriarchal dualism split the wholeness of nature. "As Queen of Sumer, Inanna is responsible to and receives her power from the resources and fertility of the land."[25] She puts on her crown, the *shugurra* the crown of Sumer (see fig. 83).

Gone is the fearful, brooding girl. "With the *shugurra* on her head, Inanna goes to the sheepfold, which is the center

of nature in Sumer. Leaning against a fruit tree, she rejoices in her own natural powers—her wondrous vulva. In Sumerian the word for sheepfold, womb, vulva, loins, and lap is the same."[26] . . . The pictograph for the sheepfold also represents the vulva (see fig. 84).

Inanna and the God of Wisdom

Eager for adventure, to test her powers, Inanna sets out to visit Enki, the God of Wisdom, who is also the God of the Waters. His city, Eridu, is located near where the fresh and salt waters meet, at the convergence of the Tigris and Euphrates rivers and the Persian Gulf. Always following his feelings and instincts, Enki is the Great Shaman.

Enki and Inanna drink together. In drunken frivolity, the overeffusive host offers the treasures of his kingdom to the young queen, the gifts of *me,* the ordering principles of civilization. The God of Wisdom gives Inanna all the knowledge necessary to rule her kingdom.[27] His last gift is "the making of decisions," without which all the other *me* are useless. When a soberer Enki realizes what he has done, he wants his riches back. The dark side of his nature takes over. Possessive, jealous, and controlling, he is the malevolent shaman who withholds rather than gives.

Inanna recognizes the god's dual nature and outwits him with the help of her confidante, the priestess Ninshubur. Together, they bring the sacred *me* back safely to Uruk where the queen offers them to her people. The youthful "Inanna flaunted her raw feminine vitality—her wondrous vulva." In battle with Enki her powers were tested, and "Inanna emerged a fuller woman."[28]

84. SHEEPFOLD WITH SHEEP AND GATEPOSTS OF INANNA, ca. **3000** B.C.E. Limestone trough. Mesopotamia.

Two lambs crawl out from either side of the sheepfold, which bears the gateposts of Inanna, indicating that the animals are the property of the goddess and her temple, young lambs, symbolically "born" from the womb of the goddess of fertility.[8]

The Courtship of Inanna and Dumuzi

Now she has earned her throne, but her bed is still empty. At first she refuses the shepherd Dumuzi, the man her brother has selected to be her husband, saying she wants to marry a farmer. Dumuzi is adamant, bragging about his assets and asserting that his family from the steppes is as good as theirs from the river delta. In the end, to avoid a quarrel, she capitulates and accepts her brother's choice. Behind this family quarrel is the historical reality of invasion. The shepherd represents the pastoralists from the north who have overcome the people who farm the rich alluvial plain.

Inanna is hesitant when they first meet, but Dumuzi's obvious delight in her arouses her passion.

Inanna speaks:

"My vulva, the horn,
The Boat of Heaven,
Is full of eagerness like the young moon.
My untilled land lies fallow.

. . . Who will plow my vulva?
Who will plow my high field?
Who will plow my wet ground?"

Dumuzi eagerly replies:

"Great Lady, the king will plow your vulva
I, Dumuzi the King, will plow your vulva."

Inanna:

"Then plow my vulva, man of my heart!
Plow my vulva!"

At the king's lap stood the rising cedar
Plants grew high by their side.
Grains grew high by their side.
Gardens flourished luxuriantly.

Inanna rejoices:

"He has sprouted; he has burgeoned;
He is lettuce planted by the water.
He is the one my womb loves best.

"My well-stocked garden of the plain,
My barley growing high in its furrow
My apple tree which bears fruit up to its crown,
He is lettuce planted by the water.

"My honey-man, my honey-man sweetens me always.
My lord, the honey-man of the gods,
He is the one my womb loves best.
His hand is honey, his foot is honey,
He sweetens me always."[29]

The issue of their union is not only offspring but luxuriant vegetation and a bountiful harvest. Their eagerness and delight in each other knows no bounds; their passion is open and joyous (see fig. 85). "The world of the senses so explodes about them . . . that they are oblivious of everything but each other." Her lover has pleased her and Inanna chooses him as her consort. Through marriage the Goddess gives her husband the strength to provide leadership, guidance, and fertility to others. She gives him the throne, scepter, staff, crook, and crown, as well as the promise of good harvests and the joys of her bed. Sadly, when the honeymoon is over and Dumuzi takes on the prescribed role of father and king, he asks to be set free. "Although the shepherd has become king and Inanna has found a consort for her royal marriage bed, the intimacy and passion of their . . . love is gone."[30]

Inanna Descends to the Great Below

The hymn cycle continues. After the marriage has been consummated, the fertility of the land and the well-being of her people ensured, Inanna makes a second descent. Unlike the first which was from heaven to earth to participate in public ritual, her second, from the earth to the underworld, is a personal journey for spiritual growth.[31] Inanna goes to learn about the Land of the Dead. She "is Queen of Heaven and Earth, but she does not know the underworld." Her understanding of life is necessarily limited.[32]

To enter the spiritual realm of the underworld, Inanna must give up her earthly powers. Her need to make the journey is compelling but she is apprehensive. In preparation, she

85. LOVERS EMBRACING ON BED, ca. 2000–1600 B.C.E. View from above. Terracotta plaque. Mesopotamia.

A bearded man cups his partner's head in the palm of one hand and rests his other hand upon her waist. She encircles her lover's waist with one arm, offering him her breast with the other, and places her foot over his. Votive plaques commemorating the sacred marriage served as auspicious amulets for their owners, providing good fortune.

gathers up the seven *me,* transformed into items of her glamorous queenly costume, her crown, her jewels, and her gown. She believes these worldly manifestations of her identity will protect her like a talisman. Inanna instructs her servant and confidant Ninshubur to remind the gods, her father and grandfather, of their daughter in case she doesn't return in three days.

The underworld, the great unknown, is the domain of Inanna's sister, Ereshkigal, who, as the Grain Goddess, once ruled in the great above. Now she has been exiled to the great below, the underworld, which has become a dread place under patriarchy, a land of no return. "In the underworld, she eats clay and drinks dirty water. She has no compassion for the relationships of others, husband and wife or parent and child."[33] Her husband, Gugalanna, the Great Bull of Heaven, is dead. Unloving, unloved, abandoned, she is full of rage, greed, and desperate loneliness.

Rather than welcome Inanna, Ereshkigal, enraged with jealousy by her younger sister's full life, instructs Neti, the gate keeper, to strip Inanna of all her finery, all her earthly attributes, her accomplishments, her identity, her cities, and her temples. She wants Inanna to experience what it is like to be rejected, to be incapable of movement or relationship.

> The descent, which Inanna began on earth by abandoning her seven cities and seven temples, is continued and paralleled in the underworld. At each of the seven gates . . . Inanna is forced to give up another one of her earthly attributes.[34]

Inanna's descent is a shamanic journey, a venturing into the void, the unknown, into the dark womb of the inner Earth for the wisdom it holds. In this symbolic death, she hangs on a peg, a rotting corpse, but gains essential insight and experience into the full cycle of existence.

No longer the commanding Queen, she can accept her vulnerability. When Inanna doesn't return, Ninshubur goes to the gods for help. All are indifferent to Inanna's fate except grandfather Enki, the God of Wisdom. He understands the full import of Inanna's message, namely that civilization in Sumer could regress to its primitive stages if she was not rescued from the realm of the dead.[35] After all, it was Inanna who had brought the *me,* the attributes of civilization, to Sumer.

Enki arranges her release. Although Inanna is reborn, she must follow the rules of the underworld and provide someone to take her place. Dumuzi, sitting on Inanna's throne, engrossed in his new role as king, has not even noticed that Inanna has gone from Earth. He has not even put on mourning clothes. Outraged, Inanna selects her husband as her replacement and in the words of the poem "fastens on him the eye of death."[36] In the world of light she repeats the actions of her dark sister, fully embodying in herself the underworld, death-dealing aspect of the Goddess.[37]

Just as Inanna needed time to descend, abandoning one city and temple after another at each level, Dumuzi must divest himself step by step of his kingship, his shepherdship, his achievements, and his virility. Fleeing in terror from the demons of the underworld who have come to fetch him, he returns to his boyhood home in the steppes, the treeless tracks of northern Sumer.

> There he calls on the familiar natural forces—plants and animals—to comfort him. He calls on his mother and sister; he has lost his strength and vitality and can no longer provide for them. Alone without power, comfort or direction, he turns inward and dreams.[38]

A prophetic dream in which he and his kingdom are slowly returned to a primordial state captures the enormity of his loss. There seems to be no escape from the forces that will carry him to his death until his compassionate sister, Geshtinanna, offers to take his place for half of every year.

> Geshtinanna, "rootstock of the grapevine," reigns over the wine whose grapes and figs are harvested from the Sumerian earth each autumn: while Dumuzi in his aspect of Damu, the power in the growing grain, reigns over the beer, whose barley grows in the earth the other six months of the year, to be harvested in the spring.[39]

Inanna and Geshtinanna together go to the edge of the steppes where they find the weeping Dumuzi. Gently, Inanna takes his hand and says the words that seal his fate. "You will go to the underworld half the year. Your sister, since she has asked, will go the other half."[40]

Inanna and Dumuzi will be united in marriage for half the year and separated for the other half. For six months Dumuzi will actively rule over Sumer and join Inanna in the sacred marriage bed, and all of Sumer will celebrate.

> The milk will flow in the sheepfold, the wheat will ripen, the apple trees will blossom. But then, as the seasons change and the harvest passes, Dumuzi will enter a period of inactivity, quietude, and meditation. He will surrender his worldly powers. . . . He will return to Ereshkigal.[41]

The scenario is a familiar one. The Year God, mortal consort of the Goddess, must be sacrificed so that the new crop will emerge from the earth.

In the wisdom of her maturity, Inanna acknowledges "the duality of life dying into death and death leading into life."[42] She knows the reality that all changes demand sacrifice.[43] Life continues, only in a different form. When the Queen of Heaven and Earth returns to the upper realms having added the Knowledge of Death to her Knowledge of Life and Love, the cycle of the Tree of Life—the *huluppa* that had given her her throne and sacred marriage bed—is now complete. Inanna can now rule over the entire cycle of fertility from birth and death to rebirth. The full cycle of the crops as well as the power of the throne of Sumer is ensured. After her journey to the Great Below, Inanna took on the powers and mysteries of death and rebirth, emerging as the Goddess who ruled over the Three Worlds: the Sky, the Earth, and the Underworld.

The Meaning of Inanna's Descents

In the *Hymn to Inanna,* the Goddess makes two descents. The first is from heaven to earth to bring prosperity to her people through her sacred marriage to the Shepherd King Dumuzi. The second is a personal journey to the underworld for initiation. There are several levels of meaning in her story. One is the historical-social, which provides insight into the culture in which the poetry was written, ca. 1750 B.C.E. However, the hymn cycle was based on a much earlier tradition. At this stage of our knowledge it is nearly impossible to fully separate the two. We must always be aware that the story is told from the point of view of the victors who suppressed the power of the Great Goddess.

The Sacred Marriage: Origin and History

The origins of the sacred marriage ritual are probably Neolithic. According to Gimbutas the presence of the masked ithyphallic god implies a festival, a wedding ceremony enacting the male god's marriage to the Great Goddess.[44] What is new at Sumer is the institutionalizing of this ritual in the political interests of the state.

The tradition of the sacred marriage at Sumer may have originated in a historical event. Sumerian king-lists, records of who ruled when and where, show a Dumuzi ruling in the Sumerian city of Uruk sometime in the first half of the third millennium B.C.E.[45] Inanna, it is generally agreed, was Uruk's guardian deity at that time and perhaps even earlier. Votive figures with the salient iconography of the Neolithic Mother Goddess found there can be dated from the fifth millennium.

As we have seen, the legendary "Dumuzi was wedded ritually to the Goddess Inanna in the city of Uruk. As one poet imagined it, it was Inanna herself who selected Dumuzi . . . for the Sacred Marriage. . . ." She cast her eyes over all the people and exalted him to the godship of the land.[46] Subsequent Sumerian kings took Dumuzi's place. The king was both human and the incarnation of the mythical Dumuzi, the Shepherd King. His identity was merged with the Vegetation God. His mother is the Lady of the Wild Cow, his father is Enki, the fertilizing waters upon which the harvest depends. Dumuzi is the god of the date palm, of the grain, and of the power of barley to produce beer. He is the vital spark of new life in nature, vegetable, and animal.[47]

As king, Dumuzi is identified with the harvest of the land. But as the mortal husband of the Great Goddess, he must die in order for earth to renew itself. His sexual energy "is needed to claim the all-giving earth, Inanna's breast, and to plow the soil, Inanna's vulva, that she may be the fertility of the land."[48]

86. INANNA WITH DATE PALM, ca. 2400 B.C.E. Fragment of a relief vessel. Mesopotamia.

The perky young ruler with flowing locks and beaming smile holds a date cluster. Stalks surrounded by blossoms grow from her shoulders, the attributes of a vegetation goddess.

In Sumer and the whole of the Near East, the symbolic mating of the Goddess with the king became an instrument of state policy, a way of legitimizing his rule: "kingship demanded a sacred foundation that could be provided only through the omnipotence of the Great Goddess."[49] Through sacrifice, the ritual death of the God King, his sacred powers were renewed and his authority over the land reestablished.

The Goddess does not merely symbolize or represent well-being; she *is* well-being. She is both the fertile womb and fertile field. Over and over again the poets praise her overflow, abundance, and prosperity, bemoaning her absence in times of calamity. She is the "life-giving flood-waters and rain clouds, on fields and meadows covered with ripe grain, on the plants and herbs that are 'the delight of the steppes.' "[50]

In the earliest myths Inanna's name was Ninanna, Lady of the Date Clusters (see fig. 86). She represented the numen or spirit of the communal storehouse for dates, "that storehouse of Eanna" that she opens for Dumuzi on the enormous pedestal vase that probably once stood in the sanctuary at Uruk (see figs. 87a and b). "Her emblem—that is to say, her pre-anthropomorphic form—confirms this, for it is . . . a gatepost with rolled up mat to serve as a door, a distinguishing mark of the storehouse."[51]

Dumuzi represents the food that is to be stored in the storehouse. His original name Amaushumgalanna means

> the one great source of the date clusters, the personified power in the one enormous bud which the date palm sprouts each year, and from which issue the new leaves, flowers, and fruits. Dumuzi-Amaushumgalanna is . . . a personification of the power behind the yearly burgeoning of the palm and its . . . yield of dates; he is . . . the power in and behind the date harvest.[52]

The marriage of "The One Great Source of the Date Clusters," to "The Lady of the Date Clusters" meant that the power of fertility and yield had been captured by the numen of the storehouse. The community, freed from the anxiety and fear of starvation, would have abundant food and drink for all time.[53] The earlier myths give us a background from which to better understand the underlying meaning of the sacred marriage ritual.

The Sacred Marriage Ritual

All year long the people brought gifts to the Goddess: fat sheep, butter, cheese, dates, fruits of all kind, beer, and wine. Now when the earth was ready to be seeded, to bring forth the grains and herbs that would nurture life, the divine spark was needed once again. Inanna "controlled the productivity of the land and the fruitfulness of the womb of man and beast."[54] Through her union with the king, the mystery of human sexuality was connected to the fecundity of nature.

". . . Inanna, the Goddess of Love, does not offer her favors freely. Not only must she be properly approached with sweet words and gifts, but she also must be properly and amply loved."[55] The rites in her temple open with songs of courtship, impassioned, lyrical verse, explicitly sexual, celebrating the delights of physical love. Dumuzi comes to Inanna bearing gifts. Their meeting at the gate of the temple storehouse is depicted on the Uruk vase (see figs. 87a and b).

The scene unfolds in three registers. At top left the bride-groom at the head of a long retinue is shown approaching carrying his wedding offerings, an abundance of foodstuffs of all kinds. Below, there are baskets, ewers, and libation jars full of food and drink; on the bottom row are sheep heavy with wool and lush ears of barley standing tall. His bride opens the gate and receives him. Behind her, in the sanctuary with its altar and sacred furniture, two priestesses officiate. The boundaries of the temple precinct are marked by the emblems of the Goddess, ringed bundles of reeds.

An anonymous poet describes the culminating events of Inanna's marriage in hymns of praise sung at the New Year's ceremony. The sacred marriage bed, hewn from the tree of life, was carefully prepared (see fig. 85).

> . . . [O]ver it was spread a specially prepared coverlet; then Inanna was washed and soaped and presumably laid on the bed; the king then "proceeded to the holy lap" with "lifted head," on ground fragrant with cedar-oil, and blissfully bedded with the goddess. The following day, a rich banquet was prepared in the large reception hall of the palace; there was much eating and drinking, music and song, as the people "parade" before the divine couple sitting side by side on their thrones.[56]

87a. BRINGING THE GIFTS TO INANNA, fourth millennium B.C.E. Alabaster vase. 3 ft. Uruk.

87b. BRINGING THE GIFTS TO INANNA, fourth millennium B.C.E. Alabaster vase. Detail.

The Role of the Hierodule

The part of the Goddess in the ritual sexual union was taken by her priestess, believed to be the embodiment of the Goddess herself. The role of the hierodule, commonly called the "sacred prostitute" in the ancient Mediterranean cultures, is little understood. She is not a prostitute, she does not sell her sexual services. Her social role is sacred. She represents the Goddess; within the context of the ritual she is the Goddess. Her sexuality is the sacred instrument of life's power, her sexual union with the king necessary to ensure the prosperity of the kingdom.

Anthropologist Frédérique Marglin conjectures that the role of the Mesopotamian hierodule may have been similar to that of the Hindu *devadasis*, professional dancers who served the deity at the temple of Jagannatha in Puri, India. The *devadasis* are considered to be the living embodiments of Jagannatha's wife Lakshmi, a goddess of prosperity, abundance, and well-being (see color plate 19). They were courtesans, concubines of the kings and priests, well educated in music, dance, and literature.

> In Indian epic literature (ca. third century B.C.E.–third century C.E.) the courtesans embody the wealth, refinement, and culture of the prosperous and well-ruled city. The active sexuality of the courtesan is the instrument that safeguards the well-being of the king and the community.[57]

The point of the ritual sexual intercourse is "not procreation but the assurance of abundant crops and the endorsement of the king's ability to rule."[58] Neither the hierodules nor the *devadasis* are supposed to be fertile, to bear children.

> The sacrifice of one's reproductive capacity is symbolically akin to death. The paradox of general fertility brought about by sexual activity of persons who have sacrificed their own fecundity . . . [is a] symbolic expression of the widespread sacrificial theme of renewed life through death.[59]

The Great Divide: Patriarchal Consciousness

In the Inanna hymns, the Goddess is no longer the sole agent of her being. She needs the help of Gilgamesh to cut down the World Tree out of which she will make her bed and her throne, the symbols of her Queenship and her womanhood. While previously her return to the upper world each spring was part of the natural cycle of the seasons, now grandfather Enki must rescue her from the underworld.

Inanna's story confronts us with the great divide between Goddess and patriarchal consciousness. We straddle both worldviews as she travels down to the underworld to experience the mysteries of death. From the vantage of the Goddess the underground is the primal womb, the matrix of all being, but to patriarchy the underworld is an alien place of horror and dread. How did such a radical transformation in consciousness come about?

We can look to the earliest layers of Sumerian mythology for some clues. Ereshkigal is an older form of the Goddess than Inanna. The syllable "ki" in her name marks her relationship to Urashki, the Sumerian Earth Goddess. Ereshkigal was once the Grain Goddess and lived in the Above; "she symbolizes the Great Round of Nature, grain above and growing, and seed below and dying to sprout again." When the sky gods prevailed, she was banished to the netherworld, now seen as a desolate alien place.[60]

To the "matriarchal consciousness" of Goddess culture, death is part of "the continuum in which different states are simply experienced as transformations of one energy." The Goddess willingly takes part in this process over which she rules.[61] Inanna ruled over the natural order of things; the pattern of nature is birth, growth, death, decay, and rebirth. "Above ground [she] is like a cornucopia, [the horn of plenty,] pouring forth" the abundant fruits of the earth. "Below ground she is passive, herself an initiate."[62] When she descended from the great above to the great below, nothing grew or procreated. The earth was barren. She hangs on a peg, a rotting corpse.

But change is the natural order. The mystery of Inanna's descent and return is the unquenchable, indwelling life. This is the basis of women's experience of childbearing and of all the blood mysteries that create and maintain life.

In Sumerian mythology, Ereshkigal and Inanna are mirror images: one is the the Queen of Heaven, the other, Queen of the Underworld. As Inanna creates, so Ereshkigal destroys. Psychologically, the two together express a bipolar wholeness of the archetypal feminine.

Under patriarchy, Ereshkigal, the former Grain Goddess, is banished to the underworld and becomes the symbol of dread death. Her message is that while life itself is ongoing, individual human life ends; there are limits. As death she is all destruction and chaos, monstrous to the patriarchal, heroic worldview with its emphasis on rational order and control.

Inanna, the embodiment of the earth's fertility, and Dumuzi, the wild bull, the symbol of male primordial energy, are yet another example of the ongoing theme of complementarity of female/male we have been following. In the fullness of her passion, Inanna calls Dumuzi "the wild bull,"[63] and her heavenly spouse, the Sky God An, is "the fecund Breed-Bull, an apt personification of the overcast skies in spring whose thunder recalls the bellowing of a bull and whose rain engenders vegetation far and wide."[64]

Yet, under patriarchy, the bull, symbol of the male life force in the Goddess culture, takes on a negative meaning—a "bull-like passion, raw desire and power, sadistic bull-dozing violence, demonic bullying."[65] Gugalanna, the Great Bull of Heaven, the repressed side of the sky god Enlil, has been banished to the underworld for his violence.

Still creation continues to depend upon the stimulating force of the masculine fertilizing power, and when the Great Bull of Heaven is killed, Inanna offers her life to renew the cycle that has stopped. Death and decay are the basis of primordial fertility rites; through this process energy is transformed from one state to another. Inanna's death in the underworld plays out the female/male exchange of energy on one level; the sacred marriage ritual is the same dynamic on another.

Under Patriarchy: A New Sociopolitical Dynamic

The exquisite lyrical poetry of the Inanna hymns describes a very personal, passionate sexual encounter reflecting intimate knowledge of a woman's psyche. Marcia Falk writing about the genre of sacred marriage poems comments on their strikingly nonsexist attitude toward heterosexual love,

> an attitude that excludes many of our modern Western stereotypes of "masculinity" and "femininity." . . . Women initiate lovemaking as often as men, both male and female voices are at times urgent and aggressive, at other times tender and vulnerable.[66]

This open attitude suggests that women were still sexually free in third-millennium Sumer, that sex was valued for pleasure as well as procreation. However, the importance of marriage in the sacred hymns (Inanna must find a husband to "plow her vulva" and share her bed) hints that female sexuality was being contained within a socially approved institution. Under patriarchy, when marriage and family became an instrument of the state, ultimately women's sexuality was controlled in the interests of property rights.

In the hymns, despite the glorification of sexuality, we also find the tell-tale signs of countervailing patriarchal attitudes. Wild nature is suspect and must be tamed before Inanna can rule. The sacred marriage ritual has become politicized. Ereshkigal's story is one of exile. For most, there is no return from the Land of the Dead.

The paradigm shift from a feminine to a masculine consciousness is underway. In the emerging Sumerian city-states we find the first documented evidence of patriarchy. Ironically Sumer has been hailed as the "cradle of civilization" with the earliest writing, the earliest monumental architecture, and centralized administration. Other firsts included war, class-structured society, and slavery. Greed and aggrandizement became the prevailing ethos of the city-states as they jockeyed with each other for land and resources.

The new hierarchical social order is reflected in the Sumerian pantheon of gods and goddesses, some of whose functions overlap. Their mythology is replete with power struggles, domestic conflict, and violence. The picture that emerges is of a polyglot polytheism, a divided rule.

Inanna, Queen of Heaven and Earth, retained many of the powers of the Great Goddess, but the extent of her domain is ambiguous, and the field is crowded with contenders. The new social meaning of the sacred marriage ritual is a clue to the way in which the Goddess's powers were co-opted under patriarchy. Although the union of male and female principals always has been part of the iconography of the Goddess, this relationship was not viewed in Neolithic times as the surrender of power but rather as a catalyst that activated new life within the earth.

In the later Sumerian sacred marriage rite, on the other hand, Inanna transfers her powers to Dumuzi who rules in her place. According to the myth Dumuzi abuses his privilege and is deposed to spend half the year in the underworld. In the social reality of the Sumerian city-state, the king whose rule has been legitimized through his ritual union with the Goddess may rule in her name but his rule is absolute.

The sociopolitical dynamic we are witnessing is one in process. The sacredness of female sexuality is still honored, but it has been channeled into a state institution. The temple and its priesthood are instruments of the state. Inanna is still the divine power, the guardian ruler of the city-state, but her military powers are now extolled.

Ironically, Inanna is the one who brings the gifts of civilization, the sacred *me,* to her city. This is the source of her fame. A close look at the list of *me* is revealing. They include:

- the rights and privileges, the duties and the trappings of priesthood and kingship
- the arts of warfare and statesmanship
- the arts of lovemaking, procreation, and family
- the arts of prostitution, sacred and profane, of the temple and tavern
- the arts of music and the artisan

Some, like the arts of warfare and statesmanship, sound disturbingly Machiavellian—the arts of deceit, the kindling of strife, of power and treachery. Others are concerned with the more positive aspects of statesmanship—the giving of judgments, the making of decisions and truth.

From the point of view of human good, "civilization" as it was understood in ancient Sumer had its limitations. Perhaps the presence of the Goddess in the Near East continued to be a benevolent force despite her taking on of warlike powers. Ultimately, in Sumer and all the ancient Near East, the Goddess's powers and values were co-opted to serve the state.

However, as Gerda Lerner in her study of the creation of patriarchy suggests, "there was a considerable time lag between the subordination of women in patriarchal society and the declassing of the goddesses . . . The power of the goddesses and their priestesses in daily life and in popular religion continued in force, even as the supreme goddesses were dethroned. It is remarkable that in societies which had subordinated women economically, educationally, and legally, the spiritual and metaphysical powers of goddesses remained active and strong."[67]

Demeter's Mysteries

The religion of the Great Goddess survived in the celebrations at the temple of the Greek Demeter at Eleusis until the fall of the Roman Empire. Men and women, philosophers and kings, came from all over the known world to be initiated into her mysteries. This placed the neophyte into direct and personal relation with the sacred. Well established by the seventh or sixth century B.C.E., the Eleusinian Mysteries were for a thousand years the center of the inner religious life.

"The growth and popularity of the mystery religions was of singular importance for the worship of the feminine divine."[1] In a world increasingly dominated by an alienation from the divine and a fear of death, the mysteries kept the spirit of the Goddess alive, honoring the sacredness of the life process. The enigma of the Eleusinian Mysteries and the extent of their appeal indicates the power the Goddess still had over the Hellenistic world (third century B.C.E. to third century C.E.).

By their very nature the mysteries were secret; initiates were forsworn not to reveal the details of their transformative experience. Obviously our knowledge is fragmentary, culled from veiled contemporary accounts, obscure literary references, the satire of playwrights and the prejudiced accounts of early Christian writers seeking to justify suppression of the mysteries. "The gap between [an outsider's] observation and the experience of those involved in [the rites] remains unbridgeable."[2] However, we do have clues in the surviving sculpture and vase paintings that commemorate key events of myth and ritual. Indeed relief sculpture found on the sanctuary grounds in Eleusis shows us the principal iconographic forms in which the Goddess was worshiped. The artists' choice of subject or theme is helpful in recovering inherent meaning because they would have selected images and symbols most relevant to their contemporaries (see figs. 94 and 95).

The wisdom of the Great Mother is the key to the well-kept secret rites that enabled men and women to overcome their fear of death. Demeter, whose lineage goes back to the Neolithic, was the only Greek goddess in whom the powers of the Great Goddess remained intact (see fig. 88). Her name is a very ancient one. *De* is the Greek word for grain and *meter*, of course, is mother.[3] Some scholars argue that she is the Earth Mother.[4] Gaia, the Earth Goddess, is her grandmother whose shadowy presence is always in the background, lending magnitude and grandeur to her mysteries. Gaia had power over the underworld because the earth is the abode of the dead. Her granddaughter was worshiped as Demeter *Chthonia* from the Greek word for in or under the earth. The dead were called *Demetereioi*, "Demeter's people."[5] Not only did Demeter bring all things to life, but when they died she received them back into her bosom.[6]

Demeter's origins are remote, going back to the Great Goddess of Old European civilization, but her sphere is not as inclusive. "She is the Goddess of the Grain, of that which grows to human benefit,"[7] not the Goddess of all creation. Her own daughter Kore (or Persephone) is the Grain Maiden, the new crop. Kore is the seed germ of grain, Demeter the mature crop. Her mysteries were connected to the agricultural cycle that later developed into an allegory of human immortality.

Classical literature is full of ecstatic accounts of the initiates' transformation at Eleusis. As Homer tells us, "Happy is he among men upon earth who has seen these mysteries,"[8] and Sophocles comments, "Thrice happy are they of men who looked upon these rites ere they go to Hades house, for they alone have true life."[9] The mysteries continued to be celebrated until their suppression by the Christian Emperor Theodosius I in 389 C.E. The sanctuary at Eleusis was burned by the Goths at the end of the fourth century.

The Eleusinian Mysteries evolved out of the religion of the agrarian peoples of Old Europe kept alive in Crete—the last stronghold of prehistoric Goddess culture throughout the many centuries—as waves of barbarian invaders, the Ionians,

88. DEMETER, ca. 340–330 B.C.E. Marble. 9 ft., 10 in. From Cnidos. Greek.

A seated figure of the Goddess majestically carved in the Classical Greek style reveals a handsome, full-bodied woman, gazing with deep set eyes into the distance.

the Achaeans, and finally the Dorians moved into Greece from 2500 to 1000 B.C.E. Accompanying the invaders was the thunderbolt God called Zeus, who ruled with his contentious pantheon from the lofty heights of Olympus, imposing a patriarchal social order and culture on the peoples whose land they conquered.

The mystery cults continued to exist outside the mainstream religions of the Greek city-states, fulfilling spiritual needs that civic religion could not. While the Eleusinian Mysteries were recognized by the Athenian government and took place under its political control, the sacred precinct and the rites remained under the supervision of the priests of Eleusis. Open to all, Greek and foreign, women and slaves, the only requirements for initiation were knowledge of the Greek language and hands free from blood—that is, from having taken a human life.

The Eleusinian Mysteries were one of many spiritual practices in the pluralistic religious climate of the Hellenistic Age, all labeled pejoratively *pagan* by the Christians whose religion supplanted theirs. Now "pagan" is simply the Latin word *paganus,* country dweller, and paganism was the religion of the country people. As we have seen at Avebury, country people continued to worship the Goddess. Although denigrated as "folk" religion rather than "high," like the great world religions Judaism and Christianity, paganism serves well the need for connection to the earth and the cosmos.

Demeter continued to be worshiped by Greek peasants at Eleusis into modern times as the "Mistress of Earth and Sea"[10] and Poseidon, Zeus's brother, was known as the Goddess's spouse.[11] Each year the villagers ritually covered her statue with flowers in order to ensure the fertility of their fields. When two Englishmen carried the statue away to a museum at Cambridge University in the early nineteenth century, the people rioted, but their protest was in vain.[12]

The Myth of Demeter and Persephone

Myth is a paradigmatic narrative by which a community tells the story of its beginnings. The Demeter-Persephone myth, which undergirds the Eleusinian Mysteries, unfolds on many levels. Demeter's story is an ancient one of the the earth's

89. THE ABDUCTION OF PERSEPHONE, ca. 2000 B.C.E. Painting on inner surface of cup. Terracotta. Minoan.

The earliest known reference to Persephone's abduction is a Minoan vase painting. Her companions gesture in alarm "as she disappears into a vagina-shaped chasm in the earth. At the lower right is a fantastic, highly sexualized flower, sent up by the earth in order to lure Kore into the trap."[9]

power to give life. It is also the earliest known story of the natural intimacy of the mother-daughter bond. The main narrative tells of the kidnapping and rape of a much beloved daughter, the mother's fruitless search, her inconsolable grief, and their eventual joyous reunion. The plot exposes the brutality of male-female relationships in a patriarchal culture and the diminution of the powers of the Goddess. Once the mother of all creatures, she is reduced to mothering only one over whose fate she has no control.[13] She cannot even locate her lost daughter. "She suffers as well the insult of having her wishes ignored, her grief trivialized, her complaint given no recognition."[14] Reduced to inchoate rage by the betrayal of the gods, she gives vent to the destructive side of her nature and, in seeking revenge, would destroy the whole human race through cruel famine.

The earliest known account of the myth is the Homeric *Hymn to Demeter,* written to explain the origin and practice of the Eleusinian Mysteries and a major source of our knowledge about those rites. "Composed for the most part around the seventh century B.C.E.," the hymns are part of an oral tradition, a larger anonymous body of verse celebrating the gods and goddesses of the Greek pantheon.[15] They vividly re-create the Olympian world of classical mythology, stories that have become for most of us in Western culture an authoritative description of the origins of religion and culture.

In the *Hymn to Demeter*, Zeus connives with his brother Hades and sanctions the kidnapping and rape of his own daughter, the beautiful Persephone whom the God of the Underworld wants for his wife (see fig. 89). One day when the fair maiden is out walking with her girlfriends in a flowery meadow, she sees a wondrous, magical, glowing narcissus. As she stoops to pluck the flower, the earth opens beneath her and Hades, with his immortal horses, bursts forth. "Begging for pity and fighting him off, she is dragged into his golden chariot . . ."[16] and carried down to his shadowy underworld kingdom.

The mountains and the seas echo with her cries. Her mother hears them but doesn't know where she has gone. For nine days (the symbolic nine of pregnancy) Demeter wanders about the earth in search of her child. No one, god or mortal, will tell her what happened. They are all afraid of Zeus. Finally, Hecate tells Demeter that she heard Persephone's cries but doesn't know where she is or who her ravisher was. Together the two goddesses go to Helios, the Sun God, who reveals the truth about Persephone's abduction and then has the temerity to try to reassure Demeter that there is no need to be angry, Hades is indeed a worthy son-in-law, a member of her own lineage.

Demeter, enraged by the perfidious Zeus, abandons the company of the Olympians and wanders about the earth disguised as an old woman beyond her childbearing years, no longer representing the fertile earth. When she comes to Eleusis, her heart overflowing with sorrow, she sits down to rest in a shady spot by the well where the women come to draw water.

She is befriended by the daughters of the King of Eleusis, who engage her to nurse their infant brother. Demeter takes comfort in caring for the child. When she contrives to make the baby prince immortal "by burying him like a brand deep in the fire," she is discovered by the frightened mother. Enraged with the mother's interference, Demeter reveals her divinity, appearing in all her glorious beauty; the palace is filled with the brilliance of lightning. Berating the Eleusinians for their ignorance of sacred things, the Goddess orders them to build a great temple in her honor and below it an altar. They do her bidding, and when the temple building is finished the Goddess retires inside still yearning for her daughter.

Finally, in desperation, she blackmails Zeus into arranging Persephone's return from the underworld. She halts the growth of all that comes from the earth for an entire year, and the famine prevents the people from sacrificing to the gods.

> . . . The cruelest of years
> Did the goddess ordain for men on the nourishing earth.
> No seed sprouted in the rich soil, for bright crowned Demeter
>   lay hidden;
> Oxen in vain dragged the bent plows through the fields,
> And white barley was scattered without avail on the ground.
> By terrible famine she would have destroyed the whole race of
>   men.[17]
> Never, she said, would she set foot on fragrant Olympus
> Or send forth the fruits of the earth in their season
> Until she had seen with her own eyes her fair-faced young
>   daughter.[18]

90. PERSEPHONE'S RETURN, ca. 440 B.C.E.
Painting on vase. Terracotta. Greek.

Persephone's return, however, is conditional. She has eaten the pomegranate seed, pressed upon her by Hades as she was leaving his realm, and so must return to the underworld for a third of every year. On a fifth-century vase painting we find Hermes, guide of souls, leading Persephone from the underground through a vagina-shaped fissure signifying rebirth. Hecate then leads the girl by torchlight to her waiting mother (see fig. 90). Demeter, grateful for her daughter's presence, accedes to the will of the gods and restores life to the crops. The hymn concludes with her gift of the Mysteries to the Eleusinian kings.

"These kings of Eleusis passed on the teachings from generation to generation, and their families continued to preside over the Mysteries until they ceased to be. Although there were other shrines to Demeter and Persephone, most notably in crevices in the earth and caves, there was only one place, Eleusis, to celebrate the Mysteries."[19]

The Eleusinian Mysteries Bring Together Two Ancient Rituals

Ritual is the enactment of myth under a highly structured situation. The object of ritual is personal transformation, bringing the worshiper into harmony with the divine. Myth is the story, the plot; ritual the experience. Much of the power of myth lies in its universal quality, its timelessness, so that each reenactment is experienced as the first time. This is the key to its transformative power. In the Eleusinian Mysteries the initiates take the role of Demeter as she searches for her lost daughter, experiencing her heartrending loss and inconsolable grief as well as the bliss of reunion with her loved one.

Demeter's story unfolds on many levels, that of the earth's fertility, of the agricultural cycle, of women's life cycle, of the natural intimacy of the mother-daughter relationship, and of the primordial relation between life and death. It tells of the flowering of her daughter's gentle nature into compassionate womanhood, the grief and loss of their separation, the desperate longing of both women for each other and their eventual ecstatic reunion. The Eleusinian Mysteries bring together two ancient rituals. The first is the personal one of a young girl's initiation into womanhood, a puberty ritual. The second is the universal rite honoring the Great Mother as the giver of grain, the staff of life.

As we have seen from Çatal Hüyük to Avebury, the sacrament of baking bread has been the focus of Goddess worship. Grain storage bins, grinding stones, and ovens are the most common furnishings of her shrines. At Çatal Hüyük, the cult statue of the birth-giving goddess was found in the grain storage bin. Baking of the bread was done in the courtyard outside the shrine. In Old Europe the shrine of the Snake Goddess, the Cosmic Creator, is dominated by a huge domed oven. In Malta, the image of the quern, the stone used to grind the grain, is carved on the base of the giant Goddess as her emblem. At Avebury, pregnant Silbury squatted down and brought forth the corn harvest. In the culminating ritual of the Eleusinian Mysteries the chief priest, the hierophant, holds two sheaves of wheat aloft in profound silence (see fig. 91).

The Mysteries at Eleusis were related to another harvest festival, for women only, of thanksgiving to Demeter honoring her as Thesmophoria, the "lawmaker." "The meaning of the name *Thesomophoria* and of Demeter's epithet Thesmorphos has been much discussed."[20] The traditional interpretation has been that "The secrets of agriculture brought by the Goddess were believed to have transformed Greece from a nomadic into a farming community. Thus 'with Demeter,' it is said, came in agriculture, settled life, marriage, and

91. DEMETER HOLDING ALOFT SHEAVES OF WHEAT, third to second century B.C.E. Bas-relief. Terracotta. Roman.

Demeter, worshiped by Romans as Ceres, has serpents around her arms like the Minoan Goddess.

the beginnings of civilized law."[21] Thesmophoria was celebrated in gratitude for Demeter's providing humankind with the capacity to grow crops, especially grain, thereby civilizing the race.

While such explanations are helpful in understanding rationalizations of later ages, they also reveal the underlying meaning of this popular ritual which retained the primal features of its origins, practices seemingly uncontaminated by later usage that must have been empowering to the participants. The rites of the Thesmophoria lasted for three days. While they continued to be enacted in urban Hellenistic Greece, they recall an earlier age, a simpler time of small matrilinear, agricultural communities. The ancient rites were preserved in such a pristine state because they connected women to life-enhancing energy, like the Hindu *shakti,* the life force within. Their elemental nature is testimony to the potency of the primal symbolism.

> These three days seem to have represented the natural cycle of the crops; from the sowing of the seeds, through the winter of waiting, to the time of "fair-birth" of the crops and their eventual harvest. The three ritual days can also be seen as

symbolizing the cycle of human reproduction, from the sexual union, through the time of pregnancy, to the time of the fair birth of the fairborn child.[22]

Pamela Berger, in recounting the story of the transformation of the protector of the crop from Grain Goddess into Christian saint suggests that the title Thesmophoria refers to Demeter's gift of rites celebrating women's mysteries.[23] The "law" she revealed is the primordial interconnection of all life.

> The festival was marked by processions, purifications, and sacrifices. Men were excluded from all ritual activities. At some point before the festival young suckling pigs were thrown down into deep underground sanctuaries, natural crevices or crypts. . . . Next to the piglets were strewn pine cones and wheat cakes in the shape of male genitals. The high point in the . . . ceremonies came on the first day when women called drawers, who had purified themselves . . . descended into the innermost sanctuaries of the chasm, carried up the rotted remains of the piglets [that had not been eaten by snakes], and laid them on the altar of Demeter and Kore. What remained was mixed with the seeds to be sown that year. The piglets' mains, the pine cones, and the wheat cakes were believed to increase the capacity of the seed to germinate, and those who could secure some of the rotted flesh to mix with the seed were assured of a good crop.
>
> The phallus-shaped pine cones and wheat cakes were obvious symbols of fertility. The snakes were seen as guardians of the inner sanctuaries and were generally viewed in the ancient world as being privy to the mysteries of the underground. At the time of sowing the powers of regeneration were assumed to pass from the fertility symbols to the piglets and to the seed. In this way, the Thesmophoria ritual was expected to aid vegetal as well as animal and human fertility.[24]

Descriptions of the ritual in primary sources are often confusing. It is not clear how long the pigs were left in the sanctuaries to rot. The flesh seems to have been regarded as some sort of offering to the earth as represented by guardian snakes.[25] The ritual is documented in a fifth-century B.C.E. vase painting showing a woman holding a pig over a trench in one hand and in her other a basket containing the *sacra*, sacred ritual objects (see fig. 92).

The pig was the cheapest and most common of sacrificial animals, one that every citizen could afford, sacred to the

92. WOMAN SACRIFICING A PIG, ca. third century B.C.E. Vase painting. Drawing after Harrison.

Vegetation Goddess since the Neolithic.[26] The fast-growing body of a pig must have impressed early agriculturalists and "its fattening must have been compared to corn growing and ripening, so that its soft fat apparently came to symbolize the earth itself, causing the pig to become a sacred animal."[27] It became the identifying emblem of Eleusis, represented on the face of its coins.

The underground sanctuary was the place deep in the earth where Persephone went. Natural clefts or chasms called *megara* were the underground dwellings of the earth goddesses Demeter and Persephone.[28] "The word itself, meaning at first a cave-dwelling, lived on in the *megaron* of kings' palaces and the temples of the Olympian gods, and the shift of meaning marks the transition from under to upper world rites."[29]

Abstinence from sex during the first day of the Thesmophoria was essential because it was believed that if women conserved their life-giving energy, the ritual invocation of the earth's powers would be more potent. The women's wombs were considered analogous to the Earth's; a seed of grain, left dormant for the long winter months, flowers in the spring becoming the harvest that nurtures the community.

On the second day, "The Fasting," the women refrained from food and drink and sat, crouching low on the ground as Demeter did in her desolate vigil by the well at Eleusis. And on the third day, "The Fair Born" or "Fair Birth," the rotten flesh was scattered on the fields to fertilize the soil and encourage new growth.

The Mysteries at Eleusis

We know somewhat more about the Eleusinian ritual than the Thesmophoria. There was no teaching, no esoteric doctrine at Eleusis. Pilgrims came for the emotional experience, their mood shifting from anxiety to rapture as they re-enacted the passion of Demeter, the descent of Kore into the underworld, and the fate of the dead. The final illumination led to personal transformation, a profound revelation of the mystery of life and death.

What was such an extraordinary experience in ancient Greece was probably ordinary for the Neolithic worshiper. In an age that no longer had faith in the gods as immanent beings fully present in everyday life, the mysteries were journeys into a consciousness that had been lost, one in which all of life was interconnected and death was part of life.

There were several degrees of initiation at Eleusis. The Mysteries were divided into two parts, the Lesser and the Greater. The Lesser Mysteries were preparatory, usually celebrated once a year in the spring, and probably included the re-enactment of the mythic narrative of Persephone's abduction and Demeter's search.[30] The Greater Mysteries were celebrated the following fall. The ceremonies continued for nine days, the same number as those of Demeter's agony when she searched in vain for her lost daughter. "From bits and pieces of evidence that have survived—artistic representations, architectural designs and scattered literary testimonies," it is possible to reconstruct some idea of what went on.[31]

The evening before the first day, the cult symbols, the sacred objects of Demeter, were brought to Athens from Eleusis by priestesses who walked the fourteen miles in solemn procession carrying the *sacra* in large, beautifully decorated baskets on their heads. The official opening was on the first day when all who were clean of hands and spoke Greek were invited to participate. On the second day the initiates were called together in Athens by the heraldic cry "To the sea, initiate!" and they went to purify themselves in the nearby Aegean. The purification was an essential feature of the Mysteries. The procession to the sea was known as "renewal" or "banishment," ritually separating the initiate from previous profane life, a crossing over. Each initiate took along a young pig with whom the purifying bath was taken. Later the pig would be sacrificed and eaten.

The Third Day was given over to prayers for the city, the Fourth Day for latecomers.[32] On the Fifth Day, the *mystai*, as the initiates were now called, crowned in myrtle and carrying torches, proceeded the fourteen miles from Athens to Eleusis where they entered the sacred grounds of Demeter, enclosed by high walls built to conceal the sacred events within. The *myste* is one "who has not seen and will not speak of the things revealed. As such, distinguished from the *epote,* who has seen but equally may not speak; the two words indicate successive grades of initiation."[33]

At nightfall, the pilgrims, with lighted torches, were led into the outer court of the sanctuary. There was singing and dancing in honor of the Goddess. The playwright Euripides wrote that on this night even the goddesses in the stormy heaven of Zeus danced to honor the golden-crowned maiden and her holy mother.[34]

On the following day, the Sixth, the aspirants fasted and offered sacrifices. The Seventh and Eighth Days were the high point, the "nights of the Mysteries." Not all *mystai* took the final initiation. Those who did entered the temple of Demeter for the central enactment of the Mysteries, "what was said," "what was enacted," and "what was shown."

The initiation took place at night. Many have tried to reconstruct what happened from the scanty and fragmentary evidence. We do have the password of the *epotai*. "I fasted, I drank the *kykeon,* I took from the chest . . . after manipulating, I placed in the basket, then removing from the basket, I replace in the chest."[35] Several scholars have identified the contents of the chest and basket as "a replica of the womb, or a phallus, or a snake, or cakes in the shape of genital organs. It is possible that the receptacles contained objects that were relics from archaic times bound up with sexual symbolism characteristic of agricultural societies."[36]

What was enacted may have included a retelling of the myth, a singing of the poet's *Hymn to Demeter,* or a more elaborate dramatization.

> Sometime during the final two days of initiation, before the beginning of the night's ceremonies and the lighting of the great fire, the *mystai* drank *kykeon,* barley water flavored with

mint. . . . Perhaps the barley was fermented and the drink intoxicating; the barley may have contained ergot, a fungus with hallucinogenic properties; we do not know. Probably the fasting prayers and anticipation of the initiates helped clarify their inner vision. We are told the initiates experienced a special seeing, the "opening of the eyes."

[Perhaps] the vision [was] the epiphany of the goddess as Earth Mother; or Persephone returning from Hades; or of the reunion of Mother and Child.[37]

In another ritual, pregnant with meaning, the *epotai* were said to cry after looking skyward, "rain," then, looking to the earth, exclaim, "conceive." Some believe that this ritual formula may have been connected with the *heiros gamos* enacted by the chief priestess and the hierophant.[38]

Ancient authors speak of the great fire burning on the roof, the smoke and flames visible from a distance,[39] the sound of a thunderlike gong. Hippolytus writing in the third century said that "during the night, in the midst of a brilliant fire celebrating the great and inexpressible mysteries, the chief priest cries out 'Holy Brimo has born a sacred child, Brimos.' . . . The goddess has acquired another name which means 'the strong one.' "[40] The mother is probably Demeter and the child, her son. New life is Mother Demeter's gift to human beings. She is said to have introduced grain agriculture. According to Homeric hymn, in her youth she bore a son, named Pluton, the personification of wealth and abundance. Her son, now called Triptolemus, "Thrice-plowed," will become the one who introduces grain and Demeter's rites to the world in her place. Associated with immortality, he is frequently represented on funeral vases. The relation between Pluton and Triptolemus is not clear; both represent treasures greatly prized—the one worldly wealth and pleasure, the other lasting life. The changing identity of Demeter's son suggests a shift in spiritual values in keeping with the changing role of the Goddess and her Divine Child in the mysteries of the Hellenistic Age. That it is Demeter's son, not daughter, who passes on her mysteries, reflects an even more fundamental change from a woman-centered world to a patriarchal one.

Some scholars say there was a viewing of the rescued Persephone in dramatic form. An epiphany of Persephone and her reunion with her mother may have been the decisive religious experience.

We do not know how this reunion was realized or what took place afterward. Nor do we know why such a vision was believed to make a radical change in the postmortem situation of the initiates. But there can be no doubt that the *epotes* perceived a divine secret which made him 'familiar' to the goddesses; he was in some way 'adopted' by the Eleusinian divinities. The initiation revealed both closeness to the divine world and continuity between life and death.[41]

Immanence of the divine and the continuity between life and death were core ideas of the Goddess religion, part of the common worldview. Suppressed by the Olympians, the mysteries preserved and made this wisdom accessible only to those initiated.

The culmination of the mysteries was the display in silence of two ears of grain by the hierophant (see fig. 90).

The most profound vision of all, the actual experience of immortality came in deep silence, when a mown ear of . . . [grain] was held up and *seen* by the initiate. Nor can words ever accompany such an experience. The ancients said that at this point the idea of immortality "lost everything confusing and became a satisfying vision."

The mown ear of . . . [grain] is a perfect symbol of immortality, of eternal rebirth. It is the fruit of life, the harvest which feeds and nourishes, it is the seed which must sink into the earth and disappear in order to give birth again. It was mown down in the moment of its ripeness, as Persephone was mown down and torn from her mother.[42]

The experience of immortality at Eleusis was linked then with the harvest and Persephone's return. The next day the initiates returned to Athens and normal life.

The Meaning of the Demeter-Persephone Myth

The Demeter-Persephone narrative is complex. The myth hinges on the violence of young women's sexual initiation and the wrenching separation from the protective mother, social realities of many women's lives under male domination. The parallel between the human and agricultural life cycle is central, the emotional intensity of the personal narrative of separation, loss, and reunion with the loved one is universalized through identification with the great round of the seasons.

> The early agricultural rites of Demeter in Crete were mimetic, that is to say, the people magically evoked by their own actions the fertility of the earth. This magic probably included invocation, singing, dancing, and lovemaking. The people celebrating their own sexuality in harmony with the creative powers of nature, as natural, human and divine.[43]

Demeter may have taken on her distinct persona in Crete. Homer sings of her lying with her mortal lover Iason in the fertile fields there. The son of that union was Pluton, the God of Wealth and Abundance. Although the Grain Goddess is a generalized character with no individual personality or narrative, Demeter's story is full of insight into a woman's situation. We do not know when archetypal figures began to take on human traits.

In the free and pleasure-loving open society of Crete, sexual rituals were not secret. They were not mysteries but were communicated freely and openly to all.[44] The rites conducted so openly in Crete were secret at Eleusis. Attitudes toward sexuality changed with the invasions and occupations of the warrior cult from the North.

Feminist philosopher Mara Keller takes a historical approach to interpretation of the myth as a mirror of the time of transition

> from the mother-rite clan cultures of the agrarian Neolithic, to the city-state societies of the Hellenic tribes based on military-right and father-right. This shift impacts on sexual experience and marital customs, as well as on economic take-over; the new male Gods typically solidified their authority in the heavens, as did the warrior-invaders on the ground, by abducting, raping and marrying women, priestesses, queens, or Goddesses of the region.[45]

In the Homeric hymn, Persephone is always referred to as Kore until her return from the underworld. Kore is a young girl of initiatory age. The term is virtually synonymous with the Greek *parthenos,* "maiden, virgin."[46] At the same time the texts are equally insistent on the fact that the maiden has reached physical maturity and is thus of marriageable age. Her companions in the meadow are the deep-breasted daughters of Oceanus.

When she returns to the upperworld, she always bears the new name, Persephone, with one exception. Zeus calls her Kore when referring to the time each year she will have to spend with Hades in the underworld. She will have to resume her role as initiate. Initiation is a liminal state, outside of ordinary experience, and must be repeated over and over to renew the mystery.

What was the nature of Persephone's sexual initiation? Archaeologist Bruce Lincoln argues that the word used in all Greek sources, *harpazein,* means "to seize, snatch, carry off," a term usually reserved for acts of war or thievery, but always acts of violence. The assault is violent, Persephone is unwilling.[47] But all these sources are the product of patriarchy when the puberty initiations of a woman-centered Goddess culture had already been transformed in alignment with the new ethos of male domination.

Keller suggests that in the earlier prepatriarchal cultures like Minoan Crete, a girl's sexual initiation would have been joyful and free. Persephone would have lain down with her lover in the fertile fields, like her mother Demeter did before her with Iason. Keller looks at the earliest known reference to the myth, an abbreviated scene painted on an earthen pot found in the palace at Phaistos, made long before Demeter was known in Greece. Usually interpreted as Persephone's abduction, it shows the maiden's two companions gazing down a huge black vagina-shaped chasm. At the lower right is a fantastic over-sized narcissus flower with an aggressively protruding stamen (see fig. 89). In the light of Keller's reinterpretation we can read this scene as a symbolic representation of Persephone's initiation into the sexual mystery.

> Death, life, male, female and, above all, the irrepressible power of reproduction—are all found in the image of the pomegranate seed. It is this seed that Persephone takes within her body—literally incorporating into her own being. With this seed, she becomes a new person: whole, mature, fertile, and infinitely more complex than before. Having tasted it, she has crossed a barrier from which there can be no turning back.[48]

Jungian Eric Neumann, whose analysis of the Goddess archetype, *The Great Mother,* is a classic, also sees Persephone's journey to the underworld as a rite of transformation into womanhood. He points to a beautiful grave stele of the early

93. DEMETER AND KORE (PERSEPHONE), early fifth century B.C.E. Bas-relief. Marble.

The two Goddesses, mother and daughter, are almost indistinguishable in appearance. Usually the maiden is characterized by the flower she carries, the mother by the fruit. Flower and fruit, narcissus and pomegranate, represent their respective roles. The redness of the pomegranate symbolizes the woman's womb, the abundance of seeds, its fertility. The narcissus expresses seduction to the sexually awakening girl.

fifth century B.C.E. in which the two goddesses, mother and daughter, "look smilingly and knowingly into each other's eyes"[49] (see fig. 93).

For Neumann, "this unity of Demeter and Kore is the central content of the Eleusinian Mysteries."[50] The goddesses belong together in their transformation from one to the other. The patriarchal overlay obscures many elements of the older women-centered culture. "Although these are late mysteries that in a certain sense were usurped by the males, it is to them that we owe much of our knowledge of the matriarchal mysteries."[51] In the prehistoric woman-centered Goddess culture, the primordial relationship was between mother and daughter who formed the nucleus of the female group. In the early patriarchal period the male is often an alien who comes from without and by violence takes the daughter from the mother. Separation and reunion, the restoration of the primary relationship to the mother, is the great motif underlying the Eleusinian Mysteries.

> Kore's resurrection from the earth—the archetypal spring motif—signifies her finding by Demeter, for whom Kore had "died," and her reunion with her. But the true mystery, through

which the primordial situation is restored on a new plane, is this: the daughter becomes identical with the mother; she becomes a mother and is so transformed into Demeter. Precisely because Demeter and Kore are archetypal poles of the Eternal Womanly, the mature woman and the virgin, the mystery of the Feminine is susceptible of endless renewal. Within the female group, the old are always Demeter, the Mother; the young are always Kore, the maiden.[52]

Persephone's rape takes on larger cosmological implications when chaos threatens as Demeter withdraws her life-giving power from the earth and the land lies barren. Ritual is often a symbolic reenactment of the beginning, the first time. Each time a woman is initiated the world is saved from chaos, for the fundamental power of creating is renewed in her being.[53] Her reemergence leads to cosmic regeneration as Demeter once again makes the earth flower.

Women's initiations "performed for the benefit of an individual are called 'rites of passage' and those performed for the benefit of the world . . . 'rites of cosmic [renewal].'"[54]

No doubt the benefit is greatest for the initiand who becomes in her own mind and that of others a goddess, a sacred object, and so forth—identifications she will carry with her beyond the ritual context and that will infuse her future actions with meaning.[55]

Initiation is a cosmic journey—a transformation, inevitably a death to the old self, and rebirth to the new. Persephone goes to the underworld an immature girl and emerges a mature woman. For the initiate, the ritual time is no time, outside of time, sacred time. "Time is annihilated for her and all those around her as they enter the world of myth, a world of [absolute] beginnings and thus rich in creative potential."[56]

The Mysteries of Demeter Tap into the Awesome Regenerative Powers of the Goddess

The mysteries of Demeter are important to our understanding of the centrality of the Goddess in human religious experience. They are a remarkable example of the continuity of Mother

94. THE REUNION OF DEMETER AND PERSEPHONE, fifth century B.C.E. Marble.

Persephone carries a lighted torch in each hand as she comes to her mother out of the darkness of the underworld. Demeter's emblems are the staff she carried when she wandered over the earth, grief-stricken, in search of her lost child, and the three sheaves of wheat represent her thanksgiving offering to humankind, the gift of agriculture upon Persephone's return.

95. DEMETER, TRIPTO-
LEMOS, AND PERSE-
PHONE, fifth century
B.C.E. Bas-relief. Marble.

The boy Triptolemos
stands between Demeter
and Persephone as they
instruct him on his mis-
sion. His journey was a
popular theme on funeral
vases found in graves
throughout the Hellenis-
tic world as far away as
Russia. In the Golden
Age of Greece, under
patriarchy, Demeter's
symbolic role as the giver
of life was taken over by a
male surrogate, her divine
son, a model for the
future Christian mystery.

Goddess religion in a male-dominated society that sought to suppress earth-centered spirituality.

Classicists, psychoanalysts, and students of comparative religion have attempted to probe the multifaceted meaning of the Eleusinian Mysteries. Mythographer Karl Kerényi finds that the mysteries reveal an ineffable, spiritualized Goddess.

> Persephone is . . . identified with the human soul which survives death, and her myth symbolizes not only the changing of the seasons but the rescue of the human soul. Certainly the mysteries seem to assure a happier time after death for those who had been initiated. The presence of Persephone seems pivotal for this blessing.[57]

Kerényi's interpretation reflects the Hellenistic search for a transcendent spirituality. By then the primal unity of the Goddess had long been shattered. According to him, at the climactic moment of the Mysteries the vision of the Goddess was of a transcendent being, no longer embodied, no longer of this earth. As long as the Mysteries continued to be celebrated, from the Hellenistic period until the fall of Rome and the end of the ancient world, there must have been a tension between Demeter, the fully embodied Earth Mother, and the mystical vision of Persephone who promised immortality. Persephone was the Goddess spiritualized but she was also the Queen of the Underworld who mediated between the Olympian gods and the Land of the Dead.

The key events of the Mysteries as they were understood in fifth-century Athens, the Golden Age of Greek civilization, are illustrated in two magnificent bas reliefs found at Eleusis. Carved in the elegant chaste style of classical Greece, they are eloquent witnesses of the ancient ritual and bring the *dramatis personae* into sharp focus (see figs. 94, 95).

The Demeter-Persephone myth, the earliest known story of the universal mother-daughter relationship, provides insight into a developmental crisis in the life of women. The Goddess was one and the Goddess was two. Demeter and Persephone were mother and daughter and also two phases in the life cycle of women. The presence of Hecate at key moments in the myth completes the trinity of the Goddess: maiden, mother, and crone, so important in ancient mythology. The continuous survival of Demeter's cult among agricultural people in

Europe despite centuries of aggressive hostility by organized Christianity suggests that the Goddess better served the spiritual needs of a people who were still connected to the earth as a living being.

Nowhere is this better illustrated than in the well-documented story of "the lady on the bus to Eleusis," which took place in February 1940. Eliade writes:

> At one of the bus stops between Athens and Corinth there came on board an old woman, "thin and dried up but with very big and keen eyes." Since she had no money to pay her fare, the driver made her leave the bus at the next stop—which was . . . Eleusis. But the driver could not get the motor started again; finally the passengers decided to chip in and pay the old woman's fare. She got back on board, and this time the bus set off. Then the old woman said to them: "You ought to have done it sooner but you are egotists; and since I am among you, I will tell you something else: you will be punished for the way you live, you will be deprived even of plants and water!" She had not finished threatening them . . . before she vanished. . . . No one had seen her get out. Then the passengers looked at one another, and they examined the ticket stub again to make sure that a ticket had indeed been issued.[58]

The story seems particularly poignant and prophetic when we consider the historical context and the ecological crisis of the end of the twentieth century. It was 1940, the eve of the agonizing years of the Nazi occupation and war. The impiety is to forget the human responsibility to honor all life.

Like the Sacred Marriage Ritual in the Near East, the celebration of Demeter's mysteries kept the spirit of the Goddess alive, but her former powers were co-opted in the service of a new ideology that reflected a different consciousness. The Mystery Religions served a people obsessed with a desire for personal immortality, spiritually adrift in a society in which traditional values no longer held.

This concept of immorality in the personal sense is totally different than the pattern of eternal rebirth in the reign of the Great Mother with its ongoing cycle of birth, death, and renewal in a collective sense. Death was not to be feared and was accepted as a natural part of life.

While we do not know what went on in the final initiation and may never know because, as archaeologist George

Mylonas has commented, the secret of the mysteries died with the last initiate, we do have the fragmentary evidence of the sculpture and ritual objects found at the sanctuary. They suggest that the power of the initiation was so compelling because it tapped into the awesome cosmic powers of the Goddess.

The Hebrew Goddess and Monotheism

CHAPTER 10

Monotheism, the belief that there is only one deity, was to prove an even more implacable foe of Goddess religion than the polytheism of the sky gods. Still the Israelites' exclusive monotheism was more wishful thinking on the part of biblical writers than a reality. The Goddess continued to play an important role in popular Hebrew religion until the fall of the First Temple and the Babylonian Exile (586 B.C.E.). "Although the Bible declares it to have been a stark choice between Yahwist monotheism and Canaanite polytheism, the situation was in reality much more blurred."[1]

In *The Hebrew Goddess* anthropologist Raphael Patai has amassed textual and archaeological evidence for the worship of a female divinity or feminine principal from Biblical times to modern Judaism and concludes that there was a Hebrew Goddess.[2] Steve Davies, a historian of religion, considers Patai's work and raises questions germane to our exploration of the nature of the Goddess and Goddess worship. Can we speak meaningfully of a Hebrew Goddess? Or are we talking about a goddess worshipped by Hebrew-speaking peoples?[3] In either case, what was the nature of the confrontation between the Goddess religion and monotheism?

To speak of a Hebrew Goddess is to make the claim that there was a distinctive goddess in the culture of the people of the Bible. Traditionally, this culture has been defined solely on the basis of Scriptures that insist on exclusive faith in Yahweh as the one and only God whose Lordship and worship differentiates the Israelites from all surrounding peoples. Yahweh was believed to have chosen the Israelites as his people.

Our understanding of early Israelite religion may have to be revised drastically. Mounting archaeological evidence, confirmed by substantial biblical allusions, suggests that the

Hebrews also worshiped the Goddess and the Canaanite thundergod Baal in rituals much like those of their polytheistic neighbors (see fig. 96).

Two Conflicting Bodies of Evidence:
Biblical and Archaeological

In reconstructing Hebrew religion we are faced with the fact that there is a conflict between two bodies of evidence, biblical and archaeological. Archaeologist William Dever tells us that "many of the biblical texts are both late and elitist—and thus may constitute less direct evidence of the actual early cult practice than archaeological discoveries."[4] Biblical authors sought to impose their view of a radical new divine reality by revising an earlier worldview. The penchant to present select information favoring their own theology did not differ from the practice of other writers in the ancient world or that of the more recent editors of the Christian canon, but their work was not disinterested history.

This explains, in part, the considerable discrepancy between archaeological finds and biblical "facts." As Canadian archaeologist John Holladay informs us, biblical description does not match what is found in the dirt. The texts may not have mirrored actual religious practice in any recognizable fashion.[5]

Biblical scholars and archaeologists have been increasingly influenced by the work of anthropologists who examine religion as a cultural system and study how people actually live and worship. Anthropological field work has given us a living context in which to consider how the texts and the evidence unearthed in excavations were used. What we "see archaeologically are the unedited fossil records of past human activity on a very wide scale. This is particularly true for *patterned* activities, that is, events taking place at the same place time after time in the same fashion. And few human activities are more 'patterned' than those connected with religious observances."[6]

From an archaeological perspective the early history of the Hebrew people is murky. No material evidence has been found to corroborate the legendary accounts of the patriarchs, of the Exodus from Egypt, or the long sojourn in the Sinai desert. Indeed the early Hebrews may have been people already settled in the hills who led a peasant revolution against the urban Canaanites. Little has survived in the material culture that distinguishes the Hebrews from the Canaanites. In order to understand the religious practices of the Hebrews, we must look at the larger context of Canaanite culture within which they developed in the period from 1500 to 1200 B.C.E., the years prior to their emergence as a contending power in that area with Yahweh as their god. The discovery some fifty years ago of the ancient city of Ugarit on the coast of Syria, once part of the land of Canaan, and its extensive literary remains is of singular importance in enriching our knowledge of the "language, literature, and culture of the Bible."[7]

Background: The Broader Context of Canaanite Culture

The sharply etched profile of the Canaanite pantheon's chief god is not so different from that of Yahweh: "a patriarchal figure, father of gods and human beings, [he is the] creator, bestower of blessing, and one who guides human destinies, stern, compassionate, wise, fearful at times."[8] His name, El, figuring prominently in the patriarchal narratives of Genesis as an epithet of Yahweh, suggests an early close identification with the Hebrew god. However, it is El's dynamic son Baal, the thundergod, and his wife, the Goddess Asherah, who are Yahweh's chief rivals.

Moreover, the names of two of the major goddesses in the Ugaritic myths—Asherah and Astarte—are the same as those mentioned in the Hebrew Bible. Asherah, the one who created the gods, is the local manifestation of the Great Goddess. A motherly goddess, she served the gods as their wet nurse. She even suckled human princes. Asherah's domain is the sea as El's is the heavens. Known as the Lady of the Sea, she is the patron of the Mediterranean port cities whose prosperity depended on the bounty of the sea and the good graces of the ruling lady. There are particular Asherahs of different cities, Sidon and Tyre for example, just as there are Virgins of Fatima and Guadalupe.[9]

Astarte is the daughter of Asherah and her husband El. The original meaning of her name was "womb" or "she who issues from the womb." She is "the inducer as well as symbol of female fertility, just as her brother-consort Baal was the inducer and symbol of male fertility. Thus the primary meaning of the names of the couple Baal and Astarte was begetter and conceiver, man and woman, husband and wife."[10]

"[The] functions and roles [of the Canaanite goddesses] clearly overlap, and they exist in changing and sometimes ambiguous relationships to the gods with whom they are associated."[11] All are aspects of the Great Goddess. Despite their different mythological roles and iconographies they were worshiped as one divine female presence.[12]

Canaanite religion is characterized by scholars as a fertility religion. When Baal is alive, "The heavens rain fat; the wadis (streams) flow with honey."[13] Drought was a devastating problem in this area and the annual drying up of the streams was explained mythologically by the death of Baal who, like Sumer's Dumuzi, died to be born again each new year.

Yahweh's role as dispenser of fertility, rain, and a good harvest was also a concern of the Hebrews, but both religions had as their central theme "cosmogony, the establishment of order and rule in the universe."[14] "Ugaritic, Mesopotamian and Israelite religion shared a common theology to the extent that kingship over the cosmos was demonstrated in battle with unruly forces, and the throne and abode of the king of the gods is established forever."[15] Clearly, the sociopolitical climate of a state modeled on autocratic divine kingship differed dramatically from that of the Goddess cultures in Old Europe and Minoan Crete.

Cosmic religions are considered by many historians of religion to be of a higher order than so-called fertility religions. However, this implies a limited concept, defining fertility solely in terms of agricultural yield and human procreation rather than as embracing all creativity, abundant well-being, and the capacity for regeneration that is the essence of life itself. Monotheistic religions relegate earthly creation to a lower order. The Goddess religion was both earthly and cosmic, the Goddess was both earth mother and cosmic life force.

The Israelites' commitment to Yahweh did not exclude other gods. In fact, until the Babylonian exile in the early sixth century, many Hebrew people worshiped in the old ways, practicing their cult in open places on peaks and hills and mountains,[16] and even in the caves below.[17] Indeed biblical sources describe the sacred stones and wooden pillars, the "asherim," of the Goddess set up next to altars to Baal upon the mountains, and upon the hills, and under every green tree.[18]

These are the places where the Goddess was universally worshiped in the ancient world. In Crete she was manifest in trees and pillars set on hilltop sanctuaries. In megalithic Western Europe she took the form of large upright stones known as menhirs sometimes carved with faces, and even necklaces, or just eyes and nose.[19] The association of the sacred female and the Goddess with the tree is a perennial theme in the Indian subcontinent from the earliest surviving artifacts of the Indus Valley civilization to contemporary village worship. The tree, like the Goddess, represents regeneration.

There is ample archaeological and textual evidence that the Goddess known under the names Asherah and Astarte was the focus of a widespread cult in ancient Israel. Asherah alone is mentioned more than forty times in the Hebrew Bible, mostly as an abomination, it is true, but the persistent concern of the biblical commentators with her presence is an indication of the extent of continuing influence.

A close look at the evidence suggests that the pillar, which may or may not have been carved, represented a divine force to be reckoned with. Asherah's pillar was even installed in the Temple of Jerusalem by Solomon's son, Rehoboam.

Asherah was associated with terebinth groves,[20] and her numinous presence was said to dwell in the leafy branches. The terebinth is a large shade tree that grew in the Mediterranean region. The first place that Abraham and Sarah stopped when they arrived in Canaan was at Shechem to consult the oracle-bearing tree, the terebinth of Moreh:[21] "Beneath the boughs of the sacred tree an oracle revealed, for the first time, the meaning of the departure from Mesopotamia"[22] that Abraham was to claim the land of Canaan for his descendants. Shechem, known as the "navel of the Land,"[23] "can be compared to Delphi, the famous oracular shrine in Greece."[24]

The Deuteronomic reformers, editors of the Hebrew canon containing Mosaic law, the fifth book of the Hebrew Bible, warned against planting the sacred trees: "You shall not plant for yourself an Asherah, any tree, beside the altar of Yahweh your god. . . . Neither shall you set up a pillar, which Yahweh your god hates."[25] The biblical text in its anxiety about idolatry is probably intentionally ambiguous about the nature of the Asherah, not making clear whether the wooden pillar was a cult figure or a cult object.

Asherah was linked to both the Hebrew Yahweh and Canaanite Baal as their consort. Recently discovered tenth-century B.C.E. inscriptions from Judea invoke the blessings of Yahweh and his Asherah testifying to their combined cult.[26] Biblical archaeologist David Noel Freedman suggests that when Yahweh defeated Baal, he claimed his consort Asherah as a prize of victory[27] just as the Indian god Indra took the Goddess Shri-Lakshmi (see color plate 19) with all her virtues of abundance and good fortune as his consort when he vanquished his cosmic rival, the god Varuna.

The Visual Evidence for the Worship of the Hebrew Goddess

As with the archaeologist, our primary resource for examining the Goddess tradition in Israelite religion is the surviving material evidence: icon, artifact, shrine, and sanctuary. The persistent presence of small female images, predominantly in clay but also in bone, ivory, and metal, found in the European cultures we have explored as well as most everywhere in Eurasia from Ireland to India, which can be dated from the Paleolithic to the Early Christian period, dramatically testify to a continuous devotion to the Goddess. Hundreds of such figures also have been found all over Israel from the period of Hebrew ascendancy in Canaan to the Babylonian exile (twelfth to sixth centuries B.C.E.). Mostly found in a domestic context rather than in shrines and sanctuaries, these small images were probably votive offerings to the Goddess.

The wooden pillars themselves never would have survived the adverse effects of the rainy winter climate, let alone centuries of purges by zealous Yahwist reformers and millennia of devastating invasions and warfare, but small clay counterparts of the larger wooden Asherah pillars are a common find in the period of the Hebrew monarchy. These depict a nude woman with prominent breasts whose lower body instead of torso and legs consists of a straight cylindrical column and flaring base (see fig. 96).

96. THE HEBREW GODDESS ASHERAH, eleventh to sixth centuries B.C.E. Terracotta. 7⅛ in. Palestine.

Small terracotta votive images, identical in form, are being found in increasing numbers at domestic sites[10] and can be identified as Asherah, the Hebrew Goddess. While their heads were made from molds, indicating large-scale manufacture, their pillar-like lower torsos were turned on a wheel like the Cretan household goddesses.

Archaeologist William Dever believes that an inscription to Yahweh and his Asherah on a large storage vessel refers to the Great Goddess. The vessel was discovered recently in a shrine attached to a caravanseri,[28] a way station where the Judean kings stopped over when they traveled from Jerusalem to Elath, the important port on their southern frontier. The iconography of the Goddess in the painting below the inscription resembles well-known Bronze Age representations of Canaanite goddesses engraved on metal pendants.[29] Like them she is bare breasted, dressed in an ankle-length, sari-style garment, and sits regally enthroned holding a lyre. But she wears a wig of tightly twisted curls like those of the pillar figures (see fig. 96), suggesting an iconography in transition.

Another important tenth-century find that appears to refer to the combined worship of Asherah and Baal/Yahweh is an elaborate terracotta stand from a Taanach shrine in northern Israel, unique in its rich imagery.[30] Taanach is the site of a famous battle between the Israelites and the Canaanites in which the prophetess Deborah was in command.[31] The Israelites probably did not occupy the city before the tenth century. Common cult objects such as incense stands have traditionally been bearers of popular iconography because they were regularly used in places of public worship. A Canaanite stand from this period was decorated with snakes, symbolic of the Goddess's powers of renewal.

The Taanach stand, almost two feet high, is capped by a shallow basin to contain the incense. Since this stand bears no trace of fire or incense, it was probably intended for offerings or libations (see fig. 97).

The identity and relationship of the deities on this complex tableau is controversial. Holladay suggests that the first and third tiers represent two aspects of Asherah, the second and fourth, Yahweh.[32] One of the principal epithets of the Canaanite goddess was "Lion Lady."[33] In Israelite culture, the tree was her most important iconic form. Holladay views the empty space on the second tier as the aniconic representation of Yahweh, the bull calf with the sun disk as his iconic form and the Temple of Solomon his house. The association of Asherah with both Baal and Yahweh is another example of the fluidity of cultic practice in the years of the Hebrew monarchy.

If we accept Holladay's reading, the imagery on the Taanach stand reveals a syncretic cult in transition, the combined

97. CULT STAND FROM TAANACH, late tenth century B.C.E. Terracotta. 21⅛ in. Palestine.

The front is decorated in four registers in high relief. A nude goddess stands *enface* on the bottom tier, her outstretched arms grasping the ears of two ferocious looking lions with bared teeth, protruding tongues, and bulbous eyes. Directly above the Goddess is an empty space framed by winged sphinxes who have lions' bodies, female heads, and Hathor headdresses.

On the third register a pair of heraldically arranged goats nibble from a stylized tree flanked by two lions who look much like those on the bottom tier. In the center of the upper register, a calf with a sun disk on its head stands between a pair of volutes that represent columns like those described at the entrance of Solomon's temple.[11]

98. Cult Statue of Bull, early twelfth century B.C.E. Bronze. Palestine.

The bronze figurine of a young bull is one of the finest pieces of sculpture dating from the Iron Age in Israel (1200–586 B.C.E.). The animal is represented naturalistically with a triangular head, narrow body, long legs, and a pronounced dewlap. The flattened muzzle has a grooved mouth and perforated nostrils. Each hollow eye socket is emphasized by a protruding ridge and originally must have been inlaid with some other material. The upright horns curve inward, with the ears below them.[12]

cult of a god and goddess, not that of a god and his consort. Her symbols are the aniconic tree and the fully anthropomorphic form of the nude female. Yahweh is present in both his invisible form and in his manifestation as bull calf. The sun disk is yet another attribute of the Near Eastern sky god.

The worship of the bull as a symbol of the male god was well known in the countries bordering the eastern Mediterranean just as it had been in nearby Mesopotamia (see fig. 98). In the second millennium B.C.E., the bull was the major cult object of the chief Canaanite god, El, and is associated with El's son, the thundergod Baal.[34]

The small statue was discovered by chance on the summit of a high ridge, one of the "high places" of cultic ritual mentioned in the Bible.

> From the remains [later] uncovered there, an open, partially paved enclosure built of stone can be reconstructed. . . . The site . . . appears to have been a center for religious ritual for a group of small settlements in the territory of the tribe of Manasseh and seems to have been in use during the time of the Judges, twelfth to eleventh century B.C.E.[35]

The bull figured prominently in the Exodus story. The Hebrew people growing anxious when Moses did not come down from the mountain, and fearing they would perish in the desert without a leader, beseeched Aaron to produce a sign from God. "Come make us gods to go ahead of us." Women gave their jewelry from which they fashioned a shining icon of the golden bull calf, the symbol of both Baal and Yahweh.

Yahweh was supposed to be invisible, appearing to his people in a cloud. Some claim that the calf was simply the pedestal of the invisible Yahweh like the cherubim who held the ark in the temple of Jerusalem.[36] Others believe that the golden calf had a much deeper meaning and was a symbol of the god of Israel.[37]

Centuries later, King Jeroboam of Israel set up two golden calves, one in Dan, the other in Bethel, so that the presence of God should be among his people; and they would not have to journey to the Temple in Jerusalem, where the Almighty dwelled in the rival kingdom of Judea. The Jerusalem Temple, built by Solomon as the house of God, was the liturgical center of the Israelite religion. When the Hebrew monarchy was divided into the northern kingdom of Israel and southern Judea after Solomon's death, the power and prestige of the Jerusalem Temple continued to be a threat to the northern ruler. Jeroboam built shrines, installed altars, and appointed priests to serve the golden calves, and he himself made sacrifices to them.

The Identity of the Hebrew Goddess

Much work needs to be done in sorting out the identities of the various Goddess figures that have been recovered in the land that was the home of the ancient Hebrews. The problem is complicated by the general fluidity in the naming of the goddesses in the Near East and the tendency for iconography and mythology to meld and merge. As her cult traveled from one people to another, the Goddess took on local coloring. The eastern Mediterranean coast was a crossroads in the ancient world and Israel was the heartland. Many different peoples lived and traveled there bringing their own sacred images with them.

Although the names of Asherah (Ashteroth), Astarte, and Anath are often combined, conflated, and confused, the most commonly found icons can be distinguished as either Asherah or Astarte.[38] Anath is mentioned directly in the Bible only as a place name, and no images found after the twelfth century B.C.E., the period of the Hebrew ascendancy, can be identified with her. Throughout the Bronze Age (2100–1300 B.C.E.), Astarte pendants (see fig. 15) and plaques are found all over the eastern shores of the Mediterranean, the area known as the Levant, most commonly represent the Goddess. Byblos on the Mediterranean coast was the center of her cult.[39] Astarte with her abstracted body and prominent sacred triangle is a direct descendant of the Ice Age ritual objects, also worn as pendants, in which the part stood for the whole. A major difference in the latter is the developed human iconography, the prominence of the head with its distinctive wig of upturned curls, a common motif of Canaanite goddesses.

The figure of Astarte was engraved on small gold pendants probably worn as protective amulets. It was found also on oval pottery plaques, mass-produced molds that are among the most common religious objects discovered in late Bronze Age levels in Israel.[40] They were used in household worship.

On the other hand, the small votive images of the twelfth to sixth centuries B.C.E. identified as Asherah (see fig. 96) are representations of the Goddess unique to Israelite culture. They have none of the motifs or attributes associated with the earlier or contemporary Canaanite goddess. The pillar form of her body already described is unmarked by any suggestion of garment or jewelry. Round corkscrew curls frame her broad face. Her incurving arms rest under her prominent breasts affirming her sacred character as source of life-giving milk. Holladay dubs her *dea nutrix,* goddess of nurture.[41] There would seem to be a Hebrew goddess after all. The local peoples evolved their own iconographic forms, the free-standing pillar/tree and the terracotta devotional icon, readily distinguishable from those of their neighbors.

The Hebrew Asherah was worshiped both in public cult and private devotion. Almost nothing specific is known about ritual context, but we can assume that the Hebrew goddess served important needs of popular religious experience not met by the official Yahwist cult. This would be particularly true for women whose need for divine protection and support was related to everyday concerns for the well-being of their families. In a seventh-century B.C.E. incantation text, the help of the Goddess Asherah is sought for women in childbirth.[42] The many finds of small clay images of pregnant women or women with children may be human or divine models (see fig. 99).

Perhaps they were like those in contemporary Bengal where women make images of the Goddess of Childbirth, Shasthi, in their own likeness, showing her pregnant, with infant(s) at her hip, and even on occasion massaging her baby (see figs. 100 and 101).

99. VOTIVE IMAGE OF PREGNANT WOMAN, sixth century B.C.E. Terracotta. From a tomb in the Phoenician cemetery at Akhziy, Israel.

100. SHASTHI, THE GODDESS OF CHILDBIRTH, WITH HER BABY, twentieth century. Terracotta. Bengal, India.

99

100

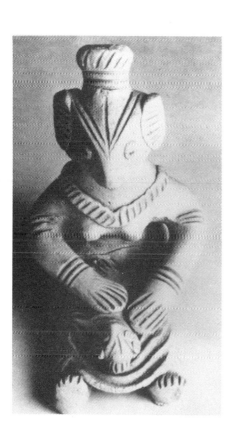

101. SHASTHI THE GODDESS OF
CHILDBIRTH MASSAGING HER BABY,
twentieth century. Terracotta. Calcutta, India.

101

This mirroring of human and divine roles makes psychological sense and is one significant reason for women's alienation in patriarchal religion where their experience of the sacred has little place. In ancient Israel women had their own domestic worship connected with the life cycle—first menstruation, sexual initiation, marriage, childbirth, and death[43]— as women have had in traditional cultures throughout the world. They met with groups of other women in small shrines; their ritual often included the making and baking of bread.[44]

The Cult of Asherah

In the Bible the Goddess is sometimes referred to as the Queen of Heaven. The fullest account of her worship by the Hebrews is from Jeremiah when the prophet is speaking out against her, telling the exiled Hebrews that Judea fell because of their neglect of Yahweh. The people's interpretation of the catastrophe may have been quite different. While recognizing that there may be divine retribution for transgressions, they believed that the sin committed had been not against Yahweh but against the Queen of Heaven. Judea fell because the people had neglected her rituals after Goddess worship had been forbidden by the Deuteronomic reforms.[45]

Jeremiah is told flatly that they will not follow his warnings but

> we shall burn incense to the Queen of Heaven, and shall pour her libations as we used to do, we, our fathers, our kings and our princes, in the cities of Judah and in the streets of Jerusalem. For then we had plenty of food, and we all were well and saw no evil. But since we ceased burning incense to the Queen of Heaven and to pour libations, we have wanted everything and have been consumed by sword and famine.[46]

As Patai says, "This unique passage allows us a glimpse of the actual ritual of the Hebrew . . . worship."[47]

Jeremiah also unwittingly gives us a charming description of a family ritual in the women's own words. The women are the ritual leaders but all family members participate. First the children gather wood and the fathers light the fire. Then the women knead dough and make cakes that are baked over the fire. When the preparations are completed, the women, assisted by the men, burn incense and pour out libations to Asherah and the other gods as well.[48]

Patai suggests that cakes offered to the Queen of Heaven might have been baked in a stone mold similar to those carved in the shape of the Goddess's body found in the kitchen of the palace at Mari in Mesopotamia. The cakes eaten by the celebrants may have been a precursor of the Christian Eucharist.[49]

Holladay looks at the archaeological record from the period of the Hebrew monarchy (eleventh to sixth centuries B.C.E.) in order to reconstruct the social organization and practice of Israelite religion.[50] After visiting architectural remains, temples, sanctuaries, shrines, and sacred precincts and examining artifacts, art, and inscriptions, he divides religious practice into establishment and nonconformist strains. Establishment religion, associated with the political states, was practiced in temples and shrines, and was primarily aniconic, without cult or votive figures. The focus of ritual was animal sacrifice.

The nonconformist tradition, a totally different form of religious expression, was practiced in open spaces, caves, and domestic quarters. Cult objects used in ritual were mostly icons. Goddess figures dominate but there were also horses, some with riders, vessels in the shape of animals, birds, and miniature furniture and lamps. Both ritual space and cult objects resemble those of Old Europe and Crete. Huge quantities of ordinary eating and drinking vessels are evidence of communal feasting. Holladay identifies the most frequent female finds, the pillar figures, as Asherah (see fig. 96). As he says, it is inconceivable that she wouldn't have had a name and who else could she be.[51]

The picture that emerges from our revised reading of the fragmentary archaeological evidence is of a popular polytheism that was violently opposed by a jealous priesthood and proselytizing prophets. The struggle is of the radically new against the entrenched and comfortable old ways.

The struggle is understandable. Familiar rites and sacred images can be trusted, particularly in times of crisis and emotional need. Yahweh was very demanding, a stern and sometimes cruel judge. The prohibition against graven images must have meant a loss of the sensual, palpable presence of the divine. The Hebrews were an agricultural people tied to the land. Yahweh was distant, removed from their daily needs.

The Confrontation of Yahweh and the Goddess

Yahweh, the god of the Israelites, was born in the milieu of herders and context of the desert.[52] He was not tied to a sanctuary, to a sacred site, or the land but to a group of men. "Nothing definite is known concerning the cult practiced by the Israelites during the forty years they spent in the desert"[53] but Yahweh was probably worshiped in a portable "tent of meeting" much like those used by pre-Islamic Arabs. When the small group that had been led by Moses entered Canaan under the leadership of Joshua (ca. 1200), they made war in the name of Yahweh, converting other tribes. But the religion of the people of the land, firmly rooted in practices sacred to an agricultural way of life, was not easily displaced.

The centuries that followed were ones of confrontation and assimilation between the radically new ways of Yahweh and the religion of the indigenous peoples. At first Baal and Yahweh were venerated side by side.[54] Baal was the "god of the land," the supreme specialist in fecundity. The early cult of the Israelites was adapted from Canaanite practice with its sacrificial system, ritual objects, and images and included both the worship of the Goddess and sacred prostitution. "The simplest form of sacrifice consisted in the offering, on a consecrated site, of different gifts or in libations of oil or water. The offerings were regarded as food for the divinity."[55] Sanctuaries built after Canaanite models included an altar, *massebahs* (standing stones), and *asherahs*.[56]

From the start the conflict between the leaders of the new religion and the worshipers of the Goddess was particularly acute because she represented values at odds with the revolutionary new ethos of monotheism in which the supreme god was separate from his creation and the moral good was situated in a higher authority. According to the biblical account, soon after they established a bridgehead in "the promised land," the Hebrews abandoned Yahweh and served Baal and the Asherahs.[57] When we assemble all the biblical evidence we find that the hills of Israel and Judea must have been covered by groves consecrated to Asherah.

Samuel, an early Hebrew leader in the days before the kings, made the first purge of idolatrous images and was rewarded by the decisive Hebrew victory over the Philistines.[58] Counterattacks against the popularity of the Goddess went on throughout the five centuries of the monarchy (eleventh to sixth centuries).

In the tenth century Solomon, at the bidding of his Sidonite wife, introduced the worship of Asherah into his kingdom and erected pillars in the high places.[59] Solomon's son, Rehoboam, under the influence of his favorite wife Maacah, even installed an image of Asherah in the temple itself.[60]

After the reign of Rehoboam, Yahwist reformers mounted a series of attacks against the Goddess that continued intermittently until the end of the monarchy and the Babylonian exile. "The worship of Asherah in the Jerusalem temple came and went with the fluctuations of power politics."[61] The zealous reforms of kings were prodded by the activities of the prophets. Isaiah and Micah, in keeping with their monotheistic opposition to any form of image worship, spoke out in particular against the Asherah cult.[62] They preached that worshiping the Asherah pillars was among the ritual sins—along with soothsaying, witchcraft, and graven images—that would bring about the destruction of Israel.[63]

The Deuteronomic reforms of the seventh century were the harshest of all. King Josiah (639–609 B.C.E.), "apparently at the insistence of the Jerusalem priesthood, on whom he may have depended for support and who no doubt lost prestige—and tithes—when many sacrifices were diverted to the numerous 'high places,' insisted on . . . an unwavering affirmation of Yahweh's exclusiveness."

He ordered the extermination of the non-Hebrew peoples who lived in Canaan, prohibited intermarriage with them, ordered their altars to be broken up, their pillars to be dashed to pieces, their Asherahs hewn down and their graven images burned.[64]

Josiah's zeal in stamping out "idolatrous practices" knew no bounds.

> . . . He brought out the image of Asherah herself from the Temple, had it burned in the Kidron Valley, ground it up into powder, and cast the dust over the graves of those who had worshiped her. Next he demolished the quarters of the Qedeshim, the sacred male prostitutes, which were in the Temple, and in which the women wove "houses" for the Asherah.
>
> Finally, he turned his attention to the countryside and cut down the Asherahs wherever they were found, filling their

places with human bones. In a similar manner he destroyed, removed, and defiled all the other high places and objects of idolatry which were originally set up by Solomon.[65]

Josiah's excesses are disturbing. Why was the Goddess so threatening that all traces of her very existence had to be eradicated? Why was she so much more feared than the male gods? There are no simple answers to these questions. The Bible is full of incredible violence and cruelty perpetrated in the name of Yahweh, probably descriptive of the social reality of that day. Yahweh's behavior is often that of a tribal chieftain toward his enemy.

The relation between gender and creation may be the critical one. We saw how in patriarchal Sumer the creative powers of the Goddess became an instrument of the state and were used to legitimize the king's rule. The god who ruled alone took unto himself all powers of generativity, cosmic and earthly, denying even the metaphoric role of the female to establish his control over creation; stamping out all cultic sexual practices was thus essential.

Elizabeth Dodson Gray calls the religion of the ancient Hebrews a "male fertility cult." The ritual of circumcision, the symbolic sacrifice of the male genital organ, is the mark of the covenant that every Hebrew male makes with his God.[66] By this act, creation was taken away from the Goddess and women were excluded from participation in the covenant.

Suppression of the Goddess and Iconoclasm

The biblical commentators seem to have confused pillars, Asherahs, and trees set up beside altars, but they did distinguish all three from graven images, sculptural representations of the divinity. The significance of the cult object in the worship of the Goddess is twofold: the embodiment of divine power in the icon, and the intimate, personal nature of image worship.

As for the Hebrew prohibition of graven images, what was it all about and how was it connected to Goddess worship? Graven images were any that were engraved or sculptured in human likeness. One of the Ten Commandments handed down by God to Moses at Mt. Sinai forbade their use. Remember, this was a seminomadic people whose God, though conceived of and comprehended in human terms, remained invisible. He appeared to his people in the desert in a cloud and could not be discerned. Images may have been forbidden to assure their loyalty to the invisible Yahweh and to prevent their creating idols or adopting the idols of other peoples with whom they came into contact during the long years of exile. When the Hebrews finally settled down in the land of Canaan, they very quickly succumbed to the temptation of image worship, which may have been a more satisfying way for them to relate to the divine.

Another critical point with regard to Hebrew iconoclasm is the relation between the prohibition of images of the divine and the suppression of Goddess worship. As we have seen, as far back as the Paleolithic the Goddess had been worshiped through votive images in the shape of the body of the Goddess. They were small enough to fit into a clasping hand; devotion was sensual. The most commonly used medium was clay, the very earth that is her body. In the pursuit of the Hebrew monotheistic ideal, the two proscriptions go hand in hand. They converge because to prohibit the making of the Goddess image is to disembody her, to sever her from her life force, which is the earth. The embodiment of the Goddess in female form, with the procreative and sexual attributes of woman, is an important element of her effectiveness as a devotional instrument. Goddess religion is not dualistic. The divine force is not distant or separate; the relationship is immediate and intimate.

The Hebrews were not the only ones to make the connection between iconoclasm and the suppression of the Goddess. Vedic India and the Protestant Reformation did also. Despite the abundance of figures from earlier and later periods, not a single anthropomorphic image has been discovered from the Vedic period in India (1200–800 B.C.E.). Minor goddesses are mentioned in the hymns but their physical attributes are very limited; there is no attempt to give them the rich visual treatment so characteristic of later Hindu descriptions of the Goddess. The Protestant Reformation rejected the cult of the Virgin and banished images from churches. One of Luther's strongest grievances against the Catholic church was idolatry, the worship of the image as divine, that is, as embodying the living presence of God.

The Goddess and the Hierodule

The Goddess was also worshiped in the form of her living representative, the priestess. In the ancient Near East, a priestess, the hierodule, took the part of the Goddess in the sacred marriage ritual and other cultic sexual activity. The Canaanite practice was taken over by the early Israelites. Hebrew scriptures tell of hierodules even in the Temple of Jerusalem. They seem to have been eliminated finally only after the Fall of the Temple and the Babylonian exile. Cultic sexual activity became synonymous with abandoning the worship of the true god and turning to the worship of false gods. The Bible considered apostasy the worst of sins. The terms used to identify the cult priestesses became insults used as invectives against the Goddess worshipers.

The disappearance of cultic sexual activity was of primary importance to the establishment of the ancient Hebrew faith. As long as the temple priestesses were the bearers of the mysterious, life-enhancing powers of creativity and procreativity, these powers could not be claimed by the creator-god. The Hebrew god took unto himself the sacred life-giving powers of the Goddess.

Conclusion

To return to Steve Davies's original question: Can we meaningfully speak of a Hebrew goddess, unique to Hebrew culture, or are we talking about a goddess worshiped by Hebrew-speaking peoples? The answer to both parts of his question is yes. My thesis is that the ancient Goddess was always one, albeit with different manifestations and iconography reflecting the culture in which she was worshiped, and that under patriarchy her identity was fragmented into different persona, each with her own name and story. Asherah of the Pillar was the Goddess of the Hebrew people, an identifiable form of the Great Goddess.

While fragmentary evidence for her cult is inconclusive, she was worshiped in high places, in the temple and the home. Her cult was long-standing. As we noted in our discussion of the Goddess in Minoan culture, the worship of the tree/pillar is an elemental form of the Goddess religion. Along with an understanding the earth and all that is on it as sacred, the numinous presence of the Goddess was experienced not only in the configurations of the landscape that were likened to her body, but also in the rocks and the trees of the land. The tree, and its derivative the pillar, are particularly potent symbols for the Goddess. Seed falls from the trees' fruit into the earth to reemerge the following season as a seedling that will grow into a tree and bear fruit.

The wooden pillars of the Goddess, known only from vague biblical descriptions, can be identified with small terracottas, with pillarlike lower torsos, votive images found along with other evidence of nonconformist or popular cult. Clay figures of pregnant females, and women with children found in domestic contexts, point to a women's religious practice centered on their own needs for life-cycle rituals.[67] Perhaps, as in village India, women had their own domestic religious practice parallel to but separate from the official state religion of Yahweh.

In continuing to worship the Goddess, women were preserving rituals that were sacred to their experience of life as cyclical, as integrated with the seasons of the earth. Close reading of the Bible reveals over and over again how the Yahwist reformers as well as the early Christians accommodated existing Goddess traditions by incorporating their rituals and sacred places, although often, it is true, reversing their values in doing so. The Israelites took over, after their fashion, the three great annual seasonal festivals of the Canaanites—*Unleavened Bread* (Passover) when springtime brought the winter rains to an end; the early summer *Weeks of Pentecost* with the first fruits of sowing; and the autumn *Ingathering* when the fruits of the land, the harvest, were brought in.[68] And the dates of the Christian Christmas and Easter were both originally days of the Pagan calendar. The syncretism between the cults of the Goddess and Yahweh, between Yahweh and Baal, for which we have only fragmentary archaeological evidence, suggests a more balanced picture of religion in ancient Israel, one more in keeping with what we know was the religious experience of other people in the larger cultural context.[69]

The Israelite religion combined the imperatives of monotheism, exclusive loyalty to one god with the hierarchical ordering and domination of patriarchy. The Lord God ruled like an absolute monarch. The Book of Genesis reverses the story of creation as experienced by men and women since the earliest intuitions of the sacred:

> The male god took over all creation.
> He created heaven and earth out of nothing, not out of his own body.
> He created by proclamation, not gestation.
> He created once and for all time, not through a dynamic process, the ongoing cycle of birth, death and regeneration.
> He created all living creatures.
> He created man first, in his own image, ordering him to fill the earth and subdue it.
> Man was to name all the living creatures, and to have his will with them.
> He created woman out of man's rib so that man would not be lonely.

> God created a beautiful garden paradise in the midst of which he placed two splendid trees: the one, the Tree of Life, the other, the Tree of the Knowledge of Good and Evil.
> Now paradise had its limitation and the fruit of the Tree of Knowledge of Good and Evil was forbidden. To eat it meant death.
> The snake, symbol of the Great Goddess, had been transformed into a veritable "snake in the grass," a seducer who tempted Eve to eat the fruit from the Tree of Knowledge of Good and Evil, and she gave Adam a bite.
> Their very first "taste" of knowledge was a painful consciousness of their nakedness. The human body was no longer good. They sewed together fig leaves and covered themselves in shame.

In his great wrath at their disobedience, God turned on man and woman. The words of his harsh judgment still ring in our ears. He cursed the earth. From now on thistles and thorns would grow upon it. Adam and all men would toil by the sweat of their brow for their bread. Eve and all women would conceive in sorrow and bear children in pain. They would desire their husbands and their husbands would rule over them. Adam, whose name means "from the dust or clay," blamed it all on the woman, whom he names Eve, "the mother of all living."

God expelled Adam and Eve from the garden, fearful lest they also eat from the Tree of Life and become immortal like him. Having eaten from the Tree of Knowledge they must die and return to the dust from whence they came.

Knowledge of good and evil included sexual knowledge. When they left the garden, Adam knew Eve for the first time and she conceived and bore Cain.

When the Christian canon was established by the church fathers in the fourth century C.E., the Hebrew Bible was included in God's revelation and Genesis became the creation story for Western culture. The unified worldview of the Goddess was replaced by a dualism opposing man to woman, life to death, human to nature, good to evil. The judgment of God was to be feared, a moral order had been established in which the human encounter with the divine was no longer life enhancing.

In Christianity all symbols of female power were suppressed or perverted, some like the snake were transformed from the positive symbol of the Goddess's powers of regeneration into the negative image of corruption and evil. The Goddess, however, was not so easily vanquished and much of her iconography, her symbols, and images were to be absorbed into the cult of the Virgin.

Is the Virgin a Goddess?
The Problem of the Immaculate Womb

✾ CHAPTER 11

The sin of Eve was overcome by the Virgin Mary, the second Eve, in whose pure *womb* the only begotten Son of God, the Redeemer, was conceived (see fig. 102). God's original creation of the earth and all its creatures had been by divine fiat. When it came to his own offspring, God went about things in a more conventional way—although not totally so, as reportedly no sexual act was involved. According to the Gospel narrative, Mary was impregnated by a spirit later imaged in the form of a bird, but still the child was conceived and nurtured in a woman's body. In Renaissance art, the birth of the divine child takes place in a cave, watched over by an ox, a regrouping of our original symbolic triad of goddess, cave, and bovine. Even St. Augustine whose hostility to bodily experience was so influential in the development of later Christian doctrine noted that the Virgin represented the earth and that Jesus was earth born.[1]

The Immaculate Womb

The Christian miracle brings together two themes associated with the worship of the Goddess in the Hellenistic world. One is death and resurrection often associated with the story of the Egyptian divinities, the Goddess Isis, her consort Osiris, and their son Horus. The other is the Virgin Goddess.

The Mother Goddess Isis ruled in Egypt with her brother-husband Osiris whose generative powers enabled the land watered by the Nile to be fertile and productive. Her cult centers on the death and resurrection of her beloved spouse. The myth was recounted and celebrated every year at the

summer festival when the crop was planted. Osiris is killed and Isis, weeping bitterly for her lost love, wanders the world in search of his body. When she finds his corpse, she restores it to eternal life, performing the rites of mummification for the first time. Through her charm and magical powers, the Goddess then reanimates his corpse and conceives their son Horus. "Thus Horus . . . the mythological counterpart of the living pharaoh, succeeds his dead father and ensures the . . . continuity and order in Egyptian life."[2]

The death and resurrection of the consort/son, the Year God who must be sacrificed in order to assure the yearly cycle

102. Giovanni di Paolo, THE ANNUNCIATION, ca. 1445. Paint on wood. Detail. Italian.

According to the Christian "cycle of Redemption: the first Eve is thrown out of Eden and closes paradise to mankind, but the Virgin Mary, the Second Eve, accepts the words of the angel and conceives the redeemer who will restore humanity to the grace of God and reopen the gates of heaven."[13]

of renewal, was absorbed into the sacred story of Christianity. Women in the Near East had continued to mourn for Tammuz (Dumuzi) up to the time of Jesus. And "although there exist no Christian examples before the Middle Ages, the image of the Pietà may have been influenced by the image of Isis and the dead Osiris" across her knees.[3]

Many goddesses were called virgin but this did not mean that chastity was considered a virtue in the pagan world. Some, like "Venus, Ishtar, Astarte, and Anath, the love goddesses of the Near East and classical mythology, are entitled virgin despite their lovers, who die and rise again for them each year." For others, like Artemis and Athena, virginity symbolized autonomy and independence, freedom to take lovers or reject them.[4] Virgin meant one-in-herself, to be true to her own nature and instinct, not maiden inviolate.

> The virgin forest is not barren or unfertilized but rather a place that is especially fruitful and has multiplied because it has taken life into itself and transformed it, giving birth naturally and taking dead things back to be recycled. It is virgin because it is unexploited, not in man's control.[5]

In the Hellenistic world asceticism was viewed as a spiritual force. "Celebrants of sacred mysteries in the ancient world often prepared themselves [for the ritual] by abstaining from food and drink as well as from sexual intercourse in order to acquire the condition of strength and purity appropriate to serving the gods" but continence did not imply moral goodness or the immorality of sex. As Marina Warner points out in her full account of the myth and cult of the Virgin Mary, *Alone of All Her Sex,* "the interpretation of the virgin birth as the moral sanction of the goodness of sexual chastity was the . . . distinctive contribution of the Christian religion to the ancient mythological formula."[6] Christianity reversed the accepted meaning and imposed asceticism on the concept of virginity.

The critical misinterpretation of Mary's physical state was a translator's error; the Hebrew word *almah,* denoting the social and legal status of an unmarried girl, was read as the Greek *parthenos* that refers to a physiological and psychological fact.[7] Parthenogenesis is the conception of a child by a female without fertilization by male seed. Societies with parthenogenic goddesses usually have elevated ideas about the status of women and downplay the biological role of the man. In Christianity, on the other hand, the childbearing woman had inferior status, her womb identified with the lower carnal order.[8] Mary, alone of her sex because of her immaculate womb, was free of carnal knowledge.

Warner notes that the Christian idea of the virgin birth gives rise to an interesting puzzle. "There is no more matriarchal image than the Christian mother of God who bore a child without male assistance."[9] But Christianity, by insisting on the chastity of the Mother Goddess, utterly transformed the meaning of the matriarchal image even though to all outward appearances it remained unchanged.[10] The image of the Mother Goddess with her child represented her sexuality and procreative power, whereas that of the Virgin and child stood for her celibacy and the will of God. She was merely the agent through which he acted.

In Hellenistic dualistic thinking, body and spirit were separated; female sexuality identified with the body and feared. The Early Christian Fathers shared this view, afraid that reason would be overthrown by passion, and sought spiritual fulfillment through detachment from earthly concerns and pleasures:

> Eve, cursed to bear children rather than blessed with motherhood, was identified with nature, a form of low matter that drags man's soul down the spiritual ladder. In the faeces and urine—Augustine's phrase—of childbirth, the closeness of woman to all that is vile, lowly, corruptible, and material was epitomized; in the "curse" of menstruation, she lay closer to the beasts; the lure of her beauty was nothing but an aspect of the death brought about by her seduction of Adam in the garden.[11]

This novel, extraordinary concept linked sexuality with death rather than life. In their ascetic revolt the early Christians needed to exempt the Mother of Christ from tainted sexuality and to proclaim her virgin purity. Her perpetual, improbable virginity became the key to a new uncorrupted, untainted spirituality through which all humanity would be redeemed from the stain of sexuality. The symbol of this new religion was the *immaculate womb* of the Virgin that made redemption possible. Fascination with the symbolic importance of the Virgin's womb inspired artists to represent it as a wondrous thing apart, clearly no ordinary female organ (see fig. 103).

103. Upper Rhenish master, THE VIRGIN MARY, ca. 1400. Painting. Germany.

The Virgin's exposed womb surrounding the fully mature infant is imaged as a golden container irradiated like the sun.

In the fourth century when the church fathers put together the official version of the Christian Bible, they found little place for Mary. While scarcely mentioned in the Gospels, the "historical" accounts of the life and teaching of Jesus, Mary's narrative was told from the beginning in another body of popular literature, the Apocrypha. By the twelfth century the tales were gathered together by Jacobus de Varagine in *The Golden Legend*. These stories of her miracles circulated and were best-sellers of their time. Despite the suppression of Goddess worship in Christianity there was an ongoing need for her earth wisdom and healing powers. Agricultural peoples continued to celebrate the seasonal festivals invoking her fecundity. Women especially sought the comfort and solace of her presence in times of pregnancy and childbirth. Many of these collected vignettes show how the Virgin gradually took on much of the power of the Goddess.

Like the Ancient Goddesses

In the earliest recorded act of homage paid to Mary, she was honored by the customary offerings to the Goddess. Epiphanius, the late fourth-century patriarch of Constantinople, "noted with outrage" that some Arab women in the neighboring countryside were offering the Virgin cakes and wine at the shrine where their ancestors had worshiped the Goddess Ashtoreth. He does not describe the shape of the cakes but firmly protests Mary's elevation to divine status. "Others in their folly, wishing to exalt the Ever-Blessed Virgin, have put her in the place of God."[12]

In habits of devotion, especially those of women, there may have been no great discontinuity between the worship of the Virgin and that of the Goddess. The Church, aware of the conservative nature of worship, and of the comfort of familiar habits, converted existing temples and shrines, built on sites whose sacred character had long been established, adapted rituals, and integrated seasonal festivals into its own devotional calendar. Sometimes the transition was gradual as new forms of worship evolved to replace the old. In other cases only the names and images changed, new ways were grafted onto the old. Shrines and temples of the Goddess were rededicated to the Virgin.

The great Gothic cathedrals, for example, were all built on sites sacred to the Goddess, over holy springs and wells. Like the Goddess, the Virgin was often of a particular place. She belonged to the parish or village or town and took its name. Her local worshipers were very possessive of her cult image that sometimes even became a prize in the interminable wars of the Middle Ages. Elaborate altarpieces portraying the Virgin and Child were often set in a familiar local landscape and included the local saints with their miracles. During the Crusades loyal sons brought back relics of the Virgin from the Holy Land.

Early Christianity was born and evolved in a world in which the power of the Goddess was still to be reckoned with. Some goddesses had a widespread following throughout the Roman Empire. Four—Isis, Artemis, Cybele, and Demeter—influenced the cult of the Virgin.

The identification of Isis with Mary (see fig. 104) was part of the syncretic development of the Madonna cult, shaping

104. ISIS NURSING HORUS, ca. 2040–1700 B.C.E. Copper. Egyptian.

Paintings and sculptures in which Isis is represented suckling her son, the god Horus, were the model for Christian icons of the Madonna and Child.

"the veneration of . . . Mary in Christian circles."[13] Egyptian scriptures read that, "In the beginning there was Isis, Oldest of the Old." She was called "the Goddess from whom all becoming arose."[14] As the Creator, she gave birth to the sun "when he rose upon the earth for the first time."[15]

Her name means chair or throne in ancient hieroglyphics, represented as a simple high seat with a short straight back and small footstool. She is the throne, the holy seat of the Pharaoh. He "received his authority by taking his place on the throne. The throne, so to speak, makes the king. In other words, the throne is his mother. The ancient Egyptians understood this idea not symbolically, but literally."[16]

Isis is characterized by her wisdom, which the Egyptians associated with magic power. "According to the religious conceptions of antiquity, real wisdom consisted of insight into the mystery of life and death. This knowledge is creative; it evokes life from death."[17] Isis was called the "Giver of Life."[18]

As her significance grew and diversified, she became the beneficial Goddess of Nature.[19] Her cult spread throughout the Mediterranean and Western Europe. In *The Golden Ass* by Apuleius, a paean of praise to her many virtues written by a second-century Roman initiate, she claims to be the universal Goddess, subsuming the attributes of all others. She tells Apuleius, in response to his inquiry, that she is Nature, the Universal Mother, mistress of all the elements, the primordial child of time, sovereign of all things spiritual, queen of the dead and also queen of the immortals, the single manifestation of all gods and goddesses.[20] By the fourth century B.C.E. her cult took the form of a mystery religion. She taught her initiates the courage and wisdom she had learned through great personal suffering, "a doctrine of piety and a consolation to men and women who find themselves in the same misfortune."[21]

In Gaul Isis was known as Our Lady of Light. The closing of the last of her temples there may have marked the end of the official worship of the Goddess in the West, but her worship continued underground almost unabated in the heterodox cult of the Black Virgin centered in France. The phenomenon of the Black Virgin as the continuity of Goddess religion in Western Europe is only now beginning to be understood.[22]

Artemis also was a nature goddess, the mother of all creatures. She came from the hinterland of Asia Minor and once may have been worshiped in the form of a tree. Her columnar lower torso is a reminder that she had formerly been carved from a tree trunk (see color plate 36). Artemis's shrine at Ephesus was one of the seven wonders of the ancient world, and Ephesus is where the Virgin Mary was traditionally believed to have spent her last years as well as the place of her assumption in bodily form to heaven. The house where Mary is said to have lived is today a place of pilgrimage. At the Council of Ephesus in 431 the Virgin was proclaimed Theotokos, the Mother of God.

The Anatolian Mother Goddess Cybele was brought to Rome from Phrygia in Asia Minor in 205 B.C.E. at the command of the Cumean sybil in order to save the city from Hannibal's invading army. Etymologically, Cybele is the Goddess of Caverns. She personified the earth in its primitive and savage state and was worshiped on the tops of mountains in the form of a black meteorite. But the Romans, uncomfortable with the raw power of the aniconic image, added the body of a woman when they installed her in a temple on the Capitoline Hill, honoring her as "Magna Mater." In the heyday of the mystery cults she became one of the leading deities of Rome and was called Augusta, the Great One; Alma, the Nourishing One; Sanctissima, the Most Holy One. Roman emperors regarded her as the supreme deity of the Empire. The first emperor, Augustus Caesar, took his title from her epithet. The Emperor Julian, the Apostate, in a beautiful hymn addressed her as Virgin, "Wisdom, Providence, Creator of our Souls." "[She] was the supreme deity of Lyons, capital of the three Gauls, where a Black Virgin cult flourishes today."[23] An enormous temple to her was built in the Forum, which was later converted into Notre Dame of Fourière (the old Forum).

"The worship of Attis, the young male consort or son of the Goddess, became increasingly important in the worship of the Magna Mater from the first through the fourth century C.E.,"[24] but his ambiguous masculinity served to highlight the female power of the Mother.[25] "According to the myth, Attis castrated himself, and some of his initiated followers, the Galli, imitated his self-sacrifice and adopted transvestite practices suitable for those who voluntarily had become eunuchs devoted to the Great Mother."[26]

The similarities between the spring rites of Attis, the celebration of his death and miraculous rebirth symbolized by the evergreen tree, and the Easter cycle of Christian holidays are striking: even details appear similar, such as Jesus' entry into Jerusalem surrounded by palm bearers, and the wooden cross as the symbol of his suffering and his chief symbol as well. The intent of both religious groups—worshippers of Attis and those of Jesus—was of spiritual rebirth.[27]

We have seen how the agricultural peoples continued to venerate Demeter as the Goddess of Grain well into the twentieth century. Sometimes Mary simply replaced Demeter as the protector of the crop. In Italy the Madonna della Spica holds sheaves of wheat in her arms. At the Shrine of Our Lady of the Prairies in North Dakota, she is represented walking barefoot through the fields holding a sheaf of wheat in her arm as she blesses the harvest (see figs. 91 and 105).

Other transformations were more subtle, part of the tradition of miracles that conventionally manifested the Virgin's powers. The grain miracles of Mary and the female saints fulfilled the deeply rooted need of agricultural peoples who had always looked to the Goddess as the guardian of their crops.[28] By the late Middle Ages stories of the grain miracles became the subject of vernacular poems and dramas and were illustrated on baptismal fonts, wall paintings, and stained-glass windows. The miracle was set within "The Flight into Egypt." Mary on her donkey passed by a field of grain and miraculous growth occurred.[29]

Demeter and the Virgin were linked in yet another way through the mysterious birth of the divine child savior, the culminating event of the Eleusinian Mysteries. At Alexandria the divine child's birth was celebrated on the Winter Solstice in the temple dedicated to Kore and Demeter. When the days began to grow long once more, the divine light was believed to be born anew (see color plate 51).

According to Neumann, the Winter Solstice, when the Goddess gives birth to the sun, stands at the center of the matriarchal mysteries. In Egyptian myth Nut swallows the sun every evening and gives birth to the new day the following morning. The myth is illustrated in an imposing fresco painted on the ceiling of the Temple of Hathor at Dendara where Nut's body arches across the whole horizon. The plants that grow up from the earth below are nurtured by both the rays of the fiery sun ball issuing from her groin and the milk pouring from her breasts.

105. Anonymous, OUR LADY OF THE PRAIRIE, twentieth century. Stone. Powers, North Dakota.

The Winter Solstice is a day of cosmic portents. "The moon is full and occupies the highest point in its cycle, the sun is at its nadir, and the constellation of Virgo rises in the east."[30] Most pagan mysteries celebrated the birth of the Divine Child at the Winter Solstice. Christians also took this day for the birth of their savior god, Jesus Christ. Centuries later they were to select the first Sunday following the full moon after the Vernal Equinox as the anniversary of the resurrection of their god, naming it Easter after the Anglo Saxon Goddess Eostre, a northern form of Astarte.[31]

To understand how such syncretism came about we must put ourselves in the mind-set of those early Christians. As we saw in the case of the Hebrew Goddess, people do not easily abandon the deities to whom they are devoted. Even when powerful new ideas are abroad and notions of the sacred are changing, the old rituals and images continue to retain their power. The commonplace "a picture is worth a thousand words" is all too true. The compelling force of the divine is still present in the old familiar icons. This may be especially so for the Goddess because her embodied form was the essential symbol of her being.

In our reconstruction of the religion of the Goddess we have focused on the visual image as the carrier of meaning and on the continuity of her iconography. As we consider the issue at hand—Is the Virgin a goddess?—the answer is to be found in the visual evidence that expresses popular religious experience and belies church doctrine.

The Power of the Image

The power of the image contradicts theology. The Virgin Mary is the most venerated image in Western culture. Her continuing importance in popular piety would appear to be more than just the assigned official role as intercessor with her son. Her images carry the embodied presence of divine female power.

Images of the Virgin were sanctified by providing them with holy origins.[32] Early tradition claims that St. Luke was told the story of Christ's birth by the Virgin herself and that he made a portrait of her from life. The prolific Luke is still credited with hundreds of statues and paintings all over the Catholic world. This legend has a critical function in establishing an all important lifeline. If the images appear miraculously or were painted by St. Luke from life, they retain the power to bring the believer into the Virgin's presence and thus experience her immanence. This is not what Christianity teaches and is idolatry. But this is how the icons of the Virgin most often functioned. The sacred image is not an illusion of reality, but reality itself.

St. Luke's portrait of the Virgin was outside the warp of time. The fifteenth-century Flemish artist Rogier van der Weyden brings the Virgin and Child into the world of his own time (see fig. 106). The earliest known image of the Virgin from the late second century showing her nursing the Christ child is painted on the walls of a Roman catacomb, the underground burial chambers where the early Christians met while their worship was still illegal. The painting, badly defaced through the ravages of time, is inscribed with the prophetic words of Isaiah, "Behold a Virgin shall be with child and shall bring forth a Son and they shall call his name Emmanuel which being interpreted is, God with us."[33]

The Virgin nursing the Christ Child is the *dea nutrix*. Her capacity to nurture is, next to her immaculate womb, the most important of her attributes. The miracle of her milk is taken literally. Her pilgrimage route in Western Europe was known as "The Milky Way." In Renaissance paintings Mary is shown as the nursing mother of the saints. The famous Cistercian abbott, St. Bernard Clairvaux, tells how he was reciting the *Ave Maris Stella* before a statue of the Virgin, when she appeared before him and, pressing her breast, let three drops of milk fall onto his lips.[34]

In the earliest collection of the miracles of the Virgin, a story is told over and over again of a man who was "dying of a putrid disease of the mouth, . . . his nose and lips have been eaten away by ulcers. His fellow monks have given him up for dead. He reproaches the Madonna, reminding her with bitterness that he has faithfully invoked her daily in the words of the women of the Gospels, 'Blessed is the womb that bore thee and the paps thou hast sucked.' "[35]

The Virgin responds to his need. With much sweetness and much delight, from her sweet bosom, she drew forth her

106. Rogier van der Weyden, ST. LUKE PAINTING THE VIRGIN, 1400–1464. Oil and tempera on panel. 54 in. × 43 in.

The artist has placed the mother suckling her infant in an elegant contemporary interior which looks out on the cityscape of Bruges. St. Luke and Mary are dressed in the fashions of the day. In this way the artist brings the Virgin and Child into the world of his own time.

breast, that is so sweet, so soft, so beautiful and placed it in his mouth [and] gently touched him all about and sprinkled him with sweet milk.[36]

And the monk miraculously recovered.

The affirmation of the childbirth and nursing of Mary is but one of the many paradoxes of the Virgin's role in Christianity. The new faith was unable to ignore the potent symbols of the women's earthly body. The womb and the breast continue as the symbols and metaphors for the Virgin as they had been for the Goddess. Still, problems of her human body plagued theologians, leading them to the most arcane and convoluted reasoning in an effort to establish doctrine that would accommodate both popular piety and their view of the new divine order.

Despite their disdain for the human body, the Early Fathers and succeeding generations of theologians couldn't get away from Mary's physicality, her all too human body, especially her womb and her breasts. For instance, did she or didn't she menstruate? In attempting to justify her physical body while denying its human functioning, the simple maiden whose virtues of humility and modesty were the very attributes that made her God's choice as the Mother of his Son, became in turn The Throne of God, The Queen of Heaven. Free from the stain of original sin, she *alone of all humankind* did not die. In her final sleep she was taken into heaven in bodily form where she was crowned by God the Father and God the Son.

The iconographic forms that evolved to express these doctrines all refer to divine status. At the Council of Ephesus in 431 she was proclaimed *Theotokos,* the god-bearer (see fig. 107). Like Isis she became the throne that legitimized her son's rule. The Council was called to settle the controversy about the nature of Christ. Was he God or was he man? By officially declaring him the son of the woman Mary and God the father he was accepted as both human and divine.

For all the theological wrangling about the necessity of Christ's being born of woman to affirm his human nature, the icon that was created to carry this message is not that of a human mother's relationship to her child. Her bearing is regal, she is holding a prince; the *Theotokos* was an image that was easily converted to the Queen of Heaven simply by placing a crown on her head.

The image of Mary as Queen of Heaven reflects not only her own power but also reveals the ambitions of the Church that Mary often symbolizes. Mary in her regal aspect embodies an assertion of the Church's power. In sculpture and wall paintings, mosaic and stained glass, she is enthroned as Queen and Empress with the symbols of universal power.

Mary first appeared as Queen, *Maria Regina,* on the walls of the church of Santa Maria Antiqua, the oldest Christian church in the Roman Forum in the first half of the sixth century.

Seated in majesty on a throne, the Virgin Queen contains a multilayered message: she belongs to a classical tradition of personifying cities and institutions as goddesses, and as such, in

107. THEOTOKOS, THE GOD BEARER, twelfth century. Wood. French.

Sitting enthroned with sacredotal gravity, she seems neither human nor motherly, exalted above all joy and suffering. She is the seat of the All Powerful, the Throne of Wisdom. The child, grave, majestic, has his hand raised. "He is already the master who commands, who teaches."[14]

the heart of Rome, she embodies the new Rome which is the Church. . . . And because she is arrayed in all the pearl-laden, jewel-encrusted regalia of a contemporary secular monarch, she also proclaims, in a brilliantly condensed piece of visual propaganda, the concept that the Church is a theocracy of which the agent and representative is the pope, the ruler of Rome.[37]

The twelfth and thirteenth centuries were the zenith of the Virgin's power. By then the experience of the pilgrims and crusaders in Byzantium, where the Virgin had long been the object of a cult of faith and love, had been absorbed by Western Christendom. And the love of the Virgin with its character of personal intimacy had brought about a cultural revival. The great cathedrals were built in her honor along the pilgrimage routes in France and Germany. In the century between 1170 and 1270 more than eighty were built in France alone. Nearly every great church belonged to Our Lady, Notre Dame.

Surely the most splendid was Chartres where she reigned supreme as the Queen of Heaven (see color plate 49). The new cathedral was built to accommodate the ever-increasing crowds, as many as ten thousand at a time, who came begging for her favors. Scenes of her life and mystery are sculpted on the great stone portals, but her most glorious image is in the luminous stained-glass window where she sits on a cushioned throne with her son in her lap. On either side the sun and the moon affirm her majesty and the winged archangels, Michael and Gabriel, offer her the scepters of spiritual and temporal power.

The twelfth-century stained glass at Chartres is famed as the most beautiful ever created. The cathedral is the Heavenly Jerusalem illumined by radiant translucent light. Chartres, as we noted earlier, was an ancient Goddess site built over a sacred spring. The foundation of the cathedral rested on its possession of two precious relics of the Virgin: the tunic she was wearing when the Angel Gabriel came to her with his momentous announcement that she was to bear God's child, and the girdle she dropped as she was carried bodily up to heaven at her Assumption. Mary dropped her girdle purposefully to the still-doubting St. Thomas as proof of her ascent.

Like the portrait taken from life, the relics were numinous with the Virgin's power, a direct gift from God to humankind. Relics miraculously held off fire, famine, plague, and invading armies. Pregnant women prayed to the Virgin's girdle so that they would feel the new life "quicken" in their womb. And for centuries peasants and queens have prayed over the Virgin's tunic that the curse of infertility be lifted from them.

When Pope Pius IX proclaimed the Immaculate Conception of the Virgin Mary in 1854 and declared she was "the only human creature ever to have been preserved from the taint of original sin," he was not referring to the miraculous conception of her son but to her own suprahuman state. She alone of all human beings was free of the will to sin. Unlike Adam and Eve, who even when they were living in the Garden in a beatific state, could choose to disobey God and sin, she was incapable of doing so. Furthermore, "God had elected her his beloved daughter from the beginning of time and predestined her to be the mother of his only-begotten Son." Incapable of sinning, she had a completely unblemished life and was the most perfect being after Jesus. Mary was conceived in all purity in the mind of the Creator, a metaphysical virgin birth of an ideal by the power of the spirit.[38]

Mary, of course, had had natural parents and was conceived in the natural way. In the painting cycle that traditionally illustrated her life, her parents Joachim and Anna are shown embracing at the Golden Gate, a visual metaphor for Mary's conception. This scene embarrassed the church and was officially banned by Innocent XI in 1677.

Such an extraordinary condition demanded a cosmic vision and seventeenth-century Spanish artists created a highly emotional devotional image based on St. John's description of the Apocalypse[39] (see fig. 108). Like the woman in Revelation the virgin is clothed in the radience of the sun and is standing on the moon. The moon had been a symbol of the Goddess since Laussel. Along with its incorporation into Mary's iconography came many associations—the cycles of menstruation, the tides, and the seasons. The moon in its constancy symbolizes eternity, in its silver whiteness, purity.

"When Pope Pius XII appeared on the balcony of St. Peter's on November 1, 1950, to address a crowd of nearly a million strong, his announcement that 'Mary [had been] . . . taken up body and soul into the glory of heaven' was greeted with thunderous clapping, with tears of joy and resonant prayers."[40] His proclamation of the "Dogma of Assumption" as an article of faith only made official a long-standing belief.

No tomb or bodily remains of the Virgin have ever been found. The actual place of her death has not been established. Many believed it was Jerusalem, others Ephesus. The Venetian Renaissance painter Titian based his great masterpiece on a vision of a twelfth-century German nun, Elizabeth of Schnonau (see fig 109). "Her flight upwards on ribbons of cirrus clouds among multitudes of caroling angels . . . signifies her passage out of time into eternity."[41]

The Assumption dogma depended on the Christian equivalence of sin with death. The Virgin's purity freed her from the dissolution of the grave. Because Adam and Eve had learned about sexuality when they disobeyed God and ate from the Tree of Knowledge of Good and Evil, all humans were doomed to return to dust at death. Mary alone is free of the sin of sexuality because of her suprahuman state. The jubilant liturgy of the Feast of the Assumption celebrated on August 15 compares Mary's womb that bore the New Law to that of the Ark of the Old Covenant, the Law of the Hebrews (see fig. 110).

> Made of "incomparable timber," inlaid with gold, the Ark was led by David into Jerusalem, where the priests sang and danced and clashed cymbals and played on harps and lyres to greet its coming, just as, the reading implies, Mary's uncorrupted body is conducted into heaven among a throng of exulting angels.[42]

The New Law removes the sting of death that the Christians feared so much. In death the body slowly dissolves into oblivion. The horror of the grave is assuaged by the promise of eternal life. Mary's bodily assumption is the promise to the virtuous. On the Day of Judgment they will be cleansed of sin, and they too will rise bodily to heaven.

The sequel to the Assumption is *The Coronation of the Virgin* in which Mary is crowned Queen of Heaven and united with the totality of the godhead. During the Counter Reformation of the seventeenth century, the Coronation of the Virgin was the theme for magnificent altarpieces like that of Velasquez who painted God the Father and God the Son jointly placing the crowns on the head of a self-possessed Mary, looking very much like the young Queen Victoria, who is seated regally on a cloud bank.

Official Christianity would, of course, protest otherwise even though the Catholic church came dangerously close to

108. Diego Velasquez, THE IMMACULATE CONCEPTION, seventeenth century. Oil on canvas. Spanish.

Mary is a young girl, neither child nor woman, as "she existed in the mind of God 'before the beginning.' "[15] Her eyes are demurely downcast, her hands come together at her breast in prayerful submission to her destiny. Like the woman in St. John's Revelation she is clothed in the radiance of the sun and is standing on the moon. Twelve stars circle her head.

declaring Mary Co-Redemtrix with Christ at Vatican II.[43] For Roman Catholics the nineteenth and first half of the twentieth centuries were the Age of Mary, but the more recent position of the Vatican has been to downplay Mariolatry. Her cult, however, seems in the ascendancy as attendance at her pilgrimage centers continues to rise.

The power of the Goddess was not denied in Christianity; she was given a new name. However, in the translation of pagan ways to Christian, the unified vision that included the sacredness of human sexuality was shattered. In the Goddess culture the life cycle, the seasonal cycle, and even the cosmic movement of the heavens were interwoven into a dense ritual fabric that grounded human existence in a rhythm of birth,

109. Titian, THE ASSUMPTION OF THE VIRGIN, 1518. Oil on canvas. Italian.

"The apostles on earth reach out in ecstasy toward the barefoot madonna, who rises, borne upwards by angels and cherubim, into the golden corona of heaven where God awaits her."[16] The Virgin's expression is transfigured as she gazes upward. A bearded Father God looks down kindly as he spreads out his cloak in welcome. The whole of the painting is suffused in a rosy golden light.

death, and regeneration. Ritual action sprang from the human necessity for food, for nurture, for the maintenance of the food supply, for procreativity and human relationships, not from a divine reality whose highest values were envisioned as beyond and outside of human life.

So the perfect Virgin is a flawed and far from perfect model for her sex. Her asexuality and virgin motherhood make it impossible for any woman to be virtuous, powerful, and sexual at one and the same time. In Christianity the power of the womb/vulva has been co-opted to serve the interests of a misogynist theology and no longer symbolizes the embodied life force of the Goddess.

Bolivian-born sculptor Marisol playfully comments on the problem of Mary as a model for women in a sculpture of the Holy Family (see color plate 50). The Virgin is splendidly costumed, her see-through womb a bejeweled, enameled wonder. The Christ child, haloed with the rays of the sun, rests serenely in his lucite cradle. By Mary's side is Joseph who, alas, has no body below his head and shoulders. As Marisol's witty art illustrates, the Christian miracle denies the full expression of our sexuality that is our birthright as women and men.

Catholic dogma proclaims the Virgin unique of all human beings, Catholic piety venerates her even above God, Western art images her as a goddess, but all this glory cannot undo the misogyny of Christian theology in which human sexuality and women's bodies are considered evil.

The Virgin and the Whore:
The Problem of the Immaculate Womb

This paradox is crystallized in the contrasting roles of the Virgin Mary and Mary Magdalene, exemplars of female piety in Christianity and the two most widely represented female figures in Christian iconography. Stereotypical symbols of the virgin and the whore, the virtuous chaste Mary and the penitent sinner Magdalene, they provide models for human behavior that severely inhibit women from experiencing themselves as fully human. Such a polarized view of women presents a double-bind for both sexes. The committed Christian is not the only victim; all in Western culture are compromised by this separation of body and spirit. Traditionally the virtuous wife could not be sexual; the sexual woman could not be virtuous. Sex outside of marriage is a mortal sin, within marriage an ambiguous blessing. In addition there is a double standard by which women are held morally accountable for

110. Vierge Ouvrante, thirteenth century; a. closed; b. open.

Nowhere is the power of the Virgin's womb more graphically symbolized than in the *Vierge Ouvrante,* a small votive sculpture that illustrates a popular but heterodox view that without her, redemption would not have taken place. When the sculpture is closed we see a fashionable Virgin offering a small globe or fruit to her child; when open we find the trinity—Father, Son, and Holy Ghost—contained within her body.

a.

b.

their sexual activity. Women's sexuality is viewed as the cause of man's continuing temptation. That women should be punished and suffer for the sin of sexuality has been considered God-given justice.

During the Renaissance, the Virgin was particularly venerated for her physical beauty. She is the central figure in magnificent altarpieces that are among the great masterpieces of Western art. In contrast, the sculptor Donatello, celebrated for his recovery of the classic perfection of the human form, made a statue of Mary Magdalene for the Baptistry in Florence, a haunting vision of a once beautiful woman ravaged by years of physical hardship and sorrow, with gaunt cheeks, sunken eyes, and thin lips set in resignation (see fig. 111). Distended veins disfigure her bony legs and feet. She is clothed only in her long golden hair full of light and life, making her body seem even more haggard by contrast. "Horrifying in its extreme emaciation, but even more so because of the spiritual desolation it radiates."[44]

The wooden sculpture still stands on view in a prominent public place. Why would a great artist at the height of his creative development turn his back on the aesthetic values that were his glory? Fortunately, the documents for the commission of the Magdalene statue survive.[45]

Midfifteenth-century Florence was devastated by the plague raging throughout Europe, bringing great suffering and in some places killing two out of every three people. The Bishop of Florence, Antoninus, a self-righteous zealot later canonized as St. Antoine, minced no words in seeking just cause and punishment. Confessor to the women of the Medici family, his letters to them baldly state his view. His wealthy penitents, like Mary Magdalene and all women, bear the guilt of female sexuality. In atonement they are to speak to no men except their husbands and their priest and leave home only to go to church.

Donatello himself had fled to the hills surrounding Florence. When he returned to his city, overwhelmed by the horror of the dead and dying all around him—the smell of death must have been everywhere—he too listened to the pious preachings of the Bishop and sought salvation in penance for his sins. At Antoninus's behest, he immortalized the penitent Magdalene who according to apocryphal literature had retreated

111. Donatello, MARY MAGDALENE, ca. 1454–55. Polychromed and gilded wood. 54 in. Baptistry of S. Giovanni, Florence.

112. Hans Baldung, THE WITCHES' SABBATH, 1510. Woodcut. German.

Brazen nakedness was another sign of witches' evil nature. Once the mark of the sacred, a nude woman's body now represented depravity. And when the invention of the printing press in the late fifteenth century revolutionized the impact of the visual arts on the masses, prints like Baldung's *The Witches' Sabbath* could be sold for pennies and had wide circulation. The bizarre images conjured up by these early printmakers have been lasting and continue to form our imaginations.

111

112

to the Egyptian desert to live the rest of her life in solitary exile following the death of Jesus.

Antoninus was a fanatic but his ideas about women were those of his age. Men's fear of their own attraction to women's earthiness and carnality continued to be projected onto the opposite sex. At no time was this paranoia more patent, more horrible than in the witch burnings that reached their peak in the sixteenth and seventeenth centuries.

The fifteenth century was a critical period in human history, of great political and religious upheaval, a time when the modern world was being birthed. The witch-hunts were an expression both of the weakening of traditional restraints and an increase in new pressures. The reasons for this mass hysteria were complex. Neo-pagan leader Starhawk links the persecution of witches to three interwoven processes:

> the expropriation of land and natural resources; the expropriation of knowledge; and the war against the consciousness of immanence, which was embodied in women, sexuality and magic. . . . Western culture underwent crucial changes that produced the particular brand of estrangement that characterizes the modern world.[46]

Witches were accused of worshiping the devil and of having actual social and sexual intercourse with him. The devil was imaged as none other than the Horned God, consort of the Goddess in Celtic religion, perverted and turned into Anti-Christ. According to Christian dogma he was evil incarnate. Witches' alleged fantastic feats like night flights on broomsticks and turning people into animals contradict ordinary grasp of reality.[47] "If crops failed, horses ran away, cattle sickened, wagons broke, women miscarried, or butter wouldn't come in the churn, a witch [could always be] blame[d]"[48] (see fig. 112).

Witch-hunts, sporadic throughout the late Middle Ages, became widespread in the late fifteenth century when Pope Innocent VII declared witchcraft a heresy and extended the power of the Inquisition to its practitioners. With the publication of the *Malleus Malificarum,* the *Hammer of Witches,* by Dominicans Kramer and Sprenger in 1486, the witch-hunters had a handbook that guided them for the next two and a half centuries. It was open season on all aberrant people, some men but mostly women of the peasant working class, the lower strata of society—midwives, herbalists, the old wise women, widows, and spinsters, women unprotected by a man.

> Estimates of the actual number of Witches executed range from 100,000 to 9,000,000. The higher estimates include many who were not officially executed but died in prison. The true number is difficult to estimate, and this fact is less important than an understanding of the climate of terror that was unleashed. Anyone—especially any woman—could be accused of being a Witch. . . . Once accused, the suspected Witch was subjected to torture. . . . Whether the accused yielded to intolerable pain and named others or confessed to whatever her

torturers suggested; whether she was mercifully strangled at the stake before burning, or burned alive, or hung, or banished, or whether she committed suicide, accusation meant ruin.[49]

When we look back across the historical time of patriarchy from the burning of the witches to the slaying of Tiamat, the Goddess Mother in the Mesopotamian creation myth, there seems almost to be some terrible inevitability, a relentless desire to crush the female essence, human and divine. The question of why is among the most puzzling of our time.[50]

Black Virgins, a Popular Heresy

The phenomenon of the Black Virgin confronts us with the survival of a popular heresy that has been a source of great embarrassment to the Church. Her origins are shrouded in mystery and the extent of her cult and influence has only begun to be known. Jungian Ean Begg has gathered together the extant evidence in his survey, *The Cult of the Black Virgin* (1985), that includes a comprehensive gazeteer of more than five hundred images mostly from Western Europe but also from Latin America. There are 302 Black Virgins in France alone (see fig. 115).

The Church has tried to explain away the blackness of these images as accidental, the result of candle smoke or exposure to the elements. But this does not make sense. If the "faces and hands of the Virgin and Child have been blackened by the elements, why has their polychromed clothing not been similarly discolored . . . [and] why has a similar process not occurred in the case of other venerated images?"[51]

Perhaps the Virgin is black because she is the Earth Goddess and the blackest earth is the richest, the most fertile. Perhaps she is black because, like the Hindu Kali, she represents the dark, the night, and death, all those other mysteries that Western culture has repressed through fear of women, of female sexuality, and of dying.

The cult of the Black Virgin marks the resurgence of the female personification of cosmic power and the female principal in a misogynous religious culture. The worship of the Black Virgin is a complex, multifaceted phenomenon that began in the early Middle Ages but has persisted into the present despite opposition, often militant, by the established Church.

Two Black Virgins, Guadalupe of Mexico and Our Lady of Czestochowa in Poland, are national symbols of increasing importance, enshrining "the major hopes and aspirations of the entire society."[52]

> During the Mexican War of Independence against Spain, her image preceded the insurgents into battle. . . . Today her image adorns house fronts and interiors, churches and home altars, bull rings and gambling dens, taxis and buses, restaurants and houses of ill repute. She is celebrated in popular song and verse. Her shrine at Tepeyac, immediately north of Mexico City, is visited each year by hundreds of thousands of pilgrims, ranging from the inhabitants of far-off Indian villages to members of socialist trade union locals.[53]

According to Guadalupe's myth of origin, the Virgin Mary appeared to Juan Diego, a humble Indian convert, and spoke to him in his native language, Nahuatl. She commanded him to seek out the Archbishop of Mexico, to inform him of her desire to see a church built in her honor on Tepeyac Hill. The archbishop was willing to see him but demanded some proof of the vision's authenticity. To convince the skeptical bishop, the Virgin wrought a miracle, making roses bloom in the arid desert. She told Diego to gather the flowers into his cloak and present the cloak to the archbishop. When he unfolded the cloak, the image of the Virgin was miraculously stamped upon it (see fig. 113).

The shrine, rebuilt several times in centuries to follow in order to accommodate ever increasing crowds of devotees, is today a basilica, the third highest kind of church in Western Christendom. Above the central altar hangs Juan Diego's cloak with the miraculous image.

The shrine at Guadalupe was not the first religious structure built on Tepeyac. In pre-Hispanic times there was a temple to the Earth Goddess Tonantzin, which means Our Mother, who, like Guadalupe, was associated with the moon and was the center of a pilgrimage cult. Some Mexican Indians to this day continue to refer to the Virgin by her Mexican name. The Virgin appeared at the site of Tonantzin's shrine only ten years after the Spanish Conquest, which had signified not only military defeat but the defeat of the old gods and the decline

113. THE VIRGIN OF GUADALUPE, twentieth century. Votive card. Mexico.

The popular devotional image shows the Virgin as she appeared to Juan Diego, a dark-skinned young woman, in the traditional iconography of the Immaculate Conception. The diminutive figure of Juan Diego is below, his arms raised as he carries his folded cloak to the bishop.

of the old ritual.[54] The myth of the apparition served as symbolic testimony to the Indians that their Goddess still lived.

Poland is another country whose people, oppressed by centuries of foreign occupation, have rallied under the patronage of the Black Madonna, Our Lady of Czestochowa, who has been venerated as the "Queen of Poland" since 1656, and is the symbol of national survival and religious liberty (see fig. 114).

The revolutionary labor movement of Poland, Solidarity, is represented by the Virgin of Czestochowa, outlawed during most of the 1980s. Members, who were unable to wear insig-

114. Pope John Paul II, seated beneath a painting of Our Lady of Czestochowa. 1979. Krakow, Poland.

Probably the wooden icon of the Virgin is of ninth century Byzantine origin with thirteenth century Italian overpaintings. It was brought to Czestochowa in 1382. A Polish prince built a shrine for her on a mountain above the city, Jasna Gora, the Hill of Light. The three slashes on her right cheek were desecrations made by Husserite robbers after which time veneration for the icon greatly increased.

nia identifying themselves as part of the movement for fear of governmental reprisal, wore buttons with the icon of the Virgin. When Solidarity leader Lech Walesa received the Nobel Peace Prize, he took the award medal to her shrine for safe-keeping. Czestochowa is the personal icon of Pope John Paul II who says he lays his devotion at her feet.

The unraveling of the Black Virgin's mysteries leads us to the underside of Christianity. Two streams of veneration of the Black Virgin can be identified. Both are viewed as heresy by the established church: One is a continuation of the earth- and women-centered Goddess religion; the other is the carrier of the esoteric teachings and spiritual practices of the Helle-nistic period.[55]

This diverse group includes the Gnostics, the Cathars, the Knights Templar, the Cult of the Holy Grail, and the Church of Mary Magdalene. Begg calls their preachings "whore wis-dom," meaning illegitimate in the eyes of the Church. The Gnostics are dualistic, believing that spirit and matter are separate and that spiritual liberation comes from knowledge. The Cathars, a Gnostic sect allied with the Troubadours and their Courts of Love, were active in the south of France dur-ing the thirteenth century. They may have practiced ritual sex. Women were admitted to their priesthood and their beliefs were so threatening that the Papacy launched a successful Crusade against them. The Templars, a Crusading Order, learned about the mystery of the female divine in the East and on their return actively promoted the cult of the Virgin. They were accused by the Inquisition of denying the validity of the sacraments as well as other unspeakable heresies like sodomy and were outlawed at the Council of Vienna in 1318.

The cult of Mary Magdalene, which worships the Black Virgin, absorbed many of the esoteric teachings. According to the Gnostic Gospels, early Christian material full of female motifs that was excluded from the official canon, Mary Mag-dalene was one of the original disciples of Jesus. In the Gospel of Mary it is hinted that they were lovers. Magdalene's cult is based on the legendary account of her settling in the area of Marseille after Jesus' death where it was believed that she had a child by Jesus. The cult of Mary Magdalene is linked to the Black Virgin because both continued to hold the female prin-ciple sacred and divine.

The worship of the Black Virgin in France goes back to the Merovingian dynasty whose kings reputedly were her patrons. Images of the Black Virgin were said to have been miraculously discovered in unfrequented spots like woods and caves where the pagan peasantry had hidden them from the zealous Christian missionaries. When the Merovingians were converted to Christianity, the icons were recovered and the clergy blessed them under Christian names, often building shrines for them just where they were found. "According to the local legends, the images refused to stay put in the parish church"[56] and disappeared, perhaps going back to their hiding places to be worshiped by the underground pagan population.

The legendary origins of these images were often fabulous. The Black Virgin of Bologne-sur-Mer (France) arrived in the seventh century in a "mysterious boat . . . without sails or crew, containing nothing but a copy of the Gospels in Syriac and a statue of the Virgin standing upright like Isis and surrounded by an extraordinary light."[57] Our Lady of Monserrat reportedly was carved by St. Luke and brought from Jerusalem to Spain by St. Peter.[58] Some say that the Black Virgin of Dijon, with pendulous breasts and a pregnant belly, was formerly a Gallo-Roman sculpture of Cybele, but Begg claims she looks more like a Teutonic witch, the cruel fantasies of the popular woodblock prints (see fig. 112) made at the height of the witch burnings in the sixteenth century.[59]

The Black Virgin of Notre Dame du Puy is of historical interest because Joan of Arc's mother prayed to her for her daughter's deliverance from the English (see fig. 115). The mother is said to have walked for a week from her farm to the Virgin's shrine.

Begg reports that many Black Virgins arrived from Byzantium in the seventh and eighth centuries at the time of the iconoclastic crisis that wracked Eastern Christendom during a period of political and theological controversy over the worship of images. The zealous iconoclasts destroyed much superb religious art. Some smaller, portable icons found their way to the West. Many of the surviving Black Virgins do appear to be Byzantine in style, although the icons themselves were paintings, not sculptures. Later the Crusaders brought back other Byzantine Virgins from the East whose style can be dated from the modes of representation prevailing from the

twelfth and thirteenth centuries where they played an important role in humanizing the image of the Virgin in Western art. The portrait of the Virgin tenderly embracing her infant son is Byzantine in origin, a major shift from the formal Theotokos in which an "aged" child sits erect in his Mother's lap, which serves as his throne. The original icons have often disappeared, destroyed by the Islamic Saracens, Protestant Huguenots, Rationalists of the Enlightenment, and the French Revolutionaries of 1789. Today they fall victim to collectors and the inflated art market.

The Black Virgins possess great power, the mana of the old goddess of life, death, and rebirth. Mana is an extraphysical power immanent in and emanating from nature, viewed as the embodiment of all elemental forces that produce and maintain the order of the universe. This is why they were so threatening to the Church.

Conclusion

If we look at what Christianity has labeled heresy, we find a different attitude toward the power of women and female sexuality. Heresy is often the inner truth of those whose way is other than that of the dominant view, like the followers of the cult of Mary Magdalene. There are two legendary versions of Magdalene's life after the death of Jesus. The one, accepted by mainstream Christianity, was Donatello's inspiration (see fig. 111); the other, telling of her journey by boat to the south of France where she had a child by Jesus, became the basis of a heretical cult. The cult of Mary Magdalene combines much of the wisdom of the old religions with the new consciousness of the power of the female expressed in courtly love, an idea that emerged in the twelfth century when Crusaders returned from the East where they had been exposed to new attitudes toward women.

The orthodox Christian notion of female sexuality is life denying, the heretical life affirming. These opposing views of the human condition, a perennial theme in myth and art, are treated in two charming sculptural reliefs, one in a French cathedral, the other once part of an early Indian monument. Both show an ascetic looking at a naked woman, but the difference in their fates in the Western and Eastern narrative is illuminating (see figs. 116, 117).

The cathedral capital shows the young man still staring open-eyed at his temptress while being abruptly pulled away by the Devil (see fig. 116).

> The artist did not know how to endow his heroine with beauty, yet has given her a sort of sinuous grace. She turns to cast an eye in the direction of her victim, letting a ribbon float behind her. But at that very moment the devil appears and grips the young man by the hair; he is now and henceforth his master. And it can be seen that the woman is his accomplice; for her hair, bristling like Satan's, makes known the daughter of hell.[60]

"For the monk" writes art historian Emile Male, "woman is almost as powerful as the devil. She is his instrument and he makes use of her to ruin saints."[61] The renowned twelfth-century cleric St. Bernard of Clairvaux warned his monks that

116

117

to "live with a woman without incurring danger is more difficult than to resuscitate the dead."[62] The great abbots and reformers of the monastic orders were afraid of women and did not want the monk to be exposed to her temptation, all too sure that he would succumb. Great precautions were taken to protect the vulnerable monks:

> The rules of Cluny did not permit a woman, for any reason whatsoever, to cross the bounds of a monastery. The rules of Cîteaux are still more severe; for a woman might not even appear there at the gate of the monastery: the brother serving as porter was instructed to refuse such a woman alms. So that in self-defense the Cistercian even goes so far as to fail in charity. If a woman comes into the church, the service is to be suspended, the abbot deposed, and the brothers sentenced to fast on bread and water.[63]

In a culture like India's that, however patriarchal, still views female sexuality as auspicious, the fate of the ascetic was very different. Indian art shows the survival of popular religious beliefs, symbols, and iconography belonging to a rich common heritage[64] that goes back to the culture of the Great Goddess. We cannot yet trace the links but the visual evidence is very convincing. Although in India the original Goddess culture was later superseded on a philosophical level by a spiritual revolution that shifted the emphasis from the outer world to self-introspection and final release, it must be remembered that "all these higher thoughts were confined to seekers of truth whose numbers must have been limited."[65] The ultimate good in Indian civilization is not release from this life but right conduct, *dharma,* which holds people together.

The well-known myth of Rishyasringa related in the Indian epics emphasizes the association of female sexuality with the life-enhancing rains. Rishi's mother, a deer, deserted her child at birth. He was raised by his father, a forest-dwelling sage, who understandably warned his son against women, keeping him apart from the society of humans. When a terrible drought ravaged a nearby kingdom, the king was told by his wise men that only Rishi's presence could save the day and bring the life-giving rains. The problem was how to lure the young ascetic out of the forest. The king sent a clever courtesan to seduce him. Rishi came upon the woman bathing in the nude in a forest pond. After luring him with tasty food and drink,

116. WOMAN, THE DEVIL'S DOOR (MULIER JANUA DIABOLI), twelfth century. Stone. Cathedral of Autun, Saône-et-Loire, France. Satan reclaims the monk tempted by the sight of nude women.

117. RISHYASRINGA, second century. Sandstone. India. The Indian ascetic gazes with pleasure and awe at the nude courtesan bathing in the forest.

new clothes and flowers, and with tender caresses, she then left under some pretext. Poor Rishi, innocent as he was in the ways of the world, went home and told his father that he had seen a wondrous creature with two horns on its chest. The father warned him that such a creature was especially dangerous, but it was too late. Rishi, passion aroused, followed the courtesan back to the king's palace and as the wise men had predicted, the rains poured down. The king gave him his daughter in marriage and the couple lived happily ever after. A fairy tale, perhaps, but one that expresses a cultural reality.

The artist has captured that moment of pure delight when Rishi sees a woman for the first time (see fig. 117). These two contrasting images epitomize the burden of Christian attitudes imposed on Western culture. We've lost the wonder and the mystery as well as the life-enhancing possibilities of sexuality.

Mary's unique status as exemplar for all her sex has penetrated Western culture and resulted in a deeply entrenched ambivalence toward women that has contributed to some of the more serious social problems of our time: the battle between the sexes and endemic violence against women. "The condition of Christian virtue as sexual abstinence is the crux of the Mary-myth."[66]

Roland Barthes, French semiologist and novelist, tells us that we lose the memory that myths were made up by human beings.[67] "The symbol [of the Virgin] is so powerful it has dynamic and irrepressible life of its own." Not just the Catholic Church believes that Mary existed from all time. Jungian psychology has made her into an archetype, a psychological truth that "determines that all men want a virgin mother, at least in symbolic form." As Barthes again comments so succinctly, the very principle of the myth is to transform history into nature.[68]

Christianity "developed an iconography that both incorporated and redefined visual elements borrowed from the Mediterranean and Near Eastern fertility religions where it grew up, though in deep antagonism to [their original meaning]."[69] The earliest surviving image of the Virgin painted on the walls of a Roman catacomb, the underground chambers where the early Christians buried their dead, shows her nursing the Christ Child, a motif of the mother with the suckling babe adopted from the Isis and Horus imagery of Egypt. But the spiritual charge is reversed, the mother becoming asexual, the son destined to be a celibate. From icons of earthly fertility, these figures became icons of spiritual transcendence.

Today, in the late twentieth century, the Goddess is re-emerging. New myths, new symbols, and new images are once again affirming the sacredness of the female body and sexuality, and indeed connecting the oppression of women to the fate of the earth. In Part Three we will continue our journey to the Goddess.

The Re-Emergence of the Goddess:

✿ PART THREE

Charles Sherman, THE NINE MUSES,
1988. Acrylic on canvas. 30 in. × 144 in.

A Symbol for Our Time

The Matriarchal Theory of Human Origins

The first signs of the Goddess's return were in the nineteenth-century Romantic Movement with its renewed appreciation of nature and emphasis on the imagination and emotions. The so-called primitive, the noble savage, was exalted by European social philosophers who were looking for universal themes of human experience to explain our mist-shrouded origins. They saw society as evolutionary from a primitive beginning to more developed civilizations, at stages of human history through which all peoples passed.

One of the most influential of the social philosophers, the Swiss scholar Johann Jakob Bachofen, maintained in *Myth, Religion and Mother Right* that the first period of human history was matriarchal and that patriarchy developed later. The keystone of his theory was "mother right," the fundamental theme of ancient myths and symbols. Linking Goddess worship with a more general theory of social development, he asserted that the early culture was characterized by widespread promiscuity reflected in the worship of female deities. Bachofen was a product of his own time, limited in his view by biased Christian attitudes toward female sexuality. He believed that the human struggle, which he saw as a natural progression to patriarchy, was to be free of the fetters of physicality that bound men and women to the earth in a relentless cycle of birth and death.

Although Bachofen's general theory is now universally discredited, his contemporary social theorists, Karl Marx and Friedrich Engels, praised it. Even Sigmund Freud thought that Goddess worship evolved out of an earlier stage of matriarchy. Bachofen's follower, British anthropologist and historian of religion James Frazer, set himself to complete his mentor's task of assembling the evidence for matriarchy among world cultures. The final edition of *The Golden Bough* (1922) ran to twelve volumes. Frazer's "stirring picture of the long evolutionary struggle of humanity toward self-understanding"[1] has penetrated popular imagination even though scholars no longer accept his comparative methodology or sweeping generalizations. Frazer's view was that by comparing the behavior of modern primitives, European peasants, and underdeveloped tribal cultures with that of historical societies in the ancient world, you could extract laws of primitive mental functioning. His fame in part rests on his having finally stripped the veil of illusion from the "real" nature of Christianity, seeing it as only one among many "pagan" rites. Religion, he believed, was the result of an imperfect understanding of the universe that modern scientific objectivity would dispel. The triumph of Darwinism provided another model for the human condition based on the premise of evolution. A "uniform progression from magic through religion to positive science seemed a plausible description of the pathway toward understanding that humanity had in fact taken."[2]

Meanwhile proponents of the matriarchal theory of origins continued to battle with those who viewed male ascendance as the natural order of things. Robert Briffault in *The Mothers* (1927) argued that matriarchy in primitive society was not simply patriarchy with a different sex in authority. His matriarchal society is

one in which female creative power is pervasive, and women have organic authority, rather than one in which the woman establishes and maintains domination and control over the man, as the man over woman in patriarchy. There would be . . . a kind of free consent to the authority of woman in a matriarchal society, because of her involvement with the essential practical and magical activity of that society.[3]

Briffault was the first to recognize what archaeologists like Mellaart and Gimbutas increasingly demonstrate: that women were the innovators of culture.

Today evolutionary social theory is no longer in vogue, and the armchair anthropology of Frazer has been out of style since the 1920s when trained anthropologists went directly into the field; but both Bachofen and Frazer raised important issues germane to our search for the meaning of the Goddess. Bachofen's view of the human quest for release from the material fetters of the Earth Mother, of transcendence as a higher order than immanence, continues to be an issue for many, raised as they were on Christian notions of contempt for the body and nature. Philosopher Ken Wilbur would split the Goddess into earthly and cosmic manifestations, cosmic being higher. Bachofen's argument that the progress from the maternal to the paternal conception of humans was the most important turning point in the history of the relations between the sexes still echoes in anthropology and among feminists searching for the origins of patriarchy.

To our late twentieth-century mind, disenchanted with both the social dynamics of monotheistic religion and the gospel of science, and starved for ritual that reifies our connection to the sacred source of our being, Frazer's exploration was on the right track. It is his methodology that is suspect; his facts gleaned from secondhand sources were often wrong and his conclusions the product of scientific materialism.

Anthropologists have now penetrated most of the world's cultures, however inaccessible and obscure. Their copious ethnography of "single, manageable cultural situations through direct fieldwork" makes it possible to come to some valid generalizations about the nature of the divine. Our growing awareness of the healing power of ritual magic and of the human necessity for personal connection to sacred sites suggests that we have much to learn from primal peoples. Today we are enriched by an explosion of knowledge about other people's symbols and ritual. The camera has brought the whole world into our living rooms.

The Archetype of the Great Mother

Anthropological studies and travel literature, as well as first-hand travel itself, are paths to the direct experience of the Goddess in our time. Another is through the psyche. The discovery of depth psychology, the study of the unconscious, reveals archetypal patterns of behavior that encode the themes of the ancient myths within our very being. While Freud, no friend to the

Goddess, thought devotion to female deities represented an infantile desire to be reunited with the mother, his colleague C. G. Jung discovered that the Goddess was a potent force in the unconscious.

Jung's theory of the feminine principle as a universal archetype, a primordial, instinctual pattern of behavior deeply imprinted on the human psyche, brought the Goddess once more into popular imagination. Jung based his psychology on religious symbolism from the prehistoric to contemporary. He held that an archetype is not "an inherited idea, but an inherited mode of psychic functioning, corresponding to that inborn *way* according to which the chick emerges from the egg; the bird builds its nest; . . . and eels find their way to the Bermudas."[4]

This is the biological aspect of the archetype, but when we look at it from the inside, from the realm of the subjective psyche, the archetype is of fundamental importance. Although not literal, these symbolic representations are real and powerful. Although not persons, these personalities, from very deep levels within, can elicit responses not possible through mere abstract thought, taking hold of the individual in a startling way and creating a condition of "being deeply moved." Jung believed that all religions rest upon archetypal foundations and, to the extent that we are able to explore them, we succeed in gaining at least a superficial glance behind the scenes of world history, and can lift a little the veil of mystery which hides the meaning of metaphysical ideas.[5]

The archetype is metaphysical because it transcends consciousness. This insight led Jung to the conclusion that one part of the psyche may be explained through recent events, but that another part reaches back to the deepest layers of human history, which is why religious myths and symbols have so much to tell us. Jungian feminists like Jean Shinoda Bolen and Christine Downing use the familiar mythology of Greek and Roman goddesses in their analysis of women's psychological development. For modern women identification with the archetypal Goddess figures provides insight into inner conflicts and can be healing.

From the Jungian perspective, the Goddess is an archetypal image at work within the human psyche that finds outward expression in the ritual, mythology, and art of early humans as well as in the dreams, fantasies, and creative works of our own time. Jungian analyst Edward Whitmont informs us that the Goddess is returning in the dreams and fantasies of his patients. "A new myth is arising in our midst and asks to be integrated into our modern frame of reference."[6]

Once again, as in prehistory and the ancient world, dreams are being used as valid sources of inner knowledge, guides to psychological healing. Jungian Esther Harding looks to the healing force of eros for both men and women, changes in psychological attitudes precipitated by the suffering and unhappiness brought about by disregarding the feminine. She suggests that the principle which in ancient and more naive days was projected in the form of a goddess is no longer seen in the guise of a deity but an inner force.[7] She was writing from the point of view of a psychotherapist in 1971 before the earth-based spirituality movement gained the momentum it now has. In his more recent work (1982) Whitmont says that his patients dream differently than they did twenty-five years before and that the Goddess is omnipresent.

In the late twentieth century there is a growing awareness that we are doomed as a species and planet unless we have a radical change of consciousness. The re-emergence of the Goddess is becoming the symbol and metaphor for this transformation of culture.

With the return of the Goddess, the new power of the feminine is being expressed in all areas of life. There is a reevaluation of the female principle in religion, in psychology, in the arts, and in the quality and relationship of humanity to the planet we live on. We are in the midst of a social revolution that will ultimately change how we see everything, as radically transformative as the smashing of the atom.

The women's movement spearheaded this revolution. Now feminists are turning to the Goddess as a model for self-transformation and empowerment. Women experience power as rooted in their biological selves, an enabling life force in contrast to the authoritative, hierarchical "power over" now so widely intrusive in our society.

Men also need the Goddess because as psychologist John Rowan says, "she represents the image of female power which is necessary to turn us round completely. . . . Unless and until both men and women genuinely believe that the female can be powerful, men are going to hang on to their power." By invoking the power of the Goddess, "men can gain immeasurably, because instead of seeing power as essentially male and essentially untrustworthy, they can relate to the much deeper and stronger female power—the power of Shakti."[8]

However, we must accept the full implications of archetypal female power, including the destructive as well as the creative and nurturing. Jungian analyst Whitmont makes a brilliant connection between the inner turbulence many of us have been experiencing and the common concern with the fate of the earth.[9]

The feminine call for a new recognition arises simultaneously with the violence that threatens to get out of hand. This strange coincidence eludes our understanding. Here mythology unexpectedly comes to our aid. . . . The archaic goddesses monitored the life cycle throughout its phases: birth, growth, love, death and rebirth. Evidently today our endangered life cycle needs divine monitoring. In the depths of the unconscious psyche, the ancient Goddess is arising. She demands recognition and homage. If we refuse to acknowledge her, she may unleash forces of destruction. If we grant the Goddess her due, she may compassionately guide us toward transformation.[10]

The emergence of the Goddess in Western consciousness has led to a new earth-based spirituality that sees humanity as part of the whole, part of the cosmos, and part of nature. The divine is within. A new understanding of the very nature of our planet as "a live Earth, in contrast to an Earth with life upon it" is changing the way scientists are studying the planet; James Lovelock's "Gaia Hypothesis," named after the Earth Goddess of early Greek myth, has made us aware of our planet as a self-creative, self-maintaining, living organism.[11]

While environmentalists have been concerned with the impact of humans on the delicate ecosystem of our wilderness since the nineteenth century, seeking to perserve our natural heritage for the pleasure of future generations, the new deep ecology and ecofeminist movements are not androcentric; they do not see humans as having any more value than animals and plants, rocks and trees. For Western culture, predicated upon a hierarchical order of all that is, this point of view has enormous implications and can eventually utterly transform our economic and social systems.

The reemergence of the Goddess in our culture has provided a paradigm for social action, the role of healer. The existing models are the shamans and exorcists of the Third World who heal both body and spirit and often serve as priestesses and priests to the Goddess. Midwives, healers, and practitioners of holistic medicine are working in new ways. Deep ecologists and ecofeminists are healing the planet, peace activists the wounds inflicted by our nation-states on one another. Artists who restore the iconography of the sacred female to contemporary culture are healing the imbalance between the masculine and the feminine that plagues our social fabric.

The Goddess has once again become a muse for the arts. She is the chief inspiration for the veritable explosion of creativity by women artists and musicians, the provocateur of those artist/activists who seek to transform our society. For a woman the discovery of the Goddess within taps into the wellsprings of her being and leads to the release of creative energies of which she may not even have been aware. This creativity long lay dormant, unrealized, because the female had been so long repressed in the culture at large that the very language in which women spoke, the images through which they expressed their inner being, were almost totally lost. The source of the artist's imagery most often is dreams, visions, trance state. The archetype of the Great Goddess, first discovered by Carl Jung, is the heritage of both men and women. Because of self-awareness engendered by the women's movement, women artists have been more receptive, more in touch with the unconscious where the primordial memory lies.

The story of the reemergence of the Goddess will be told through the lives and work of women artists who have become the prophets of our time. Their art reflects a modern sensibility different from that of the past, a self-consciousness in which individual life experience is relevant to their creative process in ways unknown to artists who served the collective needs of community and religious tradition. The first part of this book deals with the prehistoric, with archaeological evidence the primary resource. The second examines historical records that made literature and sacred text available. The third is concerned with our own time and relies heavily on the testimony of contemporary artists who are reclaiming the symbols of the sacred female.

Among historians of art and culture there is an ongoing debate as to which came first—myth, symbol, or ritual. In the late twentieth century the artist is envisioning a new mythology in the making, creating new sacred images that embody the old symbols. Art and ritual are once again working together to transform the collective consciousness.

The Way of the Goddess:
An Earth-Based Spirituality

CHAPTER 12

The Goddess is reemerging as the harbinger of a new spiritual consciousness that sees humanity as part of the whole, part of the cosmos, and part of nature. This worldview holds that the divine is immanent and all that lives is sacred. Earth-based spirituality is a growing, many faceted, grass roots movement, a neo-paganism whose practice is based on the ancient ways of the Goddess as well as a source of renewal within traditional Judaism and Christianity. Perhaps most important for our culture at large, this spirituality acknowledges the sacred dimension of women's experience long suppressed by patriarchy and monotheistic religions. The burgeoning women's spirituality movement has empowered women to transform their lives and in so doing many have become politically aware activists for social and ecological justice. The melding of spirituality and politics holds promise of revolutionizing our attitude toward life on earth.

Witches and Other Neo-Pagans

The religion of the Goddess never completely died out despite the brutal persecutions of the Inquisition and the witch burnings, but was kept alive by a handful of the faithful who practiced their rituals in small bands and preserved their knowledge of nature's teachings. The Time of Burning, of paranoia and superstition led by a fanatical and threatened Christianity, was followed by the Age of Reason, a time of disbelief. The Old Religion went underground and became the most secret of religions.

Traditions were passed down only to those who could be trusted absolutely, usually to members of the same family. Communications between covens were severed; no longer could they meet on the Great Festivals to share knowledge and exchange the results of spells or rituals. Parts of the tradition became lost or forgotten. Yet somehow, in secret, in silence, over glowing coals, behind closed shutters, encoded as fairytales and folksong, or hidden in subconscious memories, the seed was passed on.[1]

Memory of actual pagan practices and values faded; the only accounts were set down in distorted form by its enemies. The hideous stereotypes that remained seem ludicrous or tragic.[2] Language is always a problem in historical reconstruction, particularly when religious beliefs are at issue. Monotheism, a revealed tradition, breeds dogmatism, and our understanding of such terms as witch, witchcraft, and magic is encrusted by centuries of prejudice. Our dictionaries define witches as either the evil and ugly crones of fairy tales or the seductive and bewitching temptresses of television. In either case, they are supposed to possess a variety of "supernatural" powers.[3] Popular imagination still fancies them riding on broomsticks and consorting with the devil—and no wonder, since he was the old pagan horned god transformed by Christianity into evil incarnate.

"Modern Witches are thought to be members of a kooky cult, primarily concerned with cursing enemies by jabbing wax images with pins, and lacking the depth, the dignity and seriousness of purpose of a true religion."[4] These ideas about witchcraft bear little relation to the definitions given by the witches themselves.

Followers of Wicca seek their inspiration in pre-Christian sources, European folklore, and mythology. They consider themselves priests and priestesses of an ancient European shamanistic nature religion that worships a goddess who is related to the ancient Mother Goddess in her three aspects of Maiden, Mother and Crone. Many Craft traditions also worship a god, related to the ancient horned lord of the animals, the god of the hunt, the god of death and lord of the forests. Many . . . see themselves as modern-day heirs to the ancient mystery traditions of Egypt, Crete, Eleusis, and so on, as well as to the more popular peasant traditions of celebratory festivals and seasonal rites.[5]

"Only in this century have witches been able to 'come out of the broom closet,' so to speak, and counter the imagery of evil with truth."[6] Starhawk, priestess of the Craft, psychologist and political activist, believes it is important to reclaim the word "witch." For women to name themselves witch is to reclaim the right to be powerful, to reclaim a heritage as spiritual leaders, priestesses, healers, and midwives birthing human life and culture. For men, to practice the Craft is to know the feminine as divine and not to fear it. "To be a Witch is to identify with nine million victims of bigotry and hatred and to take responsibility for shaping a world in which prejudice claims no more victims."[7]

The term *witchcraft* comes from the Old English *wicce* or *wicca* referring to male or female practitioners, respectively, and can be traced back to the Indo-European root word meaning "to bend or shape." "A Witch is a 'shaper,' a creator who bends the unseen into form, and so becomes one of the Wise, one whose life is infused with magic."[8] Most coven members define witchcraft as the "Craft of the Wise . . . since the old Witches were often the wise people of the village, skilled in healing and the practical arts."[9]

Journalist Margot Adler, in her detailed historical account of the modern movement, *Drawing Down the Moon* (1987), points out that

> Misunderstandings begin at the most basic level, with the meanings of words used to describe beliefs and attitudes. . . . Take the word *magic*. Most people define it as *superstition* or *belief in the supernatural*. In contrast, most magicians, Witches, and other magical practitioners do not believe that magic has anything to do with the supernatural.[10]

Starhawk defines magic as the art of changing consciousness at will. Whatever its form, Starhawk believes "Magical techniques are effective for and based upon the calling forth of power from-within, because magic is the psychology/technology of immanence, of the understanding that everything is connected."[11] Power from within, which has many names—spirit, God, immanence, Goddess—is "what we sense in a seed, in the growth of a child, the power we feel writing, weaving, working, creating, making choices."[12] It is also darkness—fear, death, anger, hidden aspects of ourselves.

"Witchcraft has always been a religion of poetry, not the-ology,"[13] of experience, not words. There is no hierarchy, there are no centralized institutions, no monumental structures. As in Minoan Crete, the religion of the Goddess is practiced out-of-doors, in nature, even by urban Americans. While we gen-erally think of spiritual concerns as apart from the mundane, the neo-pagan worldview reaffirms the ancient idea that there is no distinction between the spiritual and material, sacred and secular.

"The Dianic tradition [of witchcraft] is a wom[a]n-cen-tered, female-only worship of women's mysteries . . ."[14] "[A] number of feminists have stated that women are Witches by right of the fact that they are women, that nothing else is needed."[15] But as Z. Budapest, High Priestess of the Susan B. Anthony Coven in San Francisco, in her compendium of Goddess rituals, spellcasting, and other womanly arts, *The Holy Book of Women's Mysteries,* tells us, Dianic witches "relate to the global Goddess as she was worshiped by all ethnic groups around the world."[16] Budapest comes from a long line of herbalists and healers, spiritual women whose descent can be traced back to the thirteenth century. She grew up in Budapest and escaped to the West after witnessing the Hun-garian Revolution in 1956.

Many women today meet in small groups to celebrate the appearance of the full moon; most would not call themselves witches. This most common of women's rituals is held when-ever possible out-of-doors in a rustic setting in the majestic moonlight. A solemn and meditative occasion, women get in touch with the mysteries within their bodies that are in rhythm with the movement of the universe.

A group of women in a feminist coven once told Adler that spiritual meant to them "the power within oneself to create artistically and change one's life."

> These women saw no contradiction between their concern for political and social change and their concern for "things of the spirit," which they equated with the need for beauty or with that spark that creates a poem or a dance. This is similar to views I have noticed among many tribal peoples who are fighting to preserve their culture.[17]

Not all neo-pagans identify with Wicca. Some name them-selves Druids after the ancient Celtic practice; others worship

19. Shri Lakshmi, Goddess of Abundance, first century c.e. Red sandstone, 43¼ in. India.

Giver of fertility and wealth, Shri Lakshmi emerges from the luxuriant lotus, the symbol of the life-giving waters. With one hand she holds her breast, the source of milk and nurture; with the other she points to her vulva, the sacred threshold of birth.

20. Frida Kahlo, My Nurse and I, 1937. Oil on sheet metal, 11¾ in. × 13¾ in. Mexico.

Kahlo imaging herself as both child and adult woman, nurses at the breast of the massive brown woman who wears the stone mask of a pre-Columbian deity. Frida's nurse is a symbol of Mexico's Indian heritage and of the Mexican earth, plants and sky. As if in sympathy with the nursing mother, milk white veins in a huge leaf in the background are engorged. The raindrops in the sky are "milk from the Virgin," thus Frida's own nurse explained to her the phenomenon of rain.[1]

21

21. TELLUS MATER (EARTH MOTHER), detail from the Altar of Peace (Ara Pacis), 13–9 B.C.E. Marble. Rome, Italy.

The bountiful Mother Goddess, embodiment of human, animal, and plant fertility, presides at the Roman Emperor Augustus' monument to the peace of the Empire.

22. Meinrad Craighead, GARDEN, 1980. Colored ink on scratchboard, 10 in. × 16 in.

Standing in her autumn garden, Mother Earth proudly offers the fruits of a rich harvest. Her body forms mirror those of a woman's reproductive system — outstretched arms reaching into baskets of eggs are the fallopian tubes and ovaries; the infant nestling in orange-red cushions, the uterus; the garden gate the opening to her birth canal.

22

23

23. SACRED LANDSCAPE: DA CHICH
ANANN, THE PAPS OF ANU, Twin Hills,
County Kerry, Ireland.

The whole of creation is the body of
the Goddess. The conical hills that rise
from the green bogs of Ireland are her
breasts. Anu may be identical with
Danu, ancestral mother of the Irish
Celts, who called themselves Danu's
Children, the Tuatha De Danann.

24. Clara Meneres, MULHER-TERRA VIVA
(WOMAN-LIVING EARTH), 1977.
Wood, acrylic, soil, grass, 120 in. × 70 in.
× 35 in. Portugal.

A Portuguese artist envisions the living earth
in female form, using sod and turf, playfully making a visual pun of the luxuriant
pubic hair.

24

25. Our Lady of the Beasts, seventh century B.C.E. Painting on terracotta funery amphora. Boetia, Greece.

A familiar image from the archaic Greek world is the Goddess who rules over the wild creatures. The great fish emblazoned on her lower body symbolizes the fertility of her womb.

26. Winifred, Milius Lubell, Potnia Theron, Mistress of the Wild Things, 1981–83. Woodcut, 7 in. × 11 in.

In her contemporary print of *The Mistress of the Wild Things,* Lubell has lovingly domesticated the wild creatures. Her goddess wears the bear mask of the Old European deity who is the nurse to the young.

27. Mayumi Oda, Treasure Ship, 1985. Silkscreen, 28 in. × 32 in.

Japanese-born Mayumi, Zen Buddhist and gardener, creates a female *bodhisattva* whose blessing is a boatload of vegetables and flowers.

28. Judy Chicago, Rainbow Warrior, 1980. Prismacolor on rag paper, 23 in. × 29 in.

In a poster, designed for the Greenpeace campaign to save the whales, the Mother-of-the-Sea gives birth to a school of fish. Her name comes from a Native American myth that tells of a rainbow warrior who will descend from the sky to save Earth's creatures when they are in danger of extinction.

29. Georgia O'Keeffe, GRAY LINE WITH BLACK, BLUE AND YELLOW, ca. 1923. Oil on canvas, 48 in. × 30 in.

O'Keeffe's monumental flower paintings can also be viewed as inviting female space.

30. Judy Chicago, THE CUNT AS TEMPLE, TOMB, CAVE AND FLOWER, ca. 1974. China paint and pen work on porcelain.

Chicago resacralizes a woman's body and female sexuality as the source of life and creativity.

29

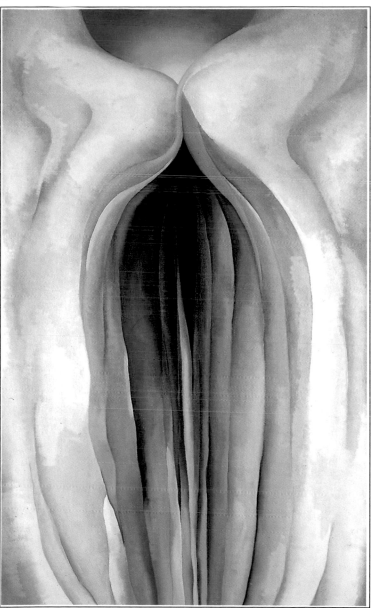

30

The Museum of Fine Arts, Houston; museum purchase with funds provided by the Agnes Cullen Arnold Endowment Fund.

31. EARTH MOTHER OF WILLENDORF, ca. 25,000 B.C.E. Limestone, 4⅛ in. Austria.

The ample volumes of the sacred female celebrate her capacity for birth and nurture.

32. SUSAN MABERRY AS THE EARTH MOTHER ON THE DAY AFTER THE NUCLEAR HOLOCAUST, 1985. Performance, *Revelations of the Flesh,* directed and produced by Cheri Gaulke, Los Angeles.

On the day after the bomb, Willendorf stands amidst the rubble, sadly contemplating the destruction of civilization.

33. THE EARTH MOTHER OF LAUSSEL, ca. 20,000–18,000 B.C.E. Limestone, 17 in. (Dordogne) France.

The natural contours of the rock wall form the ample swelling of the abdomen and thighs of this bountiful Goddess on the rock face overhanging the entrance to an Ice Age sanctuary. In her upraised hand she holds the bison horn, symbol of the crescent moon. It is marked with thirteen notches, noting the lunar months — the first calendar.

34. Ana Mendieta, GUANBANEX (left) and GUANAROCA (right), 1981. *Ruprestrian Series,* carved in living rock. Cuba.

Cuban born Mendieta carved these life-sized images in the measure of her own body on the barren hillside of her native land at the entrance of caves once sacred to the Caribbean Goddess.

35. LOUISE BOURGEOIS AS ARTEMIS, from performance, A BANQUET/FASHION SHOW OF BODY PARTS, 1980. New York City.

At the opening of an exhibition of her work, the sculptor wears the ritual garment of the Goddess, a tribute to power of the icon of Artemis.

36. ARTEMIS OF EPHESUS, first century B.C.E. Marble, 72 in. Roman.

The temple of Artemis in Asia Minor was one of the seven wonders of the ancient world. Venerated as the goddess of nature throughout the Roman Empire, she wears a mysterious ritual garment, covered with rounded forms usually believed to represent the breasts of nurture.

35

36

37. Louise Bourgeois, DESTRUCTION OF THE FATHER, detail, 1974. Latex, latex over plaster, and mixed media, 108 in. × 132 in. × 108 in.

Bourgeois creates a monumental womblike sculptural fantasy that dramatically confronts the viewer with female creative power so long oppressed by patriarchy. The title refers to her personal struggle in healing the trauma caused by her own overbearing father as well as the universal need of women to exorcise the oppressive patriarchy within.

38

38. Throne of the Queen-Priestess, Palace of Knossos, ca. 1600. Minoan Crete.

A priestess-queen probably once sat on this elegant gypsum throne, the oldest seat of royal authority found in Europe.

39. a. Suzanne Benton, The Throne of the Sun Queen, 1975. Bronze and corten steel, 10½ ft.; b. detail.

The bond between the warm nurturance of the sun and passionate intensity of women is acknowledged by the sculptor in her monumental throne to the Goddess.

39

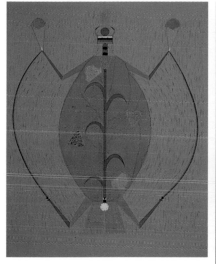

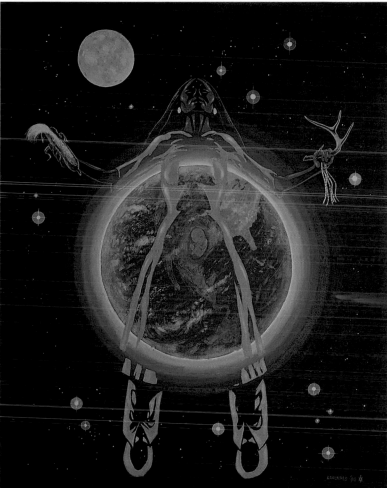

40. The Earth Mother, Earth (First Day Blessing Rite), 1910–18. Navaho sandpainting.

In Navaho tradition, a sandpainting is part of the healing ritual. The celebrant draws the Earth Mother in the cosmos, the blue disk of her body representing the sun. The white bars across the face are the dawn, the black night, blue evening light, and yellow at the mouth, sunset. The bars down each side of the face are rainbows.

The cornstalk represents the spinal column of the Earth and food. The white circle at the root of the corn is the moon. When the moon shakes its tail there is an abundance of everything.

41. John Fadden, Iakonkwe (Womankind), 1981. Acrylic on canvas, 30 in. × 24 in.

The Native American woman whose body encompasses the planet invokes the healing powers of nature so that a peaceful world may be born. Among the Iroquois, women traditionally were the providers of food and tribal elders. In one hand, as steward of the garden, she holds the sacred corn; in the other, the deer antler and string of wampum representing political power.

42

42. SNAKE GODDESS, ca. 1600 B.C.E. Faience and gold. From the temple repositories, Palace of Knossos, Crete.

Her eyes fixed in a trance-like gaze, the Minoan Goddess invokes the powers of the snakes, forces of regeneration, wrapped around her arms.

43. Margo Machido, CHARMED, 1984. Mixed media on canvas, 48 in. × 58 in.

The ancient symbols of the Goddess take on new meaning for contemporary women like Machido, for whom the snake embodies the deeply repressed pain of her emotional history that she must overcome.

44. THE SACRED LABRYS, ca. 1500 B.C.E. Gold, 3½ in. From the Temple Repositories. Palace of Knossos, Crete.

The miniature double-axe was the enigmatic emblem of the Minoan goddess, the mark of her presence in procession, both at ritual and sacred site.

45. Buffie Johnson, LABRYS, 1972. Oil on canvas, 66 in. × 84 in.

The ripe fig likened to a woman's womb because of its blood-red seedy pulp is another emblem of the Goddess. The artist has included tiny fleshy tendrils swimming over the surface of the fruit as semen making her "labrys" a symbol of the fertilized womb.

46. MALTESE GODDESS, third millennium B.C.E. Limestone.

In Malta the Goddess's powers were suggested by her voluminous form. An ancient legend told of a female giant who single-handedly moved stones weighing fifty tons and built the megalithic temple in a single night.

47. Maud Morgan, I'D LIKE TO GO TO MALTA, 1985. Oil on canvas, 65 in. × 80 in.

An artist's fantasy — if only she could go back to ancient Malta and be empowered by the monumental presence of the divine female.

43

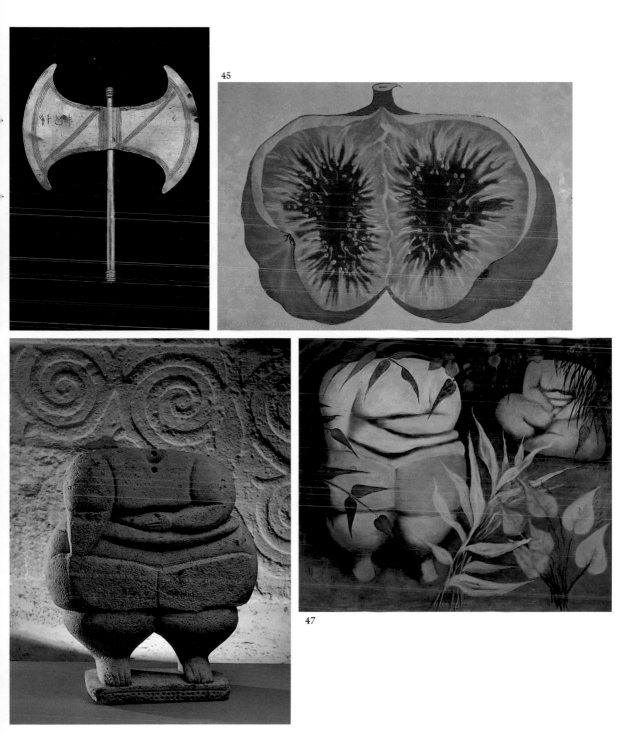

45

47

48. Yolanda Lopez, (above) THE GUADELUPE SERIES   a. *Portrait of the Artist as Virgen de Guadelupe;* b. *Margaret F. Stewart: Our Lady of Guadelupe;* c. *Victoria F. Franco: Our Lady of Guadelupe;* 1978, oil pastel on paper, 22 in. × 30 in. (at right) NUESTRA SENORA COATLICUE, 1983–88. Acrylic and oil on masonite, 48 in. × 96 in.

Lopez focuses on the paradox of the Virgin of Guadelupe, spiritual mother of Mexico, at once source of empowerment for women and symbol of colonial oppression. Juxtaposing the image of the Pre-Columbian Goddess Coatilcue within the iconography of the virgin, she comments on the sociocultural history and meaning of the image for Hispanic people. And then—incorporating portraits of herself, her mother, and her grandmother—she demystifies the power of the Church over Hispanic women, sacralizing their ordinary lives.

49

49. La Belle Verrier, 12th century. Stained glass. Chartres Cathedral, France.

In Medieval Europe, the Virgin Mary reigned supreme as the Queen of Heaven and her cult was the inspiration of the cathedral builders.

50. Marisol, The Family, 1969. Mixed media — wood, plastic, neon, and glass, 88 in. × 56 in. × 65 in.

Bolivian-born sculptor Marisol playfully spoofs "The Holy Family," as models for human life illuminating the problems posed by the immaculate conception. Mary's body is flat — two-dimensional — only her face, hands, and feet are carved in the round. Her wondrous pregnant womb, enameled and bejeweled, opens to a mirrored empty chamber within. Joseph, alas, is represented with only a head and a chest. The Christchild is a beautiful, fully human infant lying in a lucite cradle.

50

51. WINTER SOLSTICE AT NEWGRANGE, ca. 2200 B.C.E. Photograph. Megalithic barrow mound, Newgrange, Ireland.

One day a year, on the Winter Solstice when the Goddess gives birth to the new year, a shaft of light illuminates the triple spiral carved deep within the sanctuary. Christians later adjusted their calendar so that the birthday of their God would coincide with this auspicious event.

52. Meinrad Craighead, I AM SUMMER OUT OF SPRING'S DEATH, 1985. Colored ink on scratchboard.

The spiral represents the ongoing cycle of the seasons, ever-changing, ever-renewing.

51

52

the Goddess through rituals that are an evolving mix of borrowings from the Craft and Native American traditions leavened by the particular psychological and spiritual needs of our time. Adler succinctly puts her finger on why this new Paganism is so appealing.

> Modern Neo-Paganism and Witchcraft [in America is] a surprising and amazing attempt by Westerners in the heart of our industrial society to create non-authoritarian and non-dogmatic religions. . . . What's unusual about modern Pagans is that they remain anti-authoritarian while retaining rituals and ecstatic techniques that, in our culture, are used only by dogmatic religions or are the province of small and forgotten tribal groups.[18]

Starhawk, wise woman that she is, profoundly understands that ritual has the power to transform reality, to reveal the sacred. She tells us that the absolute can never be explained in words.

"The craft today is undergoing more than a revival, it is experiencing a renaissance, a re-creation."[19] Adler estimates that there are 100,000 active pagans, men and women, a live subculture, who call themselves witches, Druids, Goddess worshipers. Her study is based on extensive nationwide interviews. She visited groves and covens across the country, attending festivals and gatherings. Neo-paganism has no set creeds, no priestly establishment and is a religion of immanence, not transcendence, based on experience, not words. People who call themselves pagans "consider themselves part of a religious movement that antedates Christianity and monotheism."

> Most Neo-Pagans sense an aliveness and "presence" in nature. They are usually polytheists or animists or pantheists, or two or three of these things at once. They share a goal of living in harmony with nature and they tend to view humanity's "advancement" and separation from nature as the prime source of alienation. They see *ritual* as a tool to end that alienation. Most Neo-Pagans look to the old pre-Christian nature religions of Europe, the ecstatic religions, and the mystery traditions as a source of inspiration and nourishment. They gravitate to ancient symbols and ancient myths, to the old polytheistic religions of the Greeks, the Egyptians, the Celts and the Sumerians.[20]

Adler, herself a practicing pagan, comments with sadness on the general misunderstanding about these groups. "Words like *witch* and *pagan* do not rest easily in the mind or on the tongue."[21]

Pagans are described as weird or strange, irrational or neurotic. "The reality is very different. This *religious* movement . . . is only partly an 'occult' phenomenon. Often it is interwoven with the visionary and artistic tradition, the ecology movement, the feminist movement, and the libertarian tradition."[22] Pagans often lead quite ordinary and often successful lives in the real world, detaching themselves from many of the trends of the day, maintaining a sense of humor, a gentle anarchism, and a remarkable tolerance of diversity.

The Feminization of God: Reseeding the Judeo-Christian Mysteries

Other men and women work within organized religion to create a living spirituality that incorporates their concerns for the earth and its people into their own personal journey. They look back to the ecstatic medieval mystical traditions in Christianity and Judaism, to Hildegard of Bingen, Julian of Norwich, Mechild of Magdeburg and Meister Eckhart, and to the Kabbalists. What is so radically new for modern Christians and Jews is the feminization of God and the grounding of faith in a cosmic pantheism.

Original Blessing: A Creation Spirituality for Christians

Matthew Fox, a Dominican scholar and innovative educator, is renewing the vision of a spiritual tradition in the West, replacing the fall/original sin/redemption theology with a creation spirituality centered on that precious asset all people hold in trust and in common, the earth. He is seeking to redeem fallen nature with a living cosmology of science, mysticism, and art and preaches a global ecumenism that he calls "Geo-Justice."

Fox conceives of God as Mother, God as Child, Ourselves as God and Birthers of God's Son. Creativity is our divine birthright and responsibility.

The patriarchal tradition has pretty much ignored the implications of God's motherly side and of our responsibility to develop the mother in ourselves, whether we are women or men, married or celibate, heterosexual or homosexual.[23]

There is a potential mother in each and every one of us. Fox refers to the teachings of Rabbi Abraham Heschel:

Every soul is pregnant with the *seed* of insight. It is vague and hidden. In some people the seed grows, in others it decays. Some give birth to life. Others miscarry it. Some know how to bear, to nurse, to rear an insight that comes into being. Others do not.[24]

Fox is not speaking of literal motherhood but of nurturing and creativity. The feminist movement and with it creation-centered spirituality celebrate and are retrieving a nonliteral meaning of motherhood. Adrienne Rich defines feminism as "developing the nurturing qualities of women and men."[25] Fox asks

What would it mean to live in a nurturing society, one where even men nurtured self, one another and others? . . . From a theological point of view [it would mean] the recovery of the tradition of God as Mother.[26]

He looks to the writings of the Prophets and the Psalms, to the medieval mystics, and to the matrifocal religions of Wicca and the Native Americans for his sources. "The motherhood of God is celebrated wherever images of roundness and encircling take precedence over linear imaging. . . . Divinity is like a wheel, a circle, a whole."[27]

Fox's theology is activist and joyous. The wisdom and compassion of the Mother would "revitalize Western religion and civilization, forge new links with non-Western traditions, create gentler and more dialectical relationships to earth, to body, to pleasure, to work, to the artist within and among us."[28]

The Mother's Songs: Images of God the Mother

Another Catholic mystic, Meinrad Craighead, finds God the Mother within and paints her visions in images of extraordinary beauty, resonant with luminous earth colors, as dense and textured as medieval tapestries. Like the shamans, she looks to her dreams, reveries, and fantasies for revelation.

> I draw from my own myth of personal origin and each picture is a realization of this story and is connected to the ancient image of the Godmother in art and mythology. . . . Making is worship.[29]

Craighead's creative imagination recharges the symbols of the Great Goddess with a mystery and power that only a great art can evoke. Forty of the paintings are published with a poetic text whose words reverberate with cosmic power, *The Mother's Songs: Images of God the Mother.* Song and image are woven together. "Every page celebrates in icon and in words the female . . . divine Reality, as if to undo centuries of its repression by [the jealous] Father-God."[30]

Craighead was once a cloistered religious. For fourteen years she lived as a contemplative nun in Stanford Abbey, an English Benedictine monastery. She followed the artist's path of *via creativa,* as described by the medieval mystic Meister Eckhart, wherein the spiritual journey is an experience of birthing and creativity. Her words and images flow out from the richness of the manifest world. As psychologist Patricia Reis explains, "The 'immanent mother'—the source of all life—is perceived as a vigilant presence in all of nature. The images in [her] book, beginning from her own intimately personal vision, expand into a vastly conceived, all embracing female divinity."

> The creative spirit I know within me has the face and the force of a woman. She is my Mother, my Mothergod, my generatrix, the divine immanence I experience signified in all of creation. . . .[31]

Both the writings and the paintings spring from the place of deep memory, personal and collective, "pictures painted on the walls of my womb."[32]

> We are born remembering. We are born connected. . . . Every drawing is a quest for origin, a return to the source following the hidden threads in the labyrinthine matrix.[33]

Craighead's vision encompasses all that is alive, weaving together plant, animal, and human into a vibrant, shimmering, sometimes dizzying flux of creation. In *Garden* (see color

118. Meinrad Craighead, VESSEL, 1983.
Colored ink on scratchboard. 10 in. × 16 in.

The body of God the Mother becomes a
cauldron of creation, imaged as an earthen
pot lined with the abundant fruits of the
land: ears of corn, squash, red apples, and
bunches of purple grapes. "Vessel" was
inspired by the artist's descent into the cool
darkness of a kiva, the womblike,
underground sacred chamber of the Hopi
Indians. The artist decorates her vessel with a
row of hands, the ritual mark of woman as
far back as the Paleolithic caves.

plate 22) the towering figure of the Mother rises like a mighty
oak, spreading her powerful arms over a tangled overripe
"garden." The unborn baby nests within the womb on cushiony
lining, red with uterine blood. We read the outstretched arms
as the fallopian tubes, the egg basket as the ovaries, and the
open garden gate as the vulva and are reminded of the great
Maltese temples built in the shape of the Mother. Craighead's
Garden is a living, growing organic temple to the fecundity
of the life force.

How natural the hand is as the signature of women, the
gesture of touch that affirms the bond of relationship, of
communication, and of caring. Craighead understands that
for a woman of our time creation is not limited to procreation.

> I have never conceived, but whether or not a woman does
> conceive, she carries the germinative ocean within her, and the
> essential eggs. We have a spirituality, full from within. Whether
> we are weaving tissue in the womb or pictures in the
> imagination, we create out of our bodies.[34]

She plays with words and puns with images like one in which the overlapping faces of her mother, grandmother, and great-grandmother become one immense and winged pomegranate, carrying the seeds of her maternal origins. After leaving the monastery, Craighead returned to New Mexico, drawn like Georgia O'Keeffe to the desert landscape and the spirit of the place. Spider Woman and Changing Woman of Native American mythology inspire her paintings, and the earth that heals and gives strength is her favorite symbol (see fig. 118). In a small shrine in the western foothills in the Sangre de Cristo mountains she found Christians worshiping the Mother Earth as Our Lady of Chimayo. Pilgrims scoop up handfuls of black dirt from the earthen floor into paper bags, sacred relics to carry home.

Her art is an act of love and thanksgiving, a radiant sense of affirming the inner core of her being. She believes that art must be part of a search for truth. The outpouring of women's creativity is an expression of their spirituality making visible truths long suppressed. What is so astonishing about the creative process is that over the past twenty years as one woman artist after another began a quest for her own authentic vision, she was led back to the Goddess. As Meinrad Craighead in her deep wisdom knows: "The thread of personal myth winds through the matriarchal labyrinth, from womb to womb, to the faceless source, which is the place of origination."[35]

The Shekinah: The Feminine Face of God in Judaism

The renewed experience of God the Mother is identified by Jewish women and men as the Shekinah.[36] Her roots are venerable. She makes her first official appearance as an abstract concept denoting God's presence on earth in the writings of the rabbis, authoritative commentators on the biblical tradition, during the early years of the Jewish exile following the destruction of the second temple by the Romans in the first century C.E. In later commentaries she evolved into an independent feminine divine prompted by her compassionate nature to argue with God in defense of humankind. Raphael Patai sees her as the "direct heir to such ancient Hebrew goddesses of Canaanite origin as Asherah and Anath.[37] Later she appeared to dwell in the Tabernacle in the desert, then in Solomon's temple, and followed her people into exile. The Shekinah's role can be compared to that of the Holy Spirit, the indwelling of God in human life.

> Before long . . . this spiritual "presence" began to take on substance. Her movements from place to place could now be discerned, and having acquired a physical aspect, she became subject to historical events: more and more closely joined to the fate of Israel, she suffered its vicissitudes, accompanied the people into their exiles, and experienced the hopes and despairs with which Israel reacted to the blows dealt her by fate . . . [and] shared in the punishments meted out to God to his sinful people.[38]

Patai suggests that in biblical times, the deity was considered to comprise two persons: God and the Shekinah.[39] Then, following the fall of Solomon's temple and the Babylonian exile, she went underground for a millennium and a half.

> The God of Judaism was a lone and lofty father-figure, and whatever female divinity was allowed to exist in his shadow was either relegated to a lower plane, or her femininity was masked and reduced to a grammatical gender, as in the case of the Shekinah. Yet in spite of the masculine predominance on the highest level of the Talmudic God concept, popular belief and imagination dwelt in a world peopled and haunted by feminine numina, ranging from lowly and loathsome she-demons to exalted personifications.[40]

A thousand years into the Exile, in twelfth-century Europe, the Shekinah reemerged as a full-blown female divinity in medieval Kabbala where she occupied a central place in Jewish consciousness. In Kabbala, an esoteric, mystical system of thought more speculative than ecstatic, creation is believed to be through emanation. Popular in sixteenth- and seventeenth-century Eastern Europe, Kabbala's esoteric wisdom is appealing in modern times to those interested in the occult. In the late twentieth century the Shekinah is being reclaimed by Jewish feminists searching for a divine female presence within their own tradition. This is in part a response to the planetary crisis and to the feminist critique of patriarchal religion.

The Shekinah appeared to Los Angeles artist Gila Hirsch in an unconscious revelation that unfolded during her creative process (see fig. 119). She was doing lithography and "recalls her excitement [that] while working on the stone she was 'drawing *from* the stone rather than on the stone.'" "The night after the lithograph was completed, Hirsch dreamed that it should be called *Shekinah*. The interwoven motifs which appear here—Hebrew letters, references to time, ambiguous [snake-like] forms . . . and references to her own body—kept reappearing in subsequent work. The words *Ain Soph* were familiar to Hirsch as the everyday Hebrew expression meaning 'no end.'"[41] In her lithograph, she related the words to the seemingly endless play of images, which through free association with her dream imagery led her to discover the kabbalistic meaning of *Ain Soph* as the boundless light that emanates from the source of creation, female like the Hindu *Shakti*.

For Hirsch, as for Craighead and other artists, the act of painting is not "so much a process of invention or creation as it is one of releasing what is already known. . . . To tap these springs of personal material is to hone awareness on all levels of being. The process is enhanced by its very pursuit."[42] Her work that followed from the *Shekinah* lithograph over a five-year period led her to the erotic mystical, to the dance of life that is the movement of every living cell, which she finds imprinted in the double helix of the DNA, the genetic code of life.

"The last of this sequence was *Emergence* (1981) depicting a shadowy life-sized human form emerging from densely swaying watery reeds" (see fig. 120).

For Hirsch the discovery of the female divine source in her faith led her to a mystical union with nature. For other Jewish women the Shekinah has become a focus of worship as they evolve ritual groups that, like the *Rosh Hodesh* (New Moon) circles and the Harvest ritual of the Succoth, look back to the customs of their ancestors in the Holy Land.

Rabbi Léah Novick believes that the memory of the Shekinah was kept alive by women through oral tradition. By removing the veils rabbinic commentators had drawn over her, women have become the midwives of the Shekinah for today. They are beginning once again to hear her words in the language of our time, fleshing out her embodied presence. Novick, spiritual teacher and visionary, a leader in the Jewish renewal movement, reinterprets the Shekinah of the mystical

Kabbala in the light of contemporary Gaia consciousness. She draws on traditional Jewish teaching that nothing in nature can exist without the Shekinah, who sustains and nourishes all life on the planet. While women most identify with the Shekinah as the internalized form of god within, for Jewish men she is a beacon of transformation to a more nurturing self. Novick looks to the next generation to fully embrace the Jewish goddess. According to Novick the Shekinah is the goddess of the Jews, as distinct from the Hebrew Mother Goddess Asherah. "So long as the Jews lived an agrarian life, there was less need to define her as the source of all things in nature. The process of spelling out her attributes . . . came with the exile of the Jews from their own land."[43]

Worship of the Shekinah is joyful and celebratory as the annual cycle of traditional Jewish rituals, tied to the earth—the seasons, the harvest, the cycles of the sun and the moon—is being reconceptualized and reconciled with the seasonal round of the Goddess, the equinoxes, solstices, and quarter days. This means going back to Judaism's roots, to the original meaning of the festivals in the agrarian culture of biblical times. Novick says that if we want to save, to restore the planet, we must draw on these ancient sources.

Artist Beth Ames Swartz made a pilgrimage to Israel with her thirteen-year-old daughter to connect with the Shekinah, the female energy that is a part of their heritage. Julianne was soon to be Bat Mitzvah, the traditional Jewish initiation into the religious community, now performed for girls as well as boys. Swartz worked at ten historical sites associated with biblical women whose stories had spoken to her: Miriam, Rachel, the Queen of Sheba, the prophets Huldah and Deborah, and others.

> . . . her eye and hand and heart and soul looked for and saw . . . that the land was more than earth. . . . Each site she invested with the soul and the memory of a woman whose story, now reinterpreted in the context of her work and her thinking, could better help humankind to understand contributions fertile with more than reproductive capacity.[44]

The mystical underpinning for this complex historical, ritual, and visual project rests on Swartz's understanding of Kabbala, a vision of the restoration of unity between above

119

119. Gila Yellin Hirsch, SHEKINAH, 1976. Lithograph. 19 in. × 19 in.

The eccentric, hybrid image developed in a round format, structured around a woman's face with an infinity sign above her eyes and the inscription *Ain Soph* written backwards over her breast. Her belly is made of a shell, and the strands woven around the twelve points evoke multiple allusions to hair, serpents, or ribbons.[18]

120. Gila Yellin Hirsch, EMERGENCE, 1981. Oil on canvas. 5½ ft. × 5 ft.

The emerging figure is the artist herself who is entering a new phase of her creativity, leaving the studio to work out-of-doors in nature. Several months later she found herself at an artists' colony in the high desert of southern California, an immense, varied, and abundant landscape.

"Each morning I painted at the lily pond. The reeds in *Emergence,* which had been summoned up from an obscure inner source as I had worked in my Venice studio, were now in front of me, across the pond. I knew them intimately. I watched and recorded their light with paint as they swayed in response to the wind."[19]

and below, heaven and earth, the heights and the depths. For her each of the biblical women

> symbolized the message of the Shekinah—that God has many names and can speak through women as well as men. . . . [At each site] I performed a kabbalistic ritual [relating the woman or women honored with an appropriate Sefirah (sphere of energy)] as my starting point.[45]

Like the traditional shaman, she works within the consecrated circles, beginning a personal ritual process of ordering-dis-ordering-reordering, which will evolve months later into glowing, shimmering, three-dimensional fragments, alchemist's icons evoking the mysteries of the creation of the earth. In *Red Sea #1 Honoring Miriam,* 1980 (see color plate 10), the symbolic image of the Shekinah, in a brilliant, flowing, metallic red-orange, projects forward to catch the light, its complex trifoil form that of the female. Swartz had previously consciously resisted female imagery, but this shape manifested

120

from her unconscious seems to say, "I am a woman. I am an essence. I am part of All That Is, a source, the Shekinah."[46] *Red Sea* is a tribute to Miriam, who along with her brother Moses, was a prophet and leader of the Israelites. Like the medieval alchemist, Beth Ames Swartz works with earth, air, fire, water, and sun, transmuting them through ritual into art. Her creative process/ritual involves a birth/death/rebirth of her materials. She works on site.

First she meditates to relax her body and clear her mind. Beginning with a clean white paper placed on the ground,

> she tears and mutilates the paper, . . . buries it, rubs it with earth and glue, sprays it with metallic paint and gradually brings it, layer by layer, into a new existence. She is able to express directly through this process—the intense physical and emotional interaction with her media—her deep sense of communion with the earth itself.[47]

A displaced New Yorker living in the Southwest, Swartz first discovered the powers of nature in the Arizona desert and later while rafting down the Colorado River.

> That trip marked another huge transformation in my work. I did lots of sketching and as I studied the forms of the rocks, I began to notice feminine forms within them. It made me feel involved with the land in a new way. We climbed through three billion years of geological time, went to sleep at sunset and awoke when the sun rose. The nuances and variability of the colors were overwhelming. I experienced a special kind of connection with nature and it had a profound effect on me. . . .
>
> From this experience grew a whole body of work that shows women coming from the earth. . . . I experimented with this theme, relating myself to the topography. Going into the canyon was a turning point in my life. An archetypal female figure in a landscape setting was an elemental change in my work that showed at last I felt connected to my surroundings. I knew I was home.[48]

The Goddess on the River of Our Mind, A Buddhist Meditation

Buddhism has always had its goddesses and deep connections with nature. Tara, the Mother of Mercy and Kwan Yin, the Bodhisattva of Compassion, have traditionally been sources of comfort and salvation. In an age acutely aware of the need for female divinities, their role within Buddhist practice is becoming more important for both women and men. American women Buddhist teachers are reforming Buddhism in this country, exposing and cutting away deeply entrenched patriarchal attitudes that violate the essential wisdom so appealing to Westerners. However, conventional iconography does not always reflect a modern woman's need for spiritual identity.

Japanese-born Mayumi Oda, artist and Zen practitioner, has created a whole new pantheon of Bodhisattvas, compassionate beings whose essence is enlightenment. Drawing on the themes and motifs of traditional Japanese and Buddhist mythology, she celebrates women and the female form by changing the powerful masculine gods—the Wind God, the Thunder God, and others—into their radiant, playful, female counterparts (see fig. 121).

The artist's naked goddesses with full breasts and buttocks, apple cheeks, and red nipples, swirl colorful scarves, dancing across a golden sky, or like Venus burst from the white-crested blue sea to follow the rainbow. Her goddesses are expressions of a woman's dreams of becoming.

> When I gave birth to my first child, I felt my strength as a woman. I felt joy in being a woman and I wanted to celebrate it. I had an urge to draw a big-breasted Gaia or Earth Goddess. I needed an icon for myself with which I could identify, an image through which I could grow. I used my art to create something to grow into.[49]

Her home at Muir Beach, California, is in the shadow of Mt. Tamalpais, the sacred healing ground of the Miwok Indians, and right next door to the Green Gulch Zen Center Farm.

> The first time I saw the farm from Route 1, nestled in the bosom of the gentle, sloping hills, it reminded me of the traditional Chinese painting of paradise . . . the Redwood River runs through the Green Gulch fields, watering vegetables and flowers, and then empties into the Pacific Ocean. Under the morning fog, kale, broccoli and spinach reflect the turquoise blue of the sea. Dewdrops on their leaves look as if a crystal rosary had been scattered over them. Cauliflower looks like white coral.[50]

121. Mayumi Oda, GODDESS HEARS
PEOPLE'S NEEDS AND COMES, 1976.
Silkscreen print. 24 in. × 33 in.

Kwannon, the Japanese form of Kuan Yin,
becomes transmuted into a beguiling flautist
riding a wondrous bird across a red-orange
sun. Mayumi tells us, "The goddess is
coming to you," and asks us "Can you come
to her?"[20]

Mayumi is an Earth Mother. She grows flowers and vegetables; her gardening is a spiritual practice.

> I love to sketch lettuce and purple cabbage spreading their
> leaves open like the mandala of the Buddha fields, revealing the
> mystery of creation.

> At times when I was very sad, I painted vegetables. Even when
> I feel sad and tired, the unfolding shapes of cauliflower, lettuce
> and purple cabbage give me energy to create.[51] (See color plate
> 23.)

Mayumi is like the traditional Japanese dream vendor who
came on New Year's Day, traveling from town to town, selling
simple woodblock prints of treasure ships loaded with gods

and goddesses, sacks of rice, jewels, and flowers. People would buy the prints and place them under their pillows in hopes of having a good dream for the coming year.

Recently Mayumi has been embracing the wrathful *dakhinis* as an expression of the feminine more relevant to our time when we need the fierce energy of the female to fight the forces that oppress our planet. The Tibetan *dakhinis* are playful, wild, undomesticated forces—anger, ignorance, pride, passion, and jealousy. In order to transform these emotions into creative wisdom, they must be met and experienced as they are. The Sky Dancer, represents the Great Mother, the Perfection of Wisdom. Mayumi enlarges the traditional image of the *dakhini* found on the sacred temple hanging, the *tankha,* into a monumental figure (see fig. 122).

Mayumi talks about how her art became her pathway to self. In the late sixties and early seventies, she was a Japanese woman married to an American academic living in an unfamiliar culture at a time of social change and chaos, of student strikes and women's liberation. With two small children and a house to take care of, Mayumi felt that she was going to lose herself.

> I had very little time to create. . . . Out of desperation, my art became a survival force. Without creating art, I wouldn't be myself. The children forced me to see who I was. Being an artist wasn't a luxury anymore. I needed to see myself as positive, strong. Through creating goddesses, I became stronger. I never thought that my art should be "pretty," "beautiful" or "well-balanced." Art was a means for my survival. Through my creative process, I have been creating myself. Goddesses are projections of myself and who I want to be. Each picture represents a stage of my development, the influences I was feeling and the events that were going on around me.[52]

Mayumi articulates what so many women have felt. Their hunger, sometimes a desperate longing, is unbounded for images of strong, powerful, compassionate, but also righteously angry goddesses, models of females creating the universe, creating themselves, birthing a just society. As the poet-philosopher Adrienne Rich tells us in sadness and in truth, "The woman I needed to mother me has not yet been born."

122. Mayumi Oda, THE SKY DANCER, 1987. Acrylic on canvas. 60 in. × 92 in.

The *dakhini's* horrifying appearance is often repellent to Westerners who don't understand that her role is to lead the faithful through the encounter with death to the psychological wholeness that lies beyond.

We must mother ourselves, but the nurturing is not easy if we haven't been properly mothered.

The role of the artist in our time is to give expression to the feminine consciousness that is emerging in myriad forms after so many centuries of dormancy in the West. As it has been since the origins of human consciousness, our wont is to create the gods in our own image, and so it is that we make the Goddess today. But artistic creation is never in a vacuum; it is fueled by the storehouse of existing imagery. The archaeological recovery of the ancient images of the Goddess from which the professional artist and the artist in all of us draw our inspiration is both our gift and our blessing.

Jungians make much of archetypal imagery, but how extraordinary to encounter these psychological entities in the icons of our prehistoric ancestors, and in those living traditions where the Goddess is still worshiped. Carl Jung understood that the life of the spirit is everyone's birthright. The interconnection of all that is alive, past and present, is confirmed by the reemergence of the sacred iconography in contemporary art.

Jim Ann Howard's Confrontation with the Meaning of Death

After several self-imposed months of retreat and isolation from all the sensory stimulations of material culture that do such violence to our consciousness, the Goddess came to a reluctant Jim Ann Howard in the form of a primordial self-image. She did not believe in a deity with human form and sexuality. For her the divine was a process, not a being, and the sacred was the land. Struggling to come to terms with her feelings about death so that she could paint them, perceptions and questions that had haunted her since the death of her own father in childhood were rekindled. She remembered the out-of-body experiences of puberty and the deep voice within that her grandmother had silenced, calling it primitive and un-Christian, like the old witch doctor that used to come to cure her grandfather's cows. Jim Ann wanted to paint about these experiences. In preparation she turned inward to her intuition, once again listening to her voices.

I turned off the radio. I stopped answering the telephone. I fasted. My sleep patterns changed, I began spending ten and twelve hours a day in bed, half-awake, half-asleep, dreaming constantly. I often refused to get up until I had the right dream—the one that addressed some aspect of this painting. I resolved not to question the images that came to me, but rather to trust them and to record them.

It was agonizing. Several times she wanted to give up but

during this process there came to me an increasingly profound sense of reunion—with myself, the land and the universe.[53]

What emerged was an image of the life process itself, taking the form of a female creature rising out of the depths of the sea, one leg still rooted in the murky bottom, her toes alive and wiggling in the microscopic ooze of composition and decomposition, the compost out of which the first living organism evolved. One arm rises out of the waters to support a great cosmic spiral that fills the sky, mirroring the form of a seashell lying beside her foot, split to reveal its inner helix. Sea currents and sea life, plankton and phosphorescent fish, wash around her lower body; the clearer waters above reveal the upper torso of a fully sensuous, very womanly naked body, that of the artist whose revelation this is, painted in a luminous, earthy red.

In her other hand she holds the glowing orb of the full moon. A pair of intertwining snakes hangs round her shoulders like a feather boa, the one dark, the other light, representing the interconnection of life and death. The bull's head under her foot refers to her sexuality, to the union of male and female out of which new life is born (see fig. 123 and color plate 12).

Jim Ann's vision encompasses the symbols associated with the prehistoric Goddess and is a stunning revelation of the unity of our archetypal consciousness as women. Water is the ultimate source of all life, red the color of blood, the life fluid. The moon is the cosmic symbol of women, her bodily rhythms, like the tides, in tune with its waxing and waning. Perhaps once all women menstruated in harmony with the moon cycle. The snake who sheds its skin is a universal symbol of renewal and a manifestation of the Goddess. The spiral represents burgeoning life.

123. Jim Ann Howard, REUNION, 1988. Oil on wood panel. 92 in. × 23½ in.

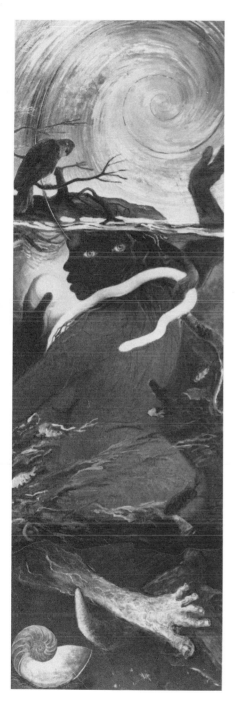

With all its compelling power, Jim Ann's vision is one not yet realized. The surface waters press down on the creature's head. Her hair is made from the roots of a leafless, dormant tree growing on the barren spit of land, awaiting the proper time and conditions to put forth its leaves and fruit.

> I chose a long narrow board to work on. . . It was important that it was of wood . . . that the surface be richly textured . . . [of] a vertical and restrictive shape. These decisions precluded any ideas of imagery. When, in the last stages of the painting, it occurred to me to carve the universal spiral from the sky to the figure's forehead as a statement of information coming from within as well as from without, I was thankful for the wooden support that I had chosen. . . . I now realize that the physical form of my piece echoes the linear, death-oriented aspect of our culture and that within its confines exists my conflicting sense of ongoingness, renewal, and life.[54]

Jim Ann Howard's Goddess correctly assesses the current state of things. She has not yet fully reestablished her territory. We have to face the death of old values before the healing can begin.

The feminine spirituality that is countering the image of the male god of patriarchy is not just for women. For many men, like Matthew Fox and his community, the vision of God the Mother is redemptive, offering them a way out of the stranglehold of patriarchal consciousness, new ways of seeing and being. For women, the image of the divine female is first and foremost a model of empowered selfhood. The Virgin Mary, however problematic she is as a model for human women, is still a powerful, nurturing, embodied force for Catholic women. But until recently Protestant and Jewish women grew up in a wasteland utterly bereft of a divine image to relate to in their essential biological selves.

With the slowly dawning new consciousness engendered by the Women's Movement, some women in the early seventies began a deliberate search for the Goddess. As they became painfully aware that their experience of the sacred had been left out of monotheistic religions, they looked to the symbols and rituals of prehistory and to the living traditions where the Goddess was still a cultural force.

Often the way of these seekers was tenuous at best, some simple half-formed ritual, some images dredged up unwittingly from the unconscious. Sometimes there was a deliberate re-creation of old iconography, almost as a talisman so that the sacred could be more palpable. Like the women of the ancient world, we need votive objects to hold in our hand and invoke the divine Mother. Every woman must internalize the image of the Goddess in order to begin to heal. For many women the journey to the Goddess is the path to wholeness, and women artists document this process. They have become the visionaries, the seers of our time.

The Goddess Within:
A Source of Empowerment for Women

CHAPTER 13

Theologian Carol Christ, a pioneer in the Women's Spirituality Movement, informs us that the simple and most basic meaning of the Goddess is female power as a legitimate, benevolent, and independent force. Her much reprinted, eloquent, and impassioned essay, "Why Women Need the Goddess," has become a credo. She begins with a quote from Ntosake Shange's Broadway play *for colored girls who have considered suicide when the rainbow is enuf.* A tall, beautiful black woman rises from despair to cry out, "I found God in myself and I loved her fiercely."[1]

> Her discovery is echoed by women around the country who meet spontaneously in small groups on full moons, solstices and equinoxes to celebrate the Goddess as symbol of life and death powers, of waxing and waning energies in the universe, and in themselves.[2]

Any woman who echoes Ntosake Shange's dramatic statement says:

> Female power is strong and creative. She is saying that the divine principle, the saving and sustaining power, is in herself, that she will no longer look to men or male figures as saviors. This meaning of the symbol of Goddess is simple and obvious . . . and stands in sharp contrast to the paradigms of female dependence on males that have been predominant in Western religion and culture.[3]

As Christ so succinctly puts it, "The real importance of the symbol of the Goddess is that it breaks the power of the patriarchal symbol of God as male over the psyche."[4]

Maud Morgan, who was seventy-seven years old when she painted her first nude self-portrait, illustrates the extraordinary power the Goddess can evoke. Morgan, a Cambridge, Massachusetts, artist, has been recognized in the establishment art world since her midtwenties. She spent a day at an exhibition of Cycladic art in a New York museum, contemplating those stunning semiabstract sculptures of the Goddess from the third millennium B.C.E. Flying home, she looked out the window and saw the iconic form of the Great Mother, stretched out the whole length of the plane, her white marble body glistening against the rosy clouds illuminated by the setting sun. As she gazed in wonder, the body of the Goddess became her own. Returning to her studio that evening, she began to paint her first nude self-portrait (see fig. 124). Exhilarated, she worked for twenty-four hours without interruption. "I felt freer than I had ever felt before in my life; I didn't give a damn."[5]

Morgan is a naturalist, a peace activist, utterly engaged in life. A documentary on her life and art filmed the previous year showed her bathing nude under a waterfall at the family summer home in Quebec. Her identification with the Goddess was so liberating that she was able then to divorce her husband from whom she had been separated for twenty-five years, to at last become her own person.

Mary Daly, author of *Beyond God the Father* (1973), points out that the model of a universe in which a male god rules the cosmos from outside serves to legitimize men's control of and women's exclusion from social institutions.

> The symbol of the Father God, spawned in the human imagination and sustained as plausible by patriarchy, has in turn rendered service to this type of society by making its mechanisms for the oppression of women appear right and fitting.[6]

The unconscious model continues to shape the perceptions even of those who have consciously rejected religious creeds. For example, as Christ says, many people have abandoned the "revealed truth of Christianity without ever questioning the underlying concept that truth is a set of beliefs revealed through the agency of a 'Great Man,' possessed of powers or intelli-

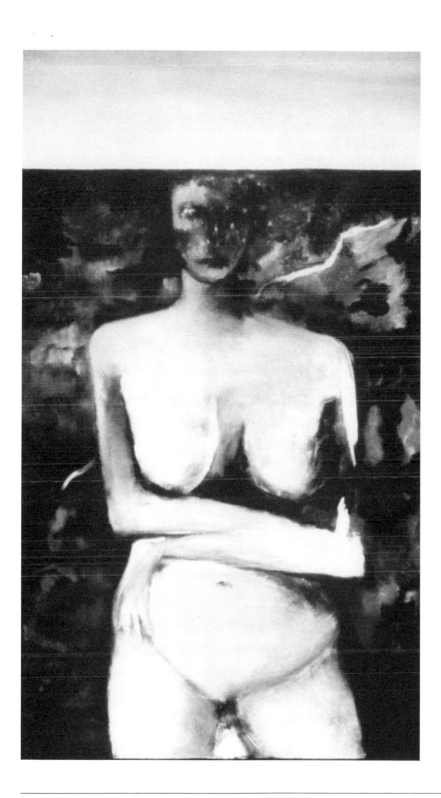

gence beyond the ordinary human scope. . . . Truth is always seen as only knowable second hand."[7]

The consciousness raising engendered by the Women's Movement in the 1960s made many painfully aware that the role of women in traditional religion was anomalous at best. For them the divine female provided a model not only for spiritual empowerment but also for an ethic centered on relationship. Women for whom faith and ethics were inevitably intertwined did not find their own rights included in the struggle for social justice. As Jewish and Christian women they could turn the other cheek but had to accept second class status. And, of course, they could not be leaders—that is, ordained as ministers, priests, or rabbis—because of their sexual identity. St. Paul forbade them to speak in church. His harsh words still rankle. Every day, orthodox Jewish males offer thanksgiving to God that they were not born women.

We have explored already the historical process through which the symbols of the Goddess were co-opted by patriarchy, their meanings often reversed to serve masculine gods. For many women in the late twentieth century, the crux of women's oppression seemed to be the gender of God. Despite theological protests that the maleness of the absolute godhead is only an accident of grammar, there was no getting around the overbearing divine persona that emerges from the biblical material, nor the fact that he chose a son as his only begotten child. The language of the Old Testament is, on the whole, unregeneratively patriarchal, a product of the historical time and culture in which it was written. The image of the Old Testament god continues to haunt Christian and Jewish women alike.

As Carol Christ says, "Religious symbol systems focused around exclusively male images of divinity create the impression that female power can never be fully legitimate, or wholly beneficent."[8] Whenever God was imaged in anthropological form in Western art he was unmistakably male, a stern old man. Attempts to purge sexist language from the scriptures and liturgy are only well-intended window dressing. No woman is fully equal before God because, despite the words in Genesis, she is not created in his image. Until recently, God's earthly surrogates, the ordained leaders of his flock, were all male. While progress has been made on the ordination of women in both Judaism and Protestantism during the last twenty-five years, Roman Catholicism still firmly denies priesthood to women because they are not of the same sex as Jesus Christ, whose ministry the priest represents.

"Imaging creates the possible. [This] powerful tool that we do not fully understand or use in our daily lives is a necessary first step in our efforts to bring about [individual and] social change." Even those of us who so urgently want to grow "and are working toward it have difficulty in comprehending and encompassing the enormity of what we are doing."[9] That is why imaging the divine as female is so essential. Until the image of the Goddess is internalized, women will be prey to self-doubt and disempowerment. Artists who are reclaiming the sacred iconography of the Goddess are creating a new social reality. As women in the ancient world were empowered by living with images of the divine female, so women today can be healed of the destructive psychological impact of our culture's pervasive negative image of the female.

The Goddess in Everywoman

When women began to look at the archaeological evidence of the prehistoric Goddess, they got in touch with long suppressed, deeply buried memories of archetypal images. Artist Mary Ann Fariello, who believes in the collective unconscious, opens herself up to the mysteries that precede memory and conjures up images that help her overcome fear (see fig. 125). Fariello was looking for an image of strength that would combat feelings of depression and negativity, but the beautiful ceramic mask modeled on her own face expresses ambivalence. The bird chained to the "mind" represents the human condition, the capacity to fly and at the same time be bound by civilization.

Artist Ann McCoy dreamed she was working on an archaeological dig restoring an ancient temple. Her guide through the sacred precinct is a draped woman whose veil hides her face. The woman bends down and lifts her skirt to expose her legs covered with fish scales. McCoy finds herself more fascinated than repelled, and notices when the woman turns her head that there are gill slits in her neck and fins protrude from behind her ears. As they speak, a procession led by a radiant child riding a donkey enters the temple grounds.

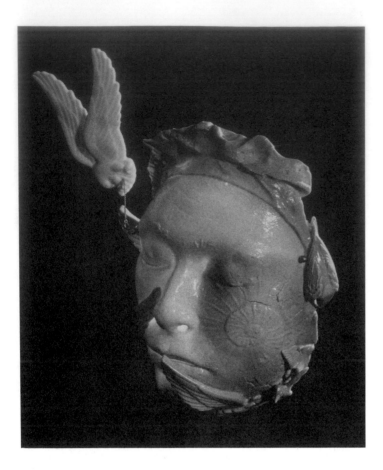

125. Mary Ann Fariello, SHROUDED MEMORIES, 1981. Porcelain mask, life size.

The porcelain mask of a woman's face, eyes closed in reflection, has a spiral shell tatooed in the cheek and a bird attached by a delicate golden chain to the forehead. The face is that of the artist. The bird and shell, primal symbols of the Goddess, were not conscious choices but appealed to her as expressions of the life force—the one the power of the heavens above and the other of the oceans below.

Using her sophisticated knowledge of both Christian and Jungian symbolism to interpret her dream, McCoy's first association was of Christ entering Jerusalem, yet there was an important difference: The radiant child was a little girl. In dreams the child often symbolizes a new idea born in the depths of the unconscious. McCoy, as was her working habit, transformed the dream imagery into her art, working with colored pencil on great white sheets of paper tacked up on the walls of her apartment (see fig. 126). The draped woman became the Fish Goddess, her head that of a recently discovered still-living archaic ancestor of the fish family. The radiant child, her head crowned in red-gold curls, now stands in innocent nakedness amidst the ruins. As in medieval alchemy, the wolf who eats rotting matter and the clear glass vials with fetuses inside symbolize the transformation of the old into the new. The age of Pisces, the fish, is coming to a close as the Goddess is reborn from the waters.

Artists habitually look at the unconscious as a source for personal expression. Some began to image themselves as the Goddess, others to re-create the ancient iconography in contemporary forms. Women began to see the wealth of Goddess imagery from the ancient Mediterranean and Third World with fresh eyes, tangible proof that "God was a woman." They bought reproductions of the icons and installed them in home altars along with personal mementos that had special meaning—shells from the beach, dried leaves and flowers, gemstones, photographs of loved ones—power objects of sacred connection.

Re-imaging the Goddess in their own likenesses was a path of self-discovery for many women artists, at times a painful confrontation with the discrepancy between the power inherent in the image and the powerlessness they felt. Each woman tapped into the power of the Goddess according to her own

126. Ann McCoy, REBIRTH OF THE GODDESS, 1986. Pencil on paper, on canvas. 9 ft. × 14 ft.

priorities. Asungi created a series of Amazons in honor of black women. "I needed to see strong, self-contained and focused black women so I reached into our tales, myths, goddesses and other spiritual realities."[10] The Goddess came to her in the guise of Katherine Dunham, the dancer who was as well a voodoo priestess (see color plate 16).

Another black artist, Faith Ringgold, made masks called "Weeping Witches" (see color plate 13) who mourn because of the double oppression of being black and female in our culture. They have their mouths open wide to symbolize women's need to speak out.[11] Ringgold, whose work mirrors the social reality of black women's lives, on a trip to Africa in 1976 saw the black woman as she is in her own environment, unafraid.

> She can go anywhere. She can get into a crowded bus with her breasts uncovered to nurse her baby, and any man there will come to her aid if she needs it.[12]

Her "witches" were inspired by African tribal masks used in women's initiation ceremonies to help the initiate get in touch with the powers of the spirits.

As a single parent trying to raise her daughter with no financial support, ceramicist Syma sorely needed the Goddess as mentor and guide. Her relationship with the Goddess is so intimate that it took her years to complete her private icon *Homage to Sophia,* which now hangs in her bedroom (see fig. 127).

Like Fariello, Syma works with a mold of her own face. Sophia started out as Syma's self-portrait as Miss America. With the artist's developing self-confidence, the ceramic face evolved into a symbol of transformation and potential. When confronted with her biggest artistic challenge, the brick sculptural pediments to be designed and executed for a row of townhouses in Boston opposite Symphony Hall, she called upon the Goddess. "I told her if she wanted to be on my building, she must help." The most prominent of the pediment reliefs shows a woman's face floating above the skyline, her hair flowing in sinuous waves across the rooftops like clouds (see fig. 128).

Sudie Rakusin's life-size oil paintings of goddesses portray women of power who gaze directly at us, confronting us with

127. Syma, HOMAGE TO SOPHIA, 1977–83. Clay and mixed media, life size. Photo by Gail Bryan. Syma's private icon is based on a ceramic mold of her own face.

128. Syma, SPIRIT OVER BOSTON, 1986. Brick. Photo by Gail Bryan.

"She's a kind of spirit over Boston." The face is another mask of the artist projected as the Goddess of the City like the patron deities of old.

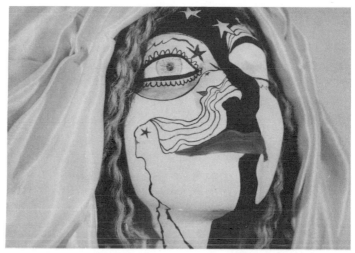

127

128

their truth, the artist's truth. Either nude or dressed in the robes of the soothsayer or priestess, they seem of our time, and yet we are unaccustomed to come upon women who reveal themselves so openly (see fig. 129). Rakusin projected onto her life-sized images her own need for wholeness and the acceptance of all that she is. She is the wild Hecate (see color plate 14).

> For years I have felt fragmented . . . competent as an artist but flawed as a woman living on the earth—not ever quite enough as a lover or friend. This last year led me into myself. . . . I have connected with my spirit, my soul and found a strength there. . . . I am learning of my power, my fire energy, the abundance in me . . . that all this energy—spiritual, psychic, emotional, creative, sexual—comes from the same source . . . and is limitless. I feel myself to be a channel, that there are messages I am to communicate. I feel driven to do this. I open willingly to these images, visions. . . . I am a Lesbian—angry at the violation of the earth, animals and women men have perpetrated. . . .
>
> I live to challenge all this. . . . We are of the goddess—strong, brave and angry. We are warriors who take risks to become. Our desires propel us. Our truths are of value, worth speaking. We love deeply and freely. In our loving we reflect back to the other the magnificence of herself and give her back her power. There is healing in this. We become whole again, going deeply into ourselves. We are all different and so very beautiful. [I]n my art I celebrate all this. . . . A cycle where what I experience and learn goes into my art . . . and as I create I discover myself.[13]

The ancient symbols of the Goddess take on new meaning for contemporary women who invoke them in times of personal crisis. Margo Machida, disoriented by the radically changing circumstances of her life when she came from a small town in the big island of Hawaii to live in New York, made a series of autobiographical paintings based on her feelings and associations of the moment. "They were like emotional Polaroids" (see fig. 130 and color plate 43). She sees the snake handling of the Minoan priestess as the test of spiritual power through an act of intense personal faith.

Coleen Kelly is another artist whose life was in turmoil. She was going through a divorce, had lost her home, and was

130. Margo Machida, CHARMED, 1984. Mixed media on canvas. 48 in. × 58 in.

"In *Charmed* I am a snake handler, which is my metaphor for the dangers of confronting self-discovery. This snake embodies the deeply repressed pain of my emotional history which I must 'handle' to achieve self-mastery and internal integration. In combining the snake image and my female form, I intentionally invoke a symbol which resonates with multiple mythological and religious associations. Although my intent is personal and secular, by linking self-image with that of a snake-handling goddess, I symbolically associate with her attributes of wisdom, strength, and regeneration."[21]

131. Coleen Kelly, THE MESSENGER: QUETZALCOATL WAS A WOMAN, 1986. Oil on canvas.

Kelly stands within the walls of the kiva, in a ritual posture, her nude body fully exposed. She is wearing a hummingbird mask. The blue hummingbird was the messenger of the Anasazi. With one hand she reaches for the serpent, the carrier of cosmic energy from the blue sky. From her other she discharges the lightning after it travels through her body. The shadow behind her is an ancestor figure; the raven in the foreground her guide into the unconscious. The hummingbird's message is that the Great Serpent God of the Aztecs, Quetzalcoatl, was a woman like herself.

taking a new path as a spiritual healer. Looking for a way to incorporate the making of art into her spiritual journey as artists still do in cultures where their role is considered sacred, she went on pilgrimage to Chaco Canyon in New Mexico, the ancient home of the Anasazi Indians, the ancestors of the Pueblo and Hopi peoples. In the ruins of a kiva, their sacred underground ceremonial center, she had a powerful vision that she later made into a painting. The four years that it took to complete the painting were a time of healing (see fig. 131).

Chyl Bergman was full of despair about the condition of our planet. Her encounter with the Dark Goddess helped her to work through some of her feelings. She spent ten days at the Council of the Feminine Fire with forty professional women who had come together to explore their inner life through ritual and dialogue in nature. They were camping out in the California hills at the Ojai Foundation, an organization committed to the process of spiritual transformation as an open and living system. It was late October and it poured rain all the time. Cold and damp, she remembered a vision that had haunted her years ago of a huge, black, very ancient creature covered with wounds, writhing in pain. She would walk around it, but whenever she got close enough to touch it, she would recoil in terror. Now she could identify her vision as Eresh-kigal and, steeped in Asian philosophy and Jungian psychology, know that an essential part of healing is to go into blackness, into the unknown.

When she returned to the studio, the energy of the council still potent, she painted a series of shadowy, abstract figures against dense, black ground, her feeling-perception of the age in which we live. Her small canvases of the Goddess were prayers of possibility. She called them after the powerful, magical names the women had chanted over and over again—Isis, Astarte, Diane, Hecate, Demeter, Kali . . . Inanna—as they

131

invoked the female force within. *Hecate* is the Dark Goddess. Life begins in the womb (see fig. 132). Her figure emerges out of a cloud of light celebrating women's growing self-respect. Bergman's black interiors are places of ritual transformation. Her images of *Hecate* recall the Paleolithic ritual objects from Czechoslovakia, in which the female form is reduced to its essential symbols, the nurturing breasts and the abstract figure with vulva slit (see figs. 5, 6). She was unaware of these obscure archaeological finds and calls their reappear-

132. Chyl Bergman (Cheryl Bowers), HECATE, 1986. Oil on canvas. 11 in. × 14 in.

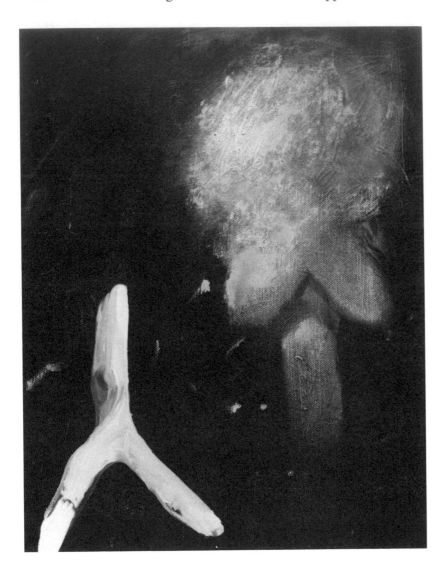

133. Audrey Flack, Isis, *1983. Acrylic on canvas. 60 in. × 60 in.*

ance in her work "morphogenetic resonances,"* believing that in this time of emerging consciousness the ancient forms are being recovered spontaneously.

Audrey Flack transformed an Egyptian death mask into an icon. An inveterate museum goer, she was attracted to the open, smiling face of an Egyptian woman painted on the outer wooden coffin in which the mummified body lay. Flack related to the dead woman as one woman to another—someone who like her had experienced birth, pain, and the death of loved ones. She used the portrait as the subject of her art (see fig. 133). She framed her Goddess with stars and Egyptian symbols like the *ankh,* the hieroglyph that stands for both female and life. The artist's inclusion of two pithy epigrams, existential statements about fate and immortality, and her naming the work after Isis whose mysteries promised life after

---

* The most fascinating—and apprehensible—treatment of this eye-opening theory is presented by Rupert Sheldrake in his book, *A New Science of Life* (Los Angeles: J. P. Tarcher, 1983). The physical and nonphysical influences of past people, events, and experiences are explained.

134

135

death, bring together her life as a painter and her life as a woman of spiritual vision. Like so many other women she seeks congruity among all aspects of her life and wants to incorporate a woman's way of seeing into mainstream art.

Mary Beth Edelson: In Search of the Goddess

New York artist Mary Beth Edelson in her search for empowerment identified with the Goddess herself.[14] Looking for an isolated Neolithic cave sanctuary where she could do a private ritual, she went to the island of Hvar in the Adriatic off the coast of Yugoslavia (see fig. 134).

> At daybreak the next morning we began the trip, climbing on and on while we and the heavy camera gear baked in the intense sun. At the top of the mountain . . . we began our descent to the barely accessible cave. The climb down was a series of straight drops. What had once been a path was now acres of mountain stone . . . Suddenly the blue Adriatic stretched before us . . . What an incredible location: the sea

134. Mary Beth Edelson, SEE FOR YOURSELF: PILGRIMAGE TO A NEOLITHIC CAVE, 1977. Private ritual in Grapceva Cave, Hvar Island, Yugoslavia. Photo by Mary Beth Edelson.

"For some years I had been attempting to make a pilgrimage to a Goddess site. I had been doing private rituals . . . for some time, both outdoors in nature and in the studio. I could feed off of them and hold them in my mind like totems but I was still hungry. I needed to do my rituals in an actual prehistoric cave; to experience a Neolithic site where I could smell the earth, poke around in the soil, breathe the air, and know that the cave air had circulated through my body and become part of me."[22]

135. Mary Beth Edelson, WOMAN RISING/ SEXUAL ENERGIES, 1974. Photograph and drawing. Private ritual. Outer Bank, North Carolina.

The female body is not a nude tantalizer, but powerful and wild, with self-generating energy. She takes a risk by not only exposing the body's naked form, but also by exposing the body's energy to potent energy forces in nature.

vista, a shelf of flat rock extending from the front of the cave, fruit and nut trees and berry bushes on either side. . . .

The cave was dazzling. It was magnificent. The main room, the great hall, sparkled and glistened with coral quartz. Stalagmites and stalactites, suggesting great temple pillars, divided the rooms into chambers. The atmosphere created a feeling of reverence and awe; . . . for me it was a holy place.[15]

She documents her rituals with a camera set on time release; the technical procedures have become second nature and do not interfere with the process. She allows the ritual to evolve naturally, getting in touch with the energy there.

I felt like the center of the universe. . . . The cave contracted and expanded with my rhythms, and shimmered on its way back and forth. I made a pact with the cave: it would tell me some of its secrets in exchange for my rituals, rituals that it had not seen for millennia. I in turn would learn some secrets now and some later—I had only to listen, to keep in touch.[16]

Through public and private rituals she seeks to exorcise the trauma women feel of being female in a world in which the norm for wholeness is male and woman is the alien other, in an art world alienated from its original sacred purposes, and a society in which it is taboo for a woman to take her spiritual destiny into her own hands. Her intent is to restore "a living mythology that cuts across many areas—political and spiritual."[17]

Her rituals are intended to connect her with the primal energies of the prehistoric Goddess. Like magic, ritual is the act of transforming consciousness. Edelson's Earth Goddess is as much a product of her personal revolt, her new female assertiveness, as it is a recognition of the universal power of the Goddess in the archaic world. "The Goddess has taken over Edelson's being, and thereby recovered her own being."[18]

Edelson photographs her body as a stand-in for the Goddess and then draws over the photograph to emphasize how she felt after the ritual.

These photographic images were defining images—*not who I am* but who *we are*. The images were presented aggressively as sexuality, mind and spirit comfortable in one body. I was summoning Goddess to make house calls, talking to Goddess with the body, and ending the dialogue with being [see fig. 135].

Woman Rising symbolizes the joy and exuberance of our new freedom as well as making a political statement for women that says "*I am,* and *I am large,* and *I am my body,* and *I am not going away.*"[19]

Betsy Damon: The 7,000-Year-Old Woman

Artist-activist Betsy Damon brought the prehistoric Goddess into the streets of New York in a modern ritual imbued with ancient meaning. Damon is at once the Goddess of Death and Rebirth, Lilith, the dark Owl Goddess, and the nourishing multibreasted virgin mother of Ephesus. She is a shaman dressed as a birdwoman, a great claw-footed owl whose layered feathers are indicated by bags of flour, colored in a range from blood red to yellow. Her white moon-face is pierced by haunting dark eyes and jet-black lips. Her movements are ponderous and slow. She crouches in the ancient birth-giving posture, within a sacred space defined by a chalk circle, cutting off the bags one by one, to reveal her nakedness in human form. The reaction of the gathering crowd was intense, curious, and hostile. Damon's sense of vulnerability was excruciating.

> The piece is about time; remembering time, moving out through time and moving back through time; claiming past time and future time . . . women's relation to time past.[20]

As "The 7,000-Year-Old Woman," she was putting female energy out into the streets at a formative time in the Women's Movement in the mid-seventies (see figs. 136, 137).

The bag is a recurring motif in Damon's work. Like the vessel and the pot, the bag symbolizes women's inner space, the womb, the container of life. Damon's imagery is archetypal; therein lies its power. Her sources are her dreams, her obsessions. In her "Shrine for Every Woman," a small cloth bag serves as a receptacle for women's stories. Damon took the portable shrine to the international women's meetings at Copenhagen and Nairobi where it became a meeting place for women of all nations to tell their stories, to reflect, to heal. The sharing of life experiences with other women cuts through isolation and makes change seem possible. Women's "silence," the wiping out of their narrative and creative work from all historical records, has been one of the most grievous patriar-

136. Betsy Damon, THE 7,000-YEAR-OLD WOMAN, 1977. Performance #2. Photograph by Su Friedrich.

chal sins, so deadening because women's culture has been rendered invisible and women know themselves only through the words of the male. A safe place in which to tell their stories, and to be heard, is a healing space.

Role-playing the Old Myths

Like the priestess of old, sculptor Suzanne Benton uses masks in ritual performances to retell ancient women's tales of recurring and timeless significance. She plays a range of mythical and legendary characters from cultures worldwide—Lilith, Sarah and Hagar, Demeter and Persephone, and the Japanese Sun Queen Amaterasu. Recasting their tales from a contemporary woman's view, she confronts "the hierarchy of social position and values in our own society, and redefines some of our unquestioned myths.

"Masks empower us to unearth our potential beings. This leap of faith permits a vision of what lies hidden even to

137. Betsy Damon, THE 7,000-YEAR-OLD WOMAN, 1977. Performance #2. Photograph by Su Friedrich.

ourselves." She is interested in encouraging an expanded sense of the archetype and in her Life Experience Workshops guides participants in the use of masks to tell their own stories. "Working with masks to explore mythic materials is a powerful tool of psychological healing. The magical aura of the mask makes possible a palpable connection to the ancient and sacred that is liberating and not easily forgotten."[21]

Benton performs her masked rituals all over the world at the sacred places were the stories were originally told. At Eleusis in Greece she played both mother and daughter in "The Tale of Persephone."

Her metal masks are unique works of art in themselves even without the body enlivening them, evoking an emotional immediacy that is at the core of myth. While working in Germany on a series of masks related to the Holocaust, she looked to Greek myths in order to comprehend the complexity of the tragedy and created a mask of Demeter as the archetypal survivor (see fig. 138).

Women and Nature

Benton's masked ritual reveals the transformation that is possible through identifying with the archetypal. Marcelina Martin's photograph captures the wonder and mystery of a woman's discovery of the sacredness of her body in nature, creating a visual experience of an inner reality that is felt but seldom shared with others except through art (see fig. 139). Martin focused on a private ritual moment as Hallie Iglehart Austen wades into a woodland pond. In this picture we are given a glimpse of the integration of personal mythology with collective mythology that so empowers women. Through the energies of ritual, the woods have become the sacred grove, the horse, bathed in the aura of summer sunlight, a totemic animal. Hallie becomes the Goddess in her sacral nakedness holding a conch, the symbol of the sacred vulva, in her upraised hand. She explains what the photograph means to her.

> Nature is our greatest teacher. As we listen to other forms of life, which often know better than we how to live in harmony, we reclaim wisdom that was once part of our ancestors' everyday life.

138. Suzanne Benton, DEMETER, 1983. Steel and copper. 12½ × 9½ × 12½ in.

The sorrowful face of the Goddess conveys the enormity of her loss. Mourning her daughter, Demeter has made the earth barren; for a whole year nothing has grown. There is no birth, human or animal. With the return of her daughter from the underworld, life begins anew. Benton identifies female power with Demeter's tale of death and resurrection.

139. Marcelina Martin, BETWEEN THE WORLDS: WOMANSPIRIT GUIDE, 1981. Photograph.

139

Boo, the white horse in *Between the Worlds,* was one such great teacher for me. . . . We would amble along at his pace, always stopping, by his choice, at this pool of water. He would stare at the water and stand stock-still for about an hour. My own meditation was on the incredible display of light in the trees above us, for Boo allowed me to lie back, our spines aligned, with my head on his rump. I lay in this vulnerable position, feeling Boo breathing under my body, trusting him not to take a step and roll me off. We both knew when it was time to move on, and I carried with me a sense of deep peace and gratitude to Boo and that place.

I am fully inhabiting my body, am myself one of the elements, stepping into the mysterious waters of timeless trance. Boo protects and guides me to the deep secrets of his sacred pool. For a moment, I know that I am free and I know that I am safe, able to move between the worlds, where magic, renewal and healing occur. This process of regeneration is our birthright, and precisely because they have been denied to us, we rediscover our heritage in our bodies and in Nature.[22]

Earth and Fire: Ana Mendieta's Ritual Sculpture

Cuban-born Ana Mendieta's work was an ongoing dialogue between the artist and the landscape. The making of her earth-body sculpture was a way of asserting her emotional ties to the earth and her mythic past. Sent by her parents from Castro's Cuba to the United States, she was a thirteen-year-old refugee and miserable in an Iowa orphanage and in foster homes. Cut off from the emotional warmth of Latin American family life, agonizingly lonely and alienated by the repressive institutional environment, Ana felt overwhelmed by the sense of having been cast out from the womb of nature (see fig. 140).

> My art is the way I re-establish the bonds that unite me to the universe. It is a return to the maternal source. Through my earth/body sculptures I become one with the earth. I become an extension of nature and nature becomes an extension of my body. This obsessive act of reasserting my ties with the earth is really the reactivation of primeval beliefs . . . [in] an omnipresent female force, the after-image of being encompassed within the womb, [and] is a manifestation of my thirst for being.[23]

140. Ana Mendieta, UNTITLED, 1977. Tree of Life series. Color photograph. Earth-body work with tree and mud executed at Old Man's Creek, Iowa City, Iowa.

Her naked body bathed in mud, she stands against an enormous tree, a living icon. The woman-and-the-tree is the Tree of Life. Like the seed, the woman holds the mystery of life in her body.

Her early work is marked by a preoccupation with blood, violence, and fertility, a characteristic of the Hispano-American fusion of Indian and Catholic religions. Once in a performance at Franklin Furnace in New York, she walked on stage to the beat of Cuban music, dipped her hands into a bucket of blood mixed with red tempera paint and marked the walls with the tracings of her outstretched arms. Her ritual gesture evoked a primordial past when women pressed their red-ochred hands against the cave walls.

In the *Silueta* series, Mendieta used the outline of her body to create the image, cutting or demarcating her silhouette into a great variety of natural materials and environments (see fig. 141). She silhouetted her body in flowers, which she then floated down a river in a raft, as on a journey to another

world. She outlined her body in candles as in a shrine. She altered a ravine and cave entrance to resemble her body, drew her figure on the stone floor of a pre-Columbian temple, and made her effigy into a volcano with a gunpowder *Silueta*.

Mendieta returned to her native Cuba and, working there for the first time, carved her images deep into the limestone caves of Jaruco, a mountainous area west of Havana that has traditionally given shelter to Cuban rebels but was once sacred to the Goddess. Her earth sculpture no longer represents a personal return to the earth but something more, the return to her homeland. The images are stronger, cruder, more sexual and more abstract than the delicate early work, as though the artist had gained strength from the direct contact with her native earth and the myths of its ancient peoples (see fig. 142

141. Ana Mendieta, UNTITLED, 1977. Silueta series. Color photograph. Gunpowder silueta executed at Old Man's Creek, Iowa City, Iowa.

She etched her form into the earth, poured gunpowder on the outline, and set it on fire, leaving a black human-shaped pit of fertile ash.

142. Ana Mendieta, Ruprestrian Series, 1981. Carved rock on cave wall. Life size. Jaruco, Cuba.

In the *Ruprestrian* series the measure of her image is still her own body. The aura is that of Laussel. Carved into the soft limestone of the cave wall, only the primal forms of the body are inscribed.

and color plate 34). She has named these images for the symbolic forces of the pre-Columbian goddesses in the language of the now extinct Tiano Indians: "Our Menstruation," "Old Mother Blood," "Moon/Luna."

Mendieta also experimented with drawings using black paint on bark paper and dry leaves, making portable work for the first time (see figs. 143, 144).

In 1983, while at the American Academy in Rome on a fellowship, Mendieta had a studio for the first time, and she began to explore the possibilities of permanent sculpture. She turned to the tree trunk as her medium, continuing her exchange between the landscape and the mythic female figure, the woman and the tree.

Her violent and tragic death in 1986 at the age of thirty-six was a terrible loss. She had just received her first commission for a monumental work that would be permanently installed in a Los Angeles park. Because of her untimely death the project will never be realized, but her proposal remains. It was to be called *La Jungla*. Seven redwood tree trunks were to be installed in a triangular patch of grass in a relationship "charged with tenseness." Each would have an image carved and burned into the exposed trunk representing the seven mystical powers of life that rule the jungle.

More than any other contemporary artist, Mendieta's work fully embodied the archetypal. She is neither re-creating nor reclaiming an ancient art; rather through her very personal

143. Ana Mendieta, THE LABYRINTH OF LIFE, 1982. Clay and earth. Executed in Iowa. 41 in. × 61 in.

and unique creative process she has given birth to a new iconography and pluralistic art singularly appropriate to our time. Radical, political, sacred, her work fuses mystery and history.

The barriers that once separated ritual and art, the performing and the visual arts are breaking down. At the same time mystery is returning as artists seek to find a way to express inner meaning in their work. Art critics have hailed the return of sacred content to art as something new. Women in search of the Goddess have been making sacred art for twenty years and the transformation of the female body has been the focus of their work.

144. Ana Mendieta, THE VIVIFICATION OF THE FLESH (LA VIVIFICACIÓN DE LA CARNE), 1981–82. Amategram series. Gouache and acrylic on amate (bark) paper. 24¾ in. × 17 in.

While the images continue to be identifiable as female figures, they are abstracted and emblematic; the reference to the artist's own body was blurred. Her images were becoming more universal.

The Resurrection of the Body and the Resacralization of Sexuality

CHAPTER 14

Affirmation of the female body as a source of pleasure and power is a major goal of the Women's Movement. Acknowledging the body as the source of knowing and a repository of lived experience has been an important breakthrough in women's search for identity. Exploring our own bodies is often the first step in self-definition.

Most women in Western culture see themselves only through the distorting gaze of a society dominated by men. While this is true for the totality of our being, it is conspicuously so for our perceptions of our bodies. The English social critic John Berger calls attention to women's habit of glancing in store windows as they pass by to check out their appearance as if they existed only in a mirrored reflection.

Our culture has been so constructed under the lens of male experience that women see themselves from the perspective of patriarchy. A woman's body is the object of male desire, fascination, and fear. A woman's nude body is a forbidden image, the theme of pornography. Pornography is not about desire but about exploitation, debasing not only the women and children involved but also the male consumer whose instincts it perverts.

The widespread violence against women in all segments of society can be linked to the ideas so deeply rooted in Judeo-Christian ethos that female sexuality is evil. While we continue to argue about the degree to which social attitudes are influenced by the visual image, we cannot deny that the themes and iconography of the visual arts reflect the culture in which they are made.

Although Western culture at large pays far too much attention to the surface appearance of things, a woman, far more than a man, is physical appearance. Artist-journalist Gail Bryan, sensitive to the camera's ability to both reveal and mask, uses the self-portrait to discover who she is. When she returned to graduate art school, her first assignment was to create a slide-show of self-portraits: She was to be physically present in every picture. The images could not be abstract in any way; shadows or props could not be used as stand-ins for body parts.

Bryan found she was paralyzed and did not know where to begin. A worldly woman, elegant, sophisticated, she was in her mid-thirties, having, like other women of our time, radically severed from her past, leaving behind many of the givens of her identity.

It was six weeks before she took her first picture. "I didn't know who I was. My body had been so packaged. I could only see myself by stripping away all the different faces—all the clothes and with them all the personas and masks that I had lived behind" (see figs. 145, 146). In the years since, she has continued to do series of self-portraits, her vehicle for the ongoing process of self-discovery.

> Photography was eminently suitable for my project. With the camera there is an instant record, there is instant involvement. Not even the hand intervenes. Everything is reduced to eye/brain.
>
> When I put myself in front of the camera, there is instant involvement. It is almost like psychodrama. . . . I do not know what I am feeling until I see the picture. . . . If I were painting or writing, there would be censors at work. In photography, there is a pared down quality and I can touch the raw material of what is there. The camera cuts right through layers of defense. It is as though my rational mind has no connection to the feeling self. It is when I see and live with the print later that my rational mind can see it . . . then I say, "Oh, that's who I am, that is what I was feeling." The camera catches my soul.[1]

There has been no place in our culture for an ordinary woman to turn for validation of bodily experience that is uniquely female. Conventional medicine has objectified and fragmented a woman's body, treating her organs and life

145. Gail Bryan, SELF-PORTRAIT WITH DAFFODILS, 1976. Black-and-white photograph.

"I set out to take a romantic picture of Spring, but the flowers became a mask. It is a women's mask, the mask of social gentility. It has to do with being a lady. And I—the real woman—am out of focus in the background. But at the same time I am pushing the trappings back in the face of correct society. This is an aggressive picture."

146. Gail Bryan, BEYOND THE MASK, 1973. Black-and-white photograph.

One face is superimposed on the other. "It was a difficult period for me. I had rejected all expected roles: elegant correct wife, academic achiever. I got involved full time in the women's movement, working for the destruction of the social fabric as it existed. I was mourning the death of the family and the integrated ideal I had seen myself as being. I felt an enormous excitement. With the stripping away of all masks, everything seemed possible but it is not easy. I came face to face with an existential void."

processes with a "scientific" detachment that excludes her psychological self. The depersonalization of the doctor/patient relationship has increased at the same time that a complex and enormously costly technology has come to dominate both diagnosis and treatment. This combination contributes to a woman's sense of alienation from her own body that, like the doctor, she has come to experience as a *problem*.

When medicine evolved as a scientific profession in the eighteenth century, the male doctors forced the female practitioners—midwives, herbalists, traditional healers—out of the field and took over all aspects of health care connected with reproduction. Eventually childbirth was removed from the home to the hospital, which has proved a mixed blessing. In psychological terms, the price has been very high; pregnancy and childbirth have been transformed into an illness. Moreover, today reproductive technology fragments not only the experience of birth but also women's role in conception and gestation. The human infant can now be conceived in a test tube, incubated in one woman's womb, and raised by another. The ugly issues raised by surrogate motherhood, in which a woman's body is rented and her child sold, have forced us at least to give pause and consider what a woman's body rights are and where technological tinkering with sacred process can lead. A woman's body is sacred not to some distant deity or to an institutionalized religion but to herself. A woman's right to control her body, her sexuality, and her reproduction is basic to the recovery of woman's full humanity. As the Boston Women's Health Collective has taught us "our bodies are ourselves."

But even for women themselves, objective anatomical knowledge of women's bodies was a dark mystery. The appearance of women's genitalia, unlike men's, which hang out, was unknown territory. Few women knew what their most sacred parts looked like. All reference to them was veiled in shame and embarrassment, their very names were unspeakable in polite company, having been made into "dirty" language of four-letter curse words. Our bodies *are* ourselves. We are sensuous beings who know the world through our senses, who know ourselves through physical intimacy.

Women's sexuality has been defined as that which gives pleasure to men. No distinction has been made between what is sexually satisfying to men and to women that might not necessarily be the same. Masters and Johnson's research validating the fact of clitoral orgasm was hailed as a revelation by many women who began to reclaim the marvelous plurality and diffusiveness of their own sexual response. To overcome Victorian prudery in which women, at least all "nice" ones, were seen as without sexual feelings has taken a long time.

Furthermore, the mind/body split in Western culture relegates emotions and body to women, rationality and spirit to men. Just how much this stereotyping results from the social construction of gender, childrearing, and limiting social roles has yet to be tested, as fathers are beginning to take a more active part in parenting and women to enter the workplace. Psychologist Carol Gilligan's research demonstrates that women tend to make moral decisions within the context of relationship rather than on the basis of abstract rules. This suggests that they respond to life in a more wholistic way. Culture has punished women for their feeling response, judging this way as less productive and valuable because in an advanced capitalistic society like ours value is gauged in terms of money earned. In this context women's work outside the marketplace is discounted.

Many women continue to be uncomfortable with their bodies. "Because women's social subordination has resulted largely from the unchangeable character of our bodies, [they] believe that it is backward to perceive any part of that character as culturally affirmative or worth retaining."[2] Many favor an unobtainable, overrated, and undesirable androgyny. Some feminists' unease with their bodies smacks of one more dualism. The wish to ignore or deny biological differences cuts women off at the neck as effectively as the diatribes of the early church fathers and the pious preachings of medieval ascetics. I suggest that women's wombs are their power centers, not just symbolically but in physical fact. When we say we act from our guts, from our deepest instincts, this is what we are speaking of. The power of our womb has been stolen from us.

Philosopher and poet Adrienne Rich asks whether women cannot

> begin, at last, to *think through the body,* to connect what has been so cruelly disorganized—our great mental capacities

hardly used, our highly developed tactile sense, our genius for close observation, our complicated, pain-enduring, multi-pleasured physicality. . . . There is for the first time today a possibility of converting our physicality into both knowledge and power.[3]

The female body is the expressive vehicle of the creative life force, the energy that activates our being. English therapist John Rowan believes that every man in Western culture also needs this connection to the vital female principle in nature and urges men to turn to the Goddess.[4] In this way men will be able to relate to human women on more equal terms, not fearful or resentful of female power. Perhaps this is how it was in prehistoric times when men and women coexisted peacefully under the hegemony of the Goddess.

When women deny all those parts of themselves said to be like nature—the relational, the carnal, the body processes and rhythms—they are denying their bodily, sensate selves.

Feminist theorists view the cultural construction of gender as the crux of the problem of women's oppression. Anthropologist Sherry Ortner's important essay, "Is Female to Male as Nature is to Culture?" was hailed as the explanation for women's almost universal lower status. Lucy Lippard challenges Ortner's conclusion.

> Ortner . . . acknowledges that the biological and psychic differences between men and women "only take on significance of superior/inferior within the framework of culturally defined value systems" (Ortner 1972:25) yet even she proceeds to follow the conventional, male-conceived path by defining culture as the transformation and transcendence of nature, wherein woman's role as synthesizer, mediator, or simply fuser of nature and culture is destined to be "transcended" rather than valued in its own right.[5]

With the growing understanding that the devaluation of nature is at the root of our ecological crisis, this argument takes on a different meaning. To be part of a culture that dominates and ravages nature no longer seems such a prize. Indeed, deep ecologists see all of humanity, both men and women, as situated within and intimately connected to nature.

Our Sexual Selves, the Truest Indicator of Our Personalities

Feminist theory that gender is a construct of culture, not biology, makes us aware once more how muddied the traditional definitions of the key words of our discourse are. In this analysis, *sex* is the biological given, the inherited physical characteristics that define us as women or men. *Gender* is the cultural definition of behavior defined as appropriate to the sexes in a given society at a given time.

Sex is a biologically based need, oriented not only toward procreation but also toward pleasure and release of tension. It involves varieties of genital and erogenous activities, not necessarily including orgasm. *Sexuality* is a more diffuse term, both including and transcending organic states, and implies erotic desire or activity, including procreation.

The word *erotic* comes from the Greek *eros*, the personification of love and creative power in all aspects. The erotic arises from our deepest instincts and is the guiding light toward understanding self and the world, as well as interpersonal communication. Since we express ourselves erotically through our sexuality, our sexuality can be understood as the truest indicator of our personality.[6] The erotic is our natural source of personal power and functions in several ways. The erotic is the power that comes from sharing deeply any pursuit with another person—be it physical, emotional, psychological, or intellectual—forming a bond between sharers and is the source of our joy.

In our culture we don't understand the roots of our sexuality and consequently fear it. We repress, deny, and subvert our erotic needs and impulses. Christianity denigrates sexuality as lust, valuing only its procreative function. Prevailing notions of power, abstract reasoning, and self-control deprecate instinct, emotion, and sensuality as weaknesses, view them as obstacles to success. The erotic has often been misnamed, considered immoral, confused with its opposite—the pornographic, a word from the Greek *pornos* for prostitute or female slave. Pornography is about power, about sex as a weapon, in the same way that rape is about violence and not sexuality at all. Pornography is the direct denial of the power of the erotic, since in emphasizing sensation without feeling, it represents the suppression of true sexuality.

We misuse seduction. To seduce is to beguile, to attract, to win over. Seduction is being in touch with your erotic power as a way to invite someone into your own space. When we misuse seduction to manipulate, we depersonalize both ourselves and the other. Sexual excitement is an inclusive creative energy. Sexuality is not a part of self to be isolated and objectified, separated from feeling. Such a split leads to making a fetish of sexuality and ultimately to abuse.

Eros holds the promise of deep connection, a cutting through the layers of caution and defensiveness that characterize our interpersonal relationships, a way out of the traps of self-absorption fostered by the stress of modern urban life. Eros is play, the fullest expression of personality in the union of body and spirit. We don't know how to play and don't even understand what it really is. Play is not passive entertainment or consumption but an activity of the spirit that allows full expression of our total being and sensibility. We might well look to the animals, a pair of birds mating, squirrels frolicking in the snow, or to the pure sensual pleasure of a kitten purring as its soft underbelly is stroked.

The Body Art of Carolee Schneemann

Artist Carolee Schneemann does know how to play, to touch, to feel, to be with all the wild abandon of a creature who is still part of nature. A delightful, beautiful, uninhibited woman, she uses her female body as a very rich resource for the making of her radical and provocative performance pieces and films. Performance art is a hybrid combining the visual arts, theater, dance, music, poetry, and ritual. While in some respects a theatrical form, this performance is free of the artificial conventions, of actors trained in ways of occupying a stage and projecting themselves to an audience. "Schneemann stresses the importance of 'movement, exercise, . . . dancing'; the physicality of the body, not its theatrical skills, is her point."[7] For her the body includes the sensual, the sexual, the erotic, pleasure, all that we found so beautifully communicated in Minoan Crete. She was one of the first artists to mine the rich Goddess lore (see fig. 147).

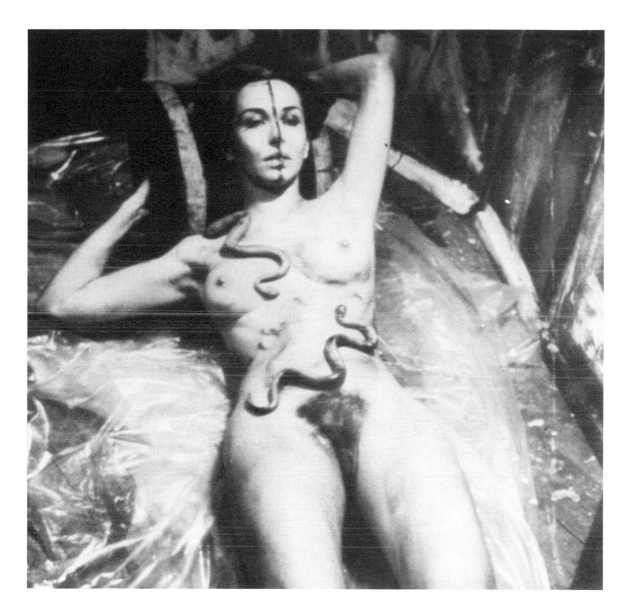

147. Carolee Schneemann, EYE BODY, 1963. Photograph of a performance.

Schneemann appeared nude with live snakes crawling on her belly and breasts in a 1963 performance called *Eye Body,* recalling the rituals of the Minoan priestess invoking the chthonic power of the serpent.

Hers was a defiant act of exorcism. She wanted to banish taboos, to free women from the bonds of male-defined pornography, to give women back their own bodies and the natural eroticism that had been suppressed in America's puritanical culture. Her imagination was haunted by images of the Cretan bull dancer—joyful, free, bare-breasted women leaping from danger to ascendancy over the bodies of the charging animals. *Eye Body* is about transformation, about identifying with intuition instead of the rational. Schneemann is in touch with her unconscious. Dreams are an important source of her imagery.

Schneemann is a painter who has enlarged the domain of her activity, using bodily gestures as her brush strokes.

> Covered in paint, grease, chalk, ropes, plastic, I establish my body as visual territory. Not only am I an image maker, but I explore the image values of flesh as the material I choose to work with. The body may remain erotic, sexual, desired, desiring but it is as well votive: marked, written over in a text of stroke and gesture discovered by my creative female will.[8]

She was challenging the traditional use of the female nude in Western art as an object to be manipulated. Schneemann was using the nude as herself—the artist, the image maker— and as a primal, archaic force. "I felt compelled to 'conceive' of my body in manifold aspects which had eluded the culture around me."[9] In the early 1960s even before Betty Friedan's *Feminine Mystique* had launched the women's movement, she understood the urgent need for every woman to reconstruct herself if she were to be free.

"Man is not the enemy"; he too is caught up in a culture that denies all expression of the feminine.

> Most men now have such guilty vague fears because they feel they must insist on their special insights and do not grasp the range, dimension of feminist change as personal transformation—which means hearing, listening to women. The enemy is man—blind determination to continue to define woman and expect her to live within by his . . . situation as if it were hers, he deflects the lessons of her unique situation with . . . his dominance. This is what we are changing—defining women through the thoughts and actions of other women.

> Men have continually re-invented, contrived the images of women because they buried, denied and repressed our experienced, invented, lived images made by ourselves. But men cannot image what it is to be a woman dreamt by a man. His long dream enshrouded our very own.[10]

Literate, articulate, aware of historical process and the implicit culture of the contemporary art world, her published writings

---

gleaned from journal entries document her struggle to reclaim women's erotic nature. "We are part of nature and of all visible and invisible forms. Our lives themselves are the materials, the stuff for our art. Our lives are art containers, life the way we shape or discover it being a form of art, the happening an intensification of our actions in life." From childhood, she saw the world as animate, expressive, alive, responsive to her desires.

> The natural world was intoxicating, giving my senses information which freed emotions for personal relationships which might one day have the rich wheeling of unpredictable qualities. My sense of my own physical life and of making things within life were always united. I began to draw before I could speak and never stopped drawing.[11]

She understands the sacredness of the ordinary and the lived experience. Performance is a ritual for her and other artists such as Mary Beth Edelson and Rachel Rosenthal who seek to connect with the presence of the ancient Goddess and the integration of body and spirit that patriarchal cultures and myths have torn asunder. "There is so much I think of in regard to the confluence of psychic and aesthetic recognition once that path between the conscious and unconscious is activated."[12]

Schneemann was a precocious child who from her earliest childhood memories reveled in the pleasure of her sexuality.

> Drawing and masturbating were the first sacred experiences I remember. Both activities began when I was about 4 years old. Exquisite sensations produced in my body and images that I made on paper, tangled with language, religion, everything that I was taught. As a result I thought that the genital was where God lived.

She grew up in the countryside in an environment that supported her naturalness. She remembered that her parents' sexual pleasure with each other was all pervasive and that she was part of that.

> [We'd] . . . all lie in bed on Sunday mornings, they would teach me to read the comics. . . . I remember the deep intimacy, sensuousness and delight. I built my own erotic fantasy life with various invisible animal and human lovers inhabiting my sheets, bed. . . .

Growing up in the country was very important.

> The animals were sexual creatures and I identified that part of my nature with them. Nudity was also clear and direct. We turned hay as adolescents. In the afternoons after working we would just take off our work clothes to swim naked in the river.

As the child of a rural physician, she was exposed to the human body as an ordinary fact of everyday life.

> My father took care of the body . . . the living body, the dying body. People would come to the house with bloody limbs . . . and we were trained to sit them down, put a towel around something that was bleeding and then run and get him. I also would peek through the keyhole of his office because it was on our side of the house. Sometimes I'd see a woman's foot sticking off the ledge of the examining table and I'd crouch there listening to him say strange things. For example, he asked one woman when she had "menstruated," and she asked, "What's that?" and I heard him say, "bleed." I had Grey's Anatomy book to look at and it gave me a peculiar inside/out visual vocabulary.

She knew she could get in touch with that naturalness by making images and by loving.

> When I was young I was called a "mad pantheist" by older friends. I didn't know what that was about (I hoped it was a female panther), but I was told that a pantheist is a nature worshiper. I had elaborate ritual places to go and lie at certain times of the day or night. There were special trees that I had to be in contact with and I would hide in a shallow well that my mother filled in with flowers. I did this at dusk because I found the transition from day to night uncertain and painful. I would get dizzy listening to the birds, smelling night aromas; . . . that was what I had to do.[13]

Schneemann works intuitively seeking to recover long buried dimensions of female experience.

> As an artist, I work intensively, reflectively; images come to me through a creative process and in concentrated states of which I am not entirely conscious, or totally comprehending. . . . Images occurred in my work without my knowledge at the time that they could be perceived as archetypal to the Goddess. . . . Coincidence, correspondence, the occurrence of "visions" given visual equivalence become significant personal

tools which can make possible a reach outside the existing conventions to reanalyze and research misappropriated, denied and obfuscated feminist aspects of our culture. To express these linkages, to demonstrate them as real and contemporary must be seen as a way of diminishing the extraordinary distance between the destroyed female culture of the past and our own present. . . .

For a performance artist the body carries the language of insight and transformation. . . . It is both a new and ancient discipline, a reintegration of physical expressions of a long lost and denied spiritual force. In pioneering, developing and demonstrating performance art and the languages of the body. . . . I have had to face resistance to my work and its unifying influence as a bridge between the split of valued-mind and distorted-body, of the respect for verbal language against the depreciation of gestural language and physical ritual.[14]

In all of Schneemann's work sex is a primary aspect. "The sexuality of her performance work results not from nudity or specific sexual behavior, but from, in a sense, converting all the bodies in the work into sexual organs."[15] She is interested in the tactile, sensual, erotic response. Her art breaks all imposed boundaries of the art world.

She also makes films, of which the most famous is *Fuses* (1965–68), showing two people, Schneemann and composer James Tenney, to whom she was then married, making love. A document about her erotic life with her husband, she expressed an intent to portray sexual experience in film from a female point of view for the first time. The seemingly random series of images was a novel experience indeed, analogous for me as a woman to that state of sensual awareness and consciousness of arousal, climax, and release in which vision is turned inward, unfocused, and color explodes. The setting is natural and domestic: the bed, the open window, the trees outside, a familiar cat. Body and face are seen in fragments, relegated to the periphery. *Fuses* is silent, the sound "no sound," like the gentle waves eternally washing on the beach, outside of time. Sequences of film were chopped, painted, dissolved, and become a material metaphor for erotic sensations. Her detailed development of a specifically natural context for the lovers' eroticism suggests that sex is not a single experience with its own limited, "proper" place and function, as is usually the case in popular or pornographic film and literature, but rather is a formative model for human apprehension of the world. She was trying to, as it were, "defuse" the representation of the sexual act, to domesticate lovemaking to show that sex is normal.

Fuses is part of a dense, multilayered *Autobiographic Trilogy* about sexuality, the web of domesticity between male and female, the nature of primitive body sensations. More than anything else, however, these films and the issues they address, come down to one thing: her experience as female.[16]

As a painter and performance artist in the early sixties Schneemann

> carved out a unique artistic cosmology based on sensual experience, and from an inherited repertoire of the unrepresentable and the historical symbolic stand-ins for women. . . . She developed a complex, at times orgiastic approach based on her own primal bodily sensations, a vocabulary stemming from the Woman as Other, as desired sexual being—all in an era predating the rise of feminism.[17]

Schneemann's work provokes, cajoles, sometimes unsettles us, demanding that attention be paid to our erotic selves, that we trust our bodies as inexhaustible sources of pleasure and knowledge and wonder. The joyousness that runs throughout her life and her work points toward her attempt to research and reinvent and reintegrate the celebration of the erotic, which was so vital a part of the culture of the Goddess.

"Revamping the World": The Resacralization of Female Sexuality Is the Challenge of Every Woman

Writer Deena Metzger urges a resacralization of female sexuality as the challenge for every woman. She deplores the mores of the recent sexual revolution. Nothing has changed.

> It is not sex we are after at all, but something far deeper.

> The task is to accept the body as spiritual and sexuality and erotic love as spiritual disciplines. It is eros which will transform our culture.[18]

> I am concerned about the possibility of seduction in a world where the belief system is puritanical, where . . . sexuality is

evil, eros is diabolical, and woman is tainted. Here we are taught that these are not attitudes nor ideas but descriptions of the order of things, that this is the nature of divine and natural laws. In this world the belief system is contradicted by instinct, and experience, by memories from the collective unconscious. And so . . . we must live in the world as heretics. My concern is heresy.[19]

Metzger has been active in transforming culture through her writings and workshops. She has developed "healing workshops" as a therapeutic means to address issues of creativity, personal transition, emotional distress, and life-threatening diseases. As a healer and psychotherapist, she works extensively with autobiography, life history, story telling, myth, and fairy tales. She seeks to "revamp the world," to restore a tradition, to reinstitute a way of seeing the world, to recover the ancient consciousness of eros.

> Sometimes according to behaviorists, feelings follow behavior, but most often the behaviors overlaid upon an alien worldview alter to correspond to the underlying thought. Contemporary sexual freedom is a case in point. For although it seeks to imitate what is thought to be pagan permissiveness, it is essentially distinct, because the symbolic magical components have not been restored. It may look like the same behavior, but it is entirely different. In fact, we do not know what appropriate behaviors, rituals, ceremonies will develop when puritanism is dislodged from the deepest levels of our psyche and when the sacredness of sexuality is restored. We cannot know what forms will develop in the contemporary world when the inclination toward bonding is not undermined by the terror of fusion. Though we talk about wholeness, oneness, holiness, we persist in developing duality, separation, division. So we do not know how we will come to express a sacred universe when it is restored. We do not know what forms sexuality as communion will take.[20]

What does it mean to revamp society? Metzger would revive the *spirit* of the sacred marriage in which the priestess, the sacred prostitute, was in the service of the Goddess and eros. Her body was the conduit to the divine.

As Metzger has told us, she is a heretic and would overthrow the existing order. Bred as we are in a sexually negative culture, it is almost impossible for us to identify with sexuality as healing in an impersonal way, to understand the role of the sacred prostitute as Metzger reconstructs it.

Heresy is thought-crime. We must change our fundamental beliefs. And that is what is so difficult.

> In the act of restoring a personal relationship to the spiritual world, we often feel as though we are defying God in the act of seeking the divine. This is a state of torment that we experience alone, ashamed, bewildered, by the extent of the internal agony, unable to formulate language to communicate the experience, unable to share the pain.[21]

What is required is internal revolution. The Goddess can be reinvoked.

> As part of this new spiritual order, we must engage in two heresies. The first more difficult task is to return to the very early, neolithic, pagan, matriarchal, perception of the sacred universe itself. The second is to re-sanctify the body. The second follows inevitably from the first. But to overthrow secular thought may be the heretical act of the century. That is why we are in so much psychic pain.[22]

The Goddess is the means by which we know the universe is sacred; through which we have the experience of the sacred. We have to live our lives so that they come into harmony with the sacred. The invocation of her image is the cry to consciousness. The ancient image of the sacred female was the vehicle that worked in people's imaginations.

Metzger sets forth a plan of action. Women must continue to talk to each other so that we don't fall back into the narrowing circle of disbelief that contradicts our instincts. We live in the void between belief and disbelief. We must tap into the memories of the collective unconscious.

Her work is political. The resacralization of the universe, of women's bodies, of female sexuality is political. The spiritual and the political were one in the culture of the Goddess. It is only with her suppression that we have come to live in a profane world.

Metzger says we must begin with "personal disarmament," imposing on ourselves the conditions we would impose on a nation-state. She believes that militarism and defensiveness are signs of our inner fear and aggression. As women we have been afraid of our own nature, which is why we so urgently need the Goddess as a model of another way of being female. One insistent voice of the women's movement has been that of equality, but equal opportunity has all too often led to women's behavior that mirrors the prevailing masculine style and only perpetuates the existing destructive culture.

Metzger describes her own recent revelation of the Goddess in a guided meditation.

> I was confronted by a large, luminous woman, approximately eight feet tall, clearly an image of a goddess. . . . Her hair was light itself. As she came close to me, I was filled with both awe at her beauty and terror at her presence. If I were to take her into me, I know my life would be altered, I would have to give up many of the masculine modes I had adopted in order to negotiate successfully in the world. The woman was powerful, but her power was of receptivity, resonance, magnetism, radiance. She had the power of eros; she drew me to her.[23]

Sadly, she concludes that she has been afraid of her own nature. Not only men have been afraid of the power of women, women too when confronted with the full dimensions of their being have backed away from the responsibility to life it entails. In a male dominated culture like ours, the encompassing power of the feminine is often just as threatening to women as to men. She is filled with awe at the task of putting on the robes of the Holy Prostitute, the woman she aspires to be.

> To come to consciousness takes an interminably long time. To bring a society to consciousness may seem to take eons. But our circumstances are so dire, we must not risk unconscious action. . . . We must allow ourselves whatever time it takes to re-establish the consciousness of the Sacred Prostitute. We must allow ourselves whatever time it takes to restore eros. . . . There is time only to work slowly. There is no time not to love.[24]

Metzger, who is Jewish, has identified with the Hebrew goddess, the Asherah, and taken as her personal icon the "tree," the form in which the Goddess manifests. *Tree* is the title of her published journal, a very moving account of her struggle with cancer and with the darker forces within her psyche. Her nude photograph on a poster published along with the book celebrates her recovery (see fig. 148).

Inscribed on the poster are her words:

> I am no longer afraid of mirrors where I see the sign of the Amazon, the one who shoots arrows. There is a fine red line

across my chest where a knife entered, but now a branch winds about the scar and travels from arm to heart. Green leaves cover the branch, grapes hang there and a bird appears. What grows in me now is vital and does not cause me harm. I think the bird is singing. . . . I have designed my chest with the care given to an illuminated manuscript. I am no longer ashamed to make love. In the night, a hand caressed my chest and once again I came to life. Love is a battle I can win. I have the body of a warrior who does not kill or wound. On the book of my body, I have permanently inscribed a tree.[25]

Eros is healing. Eros is connection. Metzger is a poet who uses her words to battle for freedom against life-denying forms of oppression. Her weapons are desire, possibility, dream, metaphor, and she wields them with a fierce determination.[26]

The Erotic and the Maternal

In the patriarchal fragmentation of the Great Goddess, the erotic and the maternal were split. The Greeks later personalized them as Aphrodite and Demeter, two discrete deities

148. Hella Hammid, TREE, 1979. Photograph.

Deena Metzger stands naked, her arms spread wide like the branches of a tree, revealing her loss of her breast to disease and surgery, proud and triumphant, the scar covered by a flowering branch tatooed on her body. "Green leaves cover the branch, grapes hang there, and a bird appears."[23]

who have become in contemporary Jungian psychological practice models for different female personalities (Bolen, Downing). Most Western women have come to believe that erotic and maternal are exclusive and separate feelings. Some feel guilty about being sexual at the expense of what they perceive as their children's needs. Freudian theory with its preoccupation with sexual pathology and "mother complexes" has made many women apprehensive about their sensuous delight in their infants' bodies. It is important for women in the recovery of their authentic feelings to acknowledge the erotic in the mother-child bond. Many women recognize the sensual pleasure of nursing; some even experience the emergence of the infant through the birth passage as sexual. Loving touch, intimate body contact, the ordinary routines of child care forge an erotic bond between mother and small child, which helps the child to thrive. Play is life enhancing. We've learned from the studies of the care of premature infants in hospital nurseries that touching and not isolation is critical to survival. Newborns are beginning to room with their mothers even in sterile hospital settings.

The French obstetrician LeBoyer advocates infant massage, taking a clue from India where mothers commonly spend hours massaging their infants' bodies, gently rubbing oil into their skin, manipulating their limbs. Their model is the Goddess of Childbirth, Shasthi, who is represented massaging her own infant in popular Bengali terracottas (see fig. 101).

The Goddess Is the Earth Mother But She Is Not Our Biological Mother

From the first, the reemergence of the Goddess has led to confusion and misunderstanding about the term *mother* in relation to the divine female. Early proponents spoke of "Mother Right" (Bachofen) in contradistinction to prevailing rights of the Father God and posited an ancient age of matriarchy preceding patriarchy. To date no archaeological, historical, or anthropological evidence has been found for any widespread female dominant cultures in which males were oppressed. Goddess cultures, as we have observed, were woman-centered and egalitarian. Jungians have espoused the Mother Goddess as an archetype, a lodestone in the collective unconscious of both men and women to be mined for psychological wholeness. So that she might more effectively serve human needs according to their therapeutic model, they have ripped asunder the unity of her being into the good mother and the bad mother whose ambivalence is symbolized by her good and bad breasts.

An antidote to the Ambivalent Mother is another popular reading of Mother Goddess as the all-loving, all-nurturing, all-caring mother we would all like to have had and continue to yearn for. The saintly Blessed Virgin Mary and the eternally compassionate Kwan Yin are the most popular manifestations of the divine female for those who worship within traditional religions. The limitation of this conception of divine power is that it ignores and obscures an essential characteristic of the wholeness we need to heal and restore balance with nature.

The association of Mother Goddess and fertility has been a problem for some women. While the Goddess, revered for her capacity to bring forth life—human, animal, and plant— has been a model of empowerment, her obvious fertility has been a problem for women who want to free themselves of any identity related to childbearing. The agony of the struggle to break out of the narrow definition of woman as wife and mother is still too raw for them. Motherhood and mothering have become problematic for these late twentieth-century women. As mother, the feminine has been "sublimated, made a fetish, exalted by male writers [and] at the same time both mother and mothers are viewed as threatening within the classic Western oedipal structure."[27]

The reemerging Goddess, metaphor, symbol, divine force, is larger than the Westernized idealized model of maternal being. When Hindus cry to Kali in their devotions "Ma! Ma!" they are not calling out to her as they would to their biological mother but to the mother of the universe, the life force that brought all into being and that sustains all that lives.

Sexuality and Procreation Are Not the Same for Women

The reclaiming of our bodies, the resacralization of our sexuality honors the sacred life force within. For women sexuality and procreation are not biologically the same even though the heterosexual act can result in pregnancy. Our new understanding of female sexuality based on psychological and physiological research that was in part engendered by the nagging questions of the women's movement, demonstrates that for women the organs of sexuality and reproduction are distinct. Although sexual activity can lead to procreation, this is not most women's usual motivation. Our sexual life is far more encompassing, closely related to our most intimate relationships. Sexual/erotic desire for most women is seated in the clitoris as well as the vagina, a quite separate organ, the vehicle for the transmission of the male seed necessary for conception. Human females are unique among primates in that their sexual desire is not determined by their fertility cycle.

The blurring of the distinctions inherent in patriarchy between male and female sexuality has obscured this important fact, eliminating it from even scientific knowledge. Surely women themselves once were aware of the source of their own bodily pleasure. When the shift of consciousness engendered by patriarchy finally became total, knowledge of women's own pleasure, of their very bodily response, was lost, their sensibility colonized. Even today in a time of sexual liberation and women's sexual freedom, when all women are "supposed" to enjoy sex, the heterosexual sex act for most men and women still is structured around male needs for satisfaction, not female. What is euphemistically called foreplay and afterplay, the stimulation of the clitoris, not the activity of the penis in the vagina, is for many women the greatest source of pleasure. Recent research demonstrates that clitoral, vaginal, and uterine stimulation, or a combination, lead to orgasm.[28]

Reflection on our new understanding of female sexuality, its diffuse nature, raises questions about heterosexuality as the norm. We know that homosexuality was widely practiced in the ancient Greek and Roman world. Men in Plato's circle and women like Sappho were bisexual. Bisexuality is coming into fashion again, a socially acceptable practice in the New Age. Can we bend our minds? Perhaps that is what we must do, so deeply rooted are our notions of human sexuality, to contemplate the possibilities for the enrichment of the human condition that such an expanded view of human sexuality opens up for pleasure and play, for deep, intimate connection, and reclaiming the mystery of our erotic natures.

The separation of sexuality and procreation, now possible with contraception, made the sexual revolution possible. The problem facing us now is the politics of sexuality, the reciprocal relations of female sexuality and the social relations of our existence.

> Sexual expression, far from having liberated women, has historically often led to increased male access to women's bodies, allowing exploitation not just sexually but economically and politically as well. To demand greater sexual freedom without formulating that demand in terms of a transformation of social relations within which sexuality is organized and articulated is to invite an intensification of old constraints on women's desire.[29]

Women's Bodies Link the Personal to the Cosmic

When women are fully in touch with the experience of their own bodies, they can reclaim the full power within and use that power not to manipulate, not to self-obsess, but to reveal the mystery it is, to transform themselves and our culture. According to the French feminist Julia Kristeva, one of the most acute of contemporary observers of female experience, women have a privileged cosmic connection because of their bodily rhythmic cycles of menstruation and pregnancy. Kristeva believes that sensing this link between the personal and the cosmic can lead to what she calls *jouissance,* a term we might try to express as joy, ecstasy, and, perhaps, serenity.[30]

Alice Jardine, a literary critic, comments on Kristeva's germinal insights and their implications for a feminist recovery of the past.

> When women allow themselves to think about their own intuitive feel for time, rather than *accepting the linear, departure-and-arrival time sense of the modern male organized world,* what they discover is something much older. *Because menstruation cycles link them more* closely to natural cycles than men, women hold a key to the past that men do not have. Their intuition, Kristeva says, "retains *repetition* and *eternity* from among the multiple modalities of time known through the history of civilization."

> Kristeva believes this exclusively female vantage point enables women to touch these *two forms of time consciousness* that men,

as non-menstruating creatures, can discern only with greater difficulty. The first, the cyclic time of *gestation* and *rhythmic* recurrence, is a "premodern form of time that coincides with the phases of the moon, the rising and setting of the sun, the passing of the seasons, and other expressions of cosmic time. . . ." Since the realization of this "cosmic connection" can produce *jouissance,* it can also open the way to a second sense of time which Kristeva calls "eternity." This is the infinite, unbounded and all encompassing time the mystics try, always unsuccessfully, to describe.

Jardine concludes that if Kristeva is correct

then women have a kind of privileged access to these other faces of time. If reclaiming these senses of time along with the sequential, arrow-flight time of the Western mind will be essential to any postmodern religious vision, then the experience of women will be an indispensable part of that vision.[31]

In our discussion of reclaiming women's bodily experience, we have circled wide, touching on some of the most radical insights of women thinkers and artists. As women and men grapple with new ways of knowing and being in the world, they churn up long forgotten dimensions of the human experience. The repression of the female has been a festering wound that has poisoned the spirit. We have paid an enormous price for what has been called civilization. This is crumbling now as we come to the end of the Judeo-Christian hegemony. The concrete changes brought about by women's massive awakening could sweep aside the established order like a tidal wave.

One stumbling block seems to be the difficulty of re-imaging, of creating new symbols, new ways of representing a new consciousness that is pluralistic. Philosopher Bruce Wilshire reminds us that at the deepest levels, our body-selves only understand concrete images and behaviors, not thoughts and ideas.[32]

Reclaiming Her Sacred Iconography:
The Artist as Prophet

The Goddess has once again become the muse. Artists are reclaiming the iconography of the sacred female out of their unconscious, channeling long-suppressed imagery in an outburst of creativity in all the visual and performing arts. Particularly relevant to our story is the work of the women of the seventies and eighties who give expression to the radically changing image of the female body in our time.

Archaeological discoveries of prehistoric goddesses brought a new vision of the female body into modern Western consciousness, an aesthetic very different than the Greek or Renaissance ideal. The prehistoric Goddess figure was an icon, the symbol of a spiritual tradition. Encoded in her physical form were values inherent in the Goddess culture. The iconography of the sacred female focused on those parts of a woman's body that had to do with the renewal of life. Nudity was sacred, not seductive. How can these symbolic values be incorporated into a new visual language of the female based on women's contemporary experience of themselves?

The arts always hold the promise of enriching our ways of seeing and being in the world. The loss of the female sensibility, that of one-half of humanity, has been tragic. Novelist Virginia Woolf understood well that the subjugation of women was both cause and symptom of a fundamental imbalance in society and subsequent lack of wholeness in the modern world that could be changed only through the introduction of women's own perception into the culture.

In the seventies, fueled by the rising expectations of the women's movement and consciousness raising, women artists took upon themselves the task of reconstructing the representation of the female. Theirs was not a concerted, premeditated, or organized movement but the idiosyncratic vision of a few women in New York City and California—adamant, courageous, outrageous. Struggling for recognition within the male-dominated art world, these women gradually came to realize that if they were to make art that expressed their unique sensibility as women, they had no choice but to create a new visual language. Women who worked within the mainstream milieu had been trapped in a vision, an aesthetic, and in a formal structure that limited the full range of self-expression. Most were not free to portray the emotional, sensual, sexual feelings of their inner landscape. The new work, as well as the older work of such established artists as Georgia O'Keeffe and Louise Bourgeois, must be considered within the context of an emerging women's culture in order to be fully understood.

"The personal is political" has been the call to arms in the Women's Movement. The woman artist's role in Western culture has become confrontational because as Judy Chicago says "we dare to redefine the nature, purpose and content of art." Artists are prescient, that is, acutely sensitive to changing culture, often expressing in both subject and style underlying currents not yet recognized by the culture at large. This is doubly so for women artists because of what the dominant image of woman in Western culture represents. Woman is everywhere present as a mediating symbol for the male but almost completely absent as an expression of female experience. In advertising art women are trivialized, their bodies and sexuality objectified, exploited, and used to sell any product from panty hose and jeans to cigarettes and whiskey.

The nude photograph of a movie starlet or an unknown model is the common man's muse. Originally conceived as a morale booster for the American serviceman during World War II, the pin-up decorated the walls of barracks, tanks, and bombers. It was the "all-American girl" freely available for fun and fantasy in a way she might never be back home. Posters and calendar pictures of female nudes can be found wherever men gather and work apart from women—in locker rooms, bars, and the cabs of long-distance trucks. The best known is Marilyn Monroe, whose face and body are probably better known than any other woman in the United States (see fig. 149).

149. MARILYN MONROE: PIN-UP.
Photograph. Copyright Tom Kelley Studios.

150. Andy Warhol, MARILYN × 100, 1962.
Acrylic and silkscreen on canvas. 81 in. ×
223½ in.

149

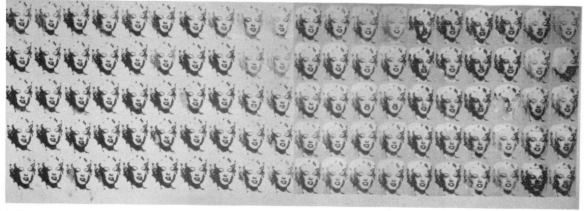

150

Since her death over twenty years ago Monroe has become the center of a cult, deified as the Sex Goddess. Ironically she took her life because she felt unable to make the human connections that would sustain her. When I began to write this book I randomly asked men who came my way—taxi drivers, undergraduates, car salesmen, the man sitting next to me at a lunchroom counter or on a cross-country plane ride, accountants, auto mechanics—who the Goddess was. No matter what their age, economic or social status, their reply was invariably, "the Hollywood Goddess" or "the Hollywood Sex Goddess." When pressed for more details, they most often identified her as Marilyn Monroe.

In a culture where women's sexuality and the relations between the sexes are so problematic, just what is the role of a Sex Goddess? The pop artists of the sixties whose theme was the banality of American culture had a field day with her image. Andy Warhol made several silkscreen prints of Monroe in which an identical photograph of her face or body was repeated over and over again, one replaceable by another like his most famous serialized image, a can of Campbell's tomato soup (see fig. 150).

A contemporary example of the ostensible use of the female nude as erotic but that is in fact pornographic is the work of Helmut Newton, a German fashion photographer frequently found in *Vogue* magazine. Newton's women, naked except for their high heels, strike menacing poses. Newton makes no pretense of his objectives, referring to his work as *nordfleish,* northern flesh. He says that he loves pale flesh—"I like cool girls"—and he wants his models to give the impression of being untouched by their surroundings and their circumstances.

In Newton's photos sexuality is a consumer product. His images of women may titillate but they also express fear and violence. I am concerned that these images do not shock others. When I saw the ten-foot-tall blowups on exhibit at the Marlborough Gallery in New York, I was revolted and enraged. When I queried the sophisticated, fashionably dressed women present, none saw anything to be disturbed about.

Too many women have bought into the dominant culture's attitude toward sexuality—to the heterosexual encounter as a war between the sexes or, at best, a game divorced from true feeling. The sexual liberation of the sixties that promised so much, fulfillment through freedom, has instead contributed to promoting sexuality as a social activity rather than the fullest expression of one's being. Sexual intimacy divorced from human connection brutalizes women for whom relationship has such high value.

The next time you pass a newsstand take a look at the pictures of women on the magazine covers. For example, *Cosmopolitan,* billing itself as the magazine "for the man-loving woman," has featured indifferently clad young women in aggressive, sexually provocative poses for some years (see fig. 151). Her stance, angular body, head-on gaze is not unlike that of Newton's "cool nudes."

Newton's images are those of male fantasy in a troubled culture that bases human relationship on exploitation. The explicit linking of female nudity and violence threatens all women.

Traditionally in Western art, the female nude has been the painter's muse, his subject *par excellence.* Since classical Greece and Rome, the artist has sought to express ideal beauty through his rendition of the female form. But his visual statement is not always so innocent. For example, the celebrated painting of female nudity, *The Turkish Bath,* by the early nineteenth-century painter, Ingres, has been praised by connoisseurs for the artist's masterful handling of the flesh tones and formal qualities of the women's bodies. But we know from the artist's records that the patron who commissioned this work was looking for something more than beauty. What the Turkish diplomat wanted was "the sight of female flesh" on display in his drawing room. Aestheticians and art historians see nothing wrong with gratifying a sensibility that disassociates a human body from a human being and uses a woman's body as the subject of a painterly exercise (see fig. 152).

In the thirties, the French surrealist Magritte created another male fantasy entitled *The Rape,* a visual pun in which a woman's face can also be read as her nude torso—bulging eyes as breasts, pug nose as navel, and pursed lips as pubic hair. The artist's treatment is playful but rape is deadly serious business, the ultimate violence of one human against another. One out of every three women in the United States will be sexually assaulted in her lifetime.

COSMOPOLITAN

Facts About the
Female Sex Drive
That Even
Sophisticated Ladies
May Not Know

Nick Nolte,
About to
Break Out in the
Superstar Derby.
Très Sexy

When Baby
Makes Three but
Also Makes
Mommy Depressed
and Restless

Is Divorce
the Answer?
The Fantasy —
and the Facts

Rona Barrett,
Hollywood's Tough
Money-and-
Power Watcher

The Riveting Story
of a Compulsive
Girl Gambler

Buddy-Flirting:
The Bold, New Way
to Have Him
Notice and Like You

Sex-ercise:
to Make Your Body
Sensuously
Catlike—and Keep
Him Purring

Models Tell
Their Secret
Makeup Tricks

A Memorable
Excerpt from
A Hostage to
Fortune. Plus an
Explosive Novel of
Love and Money

151. THE COSMOPOLITAN COVER GIRL, May 1979.

152. J. A. D. Ingres, THE TURKISH
BATH, 1820. Oil on canvas. France.

Feminist Art: The Body Politic

With the rising consciousness of the feminist movement, women began to protest actively against the male artists' privileged exploitation of women's bodies. Women artists in the United States and Western Europe began to make a new kind of art that gave expression to their feelings about themselves and their relationships. Feminist art, concerned with demythologizing, demystifying women's roles, women's bodies, and sexual stereotypes, is political in its nature, that is, with intent of realizing social change. Today, while there are many women artists, not all make feminist art, which may require a particular experience of consciousness raising, as well as a climate of collaboration and support. Now, perhaps for the first time in the history of art, women are creating a visual language through which they give form to their own experience.

Feminist Iconography

The unifying characteristic of feminist art is the primacy of content rather than style and most often begins with the artist's own body and sexuality. Each woman has had her own consciousness-raising process supported by the ideology of the women's movement. While her own body, her own sexuality, is intimate and personal, the personal becomes political by making it publicly recognizable. A core part of a woman's self-determination is the identification of her sexual nature. The creative act of transforming this sexual definition into her art affirms her being.

In *The Second Sex,* Simone de Beauvoir underscores the importance of women knowing the structure of their genitals. "The feminine sex organ is mysterious even to the woman herself. . . . Woman does not recognize herself in it and this explains in large part why she does not recognize its desires as hers."[1] The representation of women's private parts has been a forbidden subject in Western art.

Suzanne Santoro, an American sculptor living in Rome in the seventies, saw the demystification of her sexual organs as a prerequisite to self-expression. In Italy in 1970 the debate over vaginal and clitoral orgasms was well underway. Like so many women then, she had never really looked at her genitals.

153. Suzanne Santoro, FLOWER AND CLITORIS, 1974. Photograph. Rome, Italy.

When the photograph of the clitoris is placed next to a half-opened flower, we are confronted with the structural beauty of our organic selves. The multiple layering and deep unfolding is not unlike that of the flower revealing its reproductive heart, the pistil and stamen.

We were learning how important it was for women to know how they were made. I took a cast and I was amazed by the structural solidity of it—the very precise construction and form.[2]

Santoro was in a feminist group called the Rivolta Feminile. "For three years we talked about sex." In 1974, after working for several years on molds and sculptural representations of female genitals, she published *Per Una Espressione Nuova: Towards a New Expression* (Rome, 1974). This small volume intersperses a bilingual text with black-and-white reproductions of female genitals, flowers, and shells, along with traditional images of naked women (see fig. 153).

Santoro presents the vulva and clitoris in bird's-eye view, isolated clinically on white paper.

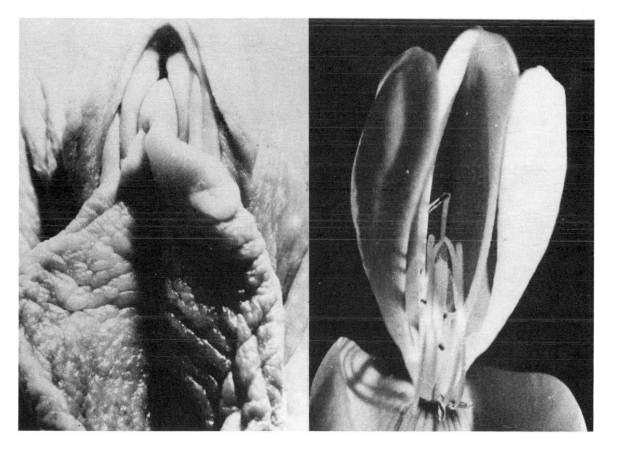

I want to present the *structure* of an image and separate it from myself. . . . The placing of the Greek figures, the flowers, and the conch shell near the clitoris is a means of understanding the structure of the female genitals.[3]

She uses these parallels between biology and nature to critique the way women have been perceived in the past. Her chain of association is evocative, poetic. "The only thing that comes near to looking like our sex in nature . . . is the muscle, leaves, dried apricots, some wild flowers."[4] The placing of the flowers and the conch near the clitoris is an invitation for the sexual self-expression that has been denied women till now, and which, she believes, leads to greater self-knowledge in other areas of our lives. "Expression begins with self-assertion and the awareness of the difference between ourselves and others."

Santoro's *Flower and Clitoris* call up visions of Georgia O'Keeffe's famous flower paintings. O'Keeffe's work since 1915 has been labeled "feminine" by critics because of its many associations with the female body (see fig. 154 and color plate 29).

O'Keeffe herself refused to make connections between her art and her female experience. She insisted that the erotic interpretation of her images of flowers and the rhythmic hills of the Southwest was in the eye of the beholder. Perhaps her reluctance to discuss the sources of her imagery stemmed from her reaction to the sexist remarks of early reviewers who little appreciated the great power of her forms. Theorist Willard Huntington Wright, scandalized, complained that "all these pictures say is 'I want to have a baby.' "[5] Still, O'Keeffe once wrote, "Before I put brush to canvas, I question 'Is this mine? Is it influenced by some idea I have acquired from some man?'. . . I am trying with all my skill to do a painting that is all of woman, as well as all of me."[6]

Many viewers were shocked by what was seen as an unprecedented if abstracted sexuality. Some understood that hers was a voice they hadn't heard before. Louis Mumford wrote, "She has invented a language, and has conveyed directly and chastely in paint experience for which language conveys only obscenities."[7]

She may have pushed aside any self-reflection that identified her art with her feelings as a woman, but O'Keeffe was very much aware of the connections of her body to the earth. To paint the female she chose to picture the land and its natural

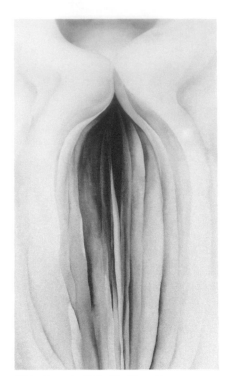

154. Georgia O'Keeffe, Grey Line with Black, Blue, and Yellow, ca. 1923. Oil on canvas.

Her flowers, fresh and fragile, interpreted as female genitalia, are part of a holistic natural order, the sensual, enveloping enlightened female principle. That O'Keeffe, a female artist who dealt with the transformation of natural phenomena in her work, would reveal the biological and cultural connection between woman and nature was not coincidental.[24]

forms. Her "extremely realistic and at the same time highly abstract pictures of the New Mexican earth, which she made her home for some fifty years, have a voluptuous spareness that unavoidably evokes a female body in contour and surface"[8] (see fig. 155).

> Sometimes I think I am half mad with love for this place. . . . My center does not come from my mind—it feels in me like a plot of warm moist well-tilled earth with the sun shining hot on it.[9]

Lucy Lippard identifies the Pedernal Mesa—a recurring image in the artist's work—as "the birthplace of the Navaho's legendary Changing Woman who represents both earth and time."[10]

O'Keeffe knew that she was creating a new iconography even though she declined to discuss it. And with good reason. Feminist art critic Arlene Raven points out that

> Accepting an interpretation of her work as feminine would have meant accepting further critical and historical isolation, which had been the lot of female artists, and the attendant narrow critical categories and general lack of seriousness with which female sensibility was and is treated.[11]

Radical feminist art criticism is willing to go beyond the narrow categories of the formalist analysis that the art world has imposed upon itself to once again consider the content of the work of art important and relevant.

155. Georgia O'Keeffe, NEAR ABIQUIU, NEW MEXICO, 1930. Oil on canvas. 16 in. × 30 in.

Judy Chicago: An Iconography for Everywoman

O'Keeffe's sensibility is shared by many women artists whose imagery resonates morphologically with their bodies. Their work has a central focus, often circular or oval, empty, with containerlike forms, not unlike the iconography of the sacred female, the vulva-womb, vessel and pot. For women, there seems to be some relation between creativity and the identification with their own bodies, their own sexuality.

Unlike the reticent O'Keeffe, contemporary feminist artists are very articulate about their creative process. The consciousness raising of the Women's Movement provided a sympathetic forum in which to talk about experience and feelings, allowing women's deeply repressed self-knowledge to surface. "Women's social, biological and political experiences are different from those of men; art is born of those experiences and must be faithful to them to be authentic."[12] Women artists have begun to make their lives the subject of their art. "Their work both *is* and *tells about* the pain of their life experience."[13]

156. Judy Chicago, THROUGH THE FLOWER, 1972. Lithograph.

"But in my images the petals of the flower are parting to reveal an inviting but undefined space, the space beyond the confines of our femininity. These works symbolized my longing for transcendence and personal growth."

an experience more shared and universal than we would have imagined before the Women's Movement.

Judy Chicago, the best known of the feminist artists, has extensively documented her own creative process as she took the leadership in creating a new iconography of the female. Like O'Keeffe, Chicago used the flower as the symbol of the female (see figs. 156, 157).

> [These] were my first steps in being able to make clear, abstract images of my point of view as a woman. . . . In my work, I felt a body identification with both the images I made and the surface on which they were painted. I felt myself to be both the image/surface and the artist working on that painting simultaneously. The canvas was like my own skin; I was the painting and the painting was me.[14]

When Chicago and Miriam Schapiro, who together taught the first feminist art programs in California, investigated the work of other women, they found the frequent use of a central image, often a flower, or abstracted flower form, sometimes

157. Judy Chicago, FEMALE REJECTION DRAWING, 1974. Prismacolor, pencil on rag paper. 29 in. × 23 in.

Rejected, the petals shrivel up. "*Female Rejection Drawing* is both *about* a woman artist's rejection and *means* being a woman, vulnerable and hurt."[25]

surrounded by folds or undulations, as in the structure of the vagina.

> . . . What we were seeing was a reflection of each woman's need to explore her own identity, to assert her sense of her own sexuality, as we had both done. But . . . the visual symbology . . . must not be seen in a simplistic sense. . . .[15]

The women's ready comments on their creative process made it clear that they were in touch with more than their genital sexuality; they had tapped their erotic power, their life force. This has a particular resonance for us in the context of our historical analysis of the iconography of the Goddess. From the earliest cave art, the symbol of the power of the Goddess was the vulva. Women artists did not intentionally set about appropriating this symbol as a new icon. The image simply emerged out of their unconscious, out of their deepest instinctual feelings as they struggled to give expression to their long-repressed sensibilities.

Raven writes about what a courageous act of self-exposure it is for a woman to positively identify herself with her work and say something that challenges the existing and prevailing worldview.[16] When she expresses herself without the support of a social, economic, and cultural base she has not participated in the mainstream of the culture. "The culture does not operate from her perspective. Her contribution has neither spoken to it, nor been understood by that system,"[17] which is just what happened to Judy Chicago.

An energetic, assertive woman freely in touch with her own sexuality, and working directly from this erotic power, Chicago evolved an abstract form, the butterfly-vagina. This symbol was to become the core of her new iconography in *The Dinner Party,* a monumental and complex work of art that is often misunderstood (see fig. 158).

"The idea is obviously not to reduce all women to cunts, as society itself often does. [Chicago] sees the butterflies as metaphysical references to the whole issue of what it means to be 'feminine,' how that word reveals the slant in our values and how those values can be challenged by using the vernacular imagery of the female. 'I was struggling with the issue of making the feminine holy.' "[18]

The Dinner Party is a multilevel symbol celebrating women— a movable feast of sculpture, needlework, ceramic tile, and painted china—outlining the history of women from prehistoric times. One of the most ambitious works of art made in the twentieth century, it succeeds as few others have in integrating a strong aesthetic with political content. By addressing both myth and reality, Chicago "attempts to transform reality by the exemplary use of art as purveyor of myth. [She] recognizes women's 'deep cultural hunger' for affirmative symbols."[19]

The universally negative response of mainstream art critics to the work and to its acknowledged political purpose is a perhaps not unexpected resistance of dominant culture to the revolt of the symbols that *The Dinner Party* represents. Most critics focused their opposition on the explicit sexual imagery of the plates. Chicago's overt symbolism hits too close to home in a society that continues to try to control women's bodies through an ongoing battle over reproduction rights. The hostility of the male critics to the iconic form of the plates, their discomfort with the insistent presence of *the* monumental symbol of female power, is one more example of how very difficult changing consciousness is. As long as men in Western culture are afraid of women's sexuality and cannot

158. Judy Chicago, Virginia Woolf, 1974–79. From *The Dinner Party*. China paint on white ceramic.

acknowledge their own feelings but instead project them onto women, they cannot be enriched and enlarged by the creative life force of the female.

The art establishment's continued hostility to Chicago's work is also related to the unresolved debate in late twentieth-century culture as to the meaning and purpose of art. The issues are complex but the key issue is clear: Do only elitist aesthetics have value?

Chicago's vision was to create a lasting monument so that women's participation in the human story would not be wiped out as in the past. "*The Dinner Party* is unique in having as one of its immediate goals the education and training of women to take command—not only of the project but, by extension, of their own work and lives."[20] Chicago thereby enlarged the domain of the artist in our time. The making of art was again to be personally transformative as it was once and continues to be in traditional cultures where art is part of ritual. Art was also to be didactic for the culture at large as in the ancient and medieval worlds, where public art affirmed the values of society in powerful iconic forms.

No mean task; but Chicago's mission is grandiose. Next she undertook to resacralize birthing, again affirming women's experience. *The Birth Project* consists mostly of embroidery and quilting with some drawings. The pieces are accompanied by the words of the needleworkers and feminist writers. The most compelling are the testimonials from women about their own experiences of childbirth.

The words do not get in the way of the art, which is powerful stuff, as preoccupied with the pain of birth as with its mystery. The images seem to shudder with life-giving energy. They have a primal quality, an elemental rawness that evokes an ancient time when the earth-based Goddess forms had not been replaced yet by patriarchal ones like God the Father giving birth to Adam by imperial gesture in the famous Michelangelo fresco in the Sistine Chapel.

Chicago says that she "approached the subject of birth with awe, terror, and fascination, and . . . tried to present different aspects of this universal experience—the mythical, the celebratory, and the painful."[21] When she began her research, she found that there were no images in Western art to draw upon. "Art usually grows from art, but this time art is going to have to grow directly from experience."[22] She herself has never

159. Judy Chicago, THE CROWNING, 1981. Prismacolor on rag paper. 24 in. × 33 in.

The birthing image is stark, powerful—an abstracted female form focused on the emerging new life. "Her hair flows out over her head like the branches of a tree. Her toes are spread and extended like roots connecting her to the earth. . . ."[26]

160. Anonymous, ADITI-UTTANAPAD, tenth century B.C.E. Bronze. South India.

The image is headless; her hands hold lotus branches symbolic of emerging life. The muscles of her abdomen are flexed in the contractions of labor and from her vulva the new life, a lotus bud, is coming forth. The icon abstracts the creative force inherent in the female body, making an analogy to the life-giving properties of nature.

159

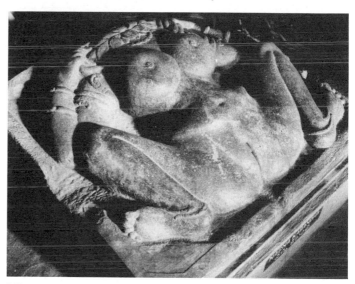

160

given birth; she immersed herself in other women's stories and witnessed several deliveries. "If men had babies, there would be thousands of images of crowning," that awesome moment when the baby's head first appears (see fig. 159).

For countless millennia of human history other cultures throughout the world have made icons for worship that show the infant's head emerging from the mother's body like the "Life-giving Goddess" of Çatal Hüyük. The Goddess in the act of giving birth is still worshiped in Hindu India (see fig. 160).

Indian iconography is the product of centuries of evolution based on an ageless mythology. The life-giving powers of Aditi are described in the ancient Vedic texts (twelfth to eighth centuries B.C.E.). Chicago's work is so important because in the West we have no such heritage.

She places the human birthing experience within the broader context of universal creation.

> I began to study pictures of the reproductive system, the birth process, and the solar system, looking for parallels in iconography. Needless to say, they were there—macrocosmic and microcosmic reflections of the creation and life process, just as I suspected. A nova looks just like an ovum, and the oceans on the earth's surface make patterns like nerve cells.

She created images in which the female form and the landscape were merged (see color plate 8).

> I was looking for a way to use the physical process of giving birth as a metaphor for the birth of the universe and of life itself. . . . I want to make forms that resonate to our substance, are recognizable at a cellular level, and . . . I want to make the creation of the universe an intimately feminine act.[23]

While Chicago's new iconography is by far the most widely known outside the art world, many other women have been drawing upon the experience of their own bodies as the subject of their art, creating images that have no precedent in Western art. Their work is very diverse, reflecting the state of anarchy in the art world—how do we define art in the post-modern world?—as well as their own efforts to break through the cultural roadblock that ignores their ways of perceiving reality.

Susan Hiller: Body Time/Cosmic Time

The aim of Susan Hiller is to reveal the extent to which conventional artists' models are inadequate because they exclude or deny part of reality. When pregnant for the first time in 1977, Hiller took her own changing body as the subject of her art, photographically documenting the changing contours of her swelling abdomen every day for the nine months of her pregnancy. At the same time she recorded her thoughts and dreams in a diary.

161. Susan Hiller, "Two," detail of TEN MONTHS, 1977–79. Artist's book and photo sequence.

162. Susan Hiller, "Eight," detail of TEN MONTHS, 1977–79. Artist's book and photo sequence.

She must have wanted this—the predicament, the contradictions. She believes physical conception must be "enabled" by will or desire, like any other creation—"pregnant with thought," "brainchild," "giving birth to an idea."

"She is the content of a mania she can observe. The object of the exercise, she must remain its subject, chaotic and tormented (*tormented* is too strong a word she decides later). She knows she will never finish in time. And meanwhile, the photographs, like someone else's glance, gain significance through perseverence."

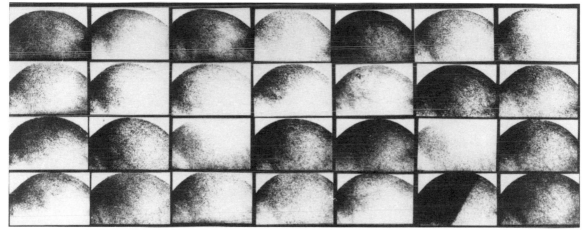

161

162

Hiller mounted the photographs and journal entries together, arranging the daily photographs with corresponding selections from her diaries into a ten-month lunar calendar of 28 days each. In this way she juxtaposed language, the way in which we order our experience, and the experience for which that ordering is not adequate. The unexpected combination of her words, her perceived reality, and her bodily experience confronts the contradictions in her life as woman-motherhood/artist-work. She is both the subject and the object of her work. When traditional boundaries are crossed or apparently opposed, categories conflated like women-artist or motherhood-work, the contradictions can become acute, especially since women's relation to the dominant culture is already marginal and problematic (see figs. 161, 162).

Ten Months takes on yet another visual reality as the sequence of swelling abdomens comes to resemble the rounded forms of the waxing moon. Women's bodily processes are intimately bound up with the cycles of the moon. Hiller says that what she is trying to do in her work is articulate what is inarticulate. Women's bodily processes *are* cyclical like the waxing and waning of the moon. We are part of nature. The period of gestation of the infant in the mother's womb was determined eons ago, long before human consciousness as we know it evolved. In our continuing evolution as social beings we must ever resolve the contradictions between our bodies through which we experience ourselves and our psyches through which we interpret that experience. The current dilemma so problematic for so many feminists is to what extent we are our bodies. Hiller's *Ten Months* tellingly situates woman/mother/artist within a universal process of gestation and birth. Utterly contemporary, Hiller, struggling with the mind/body split, takes us back to the healing of the Mysteries.

The Primal Forms of Louise Bourgeois

The primal forms of Louise Bourgeois, the doyenne of American sculptors, metamorphose the symbols of Goddess into yet more archaic forms of the elemental female (see color plates 35, 37). Bourgeois's creations are organic symbolic forms that connect us emotionally to a dimly remembered prehistory in which art was about sexuality and death. She reveals herself, her mysteries, her secrets, the dark and the ugly.

> The work of art serves a psychological function for Bourgeois, for she believes that making art is the process of giving tangible form to, and thus exorcising, the gripping, subconscious states of being that fill one with anxiety. . . . The underlying motivations for her art lie in unresolved psychological conflicts originating in her childhood years in France rather than in the psychological fabric of her adult life.[24]

Born in 1910, Bourgeois has been a productive artist for more than forty years. In considering her work as a whole, it is self-evident that her creative response was as a woman of her time—heroic, embattled, and confrontational. The titles of her works name the conflicts: *Femme Maison* (Woman

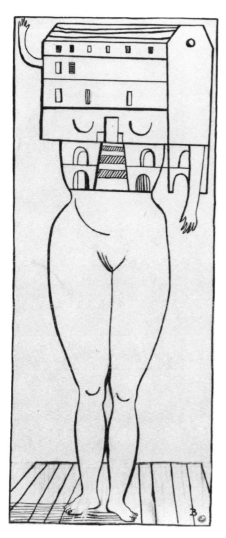

163. Louise Bourgeois, FEMME MAISON (WOMAN HOUSE), ca. 1946–47. Ink on linen. 36 in. × 14 in.

House), *Woman in the Shape of a Shuttle, Dagger Child, Femme Couteau* (Knife Woman), *The Destruction of the Father,* and *Fragile Goddess.*

She draws on the archetypal images of the mother and the phallus.

> Each period of Bourgeois' art corresponds to the hidden rhythms of her life at the time, yet like ancient animistic artists abstracting from nature, she transcends individual experience to communicate collective emotion through form. On the one hand, Bourgeois' subject is power—or power and powerlessness—and on the other, it is growth and germination.[25]

In her early paintings fragments of women were depicted against imaginary and symbolic settings in an attempt to define female reality. The *Femme Maison* (Woman House) paintings, portraying women with houses perched on their bodies in place of heads, are devastating images (see fig. 163).

> In them a woman's most obvious sign of identity, her face, has been replaced by a house. . . . Domesticity becomes the very definition of these women since they have no other means by which to speak. They are prisoners of the house and also hide behind its façade, thereby both denying and defining the female identity through this challenge to, as well as determination of, their wholeness.[26]

This was Bourgeois's reality at that time, a perception of herself, mother of small children in a foreign country, working in isolation in an art scene where there was no recognition for her reality.

In her early wood figures, works of fragility and simplicity, she explored the plight of the solitary individual isolated because of an inability to communicate. When the same wood pieces were arranged in couples or in groups, they assumed tenuous, hesitant, yet dependent relationships. "Now even though the shapes are abstract, they represent people. They are delicate as relationships are delicate. They look at each other and they lean on each other."[27]

The highly politicized atmosphere of the art scene and the Women's Movement in the late sixties and early seventies affected her work. Bourgeois took part in many of the meetings, demonstrations, exhibitions, and panel discussions. She refers to this as her "erotic period" and remembers "a certain glee, awe and fascination" with the possibility of making such explicit artistic statements, "finding them an antidote to [our culture's] generally puritanical, shy, and repressed sensibility."[28]

> There has always been a sexual suggestiveness in my work. . . . Sometimes I am totally concerned with female shapes—clusters of breasts like clouds—but often I merge the imagery—phallic breasts, male and female, active and passive.[29]

Bourgeois refers to these pieces now as " 'presexual,' meaning that they function at the most basic level of the life force itself."[30] Her iconography of a series of small female figures is strikingly reminiscent of the Paleolithic "Venus" and phallic Goddess of Old Europe (see fig. 164).

> I try to give a representation of a woman who is pregnant and who tries to be frightening. . . . She tries to be frightening but she is frightened. She's frightened for the child she carries. And she's afraid somebody is going to invade her privacy or bother her in some way and that she won't be able to defend what she's responsible for. . . .[31]

While Bourgeois's modern counterparts reclaim the fecund, voluminous organic forms of the primal mother, they express a modern woman's sensibility and anxiety. As she explains, they embody

> the polarity of woman, the destructive and the seductive. . . . A girl can be terrified of the world. She feels vulnerable because she can be wounded by the penis. So she tries to take on the weapon of the aggressor. But when a woman becomes aggressive, she becomes terribly afraid. If you are inhabited by needles, stakes, and knives, you are very handicapped. . . . The battle is fought at the terror level which precedes anything sexual[32] (see figs. 165, 166).

Bourgeois is adamant that she looks to herself for the sources of her art. Her work involves her attempt to understand herself and her needs and is a strategy for survival, expressing a personal and deeply autobiographical content. It is profoundly human. At the same time, from the wellsprings of her psyche, she has tapped into an archetypal visual language that has defined the female for millennia. Over time she has translated this vocabulary into a modern idiom that bridges the universal and the historically particular iconography of contemporary woman.

164. Louise Bourgeois, FRAGILE GODDESS, ca. 1970. Self-hardening clay. 10 in.

Fragile Goddess has the large breasts and protruding belly of pregnancy. Her arms are rudimentary, her head a projecting phallus. According to Bourgeois, this mixture of aggressiveness and vulnerability is a reference to the condition of pregnancy and its responsibilities, a woman's attempt to overcome inherent helplessness in order to protect oneself and one's children.

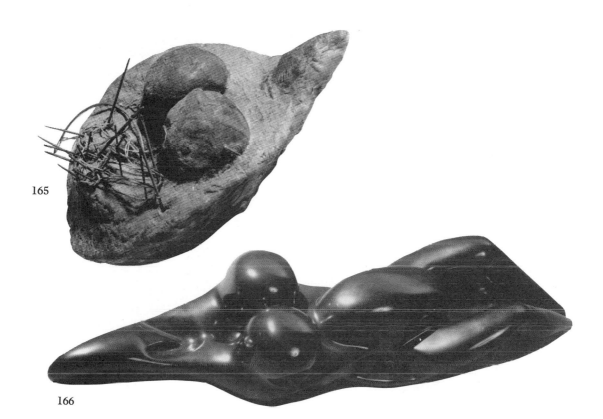

165

166

165. Louise Bourgeois, FEMME PIEU (STAKE WOMAN), ca. 1970. Wax and metal pins. 3½ in. × 2½ in. × 6 in.

Stake Woman has the look of a much-used ritual object.

166. Louise Bourgeois, FEMME COUTEAU (KNIFE WOMAN), 1981. Black marble. 5½ × 30½ × 8 in.

The five-inch *Knife Woman,* carved from rose pink marble, is small enough to be held in the clasping hand. The softly rounded volumes of the swelling abdomen and generous breasts have a lyrical beauty befitting an icon; the knifelike head is a jarring reminder of a contemporary iconography of the female in a threatening world.

Phantasmagoria: The Sexual Metaphors of Judith Bernstein

Like Bourgeois's androgynous images, the central figure of Judith Bernstein's *Venus Triptych* recalls the phallic Goddess of the early Neolithic (see figs. 167, 168).

The *Venus Triptych* is from her "Metaphorical Series," images of sex, physicality, fertility, nature, and life, all bursting with energy. Bernstein is intentionally ambiguous as she mixes human and plant forms, in fantastic combinations of bulging spheres, shadows, and lines all with multiple suggestive openings. Her large canvases explore the interplay between male and female, the literal and abstract. She sees her work as phantasmagoria, revealing the artist's innermost secrets.

A mural-sized charcoal drawing, the *Triptych* is about the relation of power and sexuality.

The male forms seem to reappear as the head of a phallus/ screw, abstracted and globular; the female, a flower form, seems to acquire a gaping genital character. Venus, who merges male with female, expresses the duality in metaphorical terms. An embodiment of the transition of roles so prevalent in contemporary culture, the image manifests a sexual self-awareness on the part of women, and the power that men have which they eventually must share.

Such an image is a primordial idea or archetype, which refers to symbolic expressions of psychic images eternally present in the collective unconscious. These symbols are manifested in the figure of the Great Mother, whether it be the ancient Venus of Willendorf or the Venus of Bernstein. . . . Like Bernstein's *Venus,* the archetypal Goddess also manifests the human experience in both feminine and masculine terms. . . .[33]

Bernstein's "Metaphorical Series" grew out of earlier work that had become her signature, bold calligraphic drawings of "phallic screws." First made in the mid-sixties as a caustic antiwar statement, they crudely elucidated the implicit relation between war, violence, and male aggression. Later, these mechanically conceived "charcoal screws" gradually meta-morphosed into hairy projectiles—visual equations of phallic power, an image whose massive energy became the icon of a sexually controversial age.[34]

Other women have also reclaimed the power of such Goddess symbols—the ubiquitous snake and the tree of life. Their restatement of familiar iconographic themes are a passionate and humorous commentary on contemporary culture. Like

167. PHALLIC GODDESS, fifth millennium B.C.E. Stone. Drawing after Guidion.

168. Judith Bernstein, VENUS TRIPTYCH, 1981–82. Charcoal on canvas. Three paintings, each 6 ft. × 6 ft.

Bernstein's Venus emerging from a dark maelstrom has the rounded female form above and phallus below. On either side are expressive, organic forms suggestive of male and female iconography.

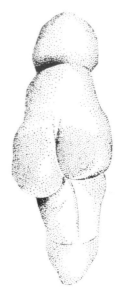

167

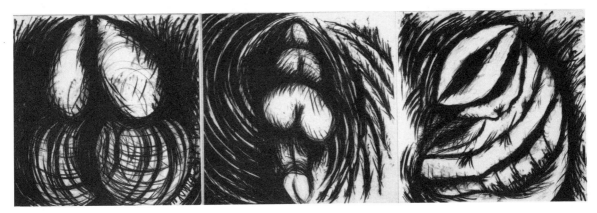

168

Bernstein, other women artists are creating a new reality by charging familiar mythical images with contemporary psychological experience.

Debra Sherwood: The Goddess Is Sometimes Out Of Joint

Sculptor Debra Sherwood's six-foot faience goddesses are technical tours de force. Like the clay she works, her images seem dug from some chthonic world inhabited by deep mysteries and dark forces. They have a strong sense of presence—fantastic, bizarre, alienated. One of her earliest, the *Snake Goddess,* is a translation of the tiny Minoan statuette on a monumental scale (see fig. 169)

The columnar, more-than-life-sized figure holds a snake, the emblem of her power, aloft in each hand, yet the face is turned to the side, the mouth pinched and small. One-half of the face is entirely black, with a vacant eye indicated by a vacant rose-colored smudge. The body is decorated with the Goddess hieroglyphs: triangles, circles, and V-shapes. Sherwood has also made a ceramic *Serpent Tree* with human arms for limbs (see fig. 170).

There is an irony in many of Sherwood's pieces. The goddesses seem to be made for celebration, but there is often a sense of foreboding or deep disturbance lurking within. These deities communicate an imbalance in our world. They point to a failing of the patriarchal order (see fig. 171).

According to Sherwood, using parallel images from the past is basic to art's universal vocabulary, but art is still inevitably of its time and our time seems out of joint. There is a dis-ease in the modern consciousness. The forces she is recalling don't always connect. Her goddesses reveal what is going on underneath, they let us into their very modern psyches.

The snake and the tree, universal symbols of regeneration, have been associated with the Goddess since the beginning. The Goddess manifest as the snake and the tree of life is also familiar in the dreams and visions of women. The coiled snake in motion is the ultimate fertility symbol. In India and in Africa the woman/tree motif symbolizing life-generating powers is still part of the spiritual landscape. Votive offerings are made to trees in the name of the Goddess, invoking her bounty.

169. Debra Sherwood, SNAKE GODDESS, 1981. Ceramic. 85 in.

170. Debra Sherwood, SERPENT TREE, 1985. Ceramic. 90 × 52 × 49 in.

171. Debra Sherwood, SEMINAL FORCES: THE PANTHEON, 1984. Six ceramic figures in front of a temple façade. Installation photograph.

169

170

171

The Tree: Universal Symbol of Regeneration

All of Nancy Azara's art is about the numinous tree. Like the ritual carver of Africa, she transforms the tree trunk into a living spiritual force (see fig. 172). Her ecstatic, prismatic colors seem to come from the white light of the sun. "The carved, oiled, and bleached wood is lavishly painted and gold-leafed . . . faces, body parts, and [symbolic] objects" seem to grow out in undulating, sensuous forms. Ripening rhythm leads in every direction: spiraling up, out, backward, down. Simultaneously ugly and beautiful, the obvious processes of gouging, scraping, and cutting are painful and even anger-provoking. But smooth and intricately detailed; their calm relieves you.[35]

In reimaging ancient archetypes, she is intent on making them relevant to contemporary experience. For Azara it is not a matter of describing spiritual experiences but of making them happen. A psychic healer, Azara works with artists and others to explore the magical power and healing properties inherent in art-making. Using meditation, guided visualization, and other exercises, she helps her clients bring images to consciousness. For women this most often means an identification with the archetypal iconography of the Goddess in bodily metaphors.

The Sacred Dance of Jean Edelstein

To come face to face with your own interior landscape and recognize it as the sacred territory of the Goddess confirms an inner spiritual presence that most Western women have been out of touch with for millennia. This is the magic stuff of oracles and soothsayers, but there is nothing supernatural about the process of discovery, merely reactivating the powers of the psyche that have lain dormant so long.

Jean Edelstein brings back the spirit of the sacred dance. Her *Earthwind* paintings explore the relation between natural forces and the human female as ritual vessel (see figs. 173, 174, 175).

"[Edelstein's] paintings are pale, like faded frescoes, with only the barest intimation of mauve or pink in the delicate

172. Nancy Azara, SUN GODDESS, 1983. Oil, tempera, and gold leaf on carved and bleached wood. 8 ft.

173

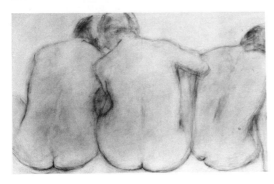

174

175

173. Jean Edelstein, EARTH, 1987. Acrylic and charcoal on canvas. 58 in. × 88 in.

"Clusters of two or three women huddle together. . . . Slow, meditative, sculptural, they are adamantly intimate. The intimacy is crucial. These women lean, touch, and whisper. Their thick bodies almost meld one into the other."[27]

174. Jean Edelstein, NOUMENON, 1987. Acrylic and charcoal on canvas.

"Groups of heavy, earthbound figures begin to rise out of a crowded, crouching stance, begin to turn, to generate tremendous and mysterious power."[28] Faceless, naked, their eerie presence recalls the sacred female of the Ice Age.

175. Jean Edelstein, WIND #13, 1987. Acrylic and charcoal on canvas. 66 in. × 88 in.

They dance in a circle, their bodies swaying in harmony to a natural rhythm like the wind. They revel in their nakedness.

washes."[36] Her work is important to reclaiming the sacred iconography of the female. There have been no images of women interacting like this in Western art since Crete. In treating the female nude as an expression of women's experience, she is resacralizing a woman's body and celebrating our pleasure in our bodies.

Nancy Spero: To the Revolution

Nancy Spero's *Chorus Line* is a grinning row of archaic Celtic images, the famous Sheela-na-gig, Goddess of fertility who once appeared on churches all over Ireland and England. Sheela-na-gig is a carving of a naked woman squatting with her knees apart, exposing her enormous vulva (see fig. 176).

Sheela's protective powers are no longer understood, her raw female sexuality no doubt troublesome. Spero has rehabilitated her image as an emblem of our time, a female who is not engaged in a cover-up (see fig. 177).

> The laugh of Medusa, as Helene Cixous explains, reveals what for men are unrepresentable: death and the feminine sex. "Let the priests tremble" Spero quotes Cixous in one of her scrolls, "we're going to show them our sexts! Too bad for them if they fall apart upon discovering that women aren't men, or that the mother doesn't have one."[37]

Nancy Spero has forged a new pictorial language for depicting women. The images she draws are adapted from archaeology, mythology, and the popular press, processed into black-and-white letterpress plates, using them over and over again much like rubber stamps. She tells women's story on long scrolls resembling those of the Chinese landscape painters. Her narratives are grounded in the nonlinear realm of prehistory with no beginning, no middle, and no end.

Her earlier work expressed a profound pessimism at the horror of the human condition, the universal violence and abuse of women. She used no color; hand printed text and image worked together giving her scrolls the immediacy of political handbills. Spero is not afraid to confront the fullness of the dark. Her goddesses projected the human reality. As she informs us throughout male literary history, gorgons, sirens, mothers of death and goddesses of night represent women who reject passivity and silence.

If Spero's earlier work focused on women's pain, the later works put forth women's pleasure and potential. We enter a world where

> naked women are unmolested; sprinting women are never tripped; laughing women remain unengaged. The image is one of freedom from every kind of physical, mental and social constraint; a freedom we do not possess but need to nurture, as an idea of a feeling, as our talisman against the oppression of habit, the grind of everyday obligation and normality.[38]

Spero has worked through some of her own pain. She has long been a leader in the feminist art movement, and in gaining recognition in the art world her vision has lightened.

> I wanted to depict women finding their voices, which partly reflected my own developing dialogue with the art world, that somehow I had a tongue and at least a part of the language of that world, there was an interchange. I'm speaking of equality and about a certain kind of power of movement in the world, and yet I'm not offering any systematic solutions.[39]

She does not offer final solutions. Her art is of the present. Her collages—overprinted, fragments, repeated images of the female body with varying meanings in different contexts— are "never going to resolve themselves, never going to offer wholeness, unity and completion."[40]

The Goddess leads the way to the revolution and women are following heads up, arms thrust back, running, leaping, dancing, celebrating their nakedness (see fig. 178 and color plate 9). "The scrolls roll on with primordial goddesses— the great goddess of Sumer, the Egyptian Goddess Nut, Artemis who 'heals women's pain,' Sheela-na-gig from the façade of a

176. Anonymous, SHEELA-NA-GIG, ninth century. Corbel on Church of St. Mary and St. David Kilpeck, Herfordshire, England.

The origins of her name are obscure but her iconography is straightforward enough. She is remembered in Ireland as the Old Woman Creatress who gave birth to all races of men.[29] Her function in the church was like that of the Gorgon on Athena's shield: to protect and ward off evil. Labeled obscene in later more prudish times, the carvings were destroyed or defaced, sometimes buried in yards of the churches they once sanctified.

176

177

177. Nancy Spero, CHORUS LINE I, 1985. Printed collage on paper. 20 in. × 110 in.

Spero's Sheela links arms with a row of identical sisters in a very comic chorus line, openly displaying that which is most taboo and laughing about it. "[H]er large-eyed face [is] a study in innocent pleasure as she exposes herself."[30] In a premodern age, the laughter she provoked, like the laughter of the carnival, defeated fear of the unknown. What was frightening or taboo in ordinary life was turned into amusing or ludicrous monstrosities.

178. Nancy Spero, TO THE REVOLUTION, 1983. Handprinting on paper. 20 in. × 9 in.

ninth-century church, along with the goddesses of the silver screen all moving in the continuous present. These goddesses of strength and healing, of female *jouissance,* these survivors, these dancers on their way to the revolution are all part of a contemporary and continuous celebration of femininity." The time is not yet, but Spero offers us a vision of what might be, "a glimpse [into] the old dream of symmetry."[41]

Spero's Goddess is the fully empowered, utterly modern woman celebrating her body, freely sexual, aware of her spiritual heritage as the embodiment of the Great Goddess, politically conscious and actively engaged in the transformation of our culture.

From the beginning of our story the female body has symbolized the sacredness of the earth. The desecration of nature is linked historically to the oppression of woman. With the growing awareness of our planet as a living organism, the Goddess has become the symbol for ecological wisdom.

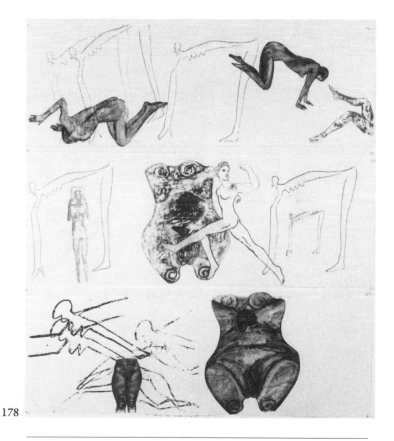

178

Gaia Consciousness: Ecological Wisdom for the Renewal of Life on Our Planet

Gaia Consciousness is a growing movement that holds promise of healing our planet. In the late twentieth century, with our very survival as a planet and species threatened by nuclear holocaust and environmental pollution, the Goddess is returning as a symbol for the resacralization of the earth. Once again we are honoring her as the source of all life (see fig. 179).

The birth of Gaia Consciousness can be traced to that incredible moment when the astronauts first landed on the moon in 1969. The dramatic photographs taken from their spaceship and later televised of the earth bathed in its own atmosphere made the astronauts' cosmic vision accessible to the whole world. The image of the continents we had all seen drawn on maps and globes in our school days now etched against the ocean shores was an awesome revelation of creation, a new icon for our time.

The photographs spawned another vision, that of scientist James Lovelock's hypothesis of the earth as a single, living organism.[1] This notion of the earth as alive is very different from our former, commonly held belief of the earth as dead matter with life on it and is changing our relationship to the planet. Lovelock named his hypothesis for the Greek Earth Goddess. He chose Gaia as a poetic or spiritual metaphor, but his naming struck a deep chord in an emerging consciousness. The moral implications of understanding that our planet is alive are enormous, and we have hardly begun to pursue them.

The astronaut's journey, like the shaman's, was literally out of this world. For both, it was a mystical experience in which the macrocosm of the universe was experienced in the micro-

"The earth, the grasses, the seas, and the infinite variety of creatures *are* her body, incarnations of her being and creativity. And all return home to her womb in death, dismemberment, extinction. In the undisturbed rhythm of earth, life and death are intertwined and balanced in a vast exchange of lives. But in this etching, the brooding figure of the great mother echoes that of the Virgin Mary in the Pieta, knees wide in the birthing posture, she gently holds in pity, love, and anguish, a glorious lifeless body, flesh of her flesh. The great mother, surrounded by and filled with animals, embodies at once both celebration and profound grief and anger."[31]

cosm of the human body. A Native American artist has envisioned the whole cosmos as a great medicine woman pregnant with the planet Earth (see color plate 41).

Women who honor their intuition have always felt themselves connected with the living earth. Poet Susan Griffin cries out from the depths of her being in affirmation.

> I know I am made from this earth, as my mother's hands were made from this earth . . . [and] this paper, these hands, this tongue speaking, all that I know speaks to me through this earth and I long to tell you, you who are earth too and listen *as we speak to each other of what we know: the light is in us.*[2]

Mexican artist Frida Kahlo painted herself as an infant suckling at an earth mother's plantlike breast (see color plate 20).

> Massive and brown, Frida's nurse is a concretization of Mexico's Indian heritage and of the Mexican earth, plants and sky. As if in sympathy with the nursing mother, milk-white veins in a huge leaf in the background are engorged. The raindrops in the sky are "milk from the Virgin"; thus had Frida's own Indian nurse explained to her the phenomenon of rain. The engorged leaf and the "Virgin's milk," the praying mantis and the metamorphosing caterpillar/butterfly that are camouflaged against the stems and leaves of plants, all express Frida's faith in the interconnectedness of every aspect of the natural world and in her own participation in that world.[3]

The legendary Frida Kahlo, tempestuous, passionate, political, has been hailed by American feminist artists as their "patrona." She was the first woman to openly paint her bodily experience and emotions. Hers is an idiom that is both naturalistic and mythic. Her life was full of intense physical pain and suffering. Badly crippled by a streetcar accident when she was seventeen, she bravely faced surgery again and again as her bones continued to deteriorate. Despite her handicap, she was active in radical politics, along with her husband, muralist Diego Rivera, fighting for social justice, and was much loved by the Mexican people. Her heritage was mixed European and Mexican; she identified with her native land and its indigenous peoples. Mexico was both her nurse and her roots.

Kahlo's deeply experienced connections to the land were organic. In another painting, *Roots*, it is she who nourishes nature.

With her elbow propped on a bed pillow, Frida dreams that her body extends over a large expanse of desert terrain. Her solitary presence in the wilderness is . . . mysteriously dreamlike and [yet] natural. . . . A window in her torso opens to reveal [not only the child she could never bear but] the rocky landscape beyond. From this mystic womb the pliant green vine emerges and spreads luxuriantly along the desert floor. Frida's blood courses in its arteries and continues in red vesicles that extend like creeping roots beyond the edges of its leaves. Frida becomes a source of life rooted in the parched Mexican earth.[4]

Like other women who open themselves up to earth's mysteries, Kahlo's identification is with a collective memory of how it was in the beginning when our earliest ancestors knew the earth as the source of all life and the ground of being.

Primal peoples everywhere have never lost this vision of the earth as the body of the Great Mother and continue to tell her story in their creation myths (see fig. 180).

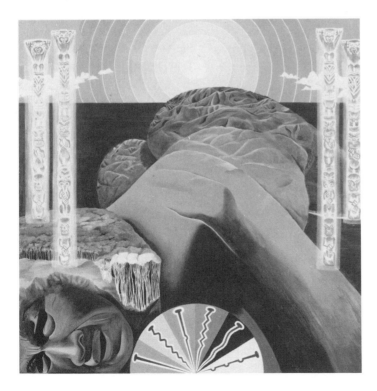

180. Robyn Kahukiwa, PAPATUANUKU, 1982. Oil on board. 114 cm × 114 cm.

Maori artist Robyn Kahukiwa reinterprets the myths of her New Zealand people through her paintings. She images her island country as the Earth Mother whose body lies on the deep blue sea against the radiating spirals of the orange-red setting sun. The Mother's face is the color of the sacred red ochre clay, her hair the mottled green-brown forest, her torso the grassy upland and serrated rocky mountains. According to Maori myth, the Earth Mother was conceived in the womb of darkness, of the night, the unknown that preceded the time of the gods.

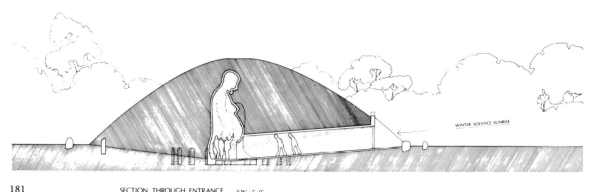

SECTION THROUGH ENTRANCE 3/16" - 1' 0"

181. Cristina Biaggi and Mimi Lobell, THE
GODDESS MOUND, 1986. Section through
entrance. Architectural drawing.

182. Cristina Biaggi and Mimi Lobell, THE
GODDESS MOUND, 1986. Entrance.
Architectural drawing.

The outside would be a large mound like
Silbury Hill in Avebury. The inside would be
the negative shape of a woman giving birth,
as the Maltese *may* have envisioned the
Goddess (see fig. 54). The figure would be
squatting in a birth-giving position, her legs
spread apart and drawn to the sides, her arms
tightly clenched under her knees. Entry
would be through a passageway leading from
the outside doorway directly into her vagina.
The inside walls would be painted an overall
red ochre color with swirling black spiral
designs like the Hypogeum at Malta.

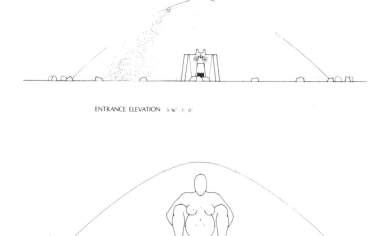

ENTRANCE ELEVATION 3 16" 1' 0"

ELEVATION OF THE GODDESS 3/16" 1' 0"

182

Sculptor Cristina Biaggi and architect Mimi Lobell designed
an earth sculpture of the Great Goddess as a temple that can
be entered (see figs. 181, 182).

Biaggi's extensive research on site at the megalithic structures in Malta and the Scottish islands gave her firsthand
experience with sacred architecture that metaphorically embodies the mysteries served. Through the construction of the
Great Goddess temple she seeks to reanimate the consciousness of architecture as a habitable structure in harmony with
the environment.

Sculpture in the Western world has lost the mystical magical presence that it had during the Neolithic period when a temple or a sculpture was considered to be the body of the deity. In creating my sculpture, I wish to bring back some of this magic and mystery. I want to create a space that inspires mystery; that evokes the dark caves of the Goddess—places of rebirth and revitalized consciousness.[5]

Biaggi is looking for a site to build her Goddess mound that can be oriented, like those of Silbury Hill and Newgrange, to the movements of the sun and moon. The great stones were set to line up with sunrise and moonrise positions on particular key days of the year. At Newgrange on the winter solstice the rising sun pours into the passageway illuminating for brief moments the triple spiral carved on the wall of the inner chamber of the earthen burial mound. The mystery immortalized at Newgrange is the earth's power to give new life to the sun (see color plate 51).

Spirit of Place

Megalithic sites have become centers of pilgrimage for those seeking the earth mysteries. Artists inspired by the energies dormant there interpret the great mounds, as Christopher Castle has done in a series of etchings based on the metaphoric connection between the movements of the celestial bodies and the landscape. *Maeve in Malta* is a graphic fantasy that illustrates important conceptual links between the burial practices of Irish and Maltese megalithic cultures.

The burial place of legendary Queen Maeve of Ireland is a huge cairn at the summit of Knockneara, dominating the area around Sligo. The stories about Maeve suggest that the historical queen was identified with the Goddess. The burial mound has yet to be opened but Castle images her lying within like the Maltese "Sleeping Lady" (see fig. 39) and links both monuments to the phases of the moon (see fig. 183).

When Judith Anderson visited Avebury at the spring equinox, she saw the Goddess rising from the landscape like a giant monolith, her body encompassing the structures in which the rituals of her life were enacted. She has captured the spirit of the place. Walking among the stones she was struck by the

183. Christopher Castle, MAEVE IN MALTA, 1985. Etching. Printed in burnt umber ink. 19¼ in. × 14⅞ in.

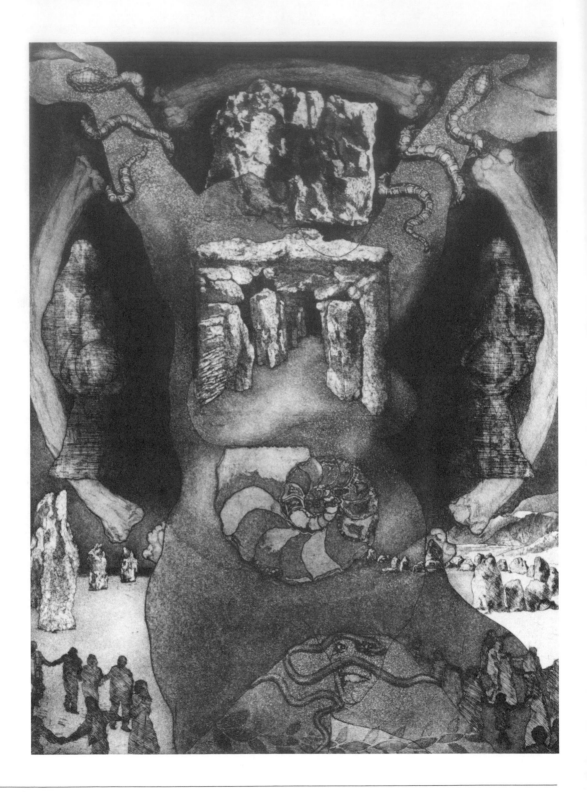

184. Judith Anderson, HER RUNES OF EARTH AND STONE, 1987. Intaglio print. 18 in. × 24 in.

silence, the awesome mystery of her body in the landscape, and by the eternal presence of the ruins. When the print was finished the artist noticed how dark it had become—"murky like the stones themselves; yet the places of light have the eerie quality of moonlight"[6] (see fig. 184).

In another of Anderson's prints, the craggy face of the Native American Earth Mother, wise Old Spider Woman, looms above the primal womb, which the artist envisions as a mandorla, a body-sized halo, enclosing the shadowy presence of the Goddess. Encircling the womb are the time-worn hands of the Mother, symbolizing her caring (see figs. 185, 186.)

185. Judith Anderson, MANDORLA OF THE SPINNING GODDESS, 1982. Etching. Intaglio print.

"We are looking at the birth of the Goddess, she who spins the web of life and death, whose womb of earth bears, sustains, and receives in death all creatures and growing things. All of these women's hands, young and old . . . are spinning and moving the threads. Our hands help create the fabric of life; in many sacred acts, our hands weave the will of the Goddess."[32]

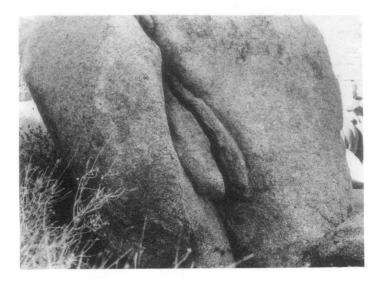

186. YONI FORMATION AT SITE 224. Crawford Ranch, Canebrake wash, San Diego County, California.

Native Americans in Southern California worshiped clefts in the rocks in the hills and mountains as the vulva of the Mother. The numinous power of the symbol as a sign for the continuation of all life in conjunction with the inherent energy of the stone has led "to the recognition and interpretation of natural features in rock as symbolic vulvas, preexistent and hence imbued with special power."[33]

For many Native Americans throughout the Western Hemisphere, corn is the power that connects the people to the Earth Mother. "She is the breath of life . . . because for them she holds the essence of the earth and conveys the power of the earth to the people. . . . Corn . . . is responsible for maintaining the linkage between the worlds."[7] Corn continues to symbolize the divine female principle among the native peoples even after four hundred years of Christian missionary activity (see color plate 40). The principal icon of Taos Pueblo Indians in New Mexico is the Corn Goddess, manifest as the Virgin Mary standing on the high altar of their church wearing a corn-yellow garment and guarded on either side by two enormous cornstalks.

Betty La Duke's poetic art reveals the interior connections of things. Plant, animal, and human life are woven together through her dreamlike imagery. She "enables us to see the Earth/the Mother/the Artist giving life, shelter and nurturance to all aspects of her creation throughout the many stages of its growth."[8]

> I slowly enter into each nature form—the earth, trees, rocks, water—letting them possess me, so that I too become the huge wave rising and falling, the redwood log whispering, the autumn tree approaching winter, the smaller rock forms as guardians of the Grand Canyon, or the birds soaring above the mountain summit.[9]

187. Betty La Duke, PERU: EARTH-MOTHER, 1984. Acrylic. 68 in. × 72 in.

"Hers is a universe in which a multitude of mythic visions come alive in the creative, female matrix"[10] (see fig. 187). La Duke's art brings together the experiences of her extensive travels, mythology, her own folklore aesthetic, and a deeply felt feminist ethic of caring.

> For many years she has spent each summer traveling in Central or South America, Asia and Africa. The sketchbooks from these trips record observations and experiences that are transformed in her studio into prints and paintings. Cross-cultural images become one-world issues: life and death, growth and decay, rites of passage and human harmony with nature, with spirits and with other humans.[11]

In West Africa La Duke went to the shrine of the River Goddess Oshun built by the German artist Suzanne Wenger in collaboration with her Yoruba assistants. Wenger has made her home in a Nigerian village since 1950, where she has been accepted as a priestess by the local people (see fig. 188).

The image of Oshun made from the mud of the river, embodies the spirit of the place, the life-giving waters that annually flood the banks bringing nurture to the surrounding farmland. Women especially come to her shrine seeking fertility or a cure from physical illnesses.

Third World peoples never lost their consciousness of the earth as the mother and the interconnection of all that lives. We have already seen how gradually over the millennia the double repression of patriarchy and monotheism disempowered the Goddess and desacralized the feminine principle.

188. Suzanne Wenger and Saka, OSHUN, GODDESS OF THE RIVER, MOTHER OF ALL, STANDING ASTRIDE A SACRED FISH, 1960–88. Mud, steel, and cement. 84 in. Photo by Su Friedrich.

Western Scientific Materialism and the Death of Nature

Gaia Consciousness runs counter to the materialist ethos dominant in the West since the seventeenth-century scientific revolution. The new science offered an increasingly mechanized concept of nature and an even greater polarization of mind and nature, reason and feeling, than that of the Greek philosophers.

That century was one of those watersheds in human evolution when everything changed drastically. By the midtwentieth century, the ideology of Western science had led us to a spiritual wasteland beyond all mystery, where nothing is sacred. The mystical traditions largely have been devalued and awareness of the sacred virtually eliminated from our consciousness. Everything could be explained away as process, biological or technical. The domination of humans over nature, now justified by both science and the Judeo-Christian worldview, has pushed us almost to the point of no return as we continue to ruthlessly despoil our natural resources and contaminate our environment. The wanton use of nuclear power as a source of energy and weaponry has brought us to the brink of extinction as a species and planet.

Our life-support systems are being violated and degraded and the ozone layer that protects us from the lethal rays of the sun has been ripped open by the fluorocarbons that fuel our spray cans, our refrigeration, and our air-conditioning systems.

The "silent spring" predicted by Rachel Carson twenty-five years ago is becoming a reality; our songbirds are being sacrificed to the voracious appetite of the fast food industry that buys beef grown on the ranches that are replacing the rain forest. "In biologist Norman Myer's estimate, our assault on the Earth constitutes the worst trauma life has suffered in all its four billion years of existence."[12]

Betsy Damon's "A Memory of Clean Water"

Betsy Damon now works to promote the awareness of the deep connection between the oppression of women and the wanton destruction of our natural resources. She is concerned

that our children will never have tasted fresh water (see fig. 189).

Memory is a 250-foot-long handmade paper casting of a stone-dry creek bed in Castle Valley, Utah. More than a mere remembrance, this monumental cast is a living presence, evoking the power and majesty of the swiftly flowing waters as they rush pell-mell down the canyon, sparkling in the brilliant sunshine and fresh, clear air, carrying with them the debris of the mountain environment. Bleached animal bones, fragile birds' feathers, slivers of mica and variegated pebbles are embedded in paper pulp, which has warm, sensuous earth colors mirroring those of the surrounding landscape: the red-browns of the canyon wall, the deep blues of the geological strata, and the yellow-green of the desert plants. She wants to make her viewer aware that the precious life-enhancing gift of nature, fresh water, is rapidly becoming a scarce resource.

190. Betsy Damon, Healing with Stones, 1985. Ritual performance. Photograph.

"Earth and stone are two forms of the same material symbolizing the same forces. Both are the sources of the world as we know it. The alchemical *petra genetrix,* or generative stone, is an incarnation of *prima materia,* the beginning, the bedrock, the Old European Great Goddess, who was both earth and sky—'unmated mother' sole creator of everything."[34]

Aware that primal peoples everywhere have "attributed to pebbles and stones, rocks and boulders, magical powers of intense energy, luck, fertility and healing,"[13] the artist did a series of public rituals in 1985, *Healing with Stones for the Survival of Our Planet* (see fig. 190).

Damon sees her role as that of a connector. Her art demands more than a mere viewing and is often participatory. Ritual is her vehicle of helping others to connect/reconnect to archetypal images.

"We Had Thought Only Little Girls Spoke with Animals"[14]

The visionary artist often dwells in her imagination at that boundary between the worlds; out of her concern for the earth has come a new enchanted art. Susan Boulet's shamanic images evoke another time, another place, in which human and animal were still of one spirit (see fig. 191).

When asked about the source of her imagery, Boulet replied that she is in touch with some kind of inner rhythm that brings up imagery appropriate for the time. "Now that we are concerned about the survival of all species, we must get to know our inner animal so we can take care of the outer ones." Nature outside the confines of the strict patriarchal faith became religion for Faith Wilding who grew up in a deeply spiritual Hutterite community in Paraguay. For the first twenty years of her life she lived in the lush jungle and communed with the plants and animals. Transplanted to California when the community came to America, she turned to feminist art, studying with Judy Chicago and Miriam Schapiro at the California Institute of the Arts in the midseventies. She began teaching the mythology of the female and doing ritual at the Women's Building in Los Angeles.

Her spring equinox ritual in 1980, *Invocation to a Burning,* was centered on the idea of rebirth from the Earth Mother.[15] A full-scale body of the Earth Mother made of wax and filled with vegetation was set on fire; the women leaped over the flames. The burning represented "an end to oppression, winter and 'our old selves.'"[16] The charred body was refilled with earth and new seeds planted. Wilding distributed the new seeds, the new life that was born out of the ashes, to women

191. Susan Seddon Boulet, MIDNIGHT SUN, 1987. Mixed media. 19 in. × 15 in.

The face of a woman emerges from the silky wolfskin, animal and human heads side by side. She holds an owl in one hand and the feathers of a hawk in the other. It is midsummer in the cold North and the midnight sun illumines the night sky.

192. Faith Wilding, LEAF-SCROLL, 1986. Detail. Gouache, ink, and gold leaf on paper. 22 in. × 75 in.

"*Leaf-scroll* consists of five cosmological world circles interspersed by large leaf-images in a cycle from birth to death. Each circle is divided into four quadrants painted yellow, blue, green, and red. At the center of the circle is a shaman figure, a human body with an animal mask. They are Deerwoman (eyes/spiritual), Rabbitman (ears/fecundity), Otterwoman (smell/wisdom), Wolfman (taste/experience), and Catwoman (touch/passion)." Six figures, half-human, half-animal, are inscribed within a circle, the microcosm surrounded by symbols of the earth, air, and fire of the universe. The sea otter is Wilding's totem animal, the link between water and air.

from all over the world who had come to the Women's International Conference at Copenhagen for a global ritual of home planting, the "Liberty Herbal."

Inspired by the work of the medieval mystic artist Hildegard von Bingen, who saw nature as a microcosm of the divine world, she works in exquisite detail like the medieval manuscript illuminators who filled the borders of their sacred texts with imagery taken directly from nature. Her *Scriptorium* paintings are an enlarged bestiary: Swan, rabbit, and deer loom life size from a patterned jewel-like ground.

When she drove across the country recently, Wilding noticed the many dead animals killed on the interstate highways and the emblematic signs marking deer crosses. Reflecting about the meaning of the loss of wild life to humans, she was aware of how powerful and yet how incredibly fragile nature is. The totemic animals in her *Leaf-scroll* represent the animal-human nature we all share (see fig. 192 and color plate 18).

For women like Wilding, Betsy Damon, and Mary Beth Edelson the spiritual is political; the experience of creating new ritual has been a significant stage in their development as visual artists.

After ten years as a performance artist, during which she mined the fertile field of Goddess myth and imagery as the sources for contemporary ritual, Edelson returned to paint-

ing. Her approach is radically innovative, as she wraps her imagery around the walls of the gallery creating sacred space. *Fish in the Sky* (see fig. 193), installed at the Danforth Museum in Framingham, Massachusetts, is an unabashedly exuberant synthesis of human and nature in a dance of life. It was inspired by a dream of fish flying with ease in the sky.

Edelson never lost touch with the Goddess. Her iconography has evolved through pilgrimage, through in-depth study of ancient sources and folklore, and through metaphysical practice. She went to a sacred Neolithic site in Yugoslavia and encountered the Goddess. Since then Edelson has been manifesting her vision in the visual language of contemporary art. Unwilling to be bound by the dictates of the mainstream art world, she has remained true to her own way of seeing. Nonetheless she is of her time. She lives and works in New York City in the center of the international art world. As an academically trained artist she has internalized the history of Western art. Her mature work is the powerful vision we have been seeking of the Goddess in our time—a compelling symbol for the interconnection of all life, for men as well as women. Her "fish" is the life force dancing across the sky.

Ecofeminism: Goddess Politics

Ecofeminism is a new political philosophy bringing together feminism and ecology, a natural coalition focused on the web of life in which all humans are embedded. A global, bio-

193. Mary Beth Edelson, FISH IN THE SKY, 1985–86. Oil on canvas. 10 ft. × 18 ft. Photograph.

Covering the entire right wall as one enters, a huge profile with flowing windblown hair metamorphoses into a streamlined fish body. In the far corner fish leap from the woman's forehead, suggesting the third eye of Eastern meditation. To the right, fish playfully swim through her skull, emerging from her ear.

centered perspective, founded on the belief in the oneness of all forms of life, ecofeminism critiques the dominant world order, envisioning a saner and more humane alternative based on a concept of power different from the prevailing one of hierarchy or "power over." This wholistic notion of power as an enabling force includes not only the rational and material but also the psychic and emotional. Activists and environmental groups like Grenham Common in England, the Green Party in Europe, and the Green Movement in the United States are committed to both personal and social change of a fundamental nature that could reshape our lives and public policy.

The term *spiritual* is controversial when applied to political movements like ecofeminism and Green Politics. The problem lies in the association of spiritual with the supernatural, a worldview that is contrary to earth-based spirituality that sees the divine as the immanent life force grounded in the natural world. Once again we are confronted with the difficulties of a truly radical shift in consciousness as emerging new concepts continually demand a letting go of old realities.

Faced with the threat to survival, some artists are leaving their studios to work directly with the public in performance and ritual, returning to the ancient role of the artist-shaman as the shaper of a new reality, a peaceful world.

Gaia Consciousness Means Peace, Not War

Painter Helene Aylon works full time for peace. The entire globe is her territory as she travels, adapting her performance pieces to the particular historical/cultural context of the place where she finds herself. Like the great icon makers of religious tradition, she has mobilized her finely tuned artistic sensibility to the transformative power of the symbol. As she evolved from process painter to political activist, she had been looking for a universal morphology, an underlying handwriting, a primary image and found it in the sac, an enclosed space, symbolic container of the life force like the womb, the cave, and the pot (see fig. 194 and color plate 6).

Impatient with her isolation and the limited public access to her work, in 1980 Aylon moved out of the studio to become more directly involved politically. Through her ritual-performances she has become a well-known figure in the international peace movement. Her performance art stems from her commitment to the feminist values of open-endedness, change, and sharing in the process of creation.

> For a long time I had been searching for some way to further the participatory aspect of my work. In the fall of 1980 I began pouring sand onto screening, observing how a sling-like sac formed from the weight. The way the sand sifted through was similar to the ways the oil descended. . . . Sand as a material was both plentiful and ubiquitous, and it lends itself to aesthetic and social statements.[17]

Since then she has been using sacs filled with sand or earth as the visual metaphor through which to call attention to our threatened planet. Her happenings are always public and directly involve her participating community and audience. She went to Israel where Arab and Jewish women working together filled cloth sacs with stones and left them in the archways of a deserted Israeli village as a sign of their wish for the end of the enmity between their peoples. They hung earth-filled sacs over the barbed wire at the Israel-Lebanon border. The image of fleeing refugees, holding their possessions in a sac or bag, is familiar in war photographs.

In 1982 Aylon organized a visit to twelve Strategic Air Command weapon sites (ironically SAC) to protest the world-wide proliferation of armaments. As her Earth Ambulance, a converted medical corps vehicle, traveled from site to site she was joined by volunteers of all ages, classes, and races who gathered earth into eight hundred pillowcases (sacs). The pillowcases donated by people along the way, who were threatened by the nuclear installations in their neighborhood, were inscribed with their dreams and nightmares about the fate of the earth.

The final stop of the rescued earth mission was the United Nations where the endangered earth was carried from the Earth Ambulance up to the Dag Hammarskjold Plaza on army stretchers. The sacs were emptied out into twelve transparent boxes; their contents became earth paintings, each with the particular tone, color, texture, and moisture of its area. The inscribed pillowcases and the earth paintings were later exhibited together. Aylon hoped her dramatic "earth rescue" would shake people out of the psychological numbing that prevents us from acting for nuclear disarmament.

194. Helene Aylon and Miriam Abramowicz, CURRENT: TWO SACS ENROUTE, 1985. Detail from video.

The following year she led a pillowcase exchange beginning with a group of American and Soviet women in the USSR. The climax of the pillowcase project took place in 1985 in Japan where women, *hibakushas,* survivors of the A-bomb, wrote their messages for peace on the sacs (see fig. 194). In a closing ritual in Kyoto, two sacs filled with sand from Hiroshima and Nagasaki, a prophetic vision of humankind's prayers for peace, were floated down the Kamagawa River en route to the cities that experienced the devastation of nuclear war.

Gaia, My Love: Shut Up or Ship Out

Rachel Rosenthal returns to theater's ancient religious function in enacting publicly the myths of the community. Her performance piece is a devastating recapitulation of popular attitudes toward our planet. Rosenthal, who has always been one of the most intelligent and politically committed of performers, builds her piece around complex issues, using nuclear imagery metaphorically, to interpret the idea of the Earth Mother and that of the apocalypse.[18]

Her performance is electric. Consummately skilled in the arts of the theater—solo performer, director, producer, script writer—she works at the cutting edge of performance art, at the interface of drama, dance, mime, and the visual arts. Her outrageous appearance fully matches her persona. Her bald head, noble and beautifully formed, is her trademark. Her eyes burn with an intensity that is searing. She stands feet apart, knees bent, arms spread wide, self-identified as Gaia, exhorting, raging, cajoling, vilifying her audience, who she says is hell-bent on destroying her (see fig. 195).

You know me . . . I'm the one you never bothered to name.

earth, with a small e
I, the first and most powerful of the Gods.
Even after you saw my loveliness from up there . . .
my comely blues my wisps of clouds,
the generosity of my life-
giving waters . . . Even then you didn't
name me.

I had a name once.
In this culture's genesis I was Gaia.
. . .
I am a cosmic body born out of cataclysm and
    catastrophe
I was seeded and, alone among the Bodies,
    was willing
I nurtured the seed in my awesome womb, . . .

I am the Matrix
You are in and of my Body
I am the Mother
I am the Daughter
I am the Lover
But scorned. I am also Lilith, the Maid of
Desolation. And I dance in the ruins of cities.[19]

In the end survival is up to us.

I am sorry.
. . .
I am sorry for you, I am sorry for me.
But then it's the same thing, isn't it?
For now *you* have the power and with the power,
the responsibility. If you cripple me beyond
repair, I will retreat back into the muds forever
and you will find yourselves my masters at last.
But you will be masters of a dead Spaceship

Earth, and at the same time its slaves. For you will need to put all your technological resources to work to maintain your life-supports, a task that I willingly performed for eons.

And yet the ultimate irony is ours.

Willy-nilly you have reintegrated the Feminine. For you yourselves are now in the role of the dreaded and hated Great Mother with all her powers of selection between Eros and Thanatos! The choice is yours!

In healing me you heal yourselves.
. . . Embrace me . . . I am you . . . *You* are Gaia now.[20]

"When she first [performed] bald in a ritual performance in the early eighties, she said that the act of having her hair cut and head shaved 'allowed dead things to be dead so that new things could grow. . . . She wanted to be open to the cosmos and its spirit, to be virile and to become androgynous."[21] Like the Cosmic Mother of Old Europe, her Gaia is a cosmogonic force. Her updating of Gaia's myth reminds us what a potent force for social change mythology can still be.

It is time to begin to spin new myths of the Goddess in our time.

195. Rachel Rosenthal, GAIA, 1983. Photograph from the performance of *Gaia, Mon Amour.* Photo by Mary Collins.

The Tantric mandala with the sacred triangle in its center, the ancient symbol of the Goddess, is projected behind her as she pleads to be healed.

Vijali: "My Art Is Torn from My Very Flesh, I Am Not Separate From It"

Vijali carves monuments to Gaia out of living rock. There is some kind of awe demonstrated in the very special relationship that she has established with the mountains. As she explores them, she inhabits them. She has carved in the Andes of Peru, in the mountains of Mexico, the hills of southern California, and on the cliffs overlooking the Pacific where the high-tide line rises to the base of her sculptured forms.

Carving these boulders had been on her mind for years. Vijali used to be a studio painter, but feeling isolated and confined like Aylon, sought a greater connection to nature. The rhythm of her work is slow, as she develops a resonance with the animals, the rocks, the weather, and the earth. The sculpture will ultimately be completed by the cyclic growth and erosion of the natural surroundings (see fig. 196).

196. Vijali Hamilton, WINGED WOMAN. Paint on granite. Box Canyon, Santa Susanna Mountains, Southern California.

A human-headed bird-goddess nests on a rocky outcropping in the wilderness, opening its rainbow-colored wing in a gesture of protection.

197. Vijali Hamilton, She Who Opens the Doors of the Earth, 1982. Granite boulders and acrylic. Yelapa, Puerta, Mexico.

"I open the boulders to show an area of space depicted as sky within the original shape. It is seeing the spirit within matter, connecting the space within the form with the whole space of the universe."

As her creative interaction with the living rock evolved, she came to view the earth as "moving, flowing energy rather than crystalized static forms as we are taught to see and psychologically validate"[22] (see fig. 197).

Vijali's Earth Mother and the World Wheel: A Global Art

Vijali's most recent project is to bring the Earth Mother into realignment with the cosmic forces. She is planning a series of twelve environmental sculptures and performances at sacred sites around the world, creating a giant medicine wheel that will circle the globe, a planetary vision of hope and transformation. Her goal is to promote peace and the relation of all peoples of the earth to each other and to the earth. The first ritual performance, "Western Gateway," took place on Harmonic Convergence Day, August 16–17, 1987, on a beautiful mountain plateau in the Santa Monica Mountains above Malibu, in southern California, land originally owned by the Chumash Indians.

Vijali has studied with Native American shamans and teachers and understands ritual art as the connection between the archaic foundations, how it was in the beginning, to the movements of the heavens above, that is, as harmonic convergence. "Western Gateway" was a collaborative event, like a tribal ceremony, integrating dance, music, visual art, and ritual. Her performances are intended to be healing, reconnecting humans with nature in a balanced way. There is widespread interest in our ancient tribal past, particularly the Native American traditions and memories of sacred ways long lost.

198. Vijali Hamilton, MEDICINE WHEEL, 1987. Environmental sculpture. Malibu, California.

At the center of the wheel is a fire pit lined with black stones. A five-foot-high lava stone rises from its center symbolizing the union of male and female. The four directions are indicated by ditches that start at the fire pit and end at the outer rim of the circle.

The east ditch is filled with gold stones symbolizing inspiration and creativity. The south contains red stones for faith and environmental lessons. The west holds black stones for inner knowing and achievement of goals. The north is filled with white stones for wisdom and strength.

The four colors also correspond to the four root races of humankind. The outer ring of the wheel is formed by twelve round stones which relate to the twelve stages of life.[35]

199. VIJALI AS THE EARTH MOTHER, 1987. Ritual performance of *World Wheel*. Malibu, California.

"Western Gateway" opens with greetings from the animal spirits of the land, then traces the evolution of human consciousness in relation to the earth from the beginning, through our present day, sober reality of disequilibrium. It concludes with a ceremonial vision of the future as Mother Earth that draws us out of confusion and imbalance and into harmony with our planet.

Vijali created a giant medicine wheel at the top of the mound as the setting for the last part of the ceremony (see fig. 198). The artist is the primordial Goddess, her body covered with earth, her hair wildly entangled in a dead branch[23] (see color plate 15 and fig. 199).

Her movements were ponderously slow, as if to the rhythm of geological time. As the crowd gathered round her on the high mound, the placement of the stone itself proved a focal point for powerful vortex. For those who understood the added implications of the wheel and the four elements, a reading of the piece gained the power of code.

These were the workings of the alchemy of ritual based on centuries of observational practice of tribal peoples whose intimate relationship and alignment with the way nature works resonates deeply with the sacredness of life.

Slowly she circled the [medicine] wheel, looking *each* person in the eye and slowing the minds of the witnessing audience so that all could enter the [liminal] space with her. She, as shaman traversing the worlds, entered a sacred time to work the wheel and effect a healing.[24]

Vijali has created a "theater of the earth." The ritual art is public, exposing in symbolic form the forces that threaten our survival. Rosenthal's Gaia scolds but Vijali heals. Participation in the dynamic process of ritual that transforms consciousness is one way of overcoming despair and empowering political action. The enormous appeal of these public ritual performances is extraordinary and prescient. They cut through deeply engrained attitudes of five thousand years of institutionalized state religion whose objective was to control and disenfranchise humans from their birthright as an integral part of the living cosmos. The Goddess is the overarching symbol for a reemerging empowerment.

The return of the shaman in the late twentieth century once again integrates the arts into the seamless fabric of the sacred, putting them to use in the service of the spirit, restoring the equilibrium that is Gaia Consciousness.

The Promise of the Goddess:
The Healing of Our Culture

I have told my story of the Goddess and in the telling have come to understand more fully why it is so important to me. We all have a personal truth within, compelling ideas that resonate with what is most sacred, with what seems right. What was most sacred for me, a Western woman of the late twentieth century, was the miracle of the birth of my children, the mystery of life conceived and nurtured in my body; the ecstasy of my sexual relationship with their father—my mate, my companion, my dearest friend and lover; and the wonder of my encounter with nature—climbing in the high places as the earth and the sky opened wide before me and walking on the beach, my internal rhythms in tune with the ebb and flow of the waves, the cycles of creation.

When such ideas are collective, we call them mythology, how it was in the beginning. We look to the tales of the divine women and men who are the players in the sacred myths as our models, seeking congruence between their ways and ours. Although the narrative is compelling, even more important for us are the visual symbols and icons through which the sacred is imaged.

The story of the Goddess belongs to the realm of all living myth. "In this realm, myth [is a truth that] retains its power long after philosophers and historians have revealed its impossibility, [continuing] to glide through our dreams, fantasies, and even our gestures."[1]

The truth of the Goddess is the mystery of our being. She is the dynamic life force within. Her form is embedded in our collective psyche, part of what it is to be human. She is Gaia, the dance of life, and her song is eros, the energy of creation.

We are only now once again admitting into our consciousness the wisdom of the ages, never lost to primal peoples, that the earth is not "a dead body, but is inhabited by a spirit that is its life and soul." This spirit perceived and experienced as the body of the Great Mother "gives nourishment to all the living things it shelters in its womb."[2]

The Goddess has come back as the beacon for the emergence of self that is not separate from the world in which our lives are embedded but a part of a greater being. In the language of the world religions, this is merging with the One. Wholeness is not the hero's journey of individuation and separation, which has been glorified since Homer. In the way of the Goddess the path leads to a consciousness that is responsible to all that is alive. What we have called matter is not separated from spirit; matter is impregnated with spirit. Perhaps what we call human is the fine-tuning of this consciousness and what we call nature is the matrix out of which this consciousness flows. Because we think symbolically and understand metaphorically, the Goddess has reemerged to guide us.

We can look to the Goddess as guardian of "the indwelling source of authentic conscience and spiritual guidance, the divinity within, the transpersonal center [which Jung calls] the Self." The rejection of traditional religious standards does not mean a rejection of ethics. The Goddess's coming means "a new ethics more deeply rooted in individual conscience."[3] In moral reasoning the highest good will no longer be an abstract force outside our own being but the wholeness of our humanity in relation to the Earth and the cosmos.

The Necessity of Reimaging

Goddess spirituality is political because it transforms our relation to society; the arts are its means of communication. The spiritual is once again being recognized as the core of art-making and art-experiencing. The image is the key to our transformation of culture. The change cannot come about without the reinforcement of new icons and symbols of female power. Jung has taught us there is a universal language of myths and symbols. Our task is to find a way to access this powerful tool of communication.

Until women can visualize the sacred female they cannot be whole and society cannot be whole. Women artists are uncovering the roots of our symbols, which have been perverted by patriarchy. As artist Jean Edelstein tells us, "their art is coming from the soul and we're trying to find the soul."[4]

The Goddess has once again become the muse to the arts. She is the chief inspiration for the veritable explosion of creativity by women artists/activists who seek to transform our society. For a woman the discovery of the Goddess within opens wellsprings of her being and leads to the release of creative energies of which she may not have been aware. The female has been so long repressed in the culture at large that the very language in which women spoke, the images through which they expressed their inner being, were almost totally lost. Tillie Olsen writes of the "silences," the poems not written, the songs not sung.

Women artists are increasingly using performance as a revolutionary strategy, often putting themselves on the line in vulnerable situations. Performance art is a return to tribal/ritual forms, an exploration of women's mythologies and lost histories, a search for metaphors that encompass our collective unconscious and our consciousness. Through art, women are recovering the ancient fabric of wholeness, of nonduality, of unity, of spirit and body, nature and culture, life and death, man and woman. Like the shaman of prehistoric and primal peoples, they are drawing on the forces of nature to heal. While modeled on the archetypal, the new art comes out of a contemporary consciousness of a historical past and a very personal, vulnerable present. They understand the imperative for new symbols that will transform our culture for a viable future.

Just as we have denied the power of the unconscious to shape our lives, so we have ignored the living forces that are not human, the power of the animals and the spirit of the place. Mythographer Joseph Campbell informs us that the animals were the first teachers of humankind. Mountains, hills, rivers, caves, and other sites having some geographical or natural particularity are often said to possess sacred power or to be places where one may make contact with the divine. Sacred sites all around the world represent touchstones of cultural values. Traditional cultural wisdom asserts that these places represent facets of nature that work to preserve the web of life itself as well as to inspire people to express their fullest potential.

Women crave accessible icons of empowerment. Very little of the outpouring of new Goddess art has been exhibited in mainstream museums and galleries. Ritual performances and happenings are often small, local events, part of workshops and festivals, that go unreported by the media. Perhaps just as the invention of the printing press revolutionized popular religious art in the sixteenth century and the lithograph in the nineteenth, the new channels of publication and distribution now evolving will bring the new sacred iconography of the female to the public in the late twentieth century.

This new iconography is a key to our power as women to name the world as we see it. In creating new symbols we are creating new ways of seeing and being in the world. But this is not just a women's culture; men need the Goddess as well. Although women took the initiative in bringing content back into art, men as well as women are making sacred art that draws on the power of nature.

In time the new iconography will include images of the male principle but they have yet to evolve. Given the distortions of Western culture in which almost all symbols and motifs of female power have been suppressed, it is not surprising that the initial thrust of the transformative process should first address this imbalance. In time the new iconography will include a new symbol of male identity, one not based on dominance and violence.

Why Men Need the Goddess: The Hero's Journey Is Not the Way to the Goddess

The myth of the hero's journey, the quest of everyman for his maleness, has not served men of our time well. The hero's journey glorified in Western tradition, extolled by mythographer Joseph Campbell as the human path, is a journey away from the Mother. The quest in search of the Father is one of exile from his female source and has led to alienation and estrangement between men and women.

Actress/playwright Donna Wilshire and philosopher Bruce Wilshire, wife and husband, grapple with gender stereotypes in our culture through an ongoing dialogue as they struggle to bring a new consciousness into their relationship of co-operation not confrontation. Bruce's passion is the radical reform of higher education; Donna performs the myths of the prehistoric Goddess in the ancient oral/dance tradition.

They acknowledge the difference between what is sacred to men and what is sacred to women. Maleness is viewed as being entirely different from femaleness, excluding all that resembles his mother or her womb.[5] The hero's odyssey takes him away from all that, to "out there" where the sky's the limit.

For 2,500 years, since the time of Aristotle, men have been talking about separation and difference and isolation as the human condition.

> When a male child separates from his mother, he becomes isolated, alienated from her and at the same time is also separated from that part of himself that was like her. Then as Freud says, he begins to associate himself with his father who is his only proper role model. Males do not simply discard the aspects of themselves that they shared with their mothers before their enforced separation, but later on after separation, those parts must be disclaimed and repressed, fought against and if need be distorted until they are unrecognized. It's as if the best way for a boy child to keep from seeing those female things in himself, all unacceptable parts of himself, is to start actively demeaning them in others, attach disgusting labels to those aspects.[6]

The Wilshires remind us that escape from the body, transcendence, is precisely the problem. Most men feel they must separate themselves from femaleness in the name of all that is masculine, all that is sacred and all that is holy. It's impossible for the male to see the whole female as holy, he fears all that body stuff, all that blood and emotion in her, dreads facing in himself the things he has learned to demean as female, dreads his vulnerability, his mortality. To be male he thinks he must be fundamentally different from her.

Seen from this point of view, it is clear that any attempt to counteract the alienation we experience in this culture must be an attempt to restore the so-called feminine aspect to men's nature—and to stop demeaning the femaleness in ourselves. But such change is difficult. Our very language is structured around dualism and hierarchy, around difference and opposition, those qualities associated with maleness identified with that which is valued more highly: mind over body; reason over emotion; hard over soft.

Individuals need not be defined as one against the other. Early humans had another model. What we now know about prehistoric peoples from the archaeological work of Gimbutas and Mellaart and from survivors of Stone Age hunting and gathering societies like the !Kung Bushmen of southwest Africa tells us that men and women once coexisted in peaceful, egalitarian collaboration.[7]

We Need a New Cosmology

Joseph Campbell says that the problem of mythology is to relate the scientific worldview to the actual living of life. We have an ancient mythology and cosmology

> . . . for the way of the seeded earth—fertility, creation, the mother goddess. And we have a mythology for the celestial lights for the heavens. But in modern times we have moved beyond the animal powers, beyond nature and the seeded earth. . . .

Myth has to deal with the cosmology of today. The scientific knowledge of reality is not incorporated into our cosmology. We need a bigger vision that includes both scientific thinking and the wisdom of the past so that ordinary people can lead visionary lives.

> The story that we have in the West, so far as it is based on the Bible, is based on a view of the universe that belongs to the first millennium B.C.E. It does not accord with our concept either of the universe or of [human] dignity. . . .

> We have today to learn to get back into accord with the wisdom of nature and realize again our [common humanity] with the animals and with the water and the sea. [This is not pantheism, nor] a personal god [who] is supposed to inhabit the world but . . . an indefinable, inconceivable mystery, thought of as a power, that is the source and supporting ground of all life and being.[8]

The symbol for this new mythology to come is the Earth seen from space (see color plate 41). We are the Earth, the

200. Judith Anderson, MYSTERY OF GENERATION, 1987. Etching. 6 in. × 24 in.

Long suppressed by nationalistic civilization, the wise grandmotherly crone and the magical pleasure loving Pan, greenman of the forests, are our natural heritage, both ordinary and profound. The child to be born suggests the miracle of new beginnings.

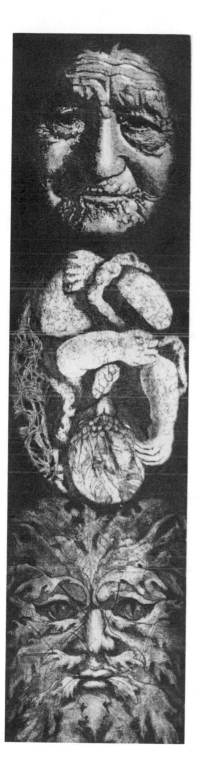

consciousness of the Earth, Mother Earth. Like so many of us, printmaker Judith Anderson is seeking a sacramental vision that honors the great web of connectedness throughout creation. Anderson's etchings and drawings are a new visual language she is gradually discovering in order to express the meanings she finds in relationships, in dreams, in women's spirituality, and in that mysterious archetypal realm where opposites are joined and where healing and creativity can flourish. In her etching *The Mystery of Generation*, "the mothers have an ancient wisdom. The fathers are grounded in earth mysteries. Their children are grounded in spirit and earth" (see fig. 200).

> How different are the gender expectations in our own culture. The earth mother is simply fertile; the father holds power through analytic detachment but there have been people and archetypes in other cultures that reveal the possibilities the print suggests. The wisdom of the grandmothers, of the crone, of women, has in other times and places been revered and men have walked in balance on their mother earth sensitive to her seasons and the mysteries of her creatures. In Europe the Green Man had many guises before he was suppressed by a relentless rationalistic civilization; the man of the forests, Pan Robin of the Green, the foliate head in cathedral carvings with vines growing from his mouth and nostrils half-hidden in leaves. Sometimes he is the noble savage, sometimes Merlin. His magic is very old. Man-made culture and the rigidity of custom have robbed women and men of some very significant natural gifts. Gifts that are at once both ordinary and profound. In the print the bird-headed child suggests a miraculous new beginning.[9]

The New Magical, Mythological Consciousness

Edward Whitmont reminds us that when old values are breaking down, the eternal problems of humankind have to be wrestled with in new ways.

> We seek new forms of self-validation and of relating to our emotional and instinctual urges. Yet paradoxically these new ways require a retrieval of old, seemingly discarded and repressed modes of functioning. The *magical, mythological,* and feminine ways of dealing with existence left behind thousands of years ago must now be reclaimed by consciousness.[10]

But compared to the past, the new consciousness will have to be endowed with greater clarity, freedom, self-awareness, and a new and different capacity to love. The Goddess has reemerged as a guide for this transformation.

We are inevitably of our time. The reemergence of the Goddess does not mean a return to the Old Religion. What it does promise is a profound healing of the malaise that permeates our social fabric and physical environment. We are in the midst of one of those epochal changes like those at the time of the coming of the Buddha and the birth of Jesus when human realities are being reshaped by a vision of far-reaching consequences.

Once again artists are the prophets and healers. A new symbology and mythology is in the making. The avante-garde is usually around the corner and out of sight for most of us. What is so telling in this revolution is that the new spirituality appears to be a grass roots phenomenon.

The Goddess has reappeared in our midst in the late twentieth century as symbol of the healing that is necessary for our survival, a transformation of consciousness that holds promise of a renewal of our culture. The emerging consciousness is pluralistic. There are many pathways that reconnect the personal to the political, the spiritual, and the sexual. There are no authorities, hierarchies, or gurus. Empowerment comes from within, from the connection to the life force.

While I have told my story primarily through women's experience and art, the life-enhancing powers of the Goddess are for men as well. Some men call themselves feminist in recognition of the political nature of the women's movement that transcends gender. In many of the men's consciousness-raising groups that are now being formed, men have taken the Horned God, the consort of the Goddess in pagan tradition, as their model. He is Pan and his way is pleasure, an active generative force.

The taming of the Goddess under patriarchy led to the gradual erosion of sexuality, the cyclical regenerative powers of the cosmos. In Minoan Crete, women and men were both frankly sexual, celebrating life through eros.

The promised healing is that in honoring all that lives— women, the earth, its manifold creatures—we will no longer need to control, oppress, despoil our planet, to make war.

We cannot—would not—wish to return to some golden prehistoric age; but in reclaiming our lost heritage we can build upon the values encoded in the prehistoric survivals. We do not have to look outside ourselves, outside our planet. What is needed is not new discoveries or technologies—only the willingness to change, to open up our hearts and honor what we already are.

Text Notes

Introduction

1. Stone 1976, xxii
2. Orenstein 1985, 456
3. Eliade 1961, 14

1. The Ice Age: The Earth as Mother

1. White 1986, 14
2. Marshall 1976
3. White 1986, 65
4. Scully 1962, 10
5. Ibid.
6. Marschack 1972, 286
7. Leroi-Gourhan 1967, 174
8. Marschack 1986 (unpub.)
9. Marschack 1972, 320–21
10. Ibid., 335
11. Campbell 1983, 67
12. Giedion 1962, 481–82

2. The Unfolding of Her Mysteries

1. von Cles-Reden 1962, 14
2. Eisler 1987, 9

3. Çatal Hüyük: Birth, Death, and Regeneration

1. Mellaart 1967, 22
2. Walker 1983, 187
3. Gimbutas 1982, 93
4. Cameron 1981, figs. 1a and 1b
5. Cameron 1981, 22ff.
6. Gimbutas 1982, 132ff.
7. Cameron 1981, 27
8. Mellaart 1967, 165
9. Ibid., 202
10. Barstow 1983, 11

4. Old Europe: Cosmic Creation and the Maintenance of Life

1. Gimbutas 1982, 238
2. Gimbutas (speech at 1988 conference)
3. Eisler 1987, 14–15
4. Srejovic 1972, 14–16
5. Ibid., 16
6. Ibid., 34
7. Ibid., 16
8. Gimbutas 1982, 110
9. Ibid., 111
10. Marschack 1972, 169–72 and fig. 62a
11. Gimbutas 1982, 112
12. Ibid.
13. Ibid., 135
14. Ibid., 94
15. Ibid., 201
16. Ibid., 158
17. Ibid., 159
18. Ibid., 196
19. Ibid., 216
20. Gimbutas 1980, 42
21. Ibid., 44
22. Gimbutas 1982, 237
23. Ibid.
24. Ibid., 9
25. Ibid., 238

5. Malta: The Temple as the Body of the Goddess

1. von Cles-Reden 1962, 70
2. Trump 1972, 24
3. Ibid., 27
4. von Cles-Reden 1962, 71
5. Biaggi 1983, 295

6. von Cles-Reden 1962, 78
7. Trump 1972, 72
8. Reis 1986 (unpub.)
9. Trump 1972, 61
10. Stone 1976, 213–14
11. Keller, unpub., 27–28
12. Sorlini 1986, 148
13. Dames 1976, 60
14. Ibid., 61
15. Sorlini 1986, 148
16. Purce 1979, 55–56
17. Ferguson 1986, 152; fig. M
18. Trump 1972, 64
19. Sorlini 1986, 148
20. Ibid., 148–49
21. von Cles-Reden 1962, 111

6. Avebury: The Great Seasonal Drama of Her Life Cycle

1. Bachofen 1967, 76
2. Dames 1977, 14–15
3. Dames 1976, 145
4. Eliade 1969, 125
5. Lincoln 1981, 17
6. Jayakar 1980, 142
7. Dames 1977
8. Marglin 1986, 309
9. Dames 1976, 12
10. Ibid., 165
11. Eliade 1958, 154, 177
12. Dames 1976, 88ff.
13. Ibid., 140
14. Ibid., 142
15. Ibid.
16. Ibid., 78
17. Dames 1977, 57
18. Walker 1988, 257–58
19. Dames 1977, 30
20. Fawcett 1970, 130
21. Dames 1977, 9–11
22. Dames 1976, 14–17
23. Ibid.
24. Ibid., 15
25. Ibid., 15–16

7. Crete: Fulfillment and Flowering

1. Hawkes 1968, 131
2. Ibid., 101
3. Ibid., 102
4. Von Matt 1968, 19
5. Levy 1963, 214
6. Scully 1962, 11
7. Scully 1982, 34–35
8. Ibid., 35
9. Hawkes 1968, 134
10. Ibid., 135
11. Ibid., 146–49
12. Ibid., 133
13. Ibid., 134
14. Levy 1963, 216
15. Walker 1983, 253
16. Hawkes 1968, 137–38
17. Ibid., 137
18. Levy 1963, 225
19. Hawkes 1968, 131–32
20. Ibid., 131
21. Ibid., 132
22. Gimbutas 1982, 186–87
23. Scully 1982, 39
24. Ibid.
25. Hawkes 1968, 124
26. Ibid., 125
27. Rohrlich-Leavitt 1977, 46
28. Ibid., 48
29. Ibid.
30. Cottrell 1963; Hood 1967; Hawkes 1968; Thomas 1973
31. Hawkes 1968, 77
32. Hawkes 1968, 155; Judge 1978, 166–67
33. Judge 1978, 166
34. Rohrlich-Leavitt 1977, 50
35. Scully 1962, 13–14
36. Waters 1963, 24
37. Huxley 1974, 157

Part Two. The Patriarchal Takeover: The Taming of the Goddess

1. Eisler 1978, 213, fn. 8
2. Gimbutas 1973, 166
3. Ibid., 201–2
4. Lerner 1986, 212
5. Ibid., 212–14
6. Ibid., 141

7. Ibid., 141–42
8. Ibid., 142
9. Ibid., 143
10. Ibid., 143–44

8. Sumer: The Descent of Inanna

1. Ochshorn 1983, 16
2. Wilshire 1988 (unpub.)
3. Wolkstein and Kramer 1983, 169
4. Ibid., xix
5. Kramer 1970, 138
6. Wolkstein and Kramer 1983, 115
7. Ochshorn 1983, 19
8. Kramer 1969(a), 11
9. Ochshorn 1981
10. Wolkstein and Kramer 1983, 123
11. Ochshorn 1983, 20
12. Ibid., 20
13. Ochshorn 1981, 47
14. Wolkstein and Kramer 1983, 125
15. Ibid., xvi
16. Ibid., 144
17. Ibid., 143
18. Ibid., 143–44
19. Ibid., 143
20. Patai 1967, 181
21. Wolkstein and Kramer 1983, 19
22. Patai 1967, 222
23. Isaiah 24:14
24. Albright 1939, 9; Patai 1967, 181–82
25. Wolkstein and Kramer 1983, 145–46
26. Ibid., 146
27. Ibid., 147–48
28. Ibid., 150
29. Ibid., 37–38
30. Ibid., 153
31. Perera 1981
32. Wolkstein and Kramer 1983, 156
33. Ibid., 158
34. Ibid.
35. Ochshorn 1983, 23
36. Wolkstein and Kramer 1983, 71
37. Perera 1981, 82
38. Wolkstein and Kramer 1983, 163
39. Ibid., 168
40. Ibid., 89
41. Ibid., 167

42. Ibid., 168
43. Perera 1981, 78
44. Gimbutas 1982, 228–30
45. Kramer 1970, 136
46. Ibid.
47. Jacobsen 1976, 25–27
48. Perera 1981, 82
49. Bolle 1965, 320
50. Kramer 1970, 138
51. Jacobsen 1976, 36
52. Ibid.
53. Ibid.
54. Kramer 1969, 49
55. Wolkstein and Kramer 1983, 155
56. Kramer 1970, 139
57. Marglin 1986, 310
58. Ibid.
59. Ibid., 311–12
60. Perera 1981, 21
61. Ibid.
62. Ibid., 47
63. Wolkstein and Kramer 1983, 44
64. Jacobsen 1976, 95–96
65. Perera 1981, 51
66. Falk 1977
67. Lerner 1986, 141–42

9. Demeter's Mysteries

1. Engelsmann 1979, 45
2. Burkert 1987, 91
3. Walker 1983, 219
4. Keller 1987, 31–32, fn. 14
5. Harrison 1927, 48–50
6. Spretnak 1984, 106
7. Downing 1984, 41
8. Homer, *Hymn to Demeter,* ll. 479–80
9. Sophocles, *Triptolemos,* fr. 837
10. Walker 1983, 220
11. Ibid., 807
12. Eliade 1982, 415
13. Weimer 1987, 7
14. Ibid., 13
15. Sargent 1973, vii

16. Homer, *Hymn to Demeter,* ll. 11.19–20

17. Ibid., ll. 2.303–8

18. Ibid., ll. 2.230–33

19. Engelsmann 1979, 50

20. Berger 1985, 71

21. Nilsson, in Engelsmann, 51–52, fn. 30

22. Keller 1986, 7

23. Berger 1985, 17

24. Ibid.

25. Harrison 1962, 123

26. Ibid., 153

27. Gimbutas 1982, 211

28. Harrison 1962, 125

29. Ibid., 126

30. Eliade 1978, 294

31. Lincoln 1981, 86

32. Engelsmann 1979, 53

33. Harrison 1962, 153

34. Luke 1987, 66

35. Eliade 1978, 296

36. Ibid.

37. Keller 1987, 52–53

38. Eliade 1978, 297

39. Ibid., 298–99

40. Luke 1987, 67

41. Eliade 1978, 299

42. Luke 1987, 67–68

43. Keller 1987, 40–41

44. Harrison 1905, 566

45. Keller 1987, 10

46. Lincoln 1981, 74

47. Ibid., 75

48. Ibid., 85

49. Neumann 1963, 307

50. Ibid.

51. Ibid., 306

52. Ibid., 308–9

53. Lincoln 1981, 107

54. Ibid., 108

55. Ibid., 188

56. Ibid., 96

57. Kerényi, in Engelsmann 1979, 57

58. Eliade 1982, 416

10. The Hebrew Goddess and Monotheism

1. Grant 1984, 61

2. Patai 1978

3. Davies, in Olson 1983, 74

4. Dever 1987, 237, fn. 4

5. Holladay 1987, 249

6. Ibid., 249

7. Miller 1987, 53

8. Ibid., 55

9. Patai 1978, 19–25

10. Ibid., 46

11. Miller 1987, 55

12. Dever 1984, 28

13. Miller 1987, 59

14. Ibid., 59

15. Ibid., 60

16. Mazar 1982, 27

17. Holladay 1987, 275

18. Deuteronomy 12:2–3; 2 Kings 16:4; 17:10–11; Isaiah 65:7; Jeremiah 2:20; 17:2; Ezekiel 6:13, 20:28; Hosea 4:13

19. Gimbutas 1987, lecture

20. Teubal 1984, 100

21. Genesis 12

22. Teubal 1984, 89–90

23. Judges 9:37

24. Teubal 1984, 90

25. Deut. 16:21–22

26. Dever 1984; Zevit 1984

27. Freedman, telephone conversation, December 1987

28. Dever 1984, 21

29. Ibid., 23, fig. 2

30. Treasures of the Holy Land 1986, 161–63

31. Judges 5

32. Holladay, telephone conversation, December 1987

33. Dever 1984, 29

34. Mazar 1982, 32

35. Treasures of the Holy Land, 1986, 154

36. Albright 1940, 229–30; Cross 1973, 73–75; de Vaux 1961, 333

37. Haran 1978, 29, n. 28; Bailey 1971, 97–115; Pfeiffer 1961

38. Patai 1967, 53

39. Walker 1983, 127

40. Albright 1971, 104–5; Teubal 1984, 27

41. Holladay 1987, 278

42. Reed 1949, 80, 81, 87

43. Bird 1987, 401

44. Ibid.

45. Patai 1978, 54
46. Jeremiah 44:15–19
47. Patai 1978, 55
48. Ibid., 55–56
49. Ibid., 57
50. Holladay 1987, 249–302
51. Ibid., 278
52. de Vaux, in Eliade 1978, 180
53. Eliade 1978, 182
54. Ibid., 184
55. Judges 6:19
56. Eliade 1978, 185
57. Judges 2:13
58. 1 Samuel 7:3–4, 10–13; 13:10
59. Ibid., 31:10
60. 1 Kings 15:13
61. Davies 1983, 72
62. Patai 1978, 35
63. Isaiah 17:8, 27:9; Micah 5:11–13
64. Deuteronomy 7:15, 12:3; Exodus 34:10
65. Patai 1978, 37
66. Dodson Gray 1982, 26
67. Bird 1987, 400–401
68. Grant 1984, 62–63
69. Dever 1984, 30

11. Is the Virgin a Goddess? The Problem of the Immaculate Womb

1. Moss and Cappannari 1982, 65
2. Meyer 1987, 155
3. Warner 1976, 209
4. Warner 1983, 47–48
5. Hall 1980, 11
6. Warner 1983, 48
7. Kristeva 1987, 101
8. Warner 1983, 58
9. Ibid., 46–47
10. Ibid., 47
11. Ibid., 58
12. Ibid., 275
13. Meyer 1987, 159
14. Stone 1976, 219
15. Budge 1969 I, 259
16. Bleeker 1983, 32
17. Ibid., 32
18. Budge 1977, 265
19. Bleeker 1983, 35
20. Graves, in Begg 1985, 61–62
21. Bleeker 1983, 38
22. Begg 1985
23. Ibid., 57
24. Salzman 1983, 65
25. Meyer 1987, 7
26. Ibid.
27. Salzman 1983, 66
28. Berger 1985, 55–56, 89
29. Ibid., 89–90
30. Neumann 1955, 313
31. Walker 1983, 267
32. Warner 1983, 292
33. Isaiah 7:14
34. Warner 1983, 197–98
35. Luke 2:27
36. Warner 1983, 198–99
37. Ibid., 104
38. Ibid., 231–47
39. Revelation 14:7
40. Warner 1983, 92
41. Ibid., 94
42. Ibid., 93
43. Eliade 1987, vol. 9, 252
44. Hartt 1988, 529
45. Hartt 1974, 383–92
46. Starhawk 1982, 185, 189
47. Ibid., 187
48. Walker 1983, 1078
49. Starhawk 1982, 187–88
50. Lerner 1986; Eisler 1987
51. Begg 1985, 6
52. Wolf 1958, 34
53. Ibid.
54. Ibid., 37
55. Begg 1985, 93–125
56. Moss 1982, 68
57. Begg 1985, 175
58. Ibid., 256
59. Ibid., 185
60. Male, in Campbell 1974, 65, fig. 56
61. Ibid., 65
62. Ibid., fig. 56
63. Ibid.
64. Chandra 1973, 1
65. Ibid.
66. Warner 1983, 335
67. Barthes 1972, 142
68. Warner 1983, 335
69. McEvilley 1987, 102

Part 3. The Re-emergence of the Goddess: A Symbol for Our Time

1. Ackerman 1987, 416
2. Ibid.
3. Rich 1986, 59–60
4. Harding 1971, ix
5. Ibid., x
6. Whitmont 1982, vii
7. Harding 1971
8. Rowan 1987, 139–41
9. Gleason 1987, 10
10. Whitmont 1982, viii
11. Sahtouris 1989, 13–14

12. The Way of the Goddess: An Earth-Based Spirituality

1. Starhawk 1979, 7
2. Ibid.
3. Adler 1986, 10–11
4. Starhawk 1979, 2
5. Adler 1986, 10–11
6. Starhawk 1979, 7
7. Ibid.
8. Ibid.
9. Adler 1986, 11
10. Ibid., 6
11. Starhawk 1982, 13
12. Ibid., 3
13. Starhawk 1979, 7
14. Budapest 1986, 3
15. Adler 1986, 178
16. Budapest 1986, 3
17. Adler 1986, 12
18. Ibid., viii–ix
19. Starhawk 1979, 8
20. Adler 1986, 4
21. Ibid., 5
22. Ibid., 6
23. Fox 1983, 222
24. Heschel, in Fox 1983, 222
25. Rich, in Fox 1983, 223
26. Fox 1983, 223
27. Ibid.
28. Ibid., 225
29. Craighead, in Reis 1986–87, 43
30. Franck 1986, 313
31. Reis 1986–87, 43
32. Craighead, in Franck 1986, 313
33. Craighead, in Reis 1986–87, 43
34. Craighead 1986, 7
35. Craighead, in Reis 1986–87, 43
36. Novick 1988
37. Patai 1967, 99
38. Ibid., 118–19
39. Ibid., 119
40. Ibid., 120
41. Wortz 1982, 25
42. Hirsch, in Wortz 1982, 14
43. Novick 1988
44. Berman, in Swartz 1981, 3
45. Swartz 1981, 12
46. Nelson 1984, 92
47. Wortz 1982, 26
48. Nelson 1984, 36
49. Oda 1984, 6–7
50. Oda 1985, 5
51. Oda, in Gates 1984, 6
52. Oda 1985, 4
53. Howard 1988, 1
54. Ibid., 2

13. The Goddess Within: A Source of Empowerment for Women

1. Christ 1987, 117
2. Ibid., 117
3. Ibid., 121
4. Christ 1987, 155
5. Morgan (personal communication)
6. Daly 1973, 13
7. Christ 1987, 63
8. Christ 1987, 118–19
9. Weaver, in Spretnak 1982, 249
10. Asungi (personal communication) 1982
11. Lippard 1976, 260
12. Monroe 1979, 414
13. Rakusin (personal communication) 1986
14. Edelson, in *Heresies* 1988, 96–99
15. Ibid., 97
16. Ibid., 98
17. Lippard 1983, 176
18. Lippard (personal communication) 1978
19. Edelson 1980, 17
20. Damon (conversation) 1988
21. Benton (personal communication) 1988
22. Austen 1988
23. Barreras del Rio and Perreault 1987, 10

14. The Resurrection of the Body and the Resacralization of Sexuality

1. Bryan 1988 (unpub.)
2. Lippard 1983, 44
3. Rich 1976, 284
4. Rowan 1987
5. Lippard 1983, 44
6. Offit 1977
7. Alloway 1980, 19
8. Schneemann 1979, 52
9. Ibid.
10. Schneemann 1977, 39
11. Schneemann 1979, 12–13
12. Schneemann, dialogue, 1988
13. Schneemann, quoted in Montano 1987, 7
14. Schneemann, interview, 1977
15. Castle 1980, 8
16. Lovelace 1986–87
17. Ibid., 2–3
18. Metzger 1986, 121
19. Ibid., 110
20. Ibid., 113–14
21. Ibid., 116
22. Ibid., 118
23. Ibid., 121–22
24. Ibid., 122
25. Metzger 1983, 219
26. Meyerhoff, in Metzger 1983
27. Jardine, in Kristeva 1981, 9
28. Doress 1987, 82
29. Van den Bosch 1984, 47
30. Kristeva 1981, 16
31. Jardine 1981, 16
32. Wilshire (personal communication)

15. Reclaiming Her Sacred Iconography: The Artist as Prophet

1. de Beauvoir 1974, 431
2. *Spare Rib,* 44
3. *Women Artists News,* Sept.–Oct. 1978, 9
4. Santoro 1974
5. Lisle 1980, 75
6. Ibid., 190
7. Lippard 1986, 695
8. Lippard 1983, 50
9. Lisle 1980, 343, 211
10. Lippard 1983, 50

11. Raven 1977, 137
12. Lippard 1983, 42
13. Johnson 1976, 1
14. Chicago 1982, 141–42
15. Chicago 1982, 143
16. Raven 1983, 14–20
17. Raven 1973, 19
18. Lippard 1980, 122
19. Ibid., 115
20. Ibid., 117
21. Chicago 1985, 7
22. Ibid., 19
23. Ibid., 13
24. Wye 1982, 14
25. Lippard 1983, 62
26. Wye 1982, 17
27. Bourgeois, quoted in Wye 1982, 60
28. Wye 1982, 27
29. Bourgeois, quoted in Wye 1982, 27
30. Wye 1982, 27
31. Bourgeois, quoted in Wye 1982, 28
32. Bourgeois, quoted in Seiberling 1974, 46
33. Stanyan 1984, 8
34. Ibid.
35. La Rose 1984, 18
36. Brown 1988, 3
37. Isaak 1987, 30–31
38. Tickner 1987, 16
39. Bird 1987, 34
40. Isaak 1987, 34
41. Ibid.

16. Gaia Consciousness: Ecological Wisdom for the Renewal of Life on Our Planet

1. Lovelock 1979
2. Griffin 1978, 227
3. Herrera 1983, 220
4. Herrera 1983, 314–15
5. Biaggi (n.d.), 2–3
6. Anderson, communication, 1988
7. Allen 1986, 22
8. Orenstein, in Guenther (n.d.), 22
9. La Duke, in Guenther (n.d.), 24
10. Guenther (n.d.), 22
11. Allan 1987, 8
12. Swimme 1987, 1

13. Lippard 1983, 16
14. Griffin 1978, 1
15. Orenstein 1987, 24; Lippard 1983, fig. 151
16. Lippard 1983, fig. 151
17. Aylon (n.d.), 3
18. Rosenthal 1987, 76
19. Rosenthal 1983, 5–6
20. Ibid., 20–21
21. Raven 1987, 71
22. Vijali (unpub.)
23. Smith 1987, 58
24. Ibid., 58

Conclusion. The Promise of the Goddess: The Healing of Our Culture

1. Lauter 1984, 73–74
2. Jung 1968, 342
3. Whitmont 1982, x
4. Edelstein, unpublished journal
5. Wilshire and Wilshire, unpublished pages, 21
6. Ibid.
7. Marshall 1976
8. Campbell 1988, 30–31
9. Anderson (unpub.)
10. Whitmont 1982

Figure Notes

Black and White

1. Gimbutas 1982, 95
2. Ibid.
3. Ibid., 201
4. Ibid., 224

5. Purce 1979, fig. 55
6. von Cles-Reden 1962, 284
7. Rohrlich-Leavitt 1977, 47–48
8. Wolkstein and Kramer 1983, 177–78
9. Lincoln 1981, fig. 25
10. Holland 1977, 124, fig. 1
11. 1 Kings 7:211–12
12. Met. Mus. of Art 1986, 153–54
13. Warner 1976, pl. 3, fig. 3
14. Male 1977, 133
15. Warner 1983, 248
16. Ibid., color pl. 5
17. Begg 1985, 213
18. Wortz 1982, 25
19. Ibid., 14
20. Oda 1981, 68
21. Machida (personal communication)
22. Edelson, in *Heresies* 1988, 96
23. Metzger pastel, 1981
24. Raven 1978, 136–38
25. Johnson 1976
26. Gloria Van Lydegraf, quoted in Chicago 1985, 34
27. Brown 1988
28. Ibid.
29. Walker 1983, 930
30. Chayet 1988, 14
31. Anderson 1988
32. Anderson 1987
33. McGowan 1975
34. Lippard 1983, 15
35. Vijali (unpub.)

Color

1. Herrera 1983, 220

Selected Bibliography

Ackerman, Robert. In Eliade, *Encyclopedia of World Religion*. New York: Macmillan, 1987.

Adler, Margot. *Drawing Down the Moon*. Boston: Beacon Press, 1987.

Albright, William Foxwell. "An Aramean Magical Text in Hebrew from the Seventh Century, B.C.," BASOR 76, 1939.

————. *From Stone Age to Christianity*. Baltimore: Johns Hopkins, 1940.

————. *The Archaeology of Palestine*. Gloucester, Mass.: Peter Smith, 1971.

Allan, Lois. "A Personal Commitment." *Artweek,* December 12, 1987.

Allen, Paula Gunn. *The Sacred Hoop: Recovering the Feminine in American Indian Traditions*. Boston: Beacon Press, 1986.

Alloway, Laurence. "Carolee Schneemann: The Body as Object and Instrument." *Art in America,* March, 1980.

Anderson, Judith. *Mandorla of the Spinning Goddess*. Unpublished, February 1987.

Austen, Hallie Iglehart. *Between the Worlds*. Unpublished, 1988.

Aylon, Helene. *Statement about Performance as Transformative Ritual*. Unpublished.

Bachofen, J. J. *Myth, Religion and Mother Right*. Trans. by Ralph Manheim. New Jersey: Princeton University Press, 1967.

Bailey, L. R. "The Golden Calf." *Hebrew Union College Annual* 42, 1971.

Barreras del Rio, Petra, and John Perrault. *Ana Mendieta: A Retrospective*. New York: New Museum of Contemporary Art, 1987.

Barstow, Ann. "The Prehistoric Goddess." In Carl Olsen, ed., *The Book of the Goddess: Past and Present*. New York: Crossroads, 1983.

Barthes, Roland. *Mythologies:* selected and translated from the French by Annette Layers. New York: Hill and Wang, 1972.

Beane, Wendell Charles. *Myth, Cult and Symbols in Sakta Hinduism—A Study of the Indian Mother Goddess*. Leiden: E. J. Brill, 1977.

de Beauvoir, Simone. *The Second Sex*. New York: Knopf, 1974.

Begg, Ian. *The Cult of the Black Virgin*. London: Routledge and Kegan Paul, 1985.

Berger, John. *Ways of Seeing*. New York: Penguin Books, 1977.

Berger, Pamela. *The Goddess Obscured: Transformation of the Grain Protectress to Saint*. Boston: Beacon Press, 1985.

Biaggi, Cristina, and Mimi Lobell. "The Goddess Mound at Vassar College." No date.

Biaggi de Blasys, Cristina. *Megalithic Sculpture that Symbolizes the Great Goddess*. Ph.D. dissertation, New York University, 1983.

Bird, Phyllis. "The Place of Women in the Israelite Cultus." In Miller, Hanson, McBride, eds., *Ancient Israelite Religion*. Philadelphia: Fortress Press, 1987.

Bleeker, C. J. "Isis and Hathor: Two Ancient Egyptian Goddesses." In Carl Olson, ed., *The Book of the Goddess: Past and Present*. New York: Crossroads, 1983.

Bolle, Kees. *The Persistence of Religion: An Essay on Tantrism and Sri Aurobindo's Philosophy*. Leiden: E. J. Brill, 1965.

Briffault, Robert. *The Mothers*. Abridged by Gordon Rottray Taylor. New York: Atheneum, 1977.

Brown, Betty Ann. "A Challenge to Feminist Positions." *Artweek,* January 9, 1988.

Burkert, Walter. *Ancient Mystery Cults*. Cambridge: Harvard University Press, 1987.

Budapest, Zsuzsanna Emese. *The Holy Book of Women's Mysteries*. Vol. 1. Oakland: Susan B. Anthony Coven 1, 1986.

Budge, E. A. Wallis. *Dwellers on the Nile*. New York: Dover Publications, 1977.

————. *Egyptian Religion*. London: Routledge and Kegan Paul, 1972; a reprint of the 1899 work.

————. *The Gods of the Egyptians*. Vol. 1, 1904. Reprint, New York: Dover, 1969.

Bynum, Caroline Walker, Stevan Aareel, and Paula Richman, eds. *Gender and Religion*. Boston: Beacon Press, 1986.

Cameron, Dorothy. *Symbols of Birth and Death in the Neolithic Era.* London: Kenyan-Deane Ltd., 1981.

———. "Generation and Regeneration: Symbols in Çatal Hüyük." Unpublished.

Campbell, Joseph. *The Masks of God: Occidental Mythology.* New York: Viking Press, 1964.

———. *The Mythic Image.* Princeton: Princeton University Press, 1983.

———. *The Way of the Animal Powers.* Vol. 1. *Historical Atlas of World Mythology.* London: Summerfield Press, 1983.

———. *The Power of Myth.* New York: Doubleday, 1988.

Cassirer, Ernst. *Philosophy of Symbolic Forms.* New Haven: Yale University Press, 1953–57.

Chandra, Moti. "Studies in the Cult of the Mother Goddess in India." *Bulletin of the Prince of Wales Museum of Western India,* 1–2, 1973.

Chayet, Sherry. "Beyond Symbolism: Spero's Work Defies Assumptions." *Syracuse Herald American Stars Magazine,* January 3, 1988.

Chicago, Judy. *The Dinner Party: A Symbol of Our Heritage.* Garden City, N.Y.: Anchor Press, 1979.

———. *Embroidering our Heritage: The Dinner Party Needlework.* Garden City, N.Y.: Anchor Press, 1980.

———. *Through the Flower: My Struggle as a Woman Artist.* Garden City, N.Y.: Anchor Press, 1982.

———. *The Birth Project.* Garden City. N.Y.: Doubleday and Company, 1985.

Christ, Carol. *Diving Deep and Surfacing: Women Writers on Spiritual Quest.* 2nd ed. Boston: Beacon Press, 1980.

———. "A Feminist Challenge: Rethinking Theology and Nature." In Judith Plaskow, Carol Christ, eds., *Weaving the Visions.* San Francisco: Harper & Row, 1989.

———. *Laughter of Aphrodite: Reflections on a Journey to the Goddess.* San Francisco: Harper & Row, 1987.

Cixous, Helene. "The Laugh of Medusa." Trans. by Keith Cohen and Paule Cohen. In *Signs.* Vol. 7, no. 1, 1981.

von Cles-Reden, Sibylle. *The Realm of the Great Goddess: The Story of Megalith Builders.* Englewood Cliffs, N.J.: Prentice-Hall, 1962.

Cohen, Joyce. *Insights.* Boston: D. R. Godine, 1978.

Cottrell, Leonard. *The Lion Gate.* London: Evans Brothers, 1963.

Craighead, Meinrad. *The Mother's Songs.* Mahwah, N.J.: The Paulist Press, 1986.

Cross, Frank. *Canaanite Myth and Hebrew Epic.* Cambridge, Mass.: Harvard University Press, 1973.

Daly, Mary. *Beyond God the Father.* Boston: Beacon Press, 1973.

Dames, Michael. *The Silbury Treasure: The Goddess Rediscovered.* London: Thames and Hudson, 1976.

———. *The Avebury Cycle.* London: Thames and Hudson, 1977.

Davies, Steve. "The Canaanite-Hebrew Goddess." In Carl Olson, ed., *The Book of the Goddess: Past and Present,* New York: Crossroads, 1983.

Dever, William G. "Asherah, Consort of Yahweh? New Evidence from Kuntillet Ajrud." BASOR 255, 1984.

———. "The Contribution of Archaeology to the Study of Canaanite and Early Israelite Religion." *Ancient Israelite Religion.* Patrick Miller, Paul D. Hanson, S. Dean McBride, eds. Philadelphia: Fortress Press, 1987.

Dodson Gray, Elizabeth. *Green Paradise Lost.* Wellesley, Mass.: Roundtable Press, 1978.

Dodson Gray, Elizabeth. *Patriarchy as a Conceptual Trap.* Wellesley, Mass.: Roundtable Press, 1982.

Doress, Paula Brown, and Diana Laskin Siegal. *Ourselves Growing Older.* New York: Simon and Schuster, 1987.

Downing, Christine. *The Goddess: Mythological Images of the Feminine.* New York: Crossroad Publishing Co., 1984.

Edelson, Mary Beth. *Seven Cycles: Public Rituals.* New York: Edelson, 1980.

———. "Pilgrimage/See for Yourself: A Journey to a Neolithic Goddess Cave." *Heresies.* Vol. 2, no. 1, reissued 1982.

———. Lecture, University of Illinois, 1986.

———. *Seven Sites: Painting on the Wall.* New York: Edelson, 1988.

Eisler, Riane. *The Chalice and the Blade: Our History, Our Future.* San Francisco: Harper & Row, 1987.

Eliade, Mircea. *Patterns in Comparative Religion.* Trans. by Rosemary Sheed. New York: Sheed and Ward, 1958.

———. *Images and Symbols: Studies in Religious Symbolism.* New York: Sheed and Ward, 1969.

———. "Earth, Water and Fertility." *A History of Religious Ideas.* Vol. 1. *From Stone Age to Eleusinian Mysteries.* Chicago: University of Chicago Press, 1978.

———. *A History of Religious Ideas.* Vol. 2. *From Gautama Buddha to the Triumph of Christianity.* Chicago: The University of Chicago Press, 1982.

Eliade, Mircea, ed. *The Encyclopedia of Religion.* New York: Macmillan, 1986.

Engelsmann, Joan Chamberlain. *Feminine Dimension of the Divine.* Philadelphia: Westminister Press, 1979.

Falk, Marcia. *The Song of Songs: Love Poems from the Bible.* New York: Harcourt Brace Jovanovich, 1977.

Fawcett, Thomas. *The Symbolic Language of Religion: An Introductory Study.* London: S.C.M. Press, 1970.

Ferguson, Ian F. G. "New Views on the Hypogeum and Tarxien." In Anthony Bonanno, ed., *Archaeology and Fertility Cult in the Ancient Mediterranean.* Amsterdam: B. P. Gruner, 1985.

Flack, Audrey. *Art and Soul: Notes on Creating.* New York: E. P. Dutton, 1986.

Fox, Matthew. *Original Blessing: A Primer in Creation Spirituality.* Santa Fe, N.M.: Bear and Company, 1983.

Franck, Frederick. "Spinner of the Red Thread." *Commonweal* 314, May 1986.

Frazer, J. G. *The Golden Bough.* London: Macmillan, 1911–15.

Freedman, David Noel. Telephone conversation, December 1987.

Gates, Barbara. "Mayumi Oda: Art Goddess on the River of Our Mind." *Inquiring Mind,* Winter 1984.

Giedion, S. *The Beginnings of Art.* Vol. 1. Princeton: Bollingen, 1957.

Gilligan, Carol. *In a Different Voice.* Cambridge, Mass.: Harvard University Press, 1982.

Gimbutas, Marija. "The Beginning of the Bronze Age in Europe and the Indo-Europeans: 3500–2500 B.C." *Journal of Indo-European Studies,* 1, 1973.

———. "The Temples of Old Europe." *Archaeology,* November–December 1980.

———. "Vulvas, Breasts and Buttocks of the Goddess Creatress: Commentary on the Origins of Art." *The Shape of the Past: Studies in Honor of Franklin D. Murphy.* G. Buccellati and C. Speroni, eds. Los Angeles: University of California, 1981.

———. *The Goddesses and Gods of Old Europe: Myths and Cult Images.* Berkeley: University of California Press, 1982.

———. Lecture, California Institute of Integral Studies. San Francisco, November 1987.

———. "Women When the World Began." Lecture, Jung Institute, San Francisco, October 1988.

Gleason, Judith. *Oya, In Praise of the Goddess.* Boston: Shambhala Publications, 1987.

Grace, Patricia. *Wahine Toa.* Auckland, New Zealand: William Collins Publishers, 1984.

Grant, Michael. *The History of Ancient Israel.* New York: Charles Scribner's Sons, 1984.

Graves, Robert. *The White Goddess: A Historical Grammar of Poetic Myth.* New York: Farrar, Straus and Giroux, 1973.

Graves, Robert, and Raphael Patai. *Hebrew Myths: The Book of Genesis.* New York: McGraw-Hill, 1966.

Griffin, Susan. *Woman and Nature.* New York: Harper & Row, 1978.

Guenther, Bruce. *Betty La Duke: Multi-Cultural Images.* Seattle: Seattle Art Museum, n.d.

Hall, Nor. *The Moon and the Virgin.* New York: Harper & Row, 1980.

Haran, M. *Temples and Temple Service in Ancient Israel: An Inquiry into the Character of Cult Phenomena and the Historical Setting of the Priestly School.* Oxford: Oxford University Press, 1978.

Harding, M. Esther. *Woman's Mysteries: Ancient and Modern.* New York: Harper & Row, 1971.

Hartt, Frederick. *Donatello: Prophet of Modern Vision.* London: Thames and Hudson, 1974.

———. *History of Italian Renaissance Art.* New York: Prentice Hall, 1988.

Harrison, Jane. *Prolegomena to the Study of Greek Religion.* 1905. Reprint, London: Merlin Press, 1980.

Hawkes, Jacquetta. *Dawn of the Gods.* New York: Random House, 1968.

Heresies. Vol. 2, no. 1. *The Great Goddess.* 1982.

Herrera, Hayden. *Frida: A Biography of Frida Kahlo.* New York: Harper & Row, 1983.

Heschel, Abraham. *The Insecurity of Freedom.* New York: Farrar, Straus and Giroux, 1972.

Holladay, John S., Jr. Telephone conversation, December 1987.

———. "Religion in Israel and Judah Under the Monarchy: An Explicitly Archaeological Approach." Ed. by Patrick D. Miller, Paul D. Hanson, and S. Dean McBride in *Ancient Israelite Religion.* Philadelphia: Fortress Press, 1987.

Holland, T. A. "A Study of Palestinian Iron Age Baked Clay Figurines, with special reference to Jerusalem Cave I." *Levant* (9), 1977.

Hood, Sinclair. *The Home of the Heroes: The Aegeans before the Greeks.* New York: McGraw-Hill, 1967.

Howard, Jim Ann. *Reunion: The Personal Death Experience.* Unpublished, 1988.

Hutchinson, R.W. *Prehistoric Crete.* Baltimore: Penguin, 1962.

Huxley, Francis. *The Way of the Sacred.* Garden City, N.Y.: Doubleday, 1974.

Iglehart, Hallie. *Womanspirit: A Guide to Woman's Wisdom.* San Francisco: Harper & Row, 1983.

Isaak, Joanna. "A Work in Common Courage." *Nancy Spero: Works Since 1950*. Syracuse, N.Y.: Everson Museum of Art, 1987.

Jacobsen, Thorkild. *The Treasures of Darkness: A History of Mesopotamian Religion*. New Haven: Yale University Press, 1976.
———. "The Graven Image." In Miller, Hanson, McBride, eds., *Ancient Israelite Religion*. Philadelphia: Fortress Press, 1987.

James, E. O. *The Cult of the Mother Goddess*. New York: Frederick A. Praeger, 1959.

Jardine, Alice. "Introduction to Julia Kristeva's 'Women's Time'." *Signs*. Autumn 1981.

Jayakar, Pupul. *The Earthen Drum*. New Delhi: National Museum, 1980.

Johnson, Kathryn C. *Changes (An Exhibition by Betsy Damon and Carol Fisher)*. College of St. Catherine. January 4–29, 1976.

Judge, Joseph. "Minoans and Mycenaeans: Greece's Brilliant Bronze Age." *National Geographic*. Vol. 153, no. 2, 1978.

Jung, Carl G. *Myths and Symbols*. New York: Dell, 1968.

Keller, Mara Lynn. "Eleusinian Mysteries: Ancient Nature Religion of Demeter and Persephone." *The Journal of Feminist Studies in Religion*. No. 1, 1987.

Kerényi, Carl. *Eleusis: Archetypal Image of Mother and Daughter*. New York: Schocken Books, 1977.

Kramer, Samuel Noah. *Cradle of Civilization*. New York: Time, Inc., 1969(a).
———. "The Dumuzi-Inanna Sacred Marriage Rite: Origin, Development, Character." Comité Belge de Recherche en Mésopotamie. *Actes de la XVIIe Rencontre Assyrologique Internationale*. Bruxelles, 30 juin–4 juillet 1969, 1970.
———. *The Sacred Marriage Rite: Aspects of Faith, Myth and Ritual in Ancient Sumer*. Bloomington: Indiana University Press, 1969(b).

Kristeva, Julia. "Stabat Mater." Susan Rubin Suileman, ed. *The Female Body in Western Culture*. Cambridge, Mass.: Harvard University Press, 1986.
———. "Women's Time." *Signs,* Autumn 1981.

La Rose, Elise. "Nancy Azara." *Arts Magazine,* September 1984.

Lauter, Estelle. *Women as Myth Makers*. Bloomington: Indiana University Press, 1984.

Lerner, Gerda. *The Creation of Patriarchy*. New York: Oxford University Press, 1986.

Leroi-Gourhan, André. *Treasures of Prehistoric Art*. New York: Harry N. Abrams, n.d.

Levy, G. Rachael. *The Gate of Horn: A Study of the Religious Conceptions of the Stone Age and Their Influences upon European Thought*. London: Faber and Faber, 1946 (Harper & Row, 1963).

Lincoln, Bruce. *Emerging from the Chrysalis: Studies in Rituals of Women's Initiation*. Cambridge, Mass.: Harvard University Press, 1981.

Lippard, Lucy. *From the Center: Feminist Essays in Women's Art*. New York: E. P. Dutton & Co. Inc., 1976.
———. "Judy Chicago's 'Dinner Party'." *Art in America*. April 1980(a).
———. "Reluctant Heroine." *The Nation*. June 7, 1980(b).
———. *Overlay: Contemporary Art and the Art of Prehistory*. New York: Pantheon, 1983.

Lisle, Laurie. *Portrait of an Artist: A Biography of Georgia O'Keeffe*. New York: Seaview Books, 1980.

Lobell, Mimi. "Spatial Archetypes." *ReVision*. Vol. 6, no. 2, Fall 1983.

Lovelace, Carrie. "The Gender and Case of Carolee Schneemann." *Millennium Film Journal*, 16, 17, 18. Fall–Winter, 1986–87.

Lovelock, J. E. *Gaia, A New Look at Life on Earth*. London: Oxford University Press, 1979.

Luke, Helen M. *The Way of Women, Ancient and Modern*. Three Rivers, Mich.: Apple Farm, 1975.

McEvilley, Thomas. "Who Told Thee That Thou Was't Naked." *Art Forum*, February 1987.

McGowan, Charlotte. *Ceremonial Fertility Sites in Southern California*. San Diego Museum Papers, No. 14, 1982.

MacNeill, M. *The Festival of Lughnasa: A Study of the Survival of the Celtic Festival of the Beginning of Harvest*. London: Oxford University Press, 1962.

Maier, Walter, III. *Asherah: Extrabiblical Evidence*. Ph.D. dissertation, 1984. Decatur, Ga.: Scholar's Press, 1986.

Male, Emile. *L'Art Religieux du XIIe Siècle en France; étude sur les origines de l'iconographie*. Paris: A. Colin, 1953.

Marglin, Frédérique. "Hieroduleia." In Mircea Eliade, ed., *The Encyclopedia of Religion*. Vol. 6, 1986.
———. *Wives of the God-King: The Rituals of the Devadasis of Puri*. New York: Oxford University Press, 1985.
———. "Yoni." In Mircea Eliade, ed., *The Encyclopedia of Religion*. 1986.

Marschack, Alexander. *Roots of Civilization*. New York: McGraw-Hill, 1972.
———. "The Eye Is Not as Clever as it Thinks." Unpublished paper.

Marshall, Lorna. *The !Kung of Nyae Nyae*. Cambridge, Mass.: Harvard University Press, 1976.

Mazer, Amihai. "The 'Bull Site'—An Iron Age in Open Cult Place." *Bulletin of American School of Oriental Research*. The Hebrew University of Jerusalem. Summer 1982.

Merchant, Caroline. *The Death of Nature*. San Francisco: Harper and & Row, 1980.

Mellaart, James. *Çatal Hüyük: A Neolithic Town in Anatolia*. New York: McGraw-Hill, 1967.

Metzger, Deena. *Tree*. Berkeley: Wingbow Press, 1983.

———. "Revamping the World: On the Return of the Holy Prostitute." *Anima* 12/2, 1986.

Meyer, Marvin W., ed. *The Ancient Mysteries: A Sourcebook*. San Francisco: Harper & Row, 1987.

Meyrs, Carol. *Discovering Eve: Ancient Israelite Women in Context*. New York: Oxford University Press, 1988.

Miller, Patrick D., Jr. "Aspects of the Religion of Ugarit." In Miller et al., eds. *Ancient Israelite Religion*. Philadelphia: Fortress Press, 1987.

Miller, Patrick D., Jr., Paul D. Hanson, and S. Dean McBride, eds. *Ancient Israelite Religion*. Philadelphia: Fortress Press, 1987.

Millett, Kate. *Sexual Politics*. New York: Doubleday, 1970.

Montano, Linda. "Interview with Carolee Schneemann." *Sex, Performance, Art in the 80's. The Flue*. Vol. 2, no. 3. Special Summer Issue, 1987.

Mookerjee, Ajit. *Kali, The Feminine Force*. New York: Destiny Books, 1988.

Morgan, Robin. *Sisterhood is Powerful*. New York: Vintage, 1970.

Moss, Leonard W., and Stephen C. Cappannari. "In Quest of the Black Virgin: She is Black Because She is Black." *Mother Worship*. Chapel Hill, N.C.: University of North Carolina Press, 1982.

Munro, Eleanor. *Originals: American Women Artists*. New York: Simon & Schuster, 1979.

Mylonas, George. *Eleusis and the Eleusinian Mysteries*. Princeton, N.J.: Princeton University Press, 1961.

Nahas, Domique, ed. *Nancy Spero's Works Since 1950*. Syracuse, N.Y.: Everson Museum of Art, 1987.

Nelson, Mary Carroll. *Connecting: The Art of Beth Ames Swartz*. Flagstaff, Ariz.: Northland Press, 1984.

Neumann, Erich. *The Great Mother*. Princeton, N.J.: Princeton University Press, (1955), 1963.

Newton, Helmut. *Big Nudes*. New York: Xavier Moreau, 1982.

Newton, Judith, and Deborah Rosenfelt. "Writing the Body: Toward an Understanding of L'Écriture Feminine." *Feminist Criticism and Social Change*. New York: Methuen, 1985.

Nilsson, M. P. *The Minoan-Mycenaean Religion and its Survival in Greek Religion*. 2nd ed. Lund, Sweden: C. W. K. Gleerup, 1950.

Ochshorn, Judith. *The Female Experience and the Nature of the Divine*. Bloomington: Indiana University Press, 1981.

———. "Ishtar and Her Cult." *Book of the Goddess Past and Present*. Carl Olson, ed. New York: Crossroads Publishing Co., 1983.

Oda, Mayumi. *Goddesses*. Berkeley: Lancaster-Miller Publishers, 1981.

———. *Retrospective*. 1985.

Offit, Avodah K. *The Sexual Self*. Philadelphia: J. B. Lippincott, 1977.

Olson, Carl. *Book of the Goddess Past and Present: An Introduction to Her Religion*. New York: Crossroads Publishing Co., 1983.

Orenstein, Gloria. "Creation and Healing: An Empowering Relationship for Women Artists." *Women's Studies International Forum*. Vol. 8, no. 5.

———. "The Symbolism of Creation and the Goddess Image in Feminist Art and Literature." Unpublished paper, Ecofeminist Conference, Los Angeles, 1987.

Patai, Raphael. *The Hebrew Goddess*. New York: Avon Books, (1967) 1978.

Perera, Sylvia Brinton. *Descent to the Goddess: A Way of Initiation for Women*. Toronto: Inner City Books, 1981.

Pfieffer, R. *Religion in the Old Testament*. New York: Harper & Row, 1961.

Pritchard, James B. *Palestinian Figurines in Relation to Certain Goddesses Known through Literature*. AOS 24. New Haven, Conn.: American Oriental Society, 1943.

Purce, Jill. *The Mystic Spiral*. London: Thames and Hudson, 1980.

Raven, Arlene. *At Home*. Long Beach, Calif.: Museum of Art, 1983.

———. "Rachel Rosenthal 'Soldier of Fortune'." *High Performance*. No. 40, 1987.

———. "Georgia O'Keeffe." *Chrysalis*. No. 2, 1977.

———. "Women's Art: The Development of a Theoretical Perspective." *Women's Space Journal*. Vol. 1, no. 1, February–March 1973.

Raven, Arlene, and Susan Rennie. "The Dinner Party Project: An Interview with Judy Chicago." *Chrysalis*. No. 4, 1978.

Ray, S. K. *The Ritual of the Bratas of Bengal.* Calcutta: Firma K. L. Mukhopadhyay, 1961.

Reed, W. L. *The Asherah in the Old Testament.* Fort Worth: Texas Christian University, 1949.

Reis, Patricia. "The Mysteries of Creativity: Self-seeding, Death and the Great Goddess." *Psychological Perspectives.*

———. "Personal Vision Becomes Art." *Gnosis.* No. 3, Fall/Winter 1986–87.

Rich, Adrienne. *Of Woman Born: Motherhood as Experience and Institution.* New York: W. W. Norton, 1986.

Rohrlich-Leavitt, Ruby. "Women in Transition: Crete and Sumer." *Becoming Visible.* Renate Bridenthal and Claudia Koonz, eds. Boston: Houghton Mifflin, 1977.

Roos, Sandra. "The Roots of Feminine Consciousness in Prehistoric Art." Unpublished manuscript, 1976.

Rosenthal, Rachel. *Gaia, mon amor: A performance by Rachael Rosenthal.* Buffalo, N.Y.: Hallwalls, 1983.

———. "L.O.W. in Gaia." *Performing Arts Journal.* No. 30, October 1987.

Rowan, John. *The Horned God: Feminism and Men as Wounding and Healing.* New York: Routledge and Kegan Paul, 1987.

Rykwert, J. *Meaning in Architecture.* Ed. Jenks and Baird, 1969.

Sahlins, Marshall. *Stone Age Economics.* Hawthorne, N.Y.: Aldine de Gruyter, 1972.

Sahtouris, Elizabeth. *Gaia: Humanity's Bridge from Chaos to Cosmos.* New York: Aslan, 1989.

Salzman, M. Rene. "Magna Mater: Great Mother of the Roman Empire." In Carl Olson, *The Book of the Goddess Past and Present.* New York: Crossroads, 1983.

Sargent, Thelma. *The Homeric Hymns.* New York: W. W. Norton, 1973.

Schneemann, Carolee. Lecture. School, Museum of Fine Arts, Boston, 1987.

———. *Homerunmuse.* 1977. Text of a performance.

———. *More than Meat Joy.* New Paltz, N.Y.: Documentext, 1979.

Scully, Vincent. *The Earth, the Temple, and the Gods.* New Haven, Conn.: Yale University Press, 1962.

———. "The Great Goddess and the Palace Architecture of Crete." *Feminism and Art History: Questioning the Litany.* Norma Braude and Mary D. Garrard, eds. New York: Harper & Row, 1982.

Seiberling, Dorothy. "The Female View of Erotica." *New York Magazine,* February 11, 1974.

Smith, Barbara T. "Art and Ceremony." *High Performance.* No. 40, 1987.

Sorlini, Guilia Battiti. "The Megalithic Temples of Malta: An Anthropological Perspective." *Archeology and Fertility Cult in the Ancient Mediterranean.* Anthony Bonanno, ed. Amsterdam: B. P. Gruner, 1985.

Spretnack, Charlene. *Lost Goddesses of Early Greece: A Collection of Pre-Hellenic Myths.* Boston: Beacon, 1984.

———. *The Politics of Women's Spirituality.* Garden City, N.Y.: Doubleday, 1982.

———. *The Spirituality of Green Politics.* Santa Fe, N.M.: Bear and Co., 1986.

———. "Ecofeminism: Our Roots and Flowering." *Reweaving the World: The Emergence of Ecofeminism.* Irene Diamond and Gloria Orenstein, eds. San Francisco: Sierra Club Books, forthcoming.

Srejovic, Dragoslav. *New Discoveries at Lepenski Vir.* London: Thames and Hudson, 1972.

Starhawk. *The Spiral Dance: A Rebirth of the Ancient Religion of the Great Goddess.* San Francisco: Harper & Row, 1979.

———. *Dreaming the Dark.* Boston: Beacon Press, 1982.

———. *Truth or Dare.* New York: Harper & Row, 1987.

Stanyon, Susan. "Judith Bernstein." *Arts Magazine,* September 1984.

Stone, Merlin. *When God was a Woman.* New York: Dial Press, 1976.

Swartz, Beth Ames. *Israel Revisited.* 1981.

Swimme, Brian. "How to Heal a Lobotomy." Ecofeminist conference, Los Angeles, 1987.

Teubal, Savina. *Sarah, the Priestess: The First Matriarch of Genesis.* Athens, Ohio: Swallow Press, 1984.

Tickner, Lisa. "Form and Content—It Doesn't Have to be a Story with a Beginning, Middle and End." *Nancy.* London: Orchard Gallery/Foyle Arts Project, 1987.

Thomas, C. G. "Matriarchy in Early Greece: The Bronze and Dark Ages." *Arethusa* 6, Fall 1973.

Thompson, Robert Farris. *Flash of the Spirit: Afro-American Art and Philosophy.* New York: Vintage, 1984.

Thompson, William Irwin. *The Time Falling Bodies Take to Light.* New York: St. Martin's Press, 1981.

Treasures of the Holy Land: Ancient Art from the Israel Museum. New York: The Metropolitan Museum of Art, 1986.

Trump, David H. *Malta: An Archaeological Guide.* London: Faber and Faber, 1972.

Van den Bosch, Annette. "Susan Hiller: Resisting Representation." *Artscribe.* No. 46, London, May–July 1984.

de Vaux, Roland. *Ancient Israel: Its Life and Institutions.* London: Darton, Longman, and Todd, 1961.

Von Matt, Leonard. *Ancient Crete.* London: Thames and Hudson, 1968.

Walker, Barbara G. *The Women's Encyclopedia of Myths and Secrets.* San Francisco: Harper & Row, 1983.

———. *The Skeptical Feminist: Discovering the Virgin, Mother and Crone.* San Francisco: Harper & Row, 1987.

———. *The Woman's Dictionary of Symbols & Sacred Objects.* San Francisco: Harper & Row, 1988.

Warner, Marina. *Alone of all her Sex: The Myth and the Cult of the Virgin Mary.* New York: Random House, 1976.

Waters, Frank. *Book of the Hopi.* New York: Viking Press, 1969.

Weimar, Joan Myers. "Mythic Parables of Female Power: Inanna, Demeter and Persephone, and the Sleeping Beauty." *Anima.* Thirteen/1, 1987.

White, Randall. *Dark Caves, Bright Visions: Life in Ice Age Europe.* New York: The American Museum of Natural History, 1986.

Whitmont, Edward C. *Return of the Goddess.* New York: Crossroads, 1982.

Wilbur, Ken. *Up from Eden.* London: Routledge and Kegan Paul, 1981.

Wilshire, Bruce. *The Moral Collapse of the University: Professionalism, Purity and Alienation.* Albany: SUNY Press, 1989.

Wilshire, Donna, and Bruce Wilshire. "Gender Stereotypes and Spatial Archetypes." *Anima,* Spring 1989.

Wilshire, Donna and Bruce. *The Great Cosmic Mother: Openness to the Past as Openness to the Future.* Unpublished paper.

Wolf, Eric. "The Virgin of Guadalupe: A Mexican National Symbol." *Journal of American Folklore,* 1958.

Wolkstein, Diane, and Samuel Noah Kramer. *Inanna: Queen of Heaven and Earth: Her Stories and Hymns from Sumer.* New York: Harper & Row, 1983.

Wortz, Melinda. *Tradition in Transition.* Irvine: University of California, Irvine, Exhibition Catalogue, January 21–February 20, 1982.

Wye, Deborah. *Louise Bourgeois.* New York: The Museum of Modern Art, 1982.

Zammit, T. *The Neolithic Temples of Hajar Qim and Mnajdra.* Valletta, Malta: Empire Press, 1927.

Zevit, Ziony. "The Khirbet el-Qom Inscription Mentioning a Goddess." BASOR 255, 1984.

❀ INDEX

Photograph and Illustration Credits

Scene from Hagia Triada Sarcophagus. Heraklion Museum, Crete. Courtesy of Robert Harding Picture Library. **70.** *Young Men and Women Bull-Leaping.* Photo courtesy of Ekdotike Athenon. **71.** *Cretan Bull Rhyton.* Photo courtesy of Ekdotike Athenon. **72.** *Pottery Group of Dancing Women from Palai Kastro.* Photo by Dimitrios Harissiadis. © George Rainbird Ltd. Courtesy of Robert Harding Picture Library. **73.** *Goddess or Her Priestess Performing a Healing Ritual.* Drawing by Patricia Reis. From *Lost Goddesses of Early Greece* by Charlene Spretnak. © 1978 by Charlene Spretnak. Illustrations ©1984 by Beacon Press. Reprinted by permission of Beacon Press. **74.** *Europa and the Bull.* Archaeology Museum, Tarquinia, Italy. **75.** *Theseus and the Minotaur.* Vatican Museums. **76.** *Cretan Coin with Labyrinth.* Drawing by Sue Sellars. **77.** *Goddess.* Courtesy of Director of Antiquities and Museums, Damascus, Syria. **78.** *Goddess or Priestess.* Courtesy of Director of Antiquities and Museums, Damascus, Syria. **79.** *City Shrine Surrounded By Signs of Inanna: The Rosettes, Her Face, and Her Gateposts.* Oriental Institute, University of Chicago. **80.** *Worshipper Petitioning Inanna.* Bible Lands Museum, Jerusalem (collection Borowski). **81.** *Planting a Tree for Inanna.* **82.** *Lilith.* **83.** *Inanna with Crown and Staff.* Musée du Louvre (#12456) Reproduced by courtesy of the Reunion des Musées Nationaux, Paris. **84.** *Sheepfold with Sheep and Gateposts of Inanna.* Photo courtesy of Hirmer Verlag, München. **85.** *Lovers Embracing on Bed.* Collection of Herr Professor Dr. Erlenmeyer, Basel, Switzerland. Photo courtesy of Erich Lessing Culture and Fine Arts Archives. **86.** *Inanna with Date Palm.* Staatliche Museen zu Berlin. **87.** *Bringing the Gifts to Inanna.* State Organization for Antiquities, Baghdad. Courtesy of Savina Teubal. **87b.** *Bringing the Gifts to Inanna (detail).* State Organization for Antiquities, Baghdad. Courtesy of Savina Teubal. **88.** *Demeter.* Reproduced by courtesy of the Trustees of the British Museum. **89.** *Persephone's Abduction.* Public domain. **90.** *Persephone's Return.*

Public domain. **91.** *Demeter Holding Sheaves of Wheat.* Museo Nazionale delle Terme. Photo courtesy of Alinari/Art Resource, New York. **92.** *Woman Sacrificing a Pig.* Drawing after Harrison. **93.** *Demeter and Kore.* Musée du Louvre. Photo courtesy of Alinari/Art Resource, New York. **94.** *The Reunion of Demeter and Persephone.* Musée du Louvre. Photo courtesy of Giraudon/Art Resource, New York. **95.** *Demeter, Triptolemos, and Persephone.* National Museum, Athens. Photo courtesy of Alinari/Art Resource, New York. **96.** *Asherah.* The Metropolitan Museum of Art, Gift of Harris D. Colt and H. Dunscombe Colt, 1934 (34.126.53). **97.** *Cult Stand from Tenach.* Courtesy of the Israel Department of Antiquities and Museums. **98.** *Cult Statue of Bull.* Courtesy of the Israel Department of Antiquities and Museums. **99.** *Votive Image of Pregnant Woman.* Courtesy of the Israel Department of Antiquities and Museums. **100.** *Shasthi, The Goddess of Childbirth, with Her Baby.* Courtesy of Ajit Mookerjee. **101.** *Shasthi, the Goddess of Childbirth Massaging Her Baby.* Public Domain. **102.** *The Annunciation.* National Gallery of Art, Washington, D.C. Samuel H. Kress Collection. **103.** *The Virgin Mary.* Staatliche Museen zu Berlin. **104.** *Isis Nursing Horus.* Egyptian Museum, Staatliche Museen Preussischer Kulturbesitz. **105.** *Our Lady of the Prairies.* Public domain. **106.** *St. Luke Painting the Virgin.* Gift of Mr. and Mrs. Henry Lee Higginson. Courtesy of Museum of Fine Arts, Boston. **107.** *Theotokos* The Metropolitan Museum of Art, Gift of J. Pierpont Morgan, 1916 (16.2.194). **108.** *The Immaculate Conception.* National Gallery, London. **109.** *The Assumption of the Virgin.* Photo courtesy of Alinari/Art Resource, New York. **110.** A and B. *Vierge Ouvrante.* Musée de Cluny. Courtesy of Giraudon/Art Resource, New York. **111.** *Mary Magdalene.* Photo courtesy of Alinari/Art Resource, New York. **112.** *The Witches' Sabbath.* Bequest of W. G. Russell Allen. Courtesy of Museum of Fine Arts, Boston. **113.** *The Virgin of Guadalupe.* Public domain. **114.** *Pope John Paul II*

Seated Beneath a Painting of Our Lady of Czestochowa. AP/Wide World Photos. **115.** *Black Virgin of Notre Dame du Puy.* Haeseler Publishers. **116.** *Woman, the Devil's Door (Mulier Janua Diaboli).* Musée du Louvre. ©Archives Photographiques, Paris/SPADEM. **117.** *Rishyasringa.* Courtesy of Chidananda Dasgupta. **118.** *Vessel.* Courtesy of Meinrad Craighead. **119.** *Shekinah.* Courtesy of Gilah Yelin Hirsch. Photo courtesy of Nick Kappes. **120.** *Emergence.* Courtesy of Gilah Yelin Hirsch. Photo by Nick Kappes. Collection of Elisabeth des Makois, Malibu, CA. **121.** *Goddess Hears People's Needs and Comes.* Courtesy of Mayumi Oda. **122.** *The Sky Dancer.* Courtesy of Mayumi Oda. **123.** *Reunion.* Courtesy of Jim Ann Howard. **124.** *Woman of the Plain.* Courtesy of Maud Morgan. **125.** *Shrouded Memories.* Photo by Pat Casey Daley. Courtesy of Mary Ann Fariello. **126.** *Rebirth of the Goddess.* Courtesy of Ann McCoy. **127.** *Astarte. Homage to Sophia.* ©Syma. Photo. ©Gail Bryan. **128.** *Spirit over Boston.* ©Syma. Photo. ©Gail Bryan. **129.** *Bend Down the Tree of Knowledge and You'll Unroost a Strange Bird.* Photo by Sheila Thomas. Courtesy of Sudie Rakusin. Collection of the Bloodroot Collective. **130.** *Charmed.* Courtesy of Margo Machida. **131.** *The Messenger: Quetzalcoatl Was a Woman.* Photo by Jan E. Watson. Courtesy of Colleen Kelley. **132.** *Hecate.* Photo by William Dewey. Courtesy of Dorothy Goldeed Gallery, Santa Monica, CA. **133.** *Isis.* Courtesy of Louis K. Meisel Gallery, New York. **134.** *See For Yourself: Pilgrimage to a Neolithic Cave.* ©Mary Beth Edelson. **135.** *Woman Rising/Sexual Energies.* ©Mary Beth Edelson. **136.** *The 7,000-Year-Old Woman.* Photo by Su Friedrich. Courtesy of Betsy Damon. **137.** *The 7,000-Year-Old Woman.* Photo by Su Friedrich. Courtesy of Betsy Damon. **138.** *Demeter.* Courtesy of Suzanne Benton. **139.** *Between the Worlds.* From Photomythology Series: "Between the Worlds." ©1981 Marcelina Martin. **140.** *Untitled.* Collection Ignacio C. Mendieta. **141.** *Untitled.* Collection Ignacio C. Mendieta. **142.** *Rupestrian Series.* Courtesy of Raquel Mendieta

Lubell. **27.** *Treasure Ship.* Courtesy of Mayumi Oda. **28.** *Rainbow Warrior.* Photo by Jon McNally. ©1980 Judy Chicago. **29.** *Gray Line with Black, Blue and Yellow.* Museum purchase with funds provided by the Agnes Cullen Arnold Endowment Fund, the Museum of Fine Arts, Houston. **30.** *The Cunt as Temple, Tomb, Cave and Flower.* ©1974 Judy Chicago. **31.** *Earth Mother of Willendorf.* Courtesy of Natural History Museum, Vienna. **32.** *Susan Maberry as the Earth Mother of Willendorf.* Courtesy of Cheri Gaulke. **33.** *The Earth Mother of Laussel.* Photo courtesy of Achille Weider, Zürich. **34.** *Ruprestrian Series.* Courtesy of Raquel Mendieta Harrington. **35.** *Louise Bourgeois as Artemis.* Photo by Duane Michals. Courtesy of *Vogue.* Copyright ©1980 by the Condé Nast Publications, Inc. **36.**

Artemis of Ephesus. Photo courtesy of Jean Edelstein. **37.** *Destruction of the Father.* Courtesy of Robert Miller Gallery, New York. **38.** *Throne of the Queen-Priestess, Palace of Knossos.* Heraklion Museum, Crete. Photo courtesy of Ekditoke Athenon. **39.** *Throne of the Sun Queen.* Courtesy of Suzanne Benton. **40.** *The Earth Mother (First Day Blessing Rite).* Courtesy of Wheelwright Museum of the American Indian, Santa Fe, New Mexico. **41.** *Iakonkwe (Womankind).* Courtesy of John Kahionhes Fadden. **42.** *Snake Goddess.* Photo courtesy of Ekditoke Athenon. **43.** *Charmed.* Courtesy of Margo Machida. **44.** *Sacred Labrys.* Theodora Wilbour Fund in memory of Zoe Wilbour, Museum of Fine Arts, Boston. **45.** *Labrys.* Courtesy of Buffie Johnson. **46.** *Maltese Goddess.* Photo

courtesy of Adam Woolfitt/Susan Griggs Agency, Ltd. **47.** *I'd Like to Go to Malta.* Courtesy of Maud Morgan. **48.** *The Guadalupe Series.* Photo by Wolfgang Dietze. Courtesy of Yolanda M. Lopez. **49.** *La Belle Verriere.* Photo courtesy of Giraudon/Art Resource, New York. **50.** *The Family.* Courtesy of Memphis Brooks Museum of Art, Memphis, Tennessee. Commissioned for Brooks Memorial Art Gallery through a grant from the National Endowment for the Arts and matching funds from the Memphis Arts Council, Brooks Fine Arts Foundation and the Brooks Art Gallery League. **51.** *Winter Solstice at Newgrange.* Courtesy of Commissioners of Public Works, Ireland. **52.** *I Am Summer out of Spring's Death.* Courtesy of Meinrad Craighead.

| 17500 | 17000 | 16500 | 16000 | 15500 | 15000 | 14500 | 14000 | 13500 | 13000 | 12500 | 12000 | 11500 | 11000 | 10500 | 10000 | 9500 | 9000 | 8500 | 8⟨ |

B.C.E.

1   THE EARTH MOTHER OF WILLENDORF.
ca. 25,000 – 30,000 B.C.E.
(text p. 6)

2   VOTIVE IMAGE OF THE GODDESS AS LIFE
GIVER, sixth century, B.C.E.
(text p. 35)

3   CROWNED SNAKE GODDESS, Neolithic
(text p. 48)

4   THE MALTESE GODDESS, ca. 3600 – 3000
(text p. 58)

5   MINOAN SNAKE GODDESS, ca. 1600 B.C.E.
(text p. 87)

6   GODDESS, mid-third millennium B.C.E.
(text p. 118)

7   DEMETER, ca. 340 – 330 B.C.E.
(text p. 145)

8   THE HEBREW GODDESS ASHERAH, eleventh
to sixth centurey B.C.E.
(text p. 172)

9   THEOTOKAS, THE GOD BEARER, twelfth
century.
(text p. 202)

10   VIERGE OUVRANTE, thirteenth century
(text p. 208)

11   Louise Bourgeois, FRAGILE GODDESS
ca. 1970 (text p. 330)

12   Debra Sherwood, Snake Goddess, 1981.
(text p. 334)

1

2

ICE AGE 35,000 B.C.E. – 9000 B.C.E.

| 17500 | 17000 | 16500 | 16000 | 15500 | 15000 | 14500 | 14000 | 13500 | 13000 | 12500 | 12000 | 11500 | 11000 | 10500 | 10000 | 9500 | 9000 | 8500 | 8⟨ |

B.C.E.